# BRIDGING
## *the* THEORY-PRACTICE
## DIVIDE *in* INTERNATIONAL
## RELATIONS

# BRIDGING
# *the* THEORY-PRACTICE
# DIVIDE *in* INTERNATIONAL
# RELATIONS

DANIEL MALINIAK, SUSAN PETERSON, RYAN POWERS,
*and* MICHAEL J. TIERNEY, *Editors*

GEORGETOWN UNIVERSITY PRESS / WASHINGTON, DC

The publisher is not responsible for third-party websites or their content. URL links were active at time of publication.

Library of Congress Cataloging-in-Publication Data

Names: Maliniak, Daniel, editor. | Peterson, Susan, 1961-editor. | Powers, Ryan, editor. | Tierney, Michael J. (Professor of government), editor.
Title: Bridging the Theory-Practice Divide in International Relations/ Daniel Maliniak, Susan Peterson, Ryan Powers, Michael J. Tierney.
Description: Washington, DC : Georgetown University Press, 2020. | Includes bibliographical references and index.
Identifiers: LCCN 2019035464 (print) | LCCN 2019035465 (ebook) | ISBN 9781626167810 (hardcover) | ISBN 9781626167827 (paperback) | ISBN 9781626167834 (ebook)
Subjects: LCSH: International relations—Study and teaching. | International relations—Research. | International relations specialists.
Classification: LCC JZ1237 .B49 2020 (print) | LCC JZ1237 (ebook) | DDC 327—dc23
LC record available at https://lccn.loc.gov/2019035464
LC ebook record available at https://lccn.loc.gov/2019035465

∞ This book is printed on acid-free paper meeting the requirements of the American National Standard for Permanence in Paper for Printed Library Materials.

21 20     9 8 7 6 5 4 3 2   First printing

Printed in the United States of America

Cover design by Jeremy John Parker.
Photo by Nico E. | Unsplash.

# CONTENTS

# ILLUSTRATIONS

## FIGURES

## TABLES

# ACKNOWLEDGMENTS

In many ways this book traces its origins to a series of conversations between faculty and students at William & Mary more than fifteen years ago. The students routinely pushed the faculty to think more deeply about our discipline and our place in it. They asked why political scientists seemed to write exclusively for others in the field and to teach their students to do the same. They repeatedly asked that their coursework (and related research opportunities) be more closely linked to the practice of international relations (IR). They asked good, smart questions: Why do professors spend so much time in class teaching us about structural realism and the various flavors of constructivism? How will this help us to do better work at the State Department, World Bank, or Amnesty International after we graduate? Does any of the research done in the IR field actually shape the thinking and behavior of policymakers? What else should we study, other than political science, to affect outcomes in the real world?

We did not always have good answers to these questions because our answers were rooted in anecdotes and second-hand observations. We had plenty of theory and good evidence about war, trade, human rights, and foreign aid, but we lacked theory and good evidence about our own discipline, which are necessary conditions for social scientific inference. To address any of these questions in a serious way, we would need a more systematic approach to studying the teaching and research practices of IR scholars and we would need data on what practitioners find most useful from their counterparts in the academy.

The Teaching, Research and International Policy (TRIP) Project grew out of those early conversations, which continued at William & Mary and, later, at the University of California, San Diego (UCSD) and the University of Wisconsin, as Dan and Ryan continued their studies. For many years, we focused most of our efforts at TRIP on disciplinary questions about the paradigmatic commitments, methodological choices, and substantive focus of IR scholars, using both surveys and content analysis of peer-reviewed journal articles.

With this book we come full circle, returning to our early conversations about the relevance of the IR discipline to the real world of international politics. This volume emerged from long-running conversations among the four of us, and with colleagues and students, about how the data we had gathered and produced on the IR discipline might speak to growing concerns about the divide between scholars and practitioners. We sought to describe and explain what many thought was a growing gap between the theory and practice of IR. Others in the discipline made a similar turn, doing the important work of trying to close this gap, particularly in the area of national security policy. Our efforts, in contrast, have focused on more fully characterizing the divide empirically and, crucially, identifying the structural forces that cause the divide and cause it to vary in magnitude over time and across issue areas. This book is a result of those efforts.

This book brings together twenty-six scholars and practitioners to explore the nature and extent of the gap across eight IR subfields: human rights, the environment, foreign aid and development, international trade, money and finance, intrastate conflict and terrorism, interstate war, and nuclear strategy. Even though this is not a book about how to bridge the gap between scholars and practitioners, we engage in a bit of bridge building of our own: we bring leading IR scholars into direct conversations with a wide range of policy practitioners. The result is a first-of-its-kind assessment of the theory-practice divide in IR that includes perspectives not only from both sides of the divide but also across a range of substantive issue areas. We hope the book itself makes a contribution to our understanding of the relationship between the theory and practice of international relations, but we are even more confident that the publicly accessible datasets on which this book is based, and which are now publicly available for other scholars to use, will make a greater long-term contribution to our understanding of the IR discipline and its interaction with the policy world.

On the long road from our initial conversations to the publication of this book we have incurred many debts. Certainly, the book would not have been possible without financial support from the Carnegie Corporation of New York, which allowed us to expand our time-series data on peer-reviewed publications, faculty views on the discipline and foreign policy issues, publications in policy journals, public opinion on foreign policy and the role of expert opinion, policymakers' views on scholarly ideas and evidence, and real-time responses by IR faculty to international events and issues in the form of "snap polls." Steve Del Rosso helped to shape this project from the outset. His continued thoughtful engagement, as evidenced by his participation in (and insightful commentary throughout) the main planning conference that led to this book, was invaluable. Steve's vision for Carnegie's International Peace and Security Program has had a powerful influence on our discipline's recent turn toward applied research. He and his colleague, Aaron Stanley, are the ideal partners—intellectual collaborators with a long-term commitment to the production of public goods. Building bridges between the academic and policy worlds of IR requires strong foundations on both sides of this gap. Carnegie has been working for more than ten years to ensure that there are strong foundations within the academy.

In the development of this book we also benefited from numerous conversations with other scholars and practitioners who have been grappling with similar questions over the past decade or more. Debbie Avant, Paul Avey, Tim Büthe, Brent Colburn, Mike Desch, Dan Drezner, Jesse Driscoll, Marty Finnemore, Frank Gavin, Jim Goldgeier, Cullen Hendrix, Mike Horowitz, Bruce Jentleson, Mara Karlin, Judith Kelley, John Kirn, Steven Linett, Renee Lipari, James Long, Michael McCoy, Marcus Newland, Dan Nielson, Amy Oakes, Brad Parks, Christian Peratsakis, Jon Pevehouse, Sneha Raghavan, Mitchell Reiss, Idean Salehyan, Jason Sharman, Jim Steinberg, Jordan Tama, Steve Van Evera, Erik Voeten, Barbara Walter, and Kate Weaver all helped shape our thinking on this important topic. We are also indebted to the contributors to this volume, whose willingness to share their research and expertise in their respective issue areas taught us much about the theory-practice divide and helped shape our arguments about it and our future data collection plans. We appreciate their patience with an unusually long review process that, ironically, highlights just one of the many differences between the worlds inhabited by our academic authors and our policy practitioner contributors.

We also owe a large debt of gratitude to a number of institutions and the people who lead them. The William & Mary Washington Center hosted the first conference of potential contributors back in 2014, which ultimately led to this book. We also thank the Reves Center for International Studies and the Office of the Dean of Arts & Sciences at William & Mary for support. William & Mary, UCSD, University of Wisconsin–Madison, Yale University, and the University of Georgia all offered supportive research environments for one or more of us during the years we spent working on this book. Finally, we are indebted to the faculty, students, and staff of the Global Research Institute at William & Mary; their work inspires and supports this research and many related areas of applied research on global issues.

We are especially indebted to a number of former students, research assistants, and staff. The work of Nicky Bell, Darin Self, Elizabeth Martin, Hannah Petrie, Kaden Paulson-Smith, Eric Parajon, and Emily Jackson in their capacities as TRIP project managers was instrumental in the production of the TRIP datasets on which this volume is based. Emily, Eric, and Hannah deserve special recognition. They exerted herculean efforts in managing four editors, twenty-six authors, eighteen chapters, and dozens of undergraduate research assistants as they helped shepherd this volume through the submission, revision, and production process. Other students and project managers who helped inspire this project and provided the sweat equity to bring it to life include Ishita Ahmed, Ben Arancibia, Alex Bellah, Peter Bergen, Will Brannon, Becca Brown, Michael Campbell, Jonathan Chan, Vera Choo, Isabelle Cohen, Nicole Cook, Anca Cretu,

Henry Crossman, Marc Dion, Aidan Donovan, Luke Elias, Jillian Feirson, Logan Ferrell, Brendan Helm, Jack Hoagland, Lindsay Hundley, Sam Hynes, Ashley Ingram, Moira Johnson, Jess Jones, Mark Jordan, Richard Jordan, Jen Keister, James Long, Sasha Maliniak, Connor McCann, Doug McNamara, Rich Nielson, Ana O'Harrow, Remington Pool, Brad Potter, Ola Pozor, Matt Ribar, Megan Smith, Kaity Smoot, Kara Starr, Alena Stern, Brandon Stewart, Hannah Thornton, Raj Trivedi, Elsa Voytas, Mike Weissberger, Emily Wilson, and Taylor Wilson. We are particularly proud that a number of these former TRIP staff members and research assistants have gone on to highly regarded international relations and political science PhD programs at Cornell, Harvard, Johns Hopkins, Ohio State, Penn, Princeton, Stanford, UCSD, Wisconsin, and elsewhere.

Because this book is the result of a long collaboration among many people, there undoubtedly are individuals we have forgotten to thank. If you're one of them, we apologize for the omission and ask that you know we are grateful for your contribution. To those we do mention here, we apologize if we have not always heeded your wise counsel; any errors or omissions, of course, remain our own.

Finally, we thank Don Jacobs at Georgetown University Press. From the first time we spoke to Don about the project, he was supportive. Throughout the review and editorial process, his steady hand provided guidance that improved the book in countless ways.

We dedicate this book to our former, current, and future students at William & Mary and the University of Georgia who continue to ask tough questions and inspire important answers.

*Daniel Maliniak*
*Susan Peterson*
*Ryan Powers*
*Michael J. Tierney*

Williamsburg, Virginia, and Athens, Georgia

# 1

# EXPLAINING THE THEORY-PRACTICE DIVIDE IN INTERNATIONAL RELATIONS
## *Uncertainty and Access*

Daniel Maliniak, Susan Peterson, Ryan Powers, and Michael J. Tierney

I s research produced by scholars of international relations (IR) relevant to contemporary policy debates? Do policymakers understand that research? If they do, is it useful to them? In recent years, commentators have bemoaned the uselessness of academic IR research to policymakers and practitioners. In early 2014, *New York Times* columnist Nicholas Kristof wrote, "My onetime love, political science . . . seems to be trying, in terms of practical impact, to commit suicide." Around the same time, David Rothkopf, then editor of *Foreign Policy*, echoed this assessment; "academic contributions," he argued, are often too "opaque, abstract, incremental, dull" to be relevant to policy practitioners (2014). After perusing an issue of the peer-reviewed journal *International Security*, influential war correspondent Tom Ricks (2014) similarly lamented the "extraordinary irrelevance of political science."

These declarations on the irrelevance of IR and political science more broadly came, ironically, at a time when many political scientists sought to move their own discipline in a more policy-relevant direction. Almost a decade earlier, Stephen M. Walt (2005) called on IR scholars to take seriously the substantive needs of policymakers even if it meant abandoning sophisticated methodological tools. Similarly, in 2009 Joseph Nye took to the *Washington Post* op-ed pages to argue that IR scholars should consider serving in government at some point in their careers. He argued that both public policy and the scholars' postgovernment scholarship would be improved by the experience. Nye's sentiments were widely held among the broader community of IR scholars at the time. A 2011 Teaching, Research, and International Policy (TRIP) survey of IR scholars at US universities (Maliniak et al. 2012) revealed that respondents overwhelmingly share these views; they perceive that there is a large gap between scholars and policymakers and that this gap should be narrowed. In all, 85 percent of IR scholars in the United States think that the academic-policy divide is as large as, or larger than, it was twenty to thirty years ago, and 92 percent believe there should be greater links between policy and academic communities (Maliniak et al. 2012).[1]

With this clear demand within the academy for increased links between scholars and policy practitioners as context, it is not surprising that a number of prominent initiatives emerged to facilitate more and deeper interaction between scholars and policymakers. Perhaps most visible has been the growing presence of political scientists and IR scholars in day-to-day policy debates taking place online and in prominent news outlets. *The Washington Post*, for example, hosts Daniel Drezner's widely read column, *The Monkey Cage*, which regularly features research and commentary from IR scholars, was self-consciously founded on the premise that political science research "gets short shrift" in the media and among policymakers (Sides 2007). Similar efforts by scholars to communicate their research, analysis, and commentary are found in other online outlets that are read extensively in policy circles. These include *War on the Rocks, Lawfare, The Conversation*, and *Political Violence at a Glance*. Similarly, an increasing number of prominent IR scholars have taken to Twitter to discuss foreign policy issues of the day with reporters and the public. In addition, some academic institutions are seeking to train students to contribute more directly to policy debates. The Bridging the Gap Project, for example, hosts well-attended workshops designed to help PhD students and faculty make their research more policy relevant and accessible to nonacademic audiences. As part of this initiative, Bridging the Gap partnered with Oxford University Press to create a new series featuring scholarly books that explore important international policy problems.

There is, in short, a vibrant and growing community of institutions and scholars making significant investments—in both time and money—to narrow the gap between scholars and policymakers. Despite these investments, as a discipline we lack systematic answers to some of the most basic questions about the nature of the theory-practice divide. How big is it? Why does it exist? Is the gap the result of incentives and constraints imposed on scholars by the academy? Or are policymakers and/or the structure of the policy problems they confront to blame? How does the nature and size of the gap vary by substantive issue area? Are some policy problems more amenable to input from scholarly experts than others? Is input from scholars only useful or possible at certain points in time?

We asked leading scholars in eight different issue areas (trade, finance and money, human rights, foreign aid and development, environment, nuclear weapons and strategy, interstate war, and intrastate conflict) to address these and similar questions in a series of research essays. We paired these scholars with veteran policy practitioners who comment on these essays and offer their own reflections on the nature of the theory-practice divide in their area of expertise. This book's chapter on the theory-practice divide in trade policy research exemplifies these contributions. Two of the discipline's most prominent scholars of trade politics, Edward D. Mansfield and Jon C. W. Pevehouse, provide a chapter on the history of the theory-practice divide in trade policy research. Ambassador Robert Zoellick, who served as US trade representative under President George W. Bush and undersecretary of state for economic and agricultural affairs for President George H. W. Bush, offers a response.[2] The resulting discussion reveals areas in which IR research on trade both affects and is affected by the policy community, but it also reminds us of areas in which scholars and policy officials remain ships passing in the night, constrained from deeper and more frequent engagement by circumstances beyond their immediate control.

To facilitate these scholar-practitioner exchanges, we asked our academic contributors to focus their efforts on producing descriptions of how research in their substantive issue area has influenced (or been influenced by) international policy. We asked practitioners from each issue area, who all had significant experience crafting, implementing, and/or advocating for specific policies, to provide commentary on where scholarly ideas, data, theories, and methods have been useful and where academics might focus their efforts to more effectively speak to the policy community. To ground the discussions empirically, we provided both the scholars and policy practitioners with access to a number of TRIP datasets and an annotated bibliography on the theory-practice divide, but we also invited them to gather their own original data, use other existing datasets, and draw on their professional experiences and those of their colleagues trying to navigate the theory-practice divide. The result of these efforts is a first-of-its kind conversation between leading IR scholars and veteran practitioners across eight substantive issue areas. We believe this book provides important new insights into the nature and size of the theory-practice divide in IR and, as important, sets the stage for future efforts to measure, understand, and, where possible, narrow the gap between theory and practice in IR.

This comparative study of the theory-practice divide highlights two features of policy problems that shape the ability and/or willingness of scholars with expertise in different substantive issue areas to influence policy and policymakers: 1) the level of uncertainty surrounding a policy problem and its proposed solutions, and 2) the level of access that scholars have to policymakers. In addition, we also highlight two sets of professional incentives that may affect IR scholars' research choices regardless of substantive issue area: 1) pressures to employ sophisticated research methods, and 2) lack of rewards for communicating research findings to the public or to practitioners outside of academia.

In this chapter, we highlight the book's novel contributions to the literature on the theory-practice divide. We then define key concepts and explain the vocabulary we use to describe various ways that scholars might be involved in the policymaking or implementation process. Next, we introduce our theory of the theory-practice divide, which is grounded in work on the role of epistemic communities and policy change. We then describe the mechanisms through which scholars and scholarship might engage, influence, and/or simply be relevant to policy debates and outcomes. Next, we reverse the causal arrow and ask how real-world events and policies might influence scholarly research. We conclude with a brief outline of the book.

## BRINGING SCHOLARS AND PRACTITIONERS FACE TO FACE OVER THE THEORY-PRACTICE DIVIDE

Until recently, most students of the relationship between the academic and policy communities of international relations argued that there is a sizable and growing gap between the two groups and that this gap was a problem.[3] Observers of the gap often blame academic norms and incentive structures for its existence and persistence (e.g., Kruzel 1994; Walt 2005, 2009; Nau 2008; Jones 2009; Nye 2009; Jentlesen and Ratner 2011). Robert Gallucci (2012), former president of the MacArthur Foundation, denounces "the incentive structure in universities and in disciplines [that] has endorsed [an] emphasis on theory and methodology." Hiring, tenure, and promotion standards earn particular scorn among critics for failing to give policy experiences sufficient weight, actively discouraging junior faculty from taking time off to gain policy experience, neglecting policy-relevant research and publications, and not hiring sufficient policy practitioners within the academy (e.g., Diamond 2002; Jentlesen 2002; Nye 2009; Walt 2009; Mahnken 2010). Scholarship is criticized for being too abstract, arcane, and theoretical (e.g., George 1997; Haass 2002; Jentlesen 2002, Mahnken 2010). Many of these arguments about the negative effects of academic culture also claim that it has created a discipline characterized by increasingly specialized and esoteric methodological approaches. John Mearsheimer calls this the "mathematization" of the discipline (Miller 2001). More recently, Michael C. Desch has argued in a number of outlets, including his chapter with Paul Avey in this volume, that the IR discipline's increasing reliance on quantitative and formal methods has contributed significantly to its declining relevance (see Avey and Desch 2014; Desch 2015, 2019a; also see Oren 2015; Walt 1999; Martin 1999).

Some works that assign responsibility to the academy for the existence and persistence of the theory-practice divide argue that the problem is less about the content of scholarly work and more about the format and/or effective communication of that research to policy officials. Much of what comes out of the academy, critics lament, simply is not readable and/or doesn't address issues of interest to practitioners (e.g., Kurth 1998; Putnam 2003; Hurrell 2011). Observers likewise bemoan the time it takes to bring peer-reviewed publications to print (Bennett and Ikenberry 2006) and argue that scholars do a poor job packaging and marketing their work for the policy community (Lepgold 1998; Eriksson and Norman 2011). Michael Barnett (2006) claims that policymakers miss the nuance in academic research for this reason; scholars need to present their findings in short, easily digestible "talking points" in outlets such as *Foreign Policy* magazine. Joseph Kruzel (1994) made a similar point decades ago, when he wrote that scholars could bridge the gap by translating their knowledge into the accessible language of op-eds, briefings, and faxes. Recently, the Bridging the Gap Project housed at American University has responded to this perceived need by teaching academics to produce and effectively communicate policy-relevant research to practitioners.

Other observers of the academic-policy divide blame policy officials and staffers for neglecting IR scholars' advice. A common refrain is that practitioners do not have the time (Lieberthal 2006; Goldman 2006; Avey and Desch 2014) and/or interest (Siverson 2000; Jentlesen and Ratner 2011) to read academic journals and books. This view is echoed by several of the practitioners who contributed to this volume. As former chief economist for the US Agency for International Development Steven Radelet notes in chapter 7, "Neither policymakers nor their staff have time to wade through 40-page papers that cover literature reviews, methodological approaches, data issues, and results. They just aren't going to do it."

This literature on the theory-practice divide is extensive, but it suffers from several limitations. First, there is a decided security bias in both the discussion of and efforts to address the gap between policymakers and scholars. Less ink has been spilled on gaps between policymakers and scholars in the trade or human rights areas. A recent review of the literature on the theory-practice divide shows that 49 percent of all articles and book chapters on the subject of the academic-policy gap have been written by experts from the security subfield (Campbell et al. 2015), even though the 2014 TRIP faculty survey showed that only about 21 percent of all IR scholars in the United States claim that international security is their primary area of research. The commentaries that we highlighted at the outset of this chapter illustrate this point; they focus almost exclusively on how scholars of international security might better serve policymakers and implementers in the security policy arena in the United States. Second, and perhaps as a consequence of the first issue, there is both a paucity of systematic data and a lack of theorizing about the nature and evolution of the theory-practice divide in IR over time or across different issue areas. Nearly all the work on the gap is based on firsthand experience in the academy, policy circles, or both (Lowenthal and Bertucci 2014). And, because the dominant explanations for the gap focus on professional incentives within the academy or the limited time that policymakers have to engage with traditional scholarly outputs, they are unable to explain variation in the gap across IR subfields. This is the case because academic incentives and policymakers' time and interests do not vary systematically, for the most part, across those subfields. These weaknesses in existing work combine to provide scholars and policymakers alike with a view of the theory-practice divide that is most relevant to scholars of US national security at particular moments. Previous work on the gap provides only partial insight into why particular scholars in particular issue areas at particular moments in time are effective in influencing policy debates, whereas others, presumably working in the shadow of the same professional incentive structure, are not. Further, this literature fails to consider how strategies for making scholarship more immediately useful to policymakers might vary by issue area or change over time.

In this volume, we begin to overcome these limitations by providing some of the first systematic measures of the nature of the theory-practice divide over time and across multiple substantive issue areas. We use empirical data to jumpstart an issue area–by–issue area conversation between scholars and policymakers on the theory-practice divide in IR. These conversations provide something for readers from both communities and offer insight into the nature and causes of the gaps that exist between scholars and policymakers in different issue areas and how they evolve over time.

The contributors to this volume use data gathered over a fifteen-year period by the TRIP project at William & Mary on the perceptions and the behavior of IR scholars.[4] These data include responses by IR scholars in thirty-six countries to more than one hundred different survey questions in six distinct omnibus surveys (fielded in 2004, 2006, 2008, 2011, 2014, and 2017). These surveys asked respondents numerous questions about their substantive research and teaching interests, their perceptions of the nature and magnitude of the theory-practice divide, and their views on whether and how scholars and policymakers should respond to that gap. A series of "snap polls" that assess scholarly opinion on contemporary international issues of immediate concern to policymakers and the public provide authors with additional information about scholars' policy preferences, the causes and anticipated effects of various policies, and expected outcomes of international crises or negotiations. Finally, a database of more than seven thousand articles published in the twelve leading peer-reviewed IR journals from 1980 to the present provide contributors with insight into the actual research outputs of IR scholars over the last forty years. For each article in this database, the TRIP project recorded data on research methodology, substantive issue area, theoretical paradigm, regional focus, time period under study, policy recommendations, and twenty-one other variables.

To this, our contributors brought a wealth of their own qualitative and quantitative data. Many of the academic authors, for instance, relied on historical evidence from both primary and secondary sources (see chapters by Murdie, Green and Hale, Schneider, Mansfield and Pevehouse, Findley and Young, and Avey and Desch). Others employ original data from structured interviews with policymakers (Schneider) or their own or others' surveys of policymakers (Avey and Desch, Kreps and Weeks). Still others employ newly collected bibliometric data (Murdie). The contributors to this volume thus present readers with what we believe to be the first attempt to *systematically* characterize the theory-practice divide in IR and then to reflect critically on that gap in conversation with veteran policy practitioners.

Our emphasis on systematic data does not imply that the conclusions drawn by our contributing authors are the final word on the theory-practice divide in IR. To the contrary, we expect the questions that we address here to be the topic of debate and inquiry for years to come. Instead, we highlight the systematic nature of the data because these data allow our contributors and readers to assess the theory-practice divide in both intertemporal and comparative perspective. This is important because, as noted previously, most of what we think we know about the academic-policy gap comes from experts in a single subfield and relies almost exclusively on case studies, reflections on personal experience, and anecdotes. The TRIP data allow our contributors to speak to questions about the size and nature of the theory-practice divide and how it might vary over time and across subfields. We hope and expect that readers will demand (and produce) more and better evidence to support a second generation of systematic empirical work on the IR discipline and the theory-practice divide.

A final contribution of this volume to our understanding of the theory-practice divide is a theory that outlines the conditions under which scholars and scholarship are most likely to influence policy outcomes. Our theoretical argument is motivated by our knowledge of and experiences in the IR discipline and the empirical regularities highlighted by our contributors. The argument we develop draws more generally on the role of epistemic communities, as well as bureaucratic incentives, in shaping policy outputs. Disciplinary incentives matter in shaping the theory-practice divide, but in this book we argue that two other factors are just as, if not more, important: variation across issues areas in levels of policy uncertainty and the porousness of the policy process. Before developing this argument more fully, we consider what it means for research to be policy relevant or influential in the policy process.

## A VOCABULARY OF THE THEORY-PRACTICE DIVIDE

When IR students ask what role scholars and scholarship play in making policy or influencing the decisions or behavior of individuals working in governmental organizations, intergovernmental organizations (IGOs), or nongovernmental organizations (NGOs), they often assume a model of influence in which policy officials pull a theoretical model off the shelf and implement policies that logically follow from it. In chapter 14, for example, Michael Findley and Joseph Young describe an experience early in their careers in which one of the authors submitted a manuscript to a peer-reviewed scholarly journal and subsequently received a revise-and-resubmit decision from the journal's editor. One of the reviewers noted that, before endorsing publication of the manuscript, the author would need to summarize the policy implications of his research. Findley and Young (in chapter 14) write, "The flawed logic suggests that scholars write an academic paper, fill it full of jargon, add some stars and bolded numbers, publish it in a gated venue, and put two paragraphs at the end of a long, oddly structured article that explains how state policies should be changed. And the 'policymakers'—presumably a Hillary Clinton or Mike Pompeo—will be paying attention and change things."

In reality, influence is often more subtle and less direct. As Findley and Young suggest, providing explicit policy prescriptions is just one way in which scholarly ideas might affect policy, and it may not be a very important one at that. Mechanisms for shaping policy range from scholars' influence on students, who may become practitioners or researchers in think tanks or government agencies, to the direct involvement of scholars in the policy process, with many points in between.[5] In discussing these different mechanisms, we find it useful to distinguish among three closely related, yet distinct, concepts: relevance, engagement, and influence. In general, although there are important differences among the three concepts, the greater the relevance of IR scholarship, the more influence scholars assert on policy; and the more they engage in the policy process, the narrower the gap between the academic and policy communities.

## Relevance

It is now de rigueur in some circles to judge contemporary IR scholarship by its "policy relevance," but the term nearly always goes undefined. When its meaning is clarified, scholars often adopt a relatively narrow definition in which relevance signals the degree to which research is problem driven and/or contains explicit policy recommendations. Desch (2019a), for example, defines policy recommendations as "the core of policy-relevance." Similarly, Daniel Byman and Matthew Kroenig (2016) write that policy-relevant scholarship is work that "produces ideas that feature in the deliberations of senior government officials as they weigh policy decisions." Andrew Bennett and G. John Ikenberry (2006) define relevance as research that "offers direct information that bears on policy choices."[6] Results from six waves of the TRIP faculty survey in the United States show that, by these definitions of relevance, most IR scholars do not believe that their research is policy relevant. From 2004 through 2017 the proportion of US scholars who describe their own research as "applied" (i.e., motivated by a policy problem) rather than "basic" (research for the sake of knowledge) has consistently hovered around one-third. In response to a different question, just 35 percent of US respondents in 2011 said their research was "primarily motivated by the policy relevance of the topic."

Figure 1.1, which is based on data from TRIP's journal article database, shows that only a small percentage of articles published in major peer-reviewed academic journals contain policy recommendations, and this number has been declining since 1980. Today, less than 5 percent of all articles in the top twelve journals in the discipline contain explicit advice for policy practitioners.

In our view (and that of many of our contributors), defining relevance as research that either is driven by specific policy problems or contains specific policy recommendations narrows the conceptual aperture too much. Policy prescriptions in peer-reviewed scholarly articles represent only one measure of the relevance of scholarly ideas. And scholars interested in communicating their findings to a policy audience in a timely manner are unlikely to embed their recommendations in a scholarly article that may take two or more years to find its way into print and is unlikely to be widely read in the policy community. In chapter 14, Findley and Young "wonder in particular whether the scholars least engaged are the ones who offer blunt policy prescriptions in articles, whereas those who are more engaged find much more subtle yet effective ways to communicate lessons learned."

In everyday usage, something is relevant to the extent that it is germane or connected to an issue under consideration, or it meets the needs of the

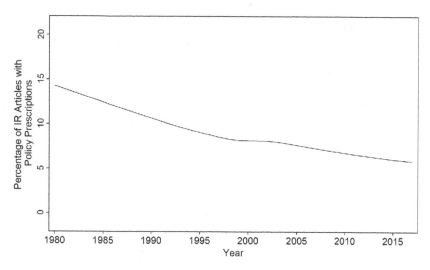

**FIGURE 1.1.** Proportion of IR articles with policy prescriptions, 1980–2017

user of the information. Research could therefore be policy relevant even if it does not contain specific policy recommendations and/or is not motivated by a particular policy problem. We thus use the terms "policy relevance" or "relevance" according to this more colloquial definition to describe academic ideas and findings that are potentially useful to policy practitioners—those tasked with making or implementing decisions within government agencies, IGOs, or NGOs—regardless of whether those ideas are ever enacted as policy.[7] In addition, practitioners also may believe that having access to systematic evidence, ideas, or methods generated by academics helps them learn lessons, understand cultural context, justify policy choices, and/or make judgments even if the scholarship does not speak directly to or provide categorical advice about a particular policy issue.[8]

Even by this broader definition, the relevance of IR scholarship is often questioned. A number of prominent "in-and-outers," individuals who alternate between policy and academic jobs, have sharply criticized IR scholarship for its lack of relevance (Nye 2008a, 2008b, 2009; Gallucci 2012). Avey and Desch's (2014) study of policymakers' views on academic research at least partially supports the anecdotal arguments: current and former US security and defense officials report that the arguments and evidence produced in history, economics, and area studies are more useful than those in political science and international affairs. These practitioners also find theoretical analysis, formal models, and quantitative analysis significantly less valuable than area studies, historical case studies, and contemporary case studies. The Avey and Desch survey is limited to senior policy officials in one issue area and asks a limited range of questions that focus on "big ideas" from the IR literature, rather than data and empirical findings produced by social scientists, but it is currently the best published evidence we have on what policy practitioners say they want from IR scholars.[9]

This broader definition of relevance also leaves room for policy-relevant insights to make their way into the hands of policymakers in forms other than peer-reviewed research outputs. For example, the TRIP project coded nearly 1,500 articles published in two major policy journals, *Foreign Affairs* and *Foreign Policy*, between 2000 and 2015. More than 41 percent of articles in these journals include explicit policy prescriptions, and just over half (53.6 percent) explicitly reference academic knowledge—that is, academic publications, academic evidence, or arguments or concepts that originate in whole or in part within the ivory tower. TRIP researchers also assembled a dataset of articles from the curriculum vitae (CVs) of about 1,500 IR scholars who had published at least one article in the top twelve peer-reviewed journals between 1980 and 2016 and who had made their CVs publicly available. We coded each CV for the number of authored or coauthored articles in policy journals. The resulting database shows that approximately 15 percent of articles published by IR scholars appear in policy, rather than scholarly, outlets. These two data points suggest that insights drawn from the academy are more widespread in policy debates than more narrow definitions of policy relevance might suggest.

## Influence

IR scholars may produce policy-relevant research that seeks to engage the policy community, but the content of foreign and international policy still may not reflect their ideas or insights. We reserve the term *influence* for ideas or empirical findings that have an effect on practitioners and/or the policies they craft. By this definition, scholarly concepts and ideas that do not shape policy officials' beliefs, conversations, or choices are said to lack influence. Findley and Young argue that this is probably the modal level of influence for academic concepts and ideas, because many academics do not seek to influence policy, whereas others want to but fail. When academic ideas change practitioners' behavior, whether in the formulation or the implementation of policy, those ideas are said to be influential.[10]

Between these two extremes are a number of direct and indirect ways in which scholarly ideas or findings affect policy and the people who craft it. We generally think we know direct influence when we see it: practitioners consult directly with academic experts or incorporate academic ideas, concepts, and/ or evidence in the decision-making process and/or policy. And, as we note in our discussion of engagement, there is some conceptual overlap in some forms of direct engagement and direct influence. Probably the least direct but most common avenue of influence involves educating students who go on to hold policy positions. IR scholars, especially those who teach at policy schools, have an enormous potential to affect policy by influencing the way their students conceptualize the major actors and processes in international politics. Those students may take policy jobs, teach other students who later enter the policy community, become activists who access the policy process, or simply influence practitioners through discussion and interaction. These effects may increase when scholars teach mid-career policy officials (Eriksson and Sundelius 2005). In all these cases, even when we do not see direct effects, we may find what, at the Strengthening the Links Conference, Stephen Del Rosso of the Carnegie Corporation of New York called "trace elements" of academic ideas in policy.[11] Research may less commonly, but still indirectly, influence policy and policymakers. Concepts, theory, or findings drawn from peer-reviewed scholarship also may help set the agenda for, or frame the terms of, policy debates. As the Avey and Desch (2014) survey of security policymakers demonstrates, policymakers are familiar with many IR concepts and theories published in academic and nonacademic outlets.

By their nature, these indirect avenues create space for policymakers to advance academic insights because of their applicability to a particular policy problem, but such insights also may have utility in private or public political battles. As Christina Boswell (2009) shows, practitioners may appropriate academic ideas to bolster their own or their agency's credibility or to lend credibility to controversial claims or high-risk decisions. Johan Eriksson and Ludvig Norman (2011) similarly show that ideas may be used for instrumental or symbolic reasons and not always in the ways intended by the scholars who originally advanced them: President George W. Bush and his advisors refuted key parts of Samuel Huntington's "clash of civilizations" thesis, but Bush still used the idea symbolically to justify what his administration portrayed as a conflict between modern, liberal ideology and terrorist ideologies. Likewise, the Bush administration sometimes invoked the democratic peace as a post hoc justification for the war in Iraq (Russet 2005).

## Engagement

Understanding the impact of IR scholarship on foreign and international policy requires understanding the relevance and influence of scholarly ideas, but it also demands consideration of the many ways in which academics participate in policymaking processes and/or attempt to shape those processes. These activities range from attempts to write for and to the policy community to participation in the policy process as a member of a government, NGO, or IGO staff.

Some IR scholars distill their research into policy briefs, op-eds, blog posts, and other works aimed directly at the policy community. In the last few years, *The Washington Post* has hired several IR and foreign affairs scholars to provide commentary on current events, either through their own column or through regular contributions to the *Post*'s blog, *The Monkey Cage*. Another blog, *Political Violence at a Glance*, includes academic analysis on violent conflict and protest. The importance of these blogs and other online outlets as a means of reaching out to policy practitioners was echoed by many participants in the Strengthening the Links Conference at William & Mary, including Peter Feaver, who in chapter 13 claims, "I know for a fact that well-placed advisors in the Obama and Trump administrations make use of *Monkey Cage.*"

Further along the continuum of scholarly engagement, members of the policy community regularly consult IR scholars through a number of channels.[12] Academics often give congressional testimony in their areas of expertise. For example, John Ruggie, professor of political science at Columbia University, offered congressional testimony in 2001 on the efficacy of the United Nations (UN) Oil for Food program in Iraq; James Fearon of Stanford University testified to Congress in 2006 on civil war and sectarian violence in Iraq; and, more recently, Georgetown Assistant Professor Oriana Mastro addressed the Senate Foreign Relations Committee on US–China relations. Academics also frequently brief NGO, IGO, and government staffs, either on or off the record. As Green and Hale note in chapter 4, many multilateral organizations allow and invite members of civil society, including academics, to attend meetings as observers, submit briefs, or participate in "side events." Further, many IR scholars "moonlight"—that is, consult—for their national governments and/or other agencies.[13] In chapter 14, Findley and Young note the example of American University scholar Stephen Tankel, who is a nonresident fellow at the Carnegie Endowment for International Peace, where he engages practitioners through targeted policy briefs. In the 2014 TRIP faculty survey, 30 percent of IR scholars across all countries said that they had consulted in the previous two years for their national government, 13 percent had consulted for an IGO, and 21 percent had consulted for an NGO.

Finally, scholars may engage the policy community by temporarily leaving their academic positions and participating directly in the policy-making process on any number of levels. Many prominent political scientists have trod this well-worn "in-and-outer" path, including Woodrow Wilson, Henry Kissinger, Joseph Nye, Stephen Krasner, Anne-Marie Slaughter, Peter Feaver, and Jeremy Weinstein. In chapter 2, Murdie notes a different type of in-and-outer personified by James Ron, whose policy experience includes stints at a number of NGOs, including Human Rights Watch, the International Committee of the Red Cross, and CARE. These in-and-outers bring their scholarly expertise to their policy positions, whether governmental or nongovernmental, and, just as important, they carry their policy experience back to the university.

## A Word about the Targets of Scholarly Attempts to Shape Policy

Gauging the impact of ideas on policy requires understanding the range of possible targets of that influence. Most of the academics, practitioners, and pundits who lament the irrelevance of IR scholarship focus mainly on the foreign policy leadership—generally, the president and his top advisors—so it would be hard not to conclude that scholars lack influence. The contributions to this volume discuss the impact of academic ideas and findings on a wide range of policy practitioners, from principal decision-makers to those who implement policy and those actors who seek to influence policy. Green and Hale note, for example, the role of private actors like the Forestry Stewardship Council in setting environmental standards and regulating externalities. Murdie discusses the impact of the language of human rights promotion advanced by IR scholars on UN and NGO staffs. In their chapter on US nuclear doctrine, Avey and Desch examine the role of defense intellectuals at RAND as a source, rather than the target, of intellectual ideas.

Throughout this book we use the term *policy practitioner* to refer to a range of individuals who engage in the practice of international politics.[14] At one end of the spectrum are *policymakers*, high-level foreign policy officials within national governments—such as presidents, prime ministers, cabinet secretaries, and ambassadors—and international organizations. Members of this group are directly involved in making foreign and international policy or advising policymaking officials. *Policy staff*, in contrast, include the much more numerous lower level personnel within national governments and international organizations who are charged with providing inputs into the policymaking process and/or implementing foreign and international policy once it has been decided. Finally, *policy advocates* are leaders and staffers within private and nonprofit organizations who may influence policy through framing, agenda setting, or lobbying national and international policymakers and staff on behalf of particular policies.

Scholarly ideas may find a receptive audience among any of these types of policy practitioners. As academic literature on domestic structures has shown (e.g., Risse-Kappen 1991; Evangelista 1995; Peterson and Wenk 2001; Cortell 2005), ideas may have a harder time reaching the top, where there are fewer points of access, but they are likely to have a significant impact if they do. In contrast, academic ideas have a greater chance of getting heard by staffers and advocates, although they must compete with many other ideas at this level, and the staffers and advocates may have less influence on policy decisions. Because they implement policy, however, staffers nonetheless may have a particularly strong impact on the content of that policy. For this reason, they may be powerful conduits for academic ideas in the policy process.

# A THEORY OF THE THEORY-PRACTICE DIVIDE

Our theory of the gap between the academic and policy communities outlines the conditions under which IR scholars and scholarship are most likely to shape policy outcomes. We argue that although academic incentives matter, variation in the theory-practice divide over time and across issue areas is driven primarily by variation in the structure of the problems confronting policymakers and the level of uncertainty surrounding the nature of and proposed solutions to those problems.

Since the seminal work on epistemic communities and international cooperation published in the 1992 special issue of *International Organization*, IR scholarship has focused on the conditions under which epistemic communities—groups of individuals with an "authoritative claim to policy relevant knowledge" in a given issue domain (Haas 1992)—can shape policy outcomes (Hass and Adler 1992). A bevy of work suggests that epistemic communities—whether defined narrowly as groups of scientists or more broadly as encompassing larger societal groups like judges, doctors, or law enforcement professionals with similarly credible claims to expertise—can influence policy outcomes (see Cross 2011 for an excellent critical discussion of this literature). Economists were instrumental in designing the Bretton Woods trade, development, and monetary institutions (Ikenberry 1992; Demekas, this volume) and later the European Monetary Union (Verdun 1999). Mathematicians and physicists developed analytical tools that spurred demands for modern arms control policy (Adler 1992; Avey and Desch, this volume). Geophysicists have provided crucial insights into how best to address global climate change, and their insights have been integrated into the terms of international agreements and domestic legislation (Allan 2017). IR scholars, in short, have long appreciated the role that epistemic communities play in shaping, and even dictating, policy outcomes.

As we illustrated previously, however, many commentators are skeptical that the epistemic community of IR scholars can have the same kind of influence on policy today. To many of the observers cited previously, the central cause of this policy irrelevance follows from the professional incentives of scholars and the disciplinary institutions in which they work. Theories of epistemic communities suggest, however, that other factors, especially features of the policy problem, may be as or more important (Haas 1990; Radaelli 1999). Indeed, although this literature suggests numerous variables that influence the relative ability of epistemic communities to affect policy outcomes, they can be broadly classified according to 1) the level of uncertainty felt by political leaders and policymakers on an issue (Haas 1990; Radaelli 1999), and 2) the level of access that the epistemic community has to key decision-makers (Haas 1990; Drake and Nicolaidis 1992; Peterson 1995). With respect to the theory-practice divide in international relations, we argue that variation in these two variables explains why the gap between the academic and policy communities varies across substantive issue areas and over time.

## Variation in the Level of Uncertainty

Scholars are likely to have more influence on policy when practitioners must address policy problems about which they have high levels of uncertainty. They may be uncertain about the nature or extent of the policy problem or the tools needed to address the problem. In these cases, policymakers and practitioners have limited "off-the-shelf" solutions. Haas (1990) argues that uncertainty stemming from the relative novelty of deciding how to address the degradation of common pool resources allowed scientists and other subject matter experts to play a key role in regional cooperation over the cleanup of the Mediterranean. As Green and Hale similarly argue in chapter 4, the emerging nature of many global environmental issues increases opportunities for IR scholars to shape policy outcomes. Likewise, when policymakers needed to design procedures for deploying nuclear weapons to complement US military doctrine or grand strategy in the 1950s and 1960s, they (thankfully) lacked a lot of "real-world" experience with nuclear war or nuclear diplomacy. In this context, as Avey and Desch show in chapter 16, government officials turned to civilian theorists, including IR scholars located in universities, to theorize about how these new weapon systems might be deployed to compel or deter a geopolitical adversary. These ideas directly and indirectly influenced policy throughout the Cold War, but especially in the 1950s and 1960s. In a similar vein, Adler (1992) argued that this same community helped construct the idea of arms control and bring it into practice. Contemporary policy problems that share similar levels of policy uncertainty may encourage scholars to produce and policymakers to demand more relevant research, and they will likely provide space for academics to have substantial policy influence. Examples of such issue areas include cybersecurity, killer robots/drones, climate change, and space policy.[15] This analysis suggests our first major argument about the role of policy uncertainty:

> 1a. *Emerging issues provide more opportunities for scholars to have influence on policymaking and policy implementation than do perennial or long-standing issues.*

A closely related argument focuses on policy problems that require highly specialized, cutting-edge technical knowledge to solve. Practitioners simply lack the specific information they need to make informed policy decisions about such issues. In chapter 4, Green and Hale explain that, in the context of climate change policy in the 1990s, the relevant authorities within states and IOs did not have "in-house expertise" from which to draw. Therefore, there were more opportunities for scholars with technical expertise to provide ideas and evidence that informed policymaking or the monitoring of policy commitments within this issue area.[16] Similarly, practitioners don't always need novel ideas or theories; sometimes they require new types of data or methods that "in-house" staff are not in a position to create or employ. As Schneider explains in chapter 6 in the context of international development policy, the use of randomized controlled trials to evaluate the impact of aid projects or the use of machine learning to categorize project-level data enable decision-makers to target resources, enhance interdonor coordination, and/or track the locations and types of Chinese development projects (also see Strange et al. 2017). Similarly, in chapter 14 Findley and Young argue that big data techniques for harvesting raw event data, employing Bayesian algorithms, and weighting different forecasts allow the Integrated Crisis Early Warning System, built by a consortium of conflict researchers at three different universities, to generate daily predictions about terrorist attacks and political instability. These forecasts are integrated into tools that allow combatant commanders to visualize data for use in operational planning and intelligence analysis. This discussion generates the following argument:

> 1b. *Highly technical issues where cutting edge methods are in demand provide more opportunities for scholars to have influence than do issues in which technical questions and existing methods are well understood by practitioners.*

## Variation in the Level of Access to Key Decision-Makers

Nuclear strategy, the design of environmental monitoring regimes, and tracking nontransparent Chinese aid require novel technical and methodological solutions, but something similar could be said for analyses of monetary or trade policy. Nevertheless, the chapters on money and trade in this book, written by both academics and practitioners, suggest that IR scholars have played only a limited role in shaping policy in their areas of expertise. These two issue areas highlight an additional important factor: the level of access that IR scholars have to policymakers. As we note in the following section, this could vary because IR scholars are displaced by scholars from another discipline, but it may also vary according to the issue area–specific differences in the level at which and the frequency with which policymakers and practitioners make decisions.

With respect to the displacement of IR scholars, we note that even if scholarly knowledge is demanded (and financed) by policy practitioners within a given issue area, the opportunities for scholars to influence policy will be constrained when some other discipline currently occupies that policy space. The chapters on trade (Pevehouse and Mansfield), finance (Pepinsky and Steinberg), and, to a lesser extent, foreign aid and development (Schneider) all conclude that either demand for scholarly knowledge and training is being largely met by the discipline of economics or, because of network effects, policymakers in these issue areas look for expertise almost exclusively among their codisciplinarians.[17] This is true even when very powerful actors within the policy community would prefer to be informed by a broad range of different disciplinary opinions (see Zoellick, this volume). This is not a story about competition as much as it is a story about finite space already being filled when IR scholars arrive at the table. In chapter 11 Demekas uses the case of the post-2008 financial crisis and the design of the Financial Stability Board to show that economists dominated the discourse around institutional design of this new governance mechanism despite the fact that expertise on political (or politicized) institutions could have been useful. Demekas (an economist) laments the fact that nobody bothered to invite the political scientists to the planning meetings.

As we note previously, the presence of competitors within a particular field may reduce the IR discipline's effectiveness in delivering policy knowledge or tools because officials have an alternative source of information (as they do in trade, money, and aid, where economists have a near monopoly on access to and influence over policy officials and staff). Nevertheless, many of our contributing authors, including the practitioners, claim that the IR discipline has much to contribute, particularly to an understanding of the politics of policy implementation. We summarize our argument about the crossdisciplinary competition as follows:

2a. *If practitioners within a given issue area have an established working relationship with another epistemic/disciplinary community, then the opportunities for influence and engagement by IR scholars will be more limited.*

The extent to which IR scholarship can be directly useful to policymakers is likely to vary as a function of the level and the rate at which policy decisions are made. Issue areas in which authority is dispersed and/or delegated to low-level actors who are empowered to make policy decisions will be characterized by a greater number of opportunities for IR scholars and scholarship to reach those individuals who make policy decisions. Issue areas in which policy decisions must be revisited on a relatively frequent basis will exhibit similar openings for academic influence. These porous issue areas also may have a greater need for outside information and expertise because the policy choices require knowledge of local or time-variant factors. Few of the chapters in this book make this argument directly, but some authors present key pieces of supporting evidence. Consider the area of foreign aid. Strategic policy decisions regarding total funding amounts and general funding priorities are taken at high levels in both Congress and the executive branch, but foreign aid agencies are given enormous leeway in designing aid interventions (Honig 2018). Aid practitioners must make hundreds or thousands of policy decisions a year and often do not have the required expertise at hand or the resources and time to invest in gaining that expertise. As Schneider notes in chapter 6, this often means that aid practitioners turn to scholars for their specialized knowledge of local conditions and training in designing interventions and evaluations. This has allowed IR scholars to make significant and direct contributions to the aid policy community in recent years.

Similarly, practitioners' receptiveness may vary across subfields based on the nature of the decisions being made. In the human rights and environment arenas, where NGOs and IGOs engage in advocacy and policymaking, scholars may engage with policy advocates and staff. The greater number of potential points of contact between academics and practitioners in these areas creates more opportunities for scholarly research to influence policy, even if that influence is sometimes at the working level. In an area like interstate war, as described by Sarah Kreps and Jessica Weeks in chapter 12, it may be harder and slower for scholarly ideas to reach the relevant decision-makers, either because decisions are taken at a higher level or because security clearances limit the number of scholars who can be involved in such conversations. That concepts like the democratic peace or the clash of civilizations *ever* reach the upper policy echelons speaks to the powerful influence of these academic ideas.

In other, less porous issue areas (e.g., nuclear weapons strategy and proliferation), policy decisions that might benefit from the insights of IR scholars are revised relatively infrequently and are taken at the very highest levels of government. Those hoping for their work to have direct impacts on nuclear security policy must convince high-level policymakers to engage with their work and do so at a time during which the government is actually open to revising nuclear security policy. The significant role that IR scholars played in nuclear strategy in the early part of the Cold War may be the exception that proves the rule. As Avey and Desch note in chapter 16, early nuclear policymakers did not have the knowledge needed to evaluate the relative wisdom of various policy choices. Early on, then, nuclear policy was a fairly porous issue area. Because nuclear policy decisions are revisited so infrequently, however, the relative porousness of this issue area declined substantially over time. IR scholars simply do not have many new opportunities to directly interact with or influence nuclear policymakers today. We therefore offer the following argument:

> 2b. *IR scholars are more likely to directly influence policy in issue areas in which policy decisions are made at relatively low levels and/or on a frequent basis.*

## Important Moderating Factors

The structural argument we present in this book does not mean that academic incentives don't matter. In fact, the explanatory power of our argument is likely to be conditional on the temporal variation in IR scholars' professional incentives to produce policy-relevant research and engage the policy community, as well as their ability to market or communicate the implications of their research in ways that are easily digested by the policy community. Unlike many existing works on the theory-practice divide that highlight the role academic incentives play, however, we argue that even when IR scholars produce policy-relevant knowledge, their ability to influence policy will be conditioned by the structure of the policy area, particularly the level of policy uncertainty and the porousness of the policy process. Nevertheless, we outline a number of important moderating factors that are explored in some of the subsequent chapters in this book. As we note in the next section, the contributing authors sometimes disagree on the explanatory value of these supply-side factors.

*Communicating theoretical arguments and research findings.* Although just one of the chapters in this volume (Kreps and Weeks, chapter 12) provides systematic evidence to support this claim, in their chapters and in presentations at our two conferences several contributors repeated an article of faith among students of the theory-practice divide: one of the key reasons that IR scholars have limited influence on policymaking and implementation stems from the fact that they cannot or will not communicate in a timely manner and in a format that can be easily consumed by practitioners.[18] In his contribution to this volume, former Principal Assistant Secretary of Defense John Harvey observes, "No one in government reads books unless they're on vacation. You need to write the one- to two-page paper that lays out the idea, states why it solves an important problem, and suggests the initial approach the official should take to get the idea in play." In this view, one issue is venue; if scholars are going to be relevant, they need to have their ideas published in places that will be read by policy officials. But there is a second, related part to this claim; to get published in *Foreign Affairs* or the *New York Times*, one needs to write in a way that is brief, clear, and accessible to nonspecialists. Within the IR discipline, many argue, ideas have become too abstract (Gallucci 2012) and methods have become too technical (Walt 2005; Nye 2008b) to be easily consumed by practitioners.

This logic helps explain funding decisions by the Carnegie Corporation of New York, a foundation dedicated to the idea that academic research can and should inform foreign policy discourse and debate. Carnegie funds the Bridging the Gap Project, which (re)trains graduate students and junior faculty to write for a public audience. Carnegie also funds an editor for the *Washington Post* blog *The Monkey Cage*. This support for a part-time editor, according to Professor Erik Voeten, one of the original editors, has made *Monkey Cage*'s "posts much more accessible to a broader audience. They also create titles and find images that attract views through social media. We have seen large increases in page-views since these editors started reframing and simplifying the posts offered to us by academics."[19]

This discussion of the first moderating factor having to do with the communication of academic theories and findings suggests the following general argument:

> 3a. *IR scholarship that is not presented in an easily consumable format will not resonate within or influence the practitioner community.*

As many of the policy practitioners (e.g., Zoellick, Harvey, and Radelet) and some of the academic contributors to this volume (e.g., Green and Hale) point out, policy problems may not respect disciplinary borders, but tenure and promotion within the academy increasingly require specialized research products for a disciplinary audience.[20] Therefore, IR scholars who are willing to cross disciplinary boundaries and consort with economists and anthropologists will be most valuable to policy practitioners, but they will be proportionately less likely to produce research prized by editors of the top

IR or political science journals and more likely to be judged as less competitive for tenure and promotion by their senior colleagues. Some internal critics of the IR discipline identify the narrowness and "professionalization" of the discipline as a key factor driving its irrelevance. As John Mearsheimer and Stephen Walt (2013, 447) explain, "One way to do this is to convince outsiders that the profession has specialized expertise. Thus, professions have powerful incentives to employ esoteric terminology and arcane techniques that make it difficult to evaluate what its members are saying."[21] The longer a subfield exists, the more likely it is to take on institutional and disciplinary features: departments within universities, tenure lines, peer-reviewed journals, and specialized conferences that are held on a regular basis. When these institutional features exist, scholars increasingly need to write for the other members of their professional guild. Alternatively, when such institutions are nascent or when they cross disciplinary divides, then validation of research is granted by groups external to the guild—including those in other disciplines and in the policy world.

The empirical patterns in this book's chapters are broadly consistent with this argument about the professionalization of the IR discipline. The subfields that are judged the most relevant and influential by our authors are newer subfields in which IR scholars have more recently begun studying these subjects, and the journals they target and the conferences they attend include scholars and practitioners from outside IR/political science. The chapters that stand out in this regard discuss human rights, environment, intrastate conflict, and development. Alternatively, the most well-established subfields (trade, finance, and interstate war) are characterized by more limited scholarly relevance and influence. The intermediate case is nuclear strategy; that new and multidisciplinary academic field had enormous influence during the early part of the Cold War, but as it aged and became institutionalized within IR, as Avey and Desch show in chapter 16, its relevance declined. In sum:

3b. *As an IR subfield matures and professionalizes, its scholarship will be less relevant to and influential for policy practitioners.*

*Professional incentives to use increasingly esoteric research methods.* The argument about the effects of the professionalization of the IR discipline is based on broad agreement among the contributors to this book, but other factors remain contested. One of the most contentious arguments relates to the effect that the methodological tools employed by IR scholars have on the ability to engage with the policy process. Specifically, the IR field's increasing reliance on quantitative or formal methods, some argue, may be inhibiting policy influence because quantitative and formal analyses are less accessible to those without specialized training. The choice of method, and increasingly the quest for causal identification, may narrow the set of questions that scholars are willing to address. This argument emerges most strongly in chapter 16 in this book, in which Avey and Desch argue that the quantification of IR correlates with a decline in IR scholars' influence on nuclear policy. To support their claim, they provide illustrative qualitative examples as well as evidence from a survey of policymakers showing what types of academic research practitioners find most and least useful.

Avey and Desch get only limited pushback on this point from the policy practitioner assigned to comment on their chapter (Harvey, chapter 17). They get substantial pushback, however, from their fellow scholar-authors. In this book and at our workshops, other academic authors often argued that if method were to blame for the theory-practice divide, then the work of econo-mists should have little influence in trade, monetary policy, and development policy because economics relies much more heavily than political science on formal theoretical models and quantitative empirical methods.[22] In fact, both IR scholars and policy practitioners who work on defense and security issues agree that economists are more influential than political scientists. When IR scholars in the United States were asked which discipline is likely to have the most influence on policy outcomes if members of that discipline agree about the effects of some policy choice, respondents answered economics more often than any other field.[23] Similarly, Avey and Desch (2013a) asked policy practitioners in the security field how useful they found "arguments and evidence" from various academic disciplines. Sixty-two percent found economics "very useful," but only 32 percent found political science "very useful."[24] These facts are hard to square with the claim that quantification drives irrelevance. Avey and Desch address the argument about economics explicitly in chapter 16. Despite pushback from their colleagues, they never-theless conclude that, over time, as strategic studies and nuclear deterrence scholarship became more influenced by economic methods, it also became less relevant to policymakers. In fact, they devote an entire section of their chapter to economics as an "intellectual dead end" as a source of influence on nuclear policy and doctrine. Disagreement over the impact of research meth-ods on the policy relevance and influence of IR scholarship also has received attention in a series of other publications on the theory-practice divide. These disputes often involve Desch and his critics (Walt 1999; Martin 1999; Avey and Desch 2014; Desch 2015; Oren 2015; Voeten 2015; Walt 2015b; Desch 2019a; Desch 2019b; Farrell and Knight 2019).[25]

This discussion suggests the following argument, which several authors test in their chapters in this book:

4. *IR scholarship that uses quantitative methods will be less relevant to and have less influence on policy and practitioners than scholarship that uses qualitative approaches.*

See table 1.1 for a summary of the arguments.

**TABLE 1.1.**   Summary of the book's arguments

| Variables of core theoretical interest | | |
|---|---|---|
| Level of policy uncertainty | 1a | Emerging issues provide more opportunities for scholars to have influence on policymaking or policy implementation than do perennial or long-standing issues. |
| | 1b | Highly technical issues where cutting-edge methods are in demand provide more opportunities for scholars to have influence than for issues where technical issues and existing methods are well understood by practitioners. |
| Porousness of the policy process | 2a | If practitioners within a given issue area have an established working relationship with another epistemic/disciplinary community, then the opportunities for influence and engagement by IR scholars will be more limited. |
| | 2b | IR scholars are more likely to directly influence policy in issue areas in which policy decisions are made at relatively low levels and/or on a frequent basis. |

| Other moderating factors | | |
|---|---|---|
| Communication and marketing research | 3a | IR scholarship that is not presented in an easily consumable format will not resonate within or influence the practitioner community. |
| | 3b | As an IR subfield matures and professionalizes, its scholarship will be less relevant to and influential for policy practitioners. |
| Professional incentives to employ esoteric models and methods | 4 | IR scholarship that uses quantitative methods will be less relevant to and have less influence on policy and practitioners than scholarship that uses qualitative approaches. |

# HOW FOREIGN AND INTERNATIONAL POLICY AND POLITICS SHAPE IR SCHOLARSHIP

In theory, at least, the relationship between the academic and policy communities of IR is a two-way street. Members of an insular academic community focused on the elegance of the discipline's theories and the power of its new methods are unlikely to produce research of interest or use to practitioners. Similarly, such scholars are unlikely to draw research inspiration from real-world problems and policies. In a world in which the gap between the two IR communities is narrower, however, international events and policy problems should motivate scholars to conduct research on questions of interest to policy practitioners.

One way to measure the extent to which scholars respond to international events and issues is simply to ask them. In the 2014 TRIP survey, we asked IR faculty whether they had responded to any major world event by making their research more relevant to policy practitioners. Across the thirty-two countries surveyed, 61 percent of all respondents said they had, whereas 67 percent of scholars working in US universities said they had engaged in more policy-relevant work because of international events.

Again, we find significant differences across IR subfields. Among the largest issue areas studied by US scholars, international security and foreign policy again top the list of scholars who report that their work responds to real-world events at 72 percent and 75 percent, respectively. International political economy comes in at 63 percent and international organization at 60 percent. This pattern holds outside the United States as well, although the percentages of scholars who say that their research reacts to international policies and problems are generally lower than in the United States. Among the smaller IR subfields in the US academy, international history (85 percent) and international law (79 percent) rank higher than security; and health (71 percent), human security (71 percent), the environment (68 percent), international relations theory (68 percent), and comparative foreign policy (67 percent) are not far behind. The pattern is similar outside the United States, although scholars of global civil society who work outside the United States are more responsive (55 percent) than faculty working in the same subfield at US universities (42 percent). Matthew Ribar (2016) moves beyond individual-level survey responses and employs the TRIP journal article database to show that "benchmark events" in the international system do shift the topics and the theories used to explain outcomes, but they do not shift the geographic focus on IR research.

The contributions to this book mirror these findings to a significant extent. In the security area Avey and Desch tell the story of the origins of an entire subdiscipline in response to the development of the atomic bomb. Mansfield and Pevehouse similarly claim that much of the research on international trade has been driven by trade policy and events and trends in the international trading system, even if this is not reflected in scholars' descriptions of their research motivation. In contrast, Findley and Young argue that although students of intrastate conflict are probably influenced by contemporary conflicts, their interest is driven less by considerations of policy practitioners' needs than by the availability within the academy of large-N datasets on conflict.

Understanding how scholars in different subfields respond to international events, as well as the extent to which scholarly research and researchers have an influence on policy, is important to comprehending and bridging the gap between the policy and academic worlds. If scholars did not respond to changes in the international system or increased demand for knowledge in the policy community by increasing their supply of policy-relevant research, it would be impossible for the academy to be relevant or to make an impact on foreign and international policy. At the same time, the increase in supply alone is not enough to increase IR scholars' influence because supply may occur in the absence of demand from practitioners for academic knowledge. Rather, as we argue in this book, the level of policy uncertainty and porousness of the decision-making process influence the extent to which academic concepts, theories, data, and methods get taken up by policy officials and other practitioners. As chapter 8 by Mansfield and Pevehouse on international trade shows, an IR discipline that is responsive to real-world events can produce policy-relevant scholarship and still fail to make an impact because there is little demand for that knowledge. Understanding the interaction of the supply and demand for knowledge from IR scholars, as we discuss in chapter 18, will be key to understanding the gap and designing strategies to close it.

## PLAN OF THE BOOK

The organization of the book mirrors the unique structure of the 2015 Strengthening the Links Conference, which brought together scholars and practitioners to discuss the relationship between the academic and policy communities within various subfields of IR. In each of eight distinct IR subfields—human rights, the environment, foreign aid and development, trade, finance and money, interstate conflict, intrastate conflict, nuclear weapons and strategy—we first present a chapter by an academic author or team that assesses the link between scholarly research and policy practices within their issue area. Each chapter is followed by a brief response from a current or former policy practitioner. The book's final chapter summarizes the empirical findings and explores common themes, asks why academic IR as a field is not more policy-relevant, explores the limits of the TRIP data, and considers areas for future research on the theory-practice divide. Finally, we consider the normative question of whether scholars *should* seek to bridge the divide and write for a policy audience. Despite the clamor in some circles for more policy-relevant research, as we noted at the beginning of this chapter, the debate about the purpose of social scientific research is far from settled. Writing for a policy audience, some IR students argue, may compromise scholars' academic objectivity and freedom, as well as the quality of their research. To presage our conclusion, the process of writing this book and our previous combined half century of studying the IR discipline convinces us that there is plenty of room in this diverse field for both applied and basic research. The field is currently experiencing a resurgence of midlevel theory, problem-driven research, and applied research, but there is space for both bridge builders and gap minders in our field.

## ENDNOTES

1. Campbell et al. (2015) show that 83 percent of all published scholarly work on the gap between policymakers and scholars portrayed the gap in a negative light, and only 8 percent of publications argued that the theory-practice divide cannot or should not be bridged.
2. Zoellick also served as president of the World Bank Group (2007–2012), deputy secretary of state (2005–2006), White House deputy chief of staff (1992–1993), and counselor of the US Department of State (1989–1992).

3. A small minority of observers claimed, however, that the gap is much smaller than is generally assumed (e.g., Heger 2014; Nau 2008; Wilson 2007). A handful of scholars (e.g., Hill and Beshoff 1994; Oren 2004, 2006; Frieden and Lake 2005; Gartzke 2011) argue that the existence of the theory-practice gap is a good thing.

4. See TRIP's Data Dashboard at https://trip.wm.edu/charts/.

5. For an analysis of academic "moonlighters," scholars who spend a portion of their time working with practitioners, and "in-and-outers," who take a leave from their academic jobs to serve full time in a policy position, see Parks and Stern (2013).

6. For a more recent and critical discussion of the concept of relevance as it is typically used in IR and political science, see Sjoberg (2015).

7. For a similar position, see Goldgeier (2012).

8. For a classic statement along these lines, see Neustadt and May (1986). For a more recent typology that distinguishes types of policy relevance, see Horowitz (2015).

9. For a more recent survey that covers more policy areas, asks more questions, and tracks the opinions of less senior policy practitioners, see Avey et al. (2019).

10. In chapter 4 of this volume, Green and Hale describe a continuum ranging from direct influence to "diffuse influence," in which policy officials adopt scholarly ideas, but not necessarily because the scholars intend this to happen.

11. This remark was made at the Strengthening the Links Conference, January, 2015, William & Mary, Williamsburg, Virginia

12. In chapter 4, Green and Hale describe this form of engagement as "engagement influence." We distinguish engagement from influence, although the two are closely related and may occur simultaneously.

13. On "moonlighters" vs. "in-and-outers," see Parks and Stern (2013).

14. We are particularly grateful to Mike Findley and Joe Young for their thoughts on different types of actors. See chapter 14 in this volume.

15. Byman and Kroenig (2016) make a similar point when they argue, "The conditions under which academic ideas are most likely to matter include discontinuous events or shocks, such as the 9/11 attacks; policy failures, such as the outbreak of an insurgency in Iraq; and unexpected decisions for which there is little initial government knowledge, such as the US decision to intervene for humanitarian purposes in Somalia." See also Horowitz (2013; 2015) and Horowitz et al. (2015) on early Cold War nuclear policy and on other emerging issues in contemporary international affairs where scholars can play an outsized role informing practitioners on various policy options.

16. Ron Mitchell (2010) and Elizabeth DeSombre (2011) come to a similar conclusion—that scholars who study international environmental issues have had substantial engagement with policymakers in the area of international environmental policy.

17. Among the practitioner chapters in these three issue areas, Radelet and Demekas see the dominant position of economists as normal, but they specify a set of emerging policy problems to which IR scholars and political scientists could contribute. By contrast, Zoellick sees any disciplinary division of labor as diminishing the possibility of both scholarly influence and good policy. Zoellick forcefully argues that complex policy problems require multidisciplinary solutions.

18. According to Pieczara and Eun (2013), this problem has worsened over the past thirty years. That is, IR scholars used to write clearly, and now they do not. For similar claims that scholars are not effectively packaging their research for policymakers' eyes, see Kruzel (1994) and Barnett (2006).

19. Private correspondence from Eric Voeten to Michael J. Tierney, November 2, 2016.
20. The argument about the value of interdisciplinary approaches to policy problems also is a common refrain from practitioners. According to Raj Shah, who led USAID's efforts to leverage knowledge in universities to improve development outcomes, and Michael Gerson (Shah and Gerson 2014), "We need engineers working with economists, anthropologists, and data scientists to solve the real-world problems of Ebola, infant mortality, and response to natural disasters. We can't do this on our own and no discipline has a monopoly of insight on how to address these kinds of problems." Robert Gallucci (2012), former assistant secretary of state and president of the MacArthur Foundation, similarly remarked, "Being really interdisciplinary is hard and requires deep engagement. The rub is that most academic experts are more interested in their theories than they are in interdisciplinary conversations or working together on problems."
21. See also Jentleson (2002); Walt (2005); Desch (2015).
22. From across the pond, Turton (2015) offers a different critique of the argument that quantification causes irrelevance. In direct response to Desch (2015), she claims that IR scholars in the UK are equally policy irrelevant in the way that Desch defines the term, but she shows that they are significantly less quantitatively oriented than their American counterparts.
23. See Jordan et al. (2009, 62). The question asked: "Assuming the members of a discipline generally agree on a policy choice, please rate the relative influence of these groups on policy outcomes in the United States. (Very Influential=3, Influential=2, Slightly Influential=1, Not influential=0)." Economists received an average score of 2.24 compared to just 1.01 for IR scholars.
24. The question asked practitioners to rate the "usefulness" of arguments and evidence from various disciplines on a four-point scale from "very useful" to "not useful at all." Although policymakers find economics, area studies, and history the most useful and political science the least useful, the separate category of "international affairs" is somewhere near the middle. See Avey and Desch (2014), figure 1.
25. Gartzke (2011) uses sophisticated quantitative techniques in his own research, but he is one of the skeptics in this conversation: "Economics became policy relevant in the first sense because it developed tools that could help policymakers better connect their actions with outcomes. These are not perfect, as recent events illustrate, but they work better than the old way of doing things (i.e., whatever we did last time, or holding one's thumb up to the wind). The problem is that political science does not yet have 'killer apps' like GDP."

# 2

# RIGHTS AND WRONGS
## Human Rights at the Intersection of the International Relations Academy and Practice

Amanda Murdie

What determines the treatment of people in a certain location? To what extent do certain international and domestic factors lead to changes in respect for individuals and their personal and collective rights? Since the creation of the United Nations (UN) and the drafting of the Universal Declaration of Human Rights (UDHR) at the end of World War II, scholars in many academic disciplines have sought to answer these questions within the framework of *human rights*.

Lawyers, philosophers, and religious scholars, among others, quickly contributed to a growing body of literature on the origins of human rights norms and their legal and ethical foundations (Bobbio 1996; Morgan 2012). Starting with a smaller footprint, researchers from various disciplines in the social sciences also began adding to the cross-disciplinary human rights scholarship. Unlike legal studies, religion, or philosophy, where concerns with values and norms often take center stage, the social sciences were historically more reluctant to focus on human rights. Due to its normative roots, human rights was often viewed to be at odds with social science's focus on "objective and empirical knowledge" (Morgan 2012, 3). The early literature on human rights in the social sciences has even been summarized as being unscientific, "inspired by activist involvement rather than the sobriety of scientific inference" (Hafner-Burton 2014, 282).

Nonetheless, there has been a recent explosion in social scientific research on human rights. This is especially true within the discipline of political science and the field of international relations (IR). Human rights research has appeared at an increasing rate in the top IR journals; it has enlivened perennial debates on the role of international institutions, norms, and nonstate actors (Keck and Sikkink 1998; Carpenter 2007; Simmons 2009).

The goal of this chapter is twofold: (1) to illustrate how the ideas from research on human rights within IR have enriched the cross-disciplinary and practitioner/policy human rights community; and (2) to examine how human rights researchers and research products compare to those in the larger IR community. Related to the first goal, there have been a plethora of recent reviews of social scientific literature on human rights, often with a strong political science or IR focus (Landman 2005; Davenport 2007; Hafner-Burton and Ron 2009; Goodman et al. 2012; Morgan 2012; Hafner-Burton 2012, 2014). I do not intend to rehash here the same literature as these informative review pieces. Instead, I simply focus on a few of the ways in which human rights scholarship in IR has added to the larger conversation on rights promotion, especially outside the ivory tower of academia.

As I explain in the following sections, human rights research within IR has had cross-disciplinary and practitioner appeal. Theoretical models developed in IR, for example, have informed some of the largest and most prominent human rights organizations and donor foundations. IR research on human rights has made its way into UN documents and reports. Even the data created by IR scholars to quantitatively research human rights abuses has been used in domestic political debates and policy statements, including the use of the Cingranelli-Richards (CIRI) Human Rights Dataset (Cingranelli et al. 2014) in the creation of the National Human Rights Programme 2014–18 in Mexico (CNNMexico 2014). In short, human rights research within IR is relevant and influential, and human rights researchers are often engaged in the policy and practitioner community (Maliniak et al. 2014).

Similar to their counterparts in the global environmental arena (Green and Hale, this volume), IR scholars and scholarship focused on human rights issues play a significant role in human rights practice. IR scholars have not been excluded from the multi- and cross-disciplinary human rights field, despite being relative latecomers. Perhaps because of the inclusive nature of human rights concepts, researchers and practitioners have largely welcomed alternative voices, including voices from IR scholars, as well as voices from the humanities and arts. At first glance, this finding may seem to contradict the argument, developed in chapter 1 of this volume, that in issue areas in which practitioners have established a working relationship with another epistemic or disciplinary community, such as the legal scholars active in the human rights area, there will be limited opportunities for IR scholars to engage and influence practice and practitioners. Unlike the privileged role of economists in the areas of trade and monetary policy (see Mansfield and Pevehouse; Pepinsky and Steinberg, this volume), however, the cross-disciplinary and inclusive history of human rights work meant that IR ideas and data have found a place in the practitioner community. The cross-disciplinary history of human rights made for a central lexicon and broad-based writing style, helping IR human rights scholarship cross disciplinary borders. The inclusive nature of human rights ideas made the practitioner community porous and open for solutions from outside the legal tradition. Moreover, the prominent role of activism within the human rights community, including the academy, means that IR scholars in this area often actively promote their normative agenda. They often do so by authoring op-eds, blog posts, and other policy publications, the easily consumable format of which is likely to resonate with practitioners (see argument 3a in chapter 1 of this volume). The importance of human rights activism also suggests that the porous nature of the human rights arena—the presence of multiple actors, including international organizations (IOs), nongovernmental organizations (NGOs), and transnational networks—provides significant opportunities for IR scholars to influence practice at the working level. This finding is consistent with argument 2b (chapter 1, this volume; also see Green and Hale; Schneider, this volume).

Regarding the second goal of the chapter, comparing human rights researchers and research products in IR to the larger field, the bottom line is surprising. Using Teaching, Research, and International Policy (TRIP) data on IR journal articles and researchers (Maliniak et al. 2011, 2018), I find that human rights scholarship in IR is, in many ways, reflective of the larger IR field, both in its epistemology and research methods. In general, I do not find that human rights scholarship is more descriptive or less positivist than other research appearing in IR journals, especially post-1990. Differences in theoretical focus do exist, however, and appear to persist over time. Although human rights literature in top-tier IR journals appears to reflect research outside of the issue area, there are differences between faculty researchers who focus on human rights and those who do not. Taken together, these findings highlight some of the peculiarities of the human rights subfield, but they also reiterate how established human rights research has become within IR. This human rights scholarship has the potential to add to mainstream IR, but it also is large and diverse enough to have cross-disciplinary and practitioner appeal.

## WHAT ARE HUMAN RIGHTS?

Before examining human rights scholarship in IR, it is important to set the conceptual boundaries of what human rights research includes. Although ideas about the rights of man have been discussed for centuries by philosophers and religious scholars, most human rights scholars define human rights as those listed in the UDHR, a nonbinding resolution of the UN that was itself the result of a cross-disciplinary collaboration across both the global North and global South (Waltz 2001; Claude and Weston 2006).[1] The UDHR contains thirty articles, covering everything from the right to life (Article 3) to the right to rest and leisure (Article 24).

Although the rights in the UDHR are supposed to be equal, indivisible, and interdependent, the political climate and realities of the time when the document was drafted introduced two fundamental divisions into human rights. First, as the UDHR was taken from a nonbinding declaration to a binding agreement, Cold War tensions created a division between (a) economic, social, and cultural rights, which were viewed as rights associated with the Soviet sphere, and (b) political and civil rights, which were rights seen as largely Western. Further divisions between rights exist in the larger human rights literature, including Vasak's (1979) popular account of "three" generations of rights: (a) political and civil rights; (b) economic, social, and cultural rights; and (c) solidarity rights, which include intergenerational rights to development and a clean environment (Wellman 2000).

Although there were many states that did not distinguish among economic, social and cultural rights, and political and civil rights, Cold War tensions and disagreements about how best to protect human rights created a delay and bifurcation in the creation of the binding treaty that was to follow the UDHR (Waltz 2001). The International Covenant on Economic, Social and Cultural Rights (ICESCR) and the International Covenant on Civil and Political Rights (ICCPR) did not enter into force until 1976. Subsequent human rights treaties have codified and focused on many additional rights. These binding treaties are largely intended to hold state parties accountable to the principles outlined in the UDHR.

A second division occurs between derogable and nonderogable rights. Most of the rights outlined in the UDHR are derogable and can be temporarily suspended at times of public emergency (Hafner-Burton et al. 2011; Richards and Clay 2012). Only a few rights—the "right to life, the right to be free from torture and other inhumane or degrading treatment or punishment, the right to be free from slavery or servitude, and the right to be free from retroactive application of penal laws"—are considered nonderogable and cannot be suspended for any reason (United Nations Department of Economic and Social Affairs 2003).[2]

Perhaps reflecting these divisions, most human rights scholarship in the social sciences, together with most practitioner advocacy, has historically focused on only a few political and civil rights, especially nonderogable rights related to a person's physical integrity. Additionally, although human rights are not granted by the state, and human rights abuses can result from actions by both state and nonstate actors, most human rights scholarship, especially within IR, has focused almost exclusively on government respect for human rights. This focus also has occurred in the practitioner community, where the UN treaty system and much of the advocacy has focused on stopping abuses by political leaders and their agents (Roth 2004).

For this project, I consider the study of any of the rights outlined in the UDHR to be human rights scholarship. I do not define human rights scholarship by scholars' use of the term "human rights" because many scholars use related terms such as "repression," "state terror," or "political terror" to refer to the same abuses of physical integrity rights (Davenport and Ball 2002; Carey and Poe 2004; Davenport 2007; Wood and Gibney 2010).[3] Additionally, the term "human security" has been critiqued within the human rights community as a "rephrase" or "bypass" of human rights language, even though "human security" typically refers to the same phenomena as are covered in traditional human rights language (Howard-Hassmann 2012). Further, I take human rights scholarship to include investigations into human rights as both the outcome variable and a causal factor.

In this regard, my definition of human rights scholarship is more encompassing than that used in the coding of the TRIP journal article database

(Maliniak, Peterson, et al. 2013). My expanded working definition allows for the inclusion of research into the repression-protest nexus (e.g., Moore 2000), genocide (Harff 2003; Krain 1997, 2005, 2012), and "human rights peace" (Sobek et al. 2006; Peterson and Graham 2011), none of which are listed as human rights scholarship in the TRIP coding of journal articles (Maliniak, Peterson, et al. 2013).[4]

Drawing on this expanded definition of human rights scholarship, I made a number of small changes when using the TRIP 2.0 journal article data and 1.0 and 2.0 faculty researcher data. First, in addition to those articles that TRIP codes as having a human rights focus, I include research where the title of the article includes any of the following terms: human rights, repression, human security, civil rights, rights, torture, physical integrity, political terror, women's rights, protection of civilians, genocide, mass killings, and political rights.[5] According to the TRIP coding of human rights, 185 articles in the database of 7,050 total articles focus on human rights. Using my more encompassing definition, there are 252 articles. In the section of this chapter that focuses on comparing human rights scholarship to other IR scholarship, I use both the TRIP measure and my more expansive measure of articles in this issue area when making my comparisons. In general, the pattern of human rights scholarship across these definitions is similar. Figure 2.1 provides the annual percentage of human rights articles in the TRIP article database of IR research. As shown, there has been a slight increase in the percentage of human rights scholarship appearing in these outlets over time.

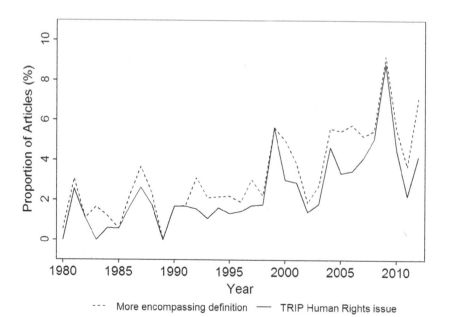

**FIGURE 2.1.** Human rights as a percentage of total IR articles, 1980–2012

As with Howard-Hassmann's (2012) discussion of the intersection of human rights and the more recent term "human security," my conceptualization of human rights researchers includes those who have research interests in human security. In the TRIP five-wave faculty survey data—which includes data from surveys given in 2004, 2006, 2008, 2011, and 2014—survey respondents could indicate that they had either a primary or secondary interest in human rights.[6] In the 2011 and 2014 surveys, respondents also could indicate whether they had a primary or secondary interest in human security.[7] When I make comparisons between human rights faculty researchers and other IR faculty researchers in the following sections, I make these comparisons with and without the inclusion of researchers that (a) identify themselves as focusing on human security, and (b) identify themselves as having secondary interests in human rights or human security.

Figure 2.2 illustrates how the percentage of TRIP faculty survey respondents who identify themselves as having a primary and/or secondary research interest in human rights has changed over time. Figure 2.2 also shows the percentage of respondents in 2011 and 2014 who identified as having a primary and/or secondary research interest in either human rights or human security.

After discussing the role that human rights research in IR has had in the practitioner/policy community, I examine these TRIP datasets in more detail in the following sections.

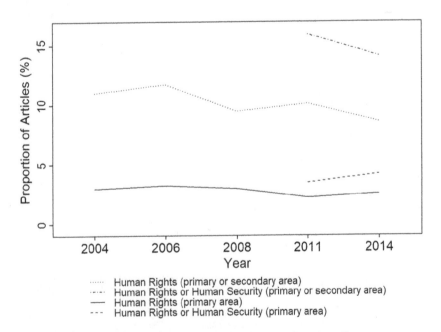

**FIGURE 2.2.**   Human security/human rights faculty research area over time

# HUMAN RIGHTS SCHOLARSHIP IN IR AND THE PRACTITIONER/POLICY COMMUNITY

Research produced by human rights IR scholars plays a large role in the practitioner/policy community. Although no comprehensive data source exists to examine whether this trend has been increasing over time, in this section I present examples of the use of IR human rights scholarship outside of academia and examples of how the practitioner/policy community has influenced the direction of academic research. The relationship between IR researchers and the practitioner/policy community appears to be relatively symbiotic in the area of human rights, with world events and the interests of the larger community influencing human rights scholarship in IR (Schmitz 2010).

Before beginning, however, let me stress that social science in general and IR in particular are not the main academic inputs into this policy area; legal scholarship still dominates the human rights policy world. For example, even though research published in cross-disciplinary journals such as *Human Rights Quarterly* has been cited hundreds of times in documents listed on the website for the UN Office of the High Commissioner for Human Rights, many of these citations are for legal scholarship. Further, each of the top three law journals has more citations in documents listed on the High Commissioner's website than the combined citation count for the top three political science journals (Google 2016a, 2016b). The dominant role of legal scholars, who were present at the creation of the field, might have crowded out IR scholars working on human rights issues. Nonetheless, it is clear that human rights IR scholarship has made its way into the policy/practitioner community and, as the following examples illustrate, influenced policy discussions. This pattern stands in stark contrast to many of the other IR issue areas, such as trade and finance, discussed in other chapters of this volume. The inclusive nature of human rights concepts, as well as the cross-disciplinary lexicon and training of many in the human rights community, could be driving this pattern. It is likely due, moreover, to the nature of human rights practice, which is populated by large numbers of NGOs, IOs, activists, and transnational advocacy networks.

One of the most influential strands of IR human rights research concerns the influence of transnational advocacy networks on improvements in a state's human rights practices. Margaret Keck and Kathryn Sikkink's (1998) book *Activists Beyond Borders: Advocacy Networks in International Politics* and the edited volume *The Power of Human Rights: International Norms and Domestic Change* (Risse et al. 1999), which were both extremely influential within the discipline, have informed many NGOs and activists about the process of improvements in human rights practices and the potential role of transnational advocacy networks. The language of human rights promotion discussed in these works is frequently referred to in UN documents and the work of NGOs and donors. For example, a recent preliminary text of a UN declaration on the rights of people to international solidarity included a reference to Keck and Sikkink (1998) (UN General Assembly 2014, A/HRC/26/34/Add.1). Likewise, a 2014 Working Group document of the UN Human Rights Commissioner, which called for the establishment of a global fund on business and human rights, cited the second edition of *The Power of Human Rights* when making the following statement: "It is recognized that one of the reasons States encounter challenges to comply with international human rights obligations is the absence of appropriate resources and capacity" (UN OHCHR 2014, SPB/SHD/MCS/ff).

Human rights scholars themselves (as "intellectuals") are actually theorized in Keck and Sikkink (1998, 9) as part of the larger transnational advocacy network for human rights promotion. Further, Keck and Sikkink (1998, 9) acknowledge that there is movement within the network from one organization or locale to another: "personnel also circulate within and among networks, as relevant players move from one to another in a version of the 'revolving door.'" This "revolving door" within the larger advocacy network describes well the movement of many IR human rights scholars from the academy to the policy community and back again. There are notable IR human rights scholars with previous experience in NGOs. James Ron is a good example; his experiences include work with Human Rights Watch, the International Committee of the Red Cross, and CARE (Ron n.d.) There are also many individuals active in UN bodies and NGOs with PhDs and research backgrounds in IR. For example, Louis N. Bickford, the program officer for the Global Human Rights Program at the Ford Foundation from 2012 to 2015, has a PhD in political science and teaches IR human rights research at New York University's Wagner School. The 2007–08 president of the UN Human Rights Council, Dorcu Costea, and the 2011–12 vice president, Anatole Fabien Nkou, both have PhDs in IR. Scott Edwards, who has a PhD in political science and who contributed a response chapter in this volume, is the director of research and a senior advisor at Amnesty International. Researchers working at many different human rights NGOs, including Amnesty International and Human Rights Watch, frequently present papers at the largest IR conference, the International Studies Association Conference.

Additionally, some IR human rights scholars have funding from the practitioner/policy community or produce works that are later adopted by this community. Sometimes, early support from the practitioner/policy community influences later IR human rights scholarship as well. For example, much IR attention has been paid to the limited and conditional role the UN international human rights treaty system has in improving human rights practices (Hafner-Burton and Tsutsui 2005; Hill 2010). Some of the early cross-disciplinary academic work on the limited effects of treaties (e.g., Bayefsky 2001; Heyns and Viljoen 2002) came after "collaboration[s] with the Office of the United Nations High Commissioner for Human Rights"

(UN ECOSOC 2000, E/2000/22 E/C.12/1999/11, 70). This work is often cited in the political science literature on human rights treaties (Landman 2004; Neumayer 2005). More recent efforts by the UN to strengthen the treaty system also include IR academics, who, along with legal scholars, have often been called on to write summary documents of academic research (UN HRC 2014b, A/HRC/AC/12/CRP.2).

Another fruitful line of IR research of interest to the UN human rights regime concerns the negative externalities of economic sanctions on human rights abuses, especially concerning the treatment of vulnerable populations (Wood 2008; Peksen 2009, 2011; Drury and Peksen 2014). A recent workshop of the UN Office of the High Commissioner for Human Rights (2009) highlighted this research. The workshop was later referenced in drafting a report for the UN Human Rights Council concerning the use of economic sanctions and other coercive measures (UN HRC 2014a, A/HRC/AC/13/CRP.2).

Outside of the UN system, the work of IR human rights scholars also has been supported by and is of interest to the larger practitioner/policy community. Among the most well known, Barbara Harff's work on genocide and Ted Gurr's work on insurgency were important in the creation of the US State Failure Task Force, which later became the Political Instability Task Force (PITF). The first footnote of Harff's 2003 *American Political Science Review* article on the risks of genocide starts with the statement that the

> study was commissioned in 1998 by the Central Intelligence Agency's Directorate of Intelligence in response to President Clinton's policy initiative on genocide early warning and prevention. It was designed by the author and carried out using her data with other data and analytic techniques developed by the State Failure Task Force . . . The author is senior consultant to the Task Force, which was established in 1994 in response to a request from senior U.S. policymakers to design and carry out a data-driven study of the correlates of state failure, defined to include revolutionary and ethnic wars, adverse or disruptive regime transitions, and genocides and politicides . . . (Harff 2003, 57).

Many other forecasting approaches to human rights abuses and insurgency have been supported by government funds, including the work of the Integrated Crisis Early Warning System (ICEWS) (O'Brien 2010). This support has been critical to the development of conflict forecasting models and events data approaches in political science (Monroe and Schrodt 2008; Gleditsch and Ward 2013). Although not all this work makes explicit reference to "human rights," much of it centers on the study of the repression-protest nexus (Shellman 2008; Metternich et al. 2013; Bell et al. 2013) and genocide. Human rights scholar David Cingranelli, for example, led a project that focused specifically on using human rights indicators to predict insurgency (Bell et al. 2013). All of these works have led to advances in the study of human rights more generally.

Human rights NGOs and institutions also have supported and utilized research from IR human rights scholars. For example, James Ron's work has been supported by the Ford Foundation (Ron n.d.). Transitional justice scholarship by teams of researchers headed by IR scholars Leigh Payne and Kathryn Sikkink has been widely cited by the International Center for Transitional Justice (see, e.g., International Center for Transitional Justice 2014). Payne's earlier work was supported by the United States Institute of Peace (Latin America Centre 2016). Many human rights NGO scholars, including myself, have been involved in the International Consortium on Closing Civic Space, an effort by the Center for Strategic and International Studies to research growing repression of civil society and activists.[8] Further, drawing on my earlier scholarship, I have worked with the Ford Foundation's Global Human Rights Portfolio, the International Council of Voluntary Agencies, and the American Jewish World Service, a leading NGO in the area of children's and women's rights. In these interactions, NGO practitioners and activists were aware of my scholarship and sought out my scholarly expertise for on-the-ground human rights situations.

The datasets created by IR scholars and used in the majority of IR human rights research have also appealed to the practitioner/policy community.[9] Two of the major datasets, the Political Terror Scale (Gibney et al. 2014) and Cingranelli-Richards (CIRI) Human Rights Dataset (Cingranelli et al. 2013) have been widely cited in newspaper reports (e.g., *New Zealand Herald* 2014; *African Manager* 2014) and UN documents (UN General Assembly 2010, A/65/165; see also Sex Workers Forum of Vienna, Austria 2013). The CIRI dataset was referenced in expert testimony about a country's court system (Chevron Corporation v. Salazar, 11 Civ. 3718). When asked about the practitioner/policy footprint of CIRI, David Richards, one of the directors of the CIRI dataset, stated:

> the list of organizations using CIRI within two years of its founding was nearly 500 in 150 countries . . . its reach ultimately extended to 170+ countries. . . . Many interactions came directly from the governments of countries themselves. I would hear from development offices, statistics bureaus, offices of Prime Ministers. . . . When asked for examples of non-academic CIRI usage, I would usually point towards the UN, World Bank (Governance Indicators), the Ibrahim Index of African Governance, the Political Instability Task Force, and the Millennium Challenge Corporation, as people know those entities. (David Richards, pers. comm. 2014)

International tribunals and truth commissions used quantitative human rights research by IR-trained scholars. Many times, the unit of analysis and level of precision necessary for international court proceedings are much different than the country year information referenced previously. For example,

Patrick Ball and his Human Rights Data Analysis Group (HRDAG) have provided evidence and technical advice for cases in the International Criminal Tribunal for the former Yugoslavia and Guatemala's Supreme Court trial of General José Efraín Ríos Montt for genocide and crimes against humanity.[10] Ball's work has appeared in human rights and IR journals, including the *Journal of Conflict Resolution* and *Human Rights Quarterly*, and there are many IR scholars involved in the group.

Recent efforts for human rights data collection in IR have further tightened links between the practitioner and the scholarly communities. The Human Rights Measurement Initiative (HRMI) is a new collaborative project between academics and practitioners to measure a comprehensive array of human rights globally.[11] HRMI is hosted by Motu Economic and Public Policy Research, a New Zealand NGO; its measurement design involves human rights academics at the University of Connecticut and the University of Georgia. Experts from many human rights NGOs, including Human Rights Watch and Amnesty International, have been involved with the project's development. Although the project will be useful for academics, its design and scope also make it valuable for the practitioner community.

Of course, the relationship between IR human rights scholarship and the larger practitioner/policy community is not one way. Human rights scholarship, even theoretical developments, have been influenced by world events and trends identified by the practitioner community. Schmitz (2011) acknowledged, for example, that the terrorist attacks on the United States on September 11, 2001, changed the behavior of human rights advocacy networks from "shaming" strategies to more local empowerment. As Schmitz remarked, post-September 11, "[s]cholars can play an important role in contributing to the ongoing shift from reactive to preventive transnational strategies" (2010, 7191). Similarly, critiques of assumptions in Keck and Sikkink's (1998) model of transnational advocacy have received much attention in IR scholarship and draw on reports from the practitioner community (Bob 2005; Murdie 2014).

Questions in the TRIP faculty survey database also indicate that "real-world" events, such as September 11 and the subsequent "war on terror," have influenced human rights researchers, both in their reading and in their teaching. Although many of the questions on the TRIP faculty surveys show that human rights researchers are no different from those who do not focus on human rights when it comes to the influence of world events, there are some notable exceptions.[12] In the 2006 survey, for example, human rights researchers reported devoting a higher percentage of their introduction to IR courses to current policies and events than their non–human rights IR counterparts.[13] And, according to the 2004 and 2006 surveys, those researchers who reported having either primary or secondary research interests in human rights were more likely to report "regularly" or "sometimes" adjusting their research as a result of real-world events.[14]

In short, the footprint of IR human rights research on the practitioner/ policy community is significant. There are two reasons for this synergy. First, human rights research, at its very core, is inclusive and cross-disciplinary. Many PhD programs in political science include cross-listed human rights courses or encourage their students to take courses on human rights in other disciplines. There is a core lexicon that researchers and practitioners learn. At both the undergraduate and graduate levels, syllabi for human rights courses often include cross-disciplinary research. Cross-disciplinary research conferences also exist (see, e.g., College of Arts & Sciences 2015). Because of this, IR scholars of human rights have found a place in a field to which they turned their attention only recently. As mentioned, the top human rights journal, *Human Rights Quarterly*, is interdisciplinary and includes research from both academics of various disciplines and practitioners. In the last two issues of 2015, for example, articles by scholars with PhDs in IR or political science were roughly one-third of the contributors; other authors included UN officials, policy analysts, NGO workers, and academics in the disciplines of law, sociology, psychology, and public health. As such, the typical IR human rights researcher has many opportunities to interact with non-IR scholars and their research, and s/he may be called on to review research from outside his/her area.

Because of the inclusive and cross-disciplinary nature of the issue area, IR researchers in this area may become accustomed to writing for a larger, non-IR audience. Publishing in cross-disciplinary academic research outlets may help improve a researcher's practitioner/policy footprint. Further, their research can be sought out and read by practitioners familiar with cross-disciplinary human rights work and publication outlets. A search on the website for the UN Office of the High Commissioner for Human Rights, for example, finds more than 500 references to *"Human Rights Quarterly"* but only four references to *"International Studies Quarterly."*

Second, activism plays a huge role in human rights improvement. According to responses given in the 2014 TRIP faculty survey, human rights researchers report advocating more in the past year than their non–human rights counterparts.[15] Experience with activism may help researchers know how to get attention outside of the academy. Prominent human rights scholars have long been contributors to IR blogs. For example, R. Charli Carpenter and Jon Western have both been permanent members of the IR blog *Duck of Minerva* for many years. Many IR human rights scholars have published op-ed pieces and policy versions related to their academic articles (see, e.g., Bob 2002; Sikkink 2011). Perhaps the nature of human rights promotion makes human rights researchers especially willing to spread the findings of their research beyond the ivory tower in formats that are easily consumable by the practitioner community. The presence of many NGOs and other nonstate actors in the human rights space, moreover, gives IR scholars more potential avenues for influence.

## ARE HUMAN RIGHTS RESEARCHERS AND THEIR RESEARCH PRODUCTS DIFFERENT FROM THE FIELD?

Although it has a long history in IR, human rights research has been seen in some circles as unscientific and motivated by an activist nature that somehow negates the scientific process (Hafner-Burton 2014). As Carey and Poe (2004, 4) point out, most social science researchers tend to steer clear of "normative judgments" and, due simply to the use of the language of human rights, "studies of human rights are normative from the onset." As Carey and Poe (2004, 4) also contend, however, normative judgments (i.e., being antiwar or anti–nuclear weapons) are not unique to the study of human rights; other IR scholars simply allow "those biases [to] frequently go unmentioned in their writings." As the previous section highlighted, human rights IR research informs the practitioner/policy community. In this section, I outline whether this research is somehow different from the rest of the IR field. Does the normative nature of human rights influence the type of IR scholar who studies the issue or the scholarship s/he produces?

To investigate these questions, I return to the TRIP journal article and faculty survey datasets (Maliniak et al. 2011, 2018). I am interested in whether human rights articles in IR journals and human rights IR faculty researchers differ from other IR articles and IR researchers in four areas: (1) epistemology, (2) research methodology, (3) theoretical perspective, and (4) willingness to offer policy prescriptions. I am interested in these four areas because (a) they allow me to provide an informed response to the critique of Hafner-Burton (2014) and others who claim that human rights IR scholarship is somehow lacking in the "sobriety of scientific inference" (282), and (b) examining these four areas may provide insights into why human rights scholarship in IR has had influence on the policy community. I run a series of cross-tabular analyses looking at how human rights articles and researchers differ from other articles/researchers in IR. Tables of these results are provided in the online appendix.

According to the conventional wisdom, one might expect human rights research, even the research appearing in IR journals, to be more nonpositivist, descriptive, and policy oriented than other IR research. Surprisingly, I find that this is not the case. Although human rights IR research is much more likely to take ideational factors seriously and typically has a constructivist bent, the conventional view of the human rights IR literature as only descriptive or nonpositivist appears to be wrong or, at the very least, dated. Underlying these statements, however, is a difference I identify between human rights research in top IR/political science journals and human rights researchers. Human rights research in IR journals appears similar to that in other areas of IR; researchers in the TRIP survey who self-identify as being human rights focused differ in epistemology and methodology.

These findings reinforce ideas about how cross-disciplinary and broad the human rights field is.

First, the TRIP journal article dataset (Maliniak, Peterson, et al. 2013) includes a dichotomous coding of whether the research is positivist or nonpositivist.[16] In the whole 1980–2012 sample, when using the TRIP human rights issue coding, the human rights IR literature is more nonpositivist than other IR literature. When you take a more encompassing view of what human rights research is and code human rights research as research with titles that include "genocide," "repression," and so forth, however, there does not appear to be a relationship between epistemology and human rights research, as compared to other issue areas of IR research. Any relationship between nonpositivist research and having a human rights issue focus appears to be time dependent and largely evident only in the pre-1990 time period. Human rights research in these journal articles, although perhaps more nonpositivist in the past, is similar today in epistemology to research in other issue areas.

When turning from human rights research that has appeared in the twelve top-tier journals to looking at the TRIP faculty surveys, a slightly different pattern emerges with respect to epistemology. To note, the TRIP faculty survey asks researchers about their epistemology in 2004, 2006, 2008, 2011, and 2014. Response options include (a) nonpositivist, (b) positivist, or (c) postpositivist.[17] In the five waves of the TRIP survey, there is a greater percentage of nonpositivist and postpositivist researchers who study human rights (primary or secondary) than who do not. This relationship is also present when I include those who say they have a primary or secondary research interest in "human security" from the 2011 survey. It is worth mentioning, however, that in the 2014 TRIP survey I do not find a statistically significant difference in epistemology between human rights and non–human rights researchers when looking only at primary research interests. When I include those who report either a primary or a secondary interest in human rights/security, I find that there is a greater percentage of nonpositivist researchers.[18] This finding does indicate that human rights researchers, as opposed to their research products in top-tier IR journals, appear to be more non-/postpositivist than their non–human rights counterparts. Their research products are probably found in other research outlets not sampled in the TRIP journal article database.[19]

Turning to research methodologies, surprisingly the TRIP journal database and other journal articles show few methodological differences between human rights and other issue areas. There is no relationship between issue focus and the use of descriptive methods.[20] There is a similar nonassociation with qualitative methodology and issue focus.[21] Not surprisingly, however, human rights research in IR journals has been less likely to use formal modeling techniques.[22] Although I do not have a strong explanation for this finding, it could be that some human rights researchers, due to their ideational bent, are less likely to positively view the assumptions of formal modeling.

Additionally, it could be that IR graduate programs that focus on human rights are not historically those with a strong formal theory component.

I also find something that goes against the conventional wisdom: With the more encompassing definition of human rights, human rights articles are actually more likely to use quantitative methods than are other IR articles.[23] This could be linked to the work of Gibney et al. (2018) and Cingranelli et al. (2014) and the ready availability of quantitative human rights data during this time period.

The 2004 survey finds that researchers with either primary or secondary interests in human rights, when asked to check all methodologies that they use, are more likely to report using quantitative approaches.[24] This result does not hold, however, if I focus only on researchers with a primary interest in human rights; I find no statistically significant difference between those with primary interests in human rights and those without. The question on research methodology was changed in the 2006 and subsequent surveys to ask for primary methodology.[25] In looking at the cross-tabular results in 2006, 2008, and 2011, a greater percentage of human rights researchers report using primarily a "legal and ethical analysis" methodology (Maliniak, Peterson, et al. 2013). This result continues to hold in the 2014 survey but only when focusing on those who report a primary or secondary interest in either human rights or human security.[26]

At their core, human rights are a social construct. I see it as no surprise, therefore, that human rights researchers and research products about human rights are more likely to focus on ideational factors than the rest of the IR field.[27] I find similar information from the TRIP faculty survey, at least when the focus is on human rights or human rights and human security as either the primary or secondary research interest.[28] Somewhat surprisingly, however, having a human rights issue focus and the use of material factors has no association in the TRIP journal article database.[29] When looking beyond the use of ideational/material factors to examine the use of various IR paradigms, both human rights articles in top IR journals and researchers are more likely to be associated with constructivism than non–human rights articles and researchers.[30] Given the role of research on nonstate actors in human rights scholarship, as outlined previously, this finding is largely consistent with conventional wisdom.

Finally, what is the relationship between human rights articles and researchers and the policy community? The TRIP surveys offer many insights on this question. Human rights articles in IR journals appear to offer policy prescriptions at a rate that is similar to non–human rights articles in IR journals.[31] The 2011 TRIP faculty survey asked related questions concerning research motivations. Human rights researchers have similar ideas about what should motivate research as their non–human rights counterparts have.[32] When the focus is not on what should motivate research but on what does motivate their research, human rights scholars are similar to non–human rights scholars; there is, however, an association between research motivation and issue area when we focus on researchers with either a primary or a secondary interest in human rights/human security.[33] In general, however, these findings do not indicate a vast difference in the motivations or policy prescriptions for human rights versus other IR research.

One difference that does come out of the TRIP faculty surveys is the difference between human rights researchers and other IR researchers on paid and unpaid consultancy. The questions asked in the survey waves differed slightly; the 2004 survey asked whether respondents consulted or worked at various organizations whereas the 2006, 2008, and 2011 surveys included separate questions for paid and unpaid consultancy undertaken in the two years before the surveys.[34] In general, although I find some evidence that human rights researchers are more likely to report having no consultancy or work partners, I also find strong evidence of some consultancy ties that could help encourage IR research in human rights to make it into the policy and practitioner communities. For example, I find much evidence of consultancy ties to NGOs, IOs, and interest groups. Given the role advocacy groups and intergovernmental organizations (IGOs) like the UN have in the human rights area, these consultancy arrangements could help foster connections between the policy and academic worlds.

## CONCLUSION

Human rights is an active research area within IR, one with vibrant debates and a growing footprint in the top journals. Since the UDHR entered into force in 1948, human rights scholarship has permeated many disciplines. Although social science in general and IR in particular were relatively late to add to the growing academic literature on human rights, their contributions have been significant, both for the field and for the practitioner/policy community. As outlined previously, human rights research in IR has influenced NGOs, IGOs, and domestic political debates. There appears to be much opportunity for future interaction with the larger rights-promotion community.

Although there are some differences in the epistemology, research methods, and theoretical perspectives of human rights researchers compared to the larger IR community, these differences are not that prominent in the work that appears in top IR journals. Whether this is a positive for the field of IR is an open question; it does, however, reiterate the diverse nature of human rights researchers in IR.

Nevertheless, cross-disciplinary work is almost taken for granted by many human rights scholars. Despite the prominence of legal scholars in the human rights arena, the cross-disciplinary and inclusive nature of the issue area has meant that IR scholars were a welcome addition to the scholarly conversation, despite IR's latecomer status.

Human rights research is an unusual issue area because of its visible normative background. This background leads many IR scholars of human rights to use their work to publicly advocate via op-eds, blogs, and other easily consumable formats. This increased engagement, combined with the presence of numerous nonstate actors in the practitioner community, have produced a prominent role for IR scholars. Although its normative background makes human rights research unusual, human rights researchers are not unique in their potential to produce scientifically valid yet "value-relevant" research (Morgan 2012, 5). This research seems to be increasing in popularity in the scholarly discipline of IR and has directly influenced the world of human rights practitioners and policy.

## ENDNOTES

1. Although the UDHR is not the only statement of rights by an IGO, it is by far the most referenced in human rights scholarship.
2. Also see Richards and Clay 2012, which outlines seven rights in the ICCPR that cannot be derogated.
3. As discussed at a planning conference for this chapter, there is often a division in the scholarly community between the study of "human rights" and "human wrongs," where the focus would be on rebellion and civil war. This is unfortunate, however, because one of the strongest predictors of human rights violations is civil unrest (Poe and Tate 1994).
4. A related issue concerns whether human rights research is classified as IR or comparative. Many researchers and publications on these topics appear to straddle fields.
5. Variable *issuearea*.
6. Using the variables *fsqg_707* for primary research interest and *fsqg_708* for secondary research interest in human rights.
7. Using the variables *fsqg_707* for primary research interest and *fsqg_708* for secondary research interest in human security in 2011, and variable *qg_118* for primary research interest and variables *qg_149_908* and *qg_149_919* for secondary research interest in 2014.
8. See Center for Strategic & International Studies. n.d. www.csis.org/programs/international-consortium-closing-civic-space-icon/icon-team.
9. See Satterthwaite and Simeone 2014 for a discussion of how social science data collection for human rights differs from fact-finding for human rights advocates. See also Fariss 2014 for a great discussion of informational issues to consider with the various human rights datasets.
10. See https://hrdag.org.
11. See https://humanrightsmeasurement.org/.
12. Results for all cross-tabular analyses on the issue of world events and human rights researchers are available in the online appendix.
13. Variable *fsqg_31_175*.
14. Variable *fsqg_320*.
15. Variable *qg_512*.
16. Variable *epistemology*.
17. Variable *fsqg_83*.
18. Variable *qg_95*.

19. An interesting extension to the TRIP article database would be to code *Human Rights Quarterly* and other human rights cross-disciplinary journals.
20. Variable *methodology_descriptive*.
21. Variable *methodology_qualitative*.
22. Variable *methodology_formal*.
23. Variable *methodology_quantitative*.
24. Variable *fsqg_87_459*.
25. Variable *fsqg_178*.
26. Variable *qg_104*.
27. Variable *ideational*.
28. It is worth noting that the TRIP faculty researcher survey only asked this question (*fsqg_84*) in 2004 and 2011.
29. Variable *material*.
30. Variables *paradigm. fsqg_706, qg_117*.
31. Variable *policyprescription*. This result holds even if I remove the journal *International Security* from the analysis.
32. Variable *fsqg_621*.
33. Variable *fsqg_626*.
34. Variable *fsqg_69* for whether respondents consulted or worked at various organizations. Variables *fsqg_1016* and *fsqg_1112* for separate questions for paid and unpaid consultancy undertaken in the two years before the surveys.

# 3

# CLOSING THE INFLUENCE GAP
## How to Get Better Alignment of Scholars and Practitioners on Human Rights

Sarah E. Mendelson

To what extent have ideas from international relations (IR) literature on human rights influenced those engaged in defending human rights, whether in governments, international organizations, or nongovernmental organizations (NGOs)? To what extent is there alignment between the time-sensitive issues that practitioners address with those studied by scholars? Under what conditions do ideas influence these different types of organizations? Definitive answers to these questions are beyond the scope of this chapter (and worthy of more investigation). Here, I offer thoughts on Amanda Murdie's "Rights and Wrongs: Human Rights at the Intersection of the International Relations Academy and Practice" (chapter 2, this volume), drawing on my twenty-five years working in academia, NGOs, think tanks, and government.

There are, of course, cases of overlapping interest and focus and examples of influence at broad and general levels. Murdie points to the award-winning work of Margaret Keck and Kathryn Sikkink (1998) on transnational advocacy networks, although it is unclear how well known their work is outside academia or how much impact that scholarship has had on the human rights community. I argue that IR scholarship on human rights does not for the most part align with what practitioners mainly focus on; I therefore find more uneven influence than Murdie. This gap ought to be better delineated and addressed both to make the academy more relevant to the human rights practitioner and to deploy specific social science methods to help solve real-world issues confronting human rights practitioners.

I identify several aspects of what I see as an influence gap, rendering the human rights practitioner community's relationship with IR scholars not entirely dissimilar to some other areas discussed in this volume, such as foreign aid (Schneider, this volume) or nuclear weapons policy (Avey and Desch, this volume). Although Murdie (p33) argues in chapter 2 that "research produced by human rights IR scholars plays a large role in the practitioner/policy community," and that "legal scholarship" plays an even larger role, there is little definition of what influence or "role" means beyond citations. In contrast with Murdie's (this volume, p33) argument that the "relationship between IR researchers and the practitioner/policy community appears to be relatively symbiotic," I find that what the academy studies does not match what practitioners confront. Here, I highlight one particularly important trend that is mission critical for human rights NGOs, consuming much time and focus—the closing space around civil society—but which has received relatively little systematic attention from IR scholars.[1]

The influence gap, however, refers not just to scholars' effects (or lack thereof) on practitioners. According to numerous accounts, human rights practitioners in NGOs experience their own limited influence with local populations. Perhaps not surprisingly, if there is scholarship that has caused practitioners to sit up and take notice, it is work—such as British political scientist Stephen Hopgood's (2013; also see Moyn 2010; Roth 2014) *The Endtimes of Human Rights*—that suggests the era of human rights is drawing to a close. Even though I find little to support Hopgood's (2014) dramatic claim that "a 150-year experiment in creating global rules to protect and defend individual human beings is coming to an end," I have documented the somber mood that has settled over the secular temple of human rights (Mendelson 2009). More strikingly, over the last decade in numerous countries, I have witnessed the perilous state of some human rights organizations and their weak links to local populations, making them easy targets for disgruntled governments. Here, I argue that social scientists could help close the influence gap by collaborating on public opinion surveys and, more generally, thoughtful design of randomized controlled trials (RCTs). The human rights (and democracy) community has not amassed a systematic understanding of what works where, when, and why. Scholars can help build an evidence base of successful interventions. Specifically, IR specialists could do more to engage the human rights community by helping construct RCTs and using survey data to enable activists to listen and respond to local populations.

Finally, there is an underexplored issue in Murdie's chapter: Why do certain ideas take hold in policy settings? Near the end of this chapter I return to this question and suggest that the role of individuals and personalities looms large and is worthy of study.

## A MISSION CRITICAL CHALLENGE: CLOSING SPACE AROUND CIVIL SOCIETY

Chief among the current challenges facing the global human rights community (and broader civil society) is a growing contagion best described as closing space around civil society. Since Vladimir Putin came to power in Russia in the early 2000s, space for civil society has been shrinking. By now, the trend has moved far beyond Russia. According to the International Center for Not-for-Profit Law, "since 2012, more than 120 laws" that touch on the Universal Declaration of Human Rights Articles 19 and 20 regarding freedom of expression, association, and peaceful assembly have been proposed or enacted in more than sixty countries (Rutzen 2015; CIVICUS 2013; Dupuy et al. 2014).

Specifically, as citizens find new ways to organize, assemble, and express themselves using social media, governments have found new ways to restrict public political space, suppress information, and label anything that they do not like as "foreign." From Russia to Zimbabwe, from Hungary to Egypt, dozens of governments are pushing back against the information power that citizens have amassed since game-changing, affordable communication technologies have come to market. Beyond the challenges of running an NGO, this phenomenon has several modalities affecting journalists, LGBTQ activists, and the physical security of human rights defenders (Petranov and Zard 2014; Cooley and Schaaf 2017). It is not an exaggeration to say that this countermovement is affecting the entire global community of human rights practitioners.

Lateral learning is alive and well among governments seeking to inhibit the work of human rights activists. In the last few years, numerous governments have replicated laws that shrink the administrative and legal space in which NGOs work. They make it difficult or impossible to get foreign funding, sometimes an organization's only source of revenue. They make it difficult to get registered or they require that all events and plans be filed ahead of time with the government. They label organizations "foreign agents" and imply or claim organizations are working on behalf of a foreign source, calling into question the NGO's loyalty and credibility (Christensen and Weinstein 2013; Carothers and Brechenmacher 2014). This trend occurs even in countries where the government itself relies on foreign assistance (Yeshanew 2012).

This issue has consumed human rights defenders in parts of the world for more than a decade, and practitioners inside and outside government increasingly view this phenomenon as a mission critical threat. President Barack Obama addressed the topic at the United Nations (UN) General Assembly and issued a Presidential Memorandum directing US government agencies, well beyond USAID and the State Department, to increase engagement with civil society around the world and push back when repressive measures are taken (White House Office of the Press Secretary 2014).

Yet a survey of IR literature uncovered relatively little work that either addressed the issue or generated remedies.[2] In the academy, closing space is a poorly understood and often overlooked threat to peaceful, prosperous development with multiple policy ramifications beyond human rights, from health to humanitarian assistance, from climate change to conflict prevention. Imagine, for example, that Liberia or Guinea had adopted laws that made it difficult or impossible for NGOs to function or receive funding from foreign sources. How would these countries have coped with the Ebola virus? If Kenya adopted such laws, how would the country handle the next famine?

# WHY IS SPACE CLOSING FOR CIVIL SOCIETY?

There appear to be numerous distinct policy drivers in various contexts, and more research is needed to delineate why the trend in closing space is occurring and what sensible remedies might be pursued. One working hypothesis is that space is closing because governments perceive the increased connectivity of citizens as a threat. Sovereignty is compromised or made more elastic in an age of citizens empowered with technology and information (Mendelson 2015). This pattern is most evident in Russia, where Putin views the internet as a "CIA project" and innovators—such as Pavel Durov who created the Russian version of Facebook, *VKontakte*—have fled Russia; however, other countries such as Turkey and China have followed suit (Hakim 2014; Goel and Kramer 2015). Power is fluid, if not shifting (Naim 2013; for an earlier argument, see Mathews 1997). *New York Times* columnist Tom Friedman (2015) goes so far as to claim "we're in the midst of a Gutenberg-scale change in how information is generated, stored, shared, protected and turned into products and services. We are seeing individuals become super-empowered to challenge governments and corporations." That power shift has many governments hostile to civil society, fearful of greater transparency revealing ill-gotten gains by corrupt government officials (Christensen and Weinstein 2013).

NGO activists also claim there is a crisis of legitimacy within civil society; space is closing in part because governments can put restrictions in place with relatively little response from populations. (The events in Ukraine in early 2014 stand in stark contrast; the balance of power between then President Viktor Yanukovich and Ukrainian society shifted markedly through the efforts of the Euromaidan movement [Mendelson and Harvey 2014; Higgins and Kramer 2015].) A vivid example of the crisis mentality came in the months before the 2014 International Civil Society Week: CIVICUS, a global alliance of civil society leaders with a large concentration from the global South, and a number of other NGOs, signed a letter suggesting the vision of human rights embodied in the Universal Declaration "lies in tatters" and that informal movements were challenging the more organized NGOs, and calling for a "radical re-haul of civil society" (*Civicus* blog 2014). This topic was also featured in a special edition of *Sur*, the international journal of human rights funded by the United Nations Foundation and the Ford Foundation (Shetty 2014).

A growing body of academic literature is beginning to address the crisis of closing space, but it generally is not authored by IR scholars. One exception, a research team led by Jim Ron, suggests that elites are more likely to know about human rights than the populations NGOs are meant to serve, and that may be a source of the problem (Ron et al. 2014a, 2014b). Another exception, Jack Snyder (2017), explores the shrinking of the vision and frames that the human rights movement has experienced in recent years. Closely related, development experts suggest that NGOs have gotten too far from the people they are meant to represent (Banks et al. 2015). Transnational NGOs have come in for perhaps the highest level of criticism in terms of accountability (Jordan and van Tuijl 2000; Piewitt et al. 2010; Slezkine 2014). And some work suggests that there is a correlation between the thin links of NGOs to local populations and the source of their funding, with development aid having a negative impact (Bano 2008; Banks et al. 2015; Jalali 2013). One author explains restrictive laws in the Ethiopian case as a result of NGOs' "accountability deficit" and "constituency-deficit" but acknowledges that Ethiopian law oversteps boundaries (Yeshanew 2012, 369, 379). Another laments the lack of "accountability" and "authenticity" to justify the NGO laws in Uganda: "This dependence syndrome [on foreign funding] undermines the independence and internal decision making capacity of NGOs. . . . [and] contributes to further weaken any social bases NGOs may have and makes them not accountable to the communities they serve, or any other domestic constituencies, but to the funder who in most cases are in foreign countries" (Tushabomwe 2014, 394).

Foreshadowing the concerns expressed by CIVICUS in 2014, Clark (2011) suggests "shifts in tactics" and argues that civil society is becoming less relevant with a loss of citizen support. Largely absent from these analyses is the way in which shifting conceptions of sovereignty and changes in the balance of power between citizens and the state, driven in part by new technologies and increased access to information by citizens, have driven the backlash, all fruitful topics for IR scholars.

## SOCIAL SCIENTISTS AND PUBLIC OPINION DATA

If relatively few IR scholars have addressed closing space or the backlash by autocrats, and if there is a crisis within civil society, whether manufactured by governments or by NGOs themselves, social scientists could play a critical role conducting public opinion surveys to help NGOs grow more resilient in the face of government restrictions. (In her own work [Davis et al. 2012], Murdie has looked at the role public opinion surveys can play.) Data on what matters and how citizens frame issues can help connect NGOs to the populations they are meant to serve. They can also be helpful to policymakers (Avey and Desch 2013b). In other words, advancing and protecting human rights need not only or mainly rely on the careful accounting of governments' noncompliance with the Universal Declaration of Human Rights that organizations such as Human Rights Watch have made central to their mandate; they ought to include large-N, random sample surveys (informed by focus groups) of what populations know and think, and how they experience human rights.[3]

Based on my own collaboration surveying on human rights in Russia, and the work that Jim Ron and his team are doing with human rights perception surveys in multiple countries, this approach seems promising (Ron and

Crow 2015). The lack of data has been an enormous problem in designing effective policies and programs. The 2015 World Development Report "Mind, Society and Behavior" (IBRD 2015) puts a great emphasis on paying "close attention to how humans actually think and decide" as opposed to making assumptions when designing programs. CIVICUS (2013, 19) also notes the importance of "public attitudes, trust, tolerance and participation" as elements that help create a healthy "enabling environment" for civil society. Opinion data can provide organizations with a baseline from which to measure the impact of campaigns.

This approach is not without challenges. Few NGOs have skilled social scientists on tap to help NGOs undertake and analyze data. Some NGOs, because of specific organizational cultures and traditions, may be uninterested in listening and responding to local populations. Donors with limited budgets may need to be persuaded that public opinion data is not a luxury item but a vital tool with which to build constituents and increase efficacy. Closing space may mean that surveys are no longer possible or that the value of popular opinion is outweighed by other repressive factors. Overall, however, listening and responding to the needs of citizens, rather than being driven by donor preferences, as has often been the case, should emerge as best practice.

## SOCIAL SCIENCE CAN HELP ADDRESS THE LEARNING GAP

Obstacles aside, the gold standard for showing impact of interventions is the RCT, yet scholars and practitioners have rarely performed such RCTs in human rights work. During my four years at USAID, I frequently encountered among practitioners and activists a learning gap (the close cousin of the influence gap) and confusion as to how to design an RCT on issues related to human rights. RCTs are common in health, education, and other aspects of development (Schneider, this volume), but in human rights and the larger democracy field, this approach is misunderstood, underdeveloped, and resisted. One activist (Gorvin 2009, 481) notes that when asked what constituted "success" or evidence of impact for Human Rights Watch, itself a sort of gold standard NGO in the human rights community, "there was a strong attachment to interpreting visibility—especially our presence in major US media outlets—as a measure of success per se." For some activists, as I found in Russia, the very notion of listening to the population, and shaping an intervention or message informed by data about public concerns challenged the identities of people who viewed themselves as dissidents driven by principle rather than strategic decision-making. The concept of serving or connecting to a population just was not in the DNA of many in the organizations (Mendelson and Gerber 2007). Alternatively, donors and activists alike fear that costs are prohibitively high, that resurveying could reveal zero impact, or that this method generates a tendency to treasure what one can measure rather than what one seeks to impact.

Although these concerns are not unwarranted, scholars could play a role in making sure that important aspects of programs are captured and a growing body of literature on what works best is developed. Younger activists are proving not only tech savvy but increasingly data driven. In Russia, the younger generation was excited about the concept of social marketing and understood the dynamics of the market and why ideas and norms may have to be sold to have influence (Mendelson and Gerber 2007).

Because NGO leaders and human rights practitioners are not usually trained social scientists, a partnership between social scientists and NGOs would go a long way to addressing this issue. Traditionally, private and public donors have not been defined in the human rights space by their interest in survey data. There are important exceptions. The Ford Foundation in the 2000s was a big supporter of such work in the United States.[4] In my time at USAID, my colleagues and I helped advance a focus on learning for which survey data will be a critical part.[5] The World Development Report 2015, "Mind, Society, and Behavior" (IBRD 2015), may help build momentum in favor of opinion surveys, and, of course, how the Sustainable Development Goals are actually implemented and measured through 2030 may help boost the demand by donors for survey data.

## IN CLOSING: IDEAS, INDIVIDUALS, AND INFLUENCE

The focus on data and organizations, especially NGOs, should not obscure the role that individuals play in influencing policymaking inside government. Simply put, certain individuals advancing specific ideas in policy positions matter enormously, and this is especially true with respect to human rights (Mendelson 1998; on ideas in foreign policy, see Goldstein and Keohane 1993). In the twenty-first century, more than ever before, given the demands generated by the sheer deluge of information, as the Avey and Desch (2013a) study suggested, policymakers read very little. There is less room for outside influences such as IR scholarship compared to earlier periods; the importance of specific individuals in positions of power may only increase over time.

One recent example of this impact of ideas and individuals was the Obama administration's establishment of the Atrocity Prevention Board (APB), a new body inside the US government that meets monthly at the assistant secretary level or above to coordinate across agencies on issues related to preventing atrocities. This effort, however maligned or misunderstood because of the ongoing war in Syria, was not the result of earlier work by social scientists such as Barbara Harff and Ted Gurr (work cited by Murdie and many others as generally influential). Rather, it was the output of think tanks in Washington working together as the Genocide Prevention Task

Force (GPTF), led by former Secretary of State Madeleine K. Albright and former Secretary of Defense William S. Cohen in 2007 and 2008, coupled with the particular role that then Special Assistant to the President and NSC Senior Director for Multilateral Affairs and Human Rights Samantha Power and NSC Director for War Crimes and Atrocities David Pressman played inside the bureaucracy in 2011 and 2012 (Murdie, this volume, p35).[6] The full impact of the APB will be difficult to gauge for outsiders; the cases will be "dogs that did not bark." The role of specific ideas and individuals are traceable, however, and rather astonishingly in this case, the concept appears to have been institutionalized. Specific fixes, such as training for USAID staff on atrocity prevention, and the continued (albeit diminished) role of the APB during the Trump administration suggest that individuals can help seed ideas that take hold.

Moreover, the degree to which IR scholarship influences UN treaty bodies or the Special Rapporteurs correlates highly with the individual in that role. Maina Kiai, the special rapporteur on freedom of assembly from 2011 to 2017, was a vital voice in the global conversation on how to push back on closing space, whereas other rapporteurs (and there are more than fifty) are far less known on issues just as critical (e.g., Kiai 2015). In short, Murdie's claim that "the footprint of IR human rights research on the practitioner/ policy community is significant" needs more robust consideration of how and why the practitioner/policy community makes decisions on various issues (Murdie, this volume, p38).

Finally, it might be worth thinking less about generating an idea that is guaranteed to find traction in the policymaking world and more about issues that are bedeviling the policymaking world and to which social scientists, and IR theorists in particular, can help identify remedies. There are ways in which a consortium or an organizational arrangement might be created to address this specific influence or legitimacy gap with which civil society activists, especially in the global South, are now so consumed. One could imagine the creation of a group working with NGOs to listen and respond to citizens using survey data along the lines of the Abdul Lateef Jamaal Poverty Action Lab at the Massachusetts Institute of Technology or Experiments in Governance and Politics but focused explicitly on human rights and surveys rather than specific interventions that social scientists show helps alleviate poverty. This Human Rights Social Science-NGO consortium would pair social scientists with NGOs. The effort might begin with a few countries or work through a series of hubs or regional platforms in which donors are already investing and evolve from there, creating peer-to-peer learning supplemented by social scientists. This collective would not by any means be the only remedy to closing space, but it might provide a concrete way to help NGOs become more sustainable, linked to the populations they are meant to be serving, and simultaneously, increase the relevance of IR scholars (and other social scientists) to human rights practitioners around the world.

# ENDNOTES

This chapter draws on a paper I prepared for another conference, titled "How Do We Know What We Know? Charting the Future for Human Rights Documentation and Analysis," held at Arizona State University, January 22–24, 2015. I thank the organizers of both conferences for the opportunity to participate, Jack Snyder and Jim Ron for comments on an earlier version of this paper, Sarah Mohamed for research assistance, and the Oak Foundation for support.

1.  Additional human rights topics demanding greater attention from IR scholars include preventing mass atrocities in Syria, the Central African Republic, South Sudan, and the Democratic Republic of Congo; abuses by Russian paramilitaries in Ukraine; human trafficking; shrinking bilateral donor budgets; historical memory as a driver of conflict; and the role of human rights in the Sustainable Development Goals.
2.  Exceptions include recently published and work in progress by James Ron, Kendra Dupuy, and Aseem Prakesh and work in progress by Alex Cooley and Jack Snyder.
3.  The various Barometers and World Values Surveys do not systematically address the sort of multifaceted or context-specific aspects of human rights that are needed, but they are a basis on which to build. The larger unaddressed mandate here is how to get activists to use the data as an important strategy in building constituencies for human rights through social marketing campaigns.
4.  See, for example, the work in the US of the "Opportunity Agenda," http://opportunityagenda.org/public_opinion. Most of the dozen-plus surveys I ran with a research team in Russia from 2002 to 2010 were supported by the Ford Foundation.
5.  See the USAID Learning Lab and USAID (2013).
6.  James P. Finkel and I were frequent attendees of APB meetings in 2012–2013, and he makes a similar point regarding GPTF and Power in Finkel (2014). I do not pretend to be an unbiased source on the APB, having been the USAID lead ahead of its creation in 2011 and then the key staffer to the USAID representative on the board in 2012–13, Deputy Administrator Donald Steinberg.

# 4

# THE STUDY AND PRACTICE OF GLOBAL ENVIRONMENTAL POLITICS

## *Policy Influence through Participation*

Jessica F. Green and Thomas Hale

U nlike war or trade, transboundary environmental problems are a relatively new feature of world politics. Despite their relative newness, environmental challenges will occupy a central and growing place in practitioners' attention for the foreseeable future. Our impact on the natural world is destabilizing human societies. The implications for world politics are profound. As an October 2014 Pentagon report noted, "Rising global temperatures, changing precipitation patterns, climbing sea levels, and more extreme weather events will intensify the challenges of global instability, hunger, poverty, and conflict. They will likely lead to food and water shortages, pandemic disease, disputes over refugees and resources, and destruction by natural disasters in regions across the globe" (US Department of Defense 2014)." International relations (IR) scholars agree. According to the TRIP data, IR scholars already see environmental issues like global climate change as the most important policy challenges of the century (Green and Hale 2017).

The implications for the study of world politics are similarly weighty. If IR cannot contribute to environmental questions that concern the survival of humanity, it will be of limited relevance to world politics. But while the study of global environmental issues has expanded in IR, global environmental politics (GEP) remains one of the more neglected subject areas in the field (Javeline 2014; Keohane 2014; Green and Hale 2017). Using the 2014 Teaching, Research, and International Policy (TRIP) faculty survey data, we classified GEP scholars as any respondent who listed "international environment" or "environment" as either a primary or secondary research area (Maliniak et al. 2014).[1] Of the 5,049 scholars with identifiable research areas, only 352 (7 percent) were classified as GEP scholars.

The underrepresentation of environmental politics is also made plain by the TRIP article database, which includes only 84 articles (1.23 percent) in the environment issue area and only 247 (3.50 percent) with a substantive focus on environmental issues. Because GEP scholars represent 7 percent of the discipline, it seems reasonable to infer that GEP scholars are underrepresented in top journals, although the comparison is inexact. Figure 4.1 shows

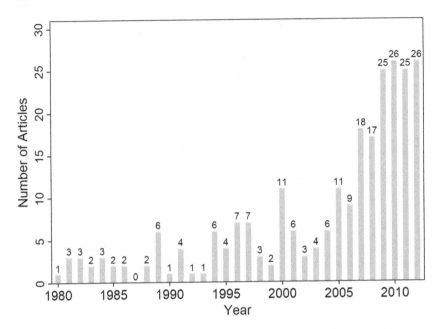

**FIGURE 4.1.** Articles with a substantive focus on the environment published in the top twelve IR journals, 1980–2012

the number of environmental articles published over time. The recent spike in environment-related articles is cause for optimism.

Thus, the data support our argument, following others, that environmental issues—not just climate change—remain at the margins of the discipline. If one goal of academic study is to contribute to broader public discussions of import (as we believe it is), then IR must engage more actively with environmental issues. We emphasize that significant environmental IR scholarship is published in specialized journals like *Global Environmental Politics*, but this work is not well represented in the top discipline-wide journals.

Given the relative lack of attention that global environmental issues receive from IR scholars, can there be much evidence for IR's influence on GEP? We argue that there has in fact been a substantial role for IR concepts and scholars in the practice of GEP. Indeed, several features of environmental politics make it particularly open to scholarly influence. Consistent with arguments 1a and 1b in chapter 1, the emerging and technical nature of environmental issues increases the opportunity for policy relevance. Because political scientists were part of the discussion early, sometimes present at the creation, they were not crowded out by natural scientists or economists. Moreover, the porous nature of the global environmental arena—its strong tradition of civil society participation and the multitude of actors involved

**TABLE 4.1.** Modes of scholarly influence on policy

|  | Intentional | Not intentional |
| --- | --- | --- |
| Necessary or sufficient | Causal | (null) |
| Facilitative | Engagement | Diffuse |

in the policy process—provides significant opportunities for influence by IR scholars, particularly at lower working levels (argument 2b). Finally, IR scholars have also been part of governmental and intergovernmental work.

Before proceeding, we must define "influence." We are interested in situations in which scholarly ideas or actions affect policy or practitioner behavior. Building on the concepts presented in chapter 1, we suggest that such influence can be roughly divided into ideal types based on two dimensions. First, does the scholar intend his/her ideas or actions to change policy? Second, how decisive is the scholarly intervention for a given outcome? These two dimensions yield three relevant types of influence (table 4.1).

First, *causal influence* occurs when scholars alter the behavior of practitioners through their ideas and actions. Betsill and Correll (2008, 24) define this type of influence as situations "when one actor intentionally communicates to another so as to alter the latter's behavior from what would have occurred otherwise." In other words, scholars take purposeful actions to alter policy or practitioner behavior, and these actions can be shown to constitute a sufficient or necessary condition for a change in policy or behavior. This is a high standard for influence; indeed, they apply their definition to NGOs, which generally have the explicit aim of influencing state policy.

We expect this type of attributable, causal influence to be rare because it likely requires academics to divert significant time from research and teaching. And it presumes that academics and their ideas wield decisive influence in complex policy processes in which many different actors compete for influence. These conditions obtain infrequently. More frequently, we expect scholars to exert "engagement influence." By this we mean that scholars' actions are geared toward changing behavior but are neither sufficient nor necessary conditions for a certain outcome; instead, they are facilitative factors. The causal chain may be complex and extended, with scholarly ideas or actions playing just one role in a larger set of interactions. For this reason, engagement influence is likely often difficult to measure directly, although we believe it is widespread and important.

In the environmental realm, engagement influence can take several forms. First, many multilateral environmental institutions allow and encourage academic observers (and other members of civil society) to participate through official submissions, "side events" at multilateral meetings, and other mechanisms. GEP scholars regularly advance ideas and policy proposals, many of which draw on academic data and analysis. Second, many international organizations include scholarly experts on committees tasked

with reviewing or implementing decisions. For example, the Intergovernmental Panel on Climate Change (IPCC), tasked with developing a scientific
consensus on the causes and impacts of climate change and the various policy
responses available, self-consciously incorporates a range of social scientists,
including IR scholars (although it includes more economists). Even though
engagement and influence are analytically distinct, scholars may have influence, often indirect, through their engagement in the policy process.

Finally, diffuse influence is perhaps the most difficult to detect empirically: scholarly ideas or actions affect policy or behavior without necessarily
intending to and without attributable causal effect. In some cases, concepts
and ideas generated by GEP scholars are reflected in policy outcomes, not
because of scholars' efforts but because academic work simply "out there"
in the world is used to craft or implement policy. For example, scholars who
name phenomena and describe their characteristics in their teaching or in
dissemination of their research may render a useful service to practitioners
who then build on this knowledge. Scholars react to developments in the policy world, and scholarly concepts and ideas leak into policy discussions and,
ultimately, policy. This highly diffuse form of (mutual) influence is likely the
most common variety, on average, across issue areas and subfields.

Our chapter explores the influence of GEP in each of the ideal types
identified. We first examine diffuse influence by reviewing the history of
GEP as a subfield. Although it is necessarily brief, we flag this history as a
contribution because we are aware of few similar intellectual histories (but
see Stevis 2014). We are not able to explicitly identify ways in which GEP
ideas have diffusely influenced outcomes, but we note how the co-evolution
of the subfield with problems and issues identified in the policy arena make
such forms of influence likely. We find increasing resonance between the two
over time. Second, we consider a rare but powerful example of causal influence: John Ruggie's role in the creation of the Global Compact. Finally,
we consider engagement influence, which we argue is particularly relevant
for GEP. The conclusion identifies opportunities for IR scholars to expand
policy-relevant research on environmental politics going forward.

## GEP SCHOLARSHIP TRACKS POLITICAL DISCUSSIONS

Has IR scholarship tracked GEP following a pattern of diffuse influence? We
answer that question by describing the co-evolution of GEP in the scholarly
and policy realms. A key challenge for this exercise is delineating the GEP
field and the role of IR scholarship within it. GEP is a large and diverse field,
branching across IR into different disciplines. Surprisingly few histories of
the field have been written.[2]

We take a chronological approach, discussing the main themes of scholarly inquiry roughly by decade, paying particular attention to when and how

political scientists contribute to and shape these discussions. We also track the extent to which scholarly discussions overlap with policy debates in the same time period.

Two core findings emerge. First, even though political scientists were relatively unengaged in GEP in early years, there has been increasing overlap between IR research on the environment and the important political developments of the time. Second, there has been a secular increase in the importance of environmental issues in policy.

## EARLY ORIGINS: FUNCTIONAL REGIMES, TRANSNATIONAL GOVERNANCE, AND EPISTEMIC COMMUNITIES, BUT FEW POLITICAL SCIENTISTS

Whereas GEP is conventionally seen to start in the postwar period, and especially after the 1970s, its precursors emerged as early as the late nineteenth century. These early origins are worth noting for two reasons. First, they show that even a century ago some of the core features of contemporary GEP—functional regimes and institutions that emphasize the role of nonstate actors and epistemic communities—were already features of the policy landscape (see Boardman 1981; Hale et al. 2013). Second, they demonstrate that political scientists were largely uninterested in these phenomena.

A number of treaties designed to conserve transboundary species emerged in the late nineteenth and early twentieth centuries. These included the 1902 Convention for the Protection of Birds Useful to Agriculture, the 1916 migratory bird treaty between the United States and the United Kingdom (on behalf of Canada and extended to Mexico in 1936), the 1911 Fur Seal Treaty, and the 1936 International Agreement for the Regulation of Whaling, which in 1947 became the stricter International Convention for the Regulation of Whaling.

At this time, a meeting of environmentalists at the 1909 International Congress for the Protection of Nature called for the creation of a general international environmental organization. World War I intervened, but environmentalists reconstituted their earlier efforts as part of the League of Nations in the 1920s. When these efforts failed to gain member state agreement, conservation groups and scientists created an information-sharing organization, the International Office for the Protection of Nature, in 1934 (Boardman 1981; Hale et al. 2013). A second attempt to create an international environmental organization in the 1940s failed to establish a strong intergovernmental body and resulted in a similar hybrid arrangement.

There is a striking absence of social scientific interest in this early environmental policymaking. For example, we find no mention of the treaties or organizations discussed previously in the *American Political Science Review* before 1950. Instead, natural scientists were the key experts influencing policy, as they remain today. As in later environmental treaties, groups of scientific experts played a key role in putting conservation on the political agenda and designing and helping to operate the resulting institutions.

## 1960S: THE POPULATION GROWTH DILEMMA

During the 1960s, environmental issues were growing beyond their initial "conservation" focus aimed at species protection and transboundary resource management. Instead, economic growth and human welfare issues took center stage, bringing an inflection point in both policy interest and scholarly work on GEP topics. Most of this work focused on the related issues of population growth and resource scarcity. Population growth was a timely topic because global rates of growth increased precipitously in the late 1950s and early 1960s. As population grew, scarcity became an issue, especially in the developing world, where rates of growth were higher and scarcity was already an issue.

Biologists Paul and Anne Ehrlich's 1968 work *The Population Bomb* was pessimistic about global prospects. The book echoed *An Essay on the Principle of Population*, in which Malthus (1798/2013) predicted that the linear increase in food supply would eventually be overtaken by the exponential growth in population, making indefinite human expansion impossible.

The so-called Club of Rome, a group of academics working at the Massachusetts Institute of Technology, delivered a similar message in *The Limits to Growth*. This work, spearheaded by natural scientists Donella and Dennis Meadows, Jorgen Randers, and William W. Behrens III, used computer models to predict how the interactions between different problems and factors would affect "the present and future predicament of man" (Meadows et al. 1974, ix). Their findings were similarly pessimistic: limits to growth would be reached within the next century.

Other works from this time examined how human behaviors beyond reproduction may exacerbate problems of scarcity. Biologist Garrett Hardin's (1968) classic work "The Tragedy of the Commons" describes how the rational behavior of individuals leads to a collectively irrational outcome, the destruction of commonly held resources. This model would later be appropriated by rational choice approaches to international cooperation.

Finally, Paul Ehrlich, John Holdren, and Barry Commoner in 1972 collectively developed the IPAT identity, which identified three key interacting factors to determine environmental impact: population, affluence, and technology (Commoner 1972; Ehrlich and Holdren 1972). They argued that controlling population growth alone would not adequately address scarcity; the use of technology and the level of affluence could have mitigating or exacerbating effects.

Political scientists largely remained absent from this discussion in which the majority of contributors were natural scientists.

# THE 1970S: THE EMERGENCE OF THE MODERN ENVIRONMENTAL MOVEMENT AND GLOBAL ENVIRONMENTAL GOVERNANCE

Environmental issues experienced a step change in political salience in the late 1960s and early 1970s and for the first time attracted the interest of political scientists. Reacting to a series of industrial disasters and warnings like Rachel Carson's *Silent Spring* (1962), the modern environmental movement emerged around the industrialized world demanding government intervention to protect air, water, and other natural resources. This grassroots movement resulted in the creation of modern environmental laws and regulatory institutions in advanced economies.

This same shift also marked a turning point for environmental politics at the international level. In 1971, scientific experts from the developing world released the Founex Report, which made three important contributions to the broader political dialogue. First, it recognized that developing countries *also* experienced "environmental" problems, although these were of a different sort than those in the developed world. Second, it laid the foundations for further discussion on the relationship between economic development and environmental protection at the upcoming United Nations (UN) Conference on the Human Environment (UNCHE), which was held in Stockholm in 1972. Third, it shifted the tenor of debates about GEP. Developing countries were no longer the object of analysis (and the source of the problem); they also were viewed as necessary participants in an ongoing discussion about solutions.

Tracking these changes in the policy world, political scientists began writing about GEP. In 1971 Harold and Margaret Sprout published *Towards a Politics of Planet Earth*. The authors pointed to the rising importance of nonmilitary issues such as the environmental impact of nuclear weapons and the rate of technological change. Lynton Caldwell's (1972) work was similarly important for the development of the field. Described as "the father of biopolitics," Caldwell is widely credited with incorporating the environmental impact statement into the National Environmental Policy Act (Haack 2014).

On the IR side, an important intervention came from a figure at the center of the discipline's scholarship-policy nexus: George Kennan. Writing in *Foreign Affairs* in 1970, Kennan called for the creation of an international environment organization to coordinate global efforts to protect the planet.

Kennan's proposal had a real-world test a few years later. In 1972, states held the first global conference on environmental issues, an environmental Bretton Woods. The Stockholm Conference on the Human Environment grew out of the problems identified in the Founex Report. One hundred thirteen nations, along with representatives of international organizations and NGOs convened to decide how to address these issues. Participating states created the UN Environment Programme (UNEP), an international institution charged with "promot[ing] international co-operation in the field of environment" (UN General Assembly 1972). From the perspective of IR scholarship, the UNCHE conference was significant in that it created the international institutional framework that would become the focus of academic research in the 1980s and 1990s.

The Stockholm Declaration recognized the important role of economic growth for developing nations. Even though a few scholars, notably those from the developing world (Castro 1972), took this as an important cue for refocusing GEP scholarship, most continued to explore questions of population and scarcity. The cleavage between developed and developing countries on the relative prioritization of growth and conservation, already visible in Stockholm, would become the enduring fault line of GEP in the decades that followed (Najam 2005).

Research on "bioenvironmentalism," which "stresses the biological limits of the Earth to support life," also flourished in the 1970s (Clapp and Dauvergne 2011, 9). These works, like their predecessors, were preoccupied with questions of resource scarcity. IR theorists entered this debate, notably through a 1977 special issue of *International Studies Quarterly* titled "The International Politics of Scarcity." The volume begins from the simple but bold premise that "it has become apparent to even the most skeptical that an international politics of scarcity, real or contrived, will be an important characteristic of the future international system" (Pirages 1977, 564). These works foreshadow ongoing research agendas in GEP: the effects of a rise in oil prices (Bobrow et al. 1977), the exploitation of ocean resources (Barkenbaus 1977), and the role of domestic politics.[3]

Thus, the 1970s marks the beginning of a corpus of work by IR scholars on GEP issues. Interestingly, however, many of these interventions do not map onto the policy discussions of the era. Rather, they respond to earlier academic work by scholars *outside* of IR.

## 1980–1990S: ENTER REGIME THEORY

As international regimes grew in the environmental arena, so did GEP theory. A number of important agreements were signed, including the Mediterranean Action Plan, the Convention on Long Range Transboundary Air Pollution, the Montreal Protocol, and several treaties governing fish species and the protection of the Antarctic (see Mitchell 2002–2016). The heyday of international environmental lawmaking was underway, coinciding with the rise of regime theory in IR.

The institutional architecture of GEP continued to expand. The UN General Assembly affirmed the need for a greater role for UNEP in establishing programmatic priorities for environmental protection in the developing world (UN General Assembly 1983). Then UN Secretary General Javier Perez de Cuellar created the World Commission on Environment and

Development (WCED), chaired by then prime minister of Norway, Gro Harlem Brundtland. The final report of the Brundtland Commission, *Our Common Future* (WCED 1987), included the seminal statement on sustainable development, which it defined as "development that meets the needs of the present without compromising the ability of future generations to meet their own needs" (WCED 1987, 9). The Brundtland Commission elaborated a vision of neoliberal environmentalism that emphasized growth for the poor and consumptive restraint by the rich (WCED 1987, 9).

The Brundtland Commission highlighted the need for international cooperation to achieve the twin goals of economic growth and environmental protection, including the need for more international and domestic environmental law and active participation of multilateral financial institutions to provide necessary funding and know-how to developing nations.

This mandate was adopted at the 1992 Rio Earth Summit, a kind of Bretton Woods for GEP, in which 172 countries agreed to an extraordinarily ambitious series of commitments to protect the global environment, including a wide-ranging aspirational text called Agenda 21, which sought to commit countries to the goals identified in the Brundtland Report. More tangibly, new regimes emerged to manage problems concerning forests, biodiversity, and climate change.

In the mid-1980s, regime theory came to the fore among IR scholars. The 1982 special issue of *International Organization* on international regimes opened a new research agenda for IR scholars. Krasner's (1983) oft-cited definition of regimes as "principles, norms, rules, and decision-making procedures around which actor expectations converge in a given issue-area" described the flurry of activity evolving in the international environmental arena. New international legal instruments, expanding mandates for existing international organizations, and increasing activity of nonstate actors were all indications of the growth of environmental regimes.

The growth in both prominence and breadth of GEP in world politics was soon followed by a similar growth in scholarly attention. Game-theoretic approaches to cooperation included examinations of environmental problems (Barrett 1994; Oye and Maxwell 1994). Regime theory conveniently provided a theoretical lens for analysis, which many GEP scholars adopted. Many historical accounts concur that work on environmental regimes is paradigmatic of GEP contributions to the broader field of IR.

The work on environmental regimes can be roughly divided according to four themes: creation, formation, compliance, and effectiveness. Early work by Oran Young (1989) presents a model of institutional bargaining that emphasizes characteristics beyond domestic politics to explain regime formation, such as the availability of solutions, perceptions of equity, and robust compliance mechanisms (Victor 2011; Hale et al. 2013). Peter Haas's (1989; also Dimitrov 2003) work on epistemic communities has made an impact in IR well beyond the GEP subfield; he emphasizes consensus among scientific experts in promoting regime formation. A number of scholars also cite the role of specific leaders as a key element in explaining the successful formation of some regimes (Mitchell 2003). Others have sought to explain why some environmental problems do *not* result in regime creation (Dimitrov 2002; Davenport 2005).

GEP scholars also view regime design as a function of the type of environmental problem addressed.[4] Mitchell's study of MARPOL shows how technology standards were able to dramatically reduce marine pollution (Mitchell 1994). Victor and Coben (2005, 25) offer a cogent critique of the Kyoto Protocol based on a mismatch of problem to solution. Young (2002) has described these design issues as a question of "institutional fit." Others view the question of fit through an ecology lens, examining whether institutional solutions respond to the ecological scale of the problem (Galaz et al. 2008; Gupta 2008; Andonova and Mitchell 2010).

Within the regime literature, GEP scholars have perhaps been most focused on questions of regime effectiveness. Effectiveness is defined differently by different scholars. The two primary distinctions are between adoption of and adherence to rules and measurable improvements in environmental outcomes (see Haas et al. 1993; Jacobson and Weiss 1995; Miles et al. 2001). The latter is particularly challenging because it requires comparison to a counterfactual (environmental outcomes in the absence of the treaty) and acknowledgment that other factors beyond the regime may contribute to environmental degradation (Mitchell 2003, 444). Finally, because treaty compliance may be an endogenous behavior, it is difficult to show that regimes truly "constrain" behavior, rather than simply screen the participating actors (von Stein 2005). Mitchell's (2003, 447) meta-analysis demonstrates the difficulties of evaluating effectiveness. Several of his examples show conflicting conclusions about the same regime or dramatic changes in the assessment over time.

For these reasons, drawing sweeping conclusions about the effectiveness of environmental regimes is challenging. A few works have put forth frameworks that suggest useful starting points. Haas, Keohane, and Levy (1993) found regimes to be most effective when the "3Cs" were in effect: environmental *concern*, a hospitable *contractual* environment, and adequate levels of national *capacity*. Jacobson and Brown Weiss (1995) cite country-level factors, international context, regime design, and the character of the regulated activity. The majority of work tends to be qualitative and comparative, seeking to draw generalizable conclusions from successes and failures. Other work evaluates effectiveness quantitatively. Breitmeier et al. (2006) compiled a database of international environmental regimes that aims to provide a broader picture of effectiveness across issue areas. Mitchell's International Environmental Agreements Database provides a tremendous resource for GEP scholars studying various regime characteristics (Mitchell 2003, 2006, 2010).[5]

This brief review only scratches the surface of a vast body of literature on environmental regimes. Although GEP scholars' contributions coincided with a dramatic growth in environmental regimes, the links to policy discussions are tenuous. The period is characterized more by parallel trajectories than meaningful interaction.

## 2000S TO THE PRESENT: THE LIMITS OF REGIMES AND REGIME THEORY

The sense of possibility that characterized GEP in the early 1990s did not endure. Countries have met countless times to negotiate measures to strengthen and implement the regimes they created in and around the Rio summit, but few successes emerged. The number of new treaties began to decline (see figure 4.2), as countries proved unable to find agreements that accommodated the divergent needs of developed and developing countries, especially as environmental issues penetrated deeper into the core economic interests of states. Some academic observers began to speak of "gridlock" in environmental governance (Victor 2011; Hale et al. 2013). While regime theory blossomed—IR scholars were developing ever more sophisticated analyses of regime design and effectiveness—environmental regimes themselves were stagnating. Arguably, however, political scientists were too focused on the functionalist logics guiding institutional design and less engaged in thinking through the political conditions under which such ideas could be realized.

At the same time, practitioners' and scholars' attention increasingly focused on other forms of global governance. The 2002 World Summit on Sustainable Development touted the importance of public-private partnerships

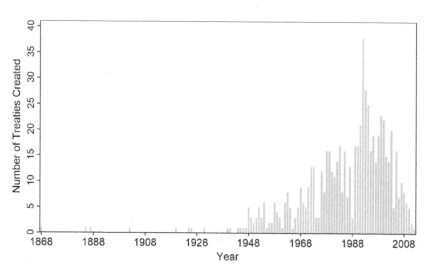

**FIGURE 4.2.**   Environmental treaties created per year, 1868–2012 (*N* = 670)

in harnessing financing and expertise for promoting "green growth." NGOs, private firms, and states increasingly collaborated on joint initiatives to manage environmental problems. For instance, the Small Grants Program of the Global Environment Facility provides project financing to NGOs and community organizations to promote sustainable development, with a co–decision-making role for national governments (Andonova and Mitchell 2010). Similarly, the Global Reporting Initiative, designed by an international NGO in consultation with a broad network of stakeholders, provides a framework for organizations to evaluate and report on their sustainability. This period has also been marked by a precipitous growth in entrepreneurial private authority, situations in which nonstate actors serve as de facto regulators, creating rules on everything from tropical commodities to carbon (Green 2014).

This shift, also seen in other issue areas (especially health, human rights, and various aspects of financial and commercial regulation) has now led to a formidable IR literature on private entrepreneurial authority and other forms of transnational governance. These works examine how NGOs, firms, and other sub-/nonstate actors and networks create voluntary standards to regulate environmental externalities (see Vogel 2008). A large swath of this work has focused on forestry and, in particular, the Forestry Stewardship Council (see, e.g., Cashore et al. 2004). Another burgeoning body of work focuses on entrepreneurial authority and climate change (Hoffman 2011; Meckling 2011; Bulkeley et al. 2012; Green 2014). Still other scholars examine private standards on the sustainable production of commodities such as coffee, tea, fisheries, palm oil, and organics, among others (Dingwerth and Pattberg 2009; Fransen 2011; Auld 2014).

GEP scholarship has also responded to the growth in institutional complexity that accompanies the rise in nonstate and transnational actors. A growing body of work examines the ways in which international organizations can help "orchestrate" activity among NGOs and other nonstate actors (Abbott et al. 2014; Hale and Roger 2014). Other scholars have studied the proliferation of nonstate actors at various levels of governance working transnationally to address environmental problems (Betsill and Bulkeley 2006; Hadden 2015).

Another hallmark of the last decade is the growing density of the international arena, in which laws and regimes increasingly "bump into" each other. Questions about whether free trade can be curtailed in the name of environmental preferences have surfaced in a number of issues over the last two decades (see O'Neill 2009, chap. 5). Most recently, the European Union (EU) sought to require flights traveling through European airspace to purchase emissions allowances. This extraterritorial application of EU law almost sparked a trade war, with opposing countries claiming that requiring the purchase of allowances could constitute a restriction in trade. Writing about the plant biodiversity regime, Raustiala and Victor (2004) coined the term "regime complex" to describe the increasingly overlapping nature of international rules and institutions, a concept that has been applied beyond the environmental realm.

Environmental issues increasingly overlap with security concerns (see, e.g., Homer-Dixon 1991). IR scholars were among the first to recognize the threat that climate change posed to national security (Hendrix and Glaser 2007; Busby 2008) and forcefully made the case to the defense establishment (Busby 2007). The Pentagon's response has been significant. It may be the case that IR scholars' traditional authority on security matters gave the field additional credibility when practitioners considered this aspect of GEP.

## CAUSAL INFLUENCE: A RARITY IN GEP

Thus far, we have demonstrated that there is ample evidence of GEP scholarship tracking trends in the political arena consistent with our concept of diffuse influence. We now examine causal and engagement influence. We find few instances of causal influence, but as the editors argue in chapter 1, this reflects structural constraints and professional incentives as much as the ability of scholars to affect influence in the policy process.

Much of the discussion of policy relevance explicitly or implicitly posits an attributable, causal relationship between a scholar and his or her work, on the one hand, and a policy outcome, what we have termed "causal influence," on the other. For example, in the UK's Research Excellence Framework (the evaluative process through which the government awards funding to universities), impact counts for 20 percent of an institution's score and is defined as "an effect on, change or benefit to the economy, society, culture, public policy or services, health, the environment or quality of life, beyond academia" (Research Excellence Framework 2012). In the United States, Congress has sought to limit National Science Foundation support for political science to research that directly contributes to national security and economic growth (NSF 2013).

Academics may sometimes achieve this form of influence, but such cases are rare for several reasons. First, direct influence is typically time intensive, creating large opportunity costs for academics who could earn greater professional rewards from research published in top journals. This incentive structure particularly discourages younger scholars who are typically seeking to establish reputations in the field and secure tenured or tenure-track jobs.

Second, academics have less time to devise and advocate policy proposals than their counterparts in NGOs, lobbies, or think tanks; they also have less experience doing so and fewer personal connections to practitioners. We can expect, moreover, that academics will have less aptitude for policy work than individuals who have selected into more policy-focused lines of work.

The final point is a consequence of the previous two. Academics are on average *relatively* less effective at direct policy work than other actors, so their causal impact may be overshadowed. Policymaking typically involves a struggle between different actors seeking to influence outcomes. For important policies, such competition is fierce, even among actors who share policy goals but compete for prestige or funding from donors. In such an environment, it is unlikely that policy work by academics will be the decisive factor influencing an outcome. In other words, even if academics devote time and energy to policy work, there are systematic reasons to expect limited causal influence.

Causal influence has rarely occurred in global environmental politics for the reasons explained previously. Nevertheless, we offer one example of causal influence—John Ruggie's efforts to create the UN Global Compact, a set of voluntary standards for multinational corporations.

For many years, the UN has sought to regulate the activities of multinational corporations. In the 1970s, these efforts were driven by developing countries seeking to advance a "New International Economic Order" (UN General Assembly 1974), but this proposal floundered once the oil crisis of the early 1970s passed. In the 1990s, new efforts arose to regulate the impact of multinational corporations on human rights and the natural environment, driven chiefly by northern civil society groups. Many of these efforts took the form of voluntary regulatory standards, which sometimes included transparency or other nonjuridical enforcement provisions (Abbott and Snidal 2009; Auld et al. 2008).

An IR scholar, Harvard Professor John Ruggie, devised, advocated, and led the implementation of one of the most central and often-studied voluntary standards. Ruggie has contributed to the literature on epistemic communities and international regimes; he is perhaps best known for explaining how "embedded liberalism"—the way in which the redistributive functions of the welfare state enabled economic integration—underpinned the postwar global economic order (Ruggie 1982). In 1997 he became UN assistant secretary-general for Strategic Planning, a post created for him by then Secretary-General Kofi Annan.

In this role, Ruggie devised and oversaw the implementation of the UN Global Compact, a set of ten principles derived from labor, human rights, and environmental treaties that 12,000 companies have elected to adopt as of 2018 (on the genesis of the Global Compact, see Andonova 2017).[6] Signatory companies are not subject to "hard" enforcement provisions but rather must provide periodic updates on their progress, and they can benefit from dissemination of best practices. The Global Compact stands out among voluntary regulatory schemes in that it carries the official imprimatur of the UN. In Ruggie's view, the Global Compact is an attempt to operationalize, in a globalized world, the "embedded liberalism" compromise between social values and market exigencies he identified in his previous scholarship (Ruggie 2004).[7]

What explains the success of Ruggie's efforts to exert causal influence? Perhaps unsurprisingly, they came at a stage in Ruggie's career when he was well established within the discipline and able to devote considerable time to policy work. Ruggie's personal commitment to these issues and entrepreneurial spirit also sets him apart from many other scholars in the discipline.

## ENGAGEMENT INFLUENCE

Interaction has been the source of the most important form of academic influence in GEP. Such influence is less direct than causal influence. It recognizes that many academics participate in policy processes and influence them in ways other than attributable, "but for" causation. When scholars engage in the policy world, they may shape practitioners' information or beliefs, defining and differentiating potential options or strategies, evaluating past performance, or contextualizing the dilemmas practitioners face by relating them to similar cases in history, other issue areas, or other parts of the world.

Engagement influence is likely more common in environmental politics than in IR for three reasons. First, the identification of GEP problems and policy responses are fundamentally scientific in nature. As the editors note in chapter 1, as issues become more technical, more opportunities arise for scholars to have influence (argument 1b). Because of the scientific nature of global environmental issues, strong epistemic communities of experts pervade the issue area. Although these groups have traditionally been dominated by natural scientists, they have increasingly welcomed and prioritized social science, including IR. Second, academics who study environmental politics tend to have strong personal commitments to environmental protection. This gives them, on average, a greater interest and willingness to engage in environmental policy work. Moreover, because civil society activism plays a central role in environmental politics (cf. chapter 2 on human rights), scholars have ready channels through which to engage. Third, and related, environmental policymaking arenas are often more accessible to a wider range of actors than other spheres of politics. As the editors argue in chapter 1, more porous issue areas, those in which decision-making authority is dispersed or delegated, create greater opportunities for IR scholars and scholarship to reach policymakers (argument 2b). Multilateral environmental meetings and international organizations have a strong tradition of civil society participation, and the multitude of actors involved in the policy process gives academics a surfeit of interlocutors for engagement and influence. In the following section, we highlight how these mechanisms have operated in several policy areas.

## Reliance on Technical Expertise, Including Social Science

The science-policy nexus is perhaps the most important avenue for engagement influence in GEP and has been the focus of scholars for a quarter century.[8] Given the technical nature of environmental problems, scientific assessments are a key political and institutional component of the policy-making process.

Recent IR scholarship examines whether and how large-scale scientific assessments of environmental issues can influence policy. The *explicit* goal of these bodies is to feed information into the policymaking process (Mitchell 2006, 3). Scientific assessments are commonplace in environmental politics; Mitchell (2006) estimates that there were between two and three active assessments per year between the 1980s and 1990s. Interestingly, he finds that these assessments are "social processes rather than published products" (Mitchell 2006, 14). That is, interaction is a key prerequisite of influence. Assessments that are credible, salient, and generated through legitimate means are more likely to have influence than those that are not.

Although we cannot track IR scholars' participation across all of these assessments, there is evidence of their participation. For instance, a number of political scientists have served on the IPCC, including David Victor, Matthew Paterson, Marc Levy, Navroz Dubash, Thomas Brewer, and Axel Michaelowa.

In addition to scientific assessments, IR scholars also have been active participants in multilateral negotiations. Ted Parson participated in the ozone negotiations and wrote a prize-winning political science book on the topic (Parson 2003). Detlef Sprinz, a political scientist at the University of Potsdam, has served as chairman of the Scientific Committee of the European Environment Agency. Axel Michaelowa at the University of Zurich has held a number of climate-related policy positions, including on the IPCC and the Clean Development Mechanism (CDM) executive board.

Furthermore, work on delegation to nonstate actors indicates that states delegate to nonstate actors, including experts, to help implement multilateral environmental agreements (Green 2008, 2014). A study of delegation to nonstate actors in multilateral environmental agreements from 1902 to 2002 demonstrates that states most frequently delegate to private actors to help implement treaties, rather than tasking them with rule-making, adjudication, enforcement, or monitoring. Moreover, once treaties have entered into force, and states must get down to the intricacies of achieving goals outlined in the treaty, they are more likely to delegate to nonstate actors, especially in areas that involve species management (Green and Hale 2017).

## Personal Commitments to Environmental Practice

Are GEP scholars more driven by personal commitment to environmental protection than, say, trade scholars are to free trade? The TRIP faculty survey data offer some evidence that they are.

In table 4.2 we report scholars' self-identified motivations for undertaking research. As described previously, we use only the most recent year a scholar answered a question to avoid double counting individuals, while obtaining the largest possible sample. Because different questions are asked in

**TABLE 4.2.** GEP scholars vs. non-GEP scholars

| | GEP scholars | Non-GEP scholars | |
|---|---|---|---|
| **Research motivations** | | | |
| Appeal to popular audience | 2% | 3% | |
| Issue area | 45% | 39% | * |
| Methodology | 0% | 3% | *** |
| Other | 11% | 9% | |
| Paradigm | 3% | 5% | * |
| Policy relevance/current events | 36% | 33% | |
| Region | 3% | 7% | *** |
| Sample size | 207 | 2,710 | |
| **Ideal relationship between academic and policy communities** | | | |
| There should be a higher wall of separation between the two. | 7% | 11% | * |
| There should be a larger number of links between the two. | 93% | 89% | * |
| Sample size | 145 | 1,985 | |

*Note:* Wald tests were conducted to identify significant differences. *** $p < 0.01$; ** $p < 0.05$; * $p < 0.1$.

different years and different scholars respond in different years, sample sizes vary by question. We conducted a Wald test to see if the identified differences between GEP and non-GEP scholars are significant. This test was limited, however, due to the small numbers of GEP scholars in our analysis samples.[9]

Consistent with our expectation, GEP scholars on average showed more commitment to their issue area than non-GEP scholars, with 45 percent citing issue area as a motivation for research compared to 39 percent of non-GEP scholars. At the same time, GEP scholars were less likely to be driven by methodology or paradigm than non-GEP scholars. There was no statistically significant difference between GEP and non-GEP scholars, however, on the influence of policy relevance and current events on their research motivations.

GEP scholars were slightly more likely to favor increased links between academic work and the policy world (93 percent compared to 89 percent), but they did not differ significantly from other scholars as to the form those links should take.

## Permeability of Environmental Policymaking

International environmental politics are extraordinarily permeable. This quality allows interested academics to get involved with relatively few barriers to entry, facilitating engagement influence. Several features of the field create this accessibility.

First, since the 1972 Stockholm conference, much of global environmental policymaking has centered around multilateral institutions, especially the UN. Activist groups have successfully lobbied the UN for access to negotiations. In a multiyear study of fifty international organizations, Tallberg et al. (2013) finds that environmental institutions (along with human rights and development entities) are consistently more likely to involve transnational actors. Important climate change summits, for example, can attract tens of thousands of nonstate actors, including many academics. Approximately 150 universities are officially registered observers of the UN Framework Convention on Climate Change.[10]

The TRIP surveys add evidence for this claim. GEP scholars were not generally more or less likely to engage in paid consulting work in the policy world than their non-GEP colleagues. The one exception, however, is international organizations, where 15 percent of GEP scholars report that they had worked as paid consultants in the previous two years compared to 10 percent of non-GEP scholars. This difference is consistent with our argument that global environmental policymaking is relatively permeable to academics.

Second, as noted previously, environmental politics is increasingly characterized by complexity, with many different institutional layers—intergovernmental, domestic, transnational, and so forth—playing a role in dense regime complexes. This proliferation of institutions and policy processes creates many potential access points for academics. A scholar interested in engaging in policy work on marine species protection, for example, may approach a number of relevant intergovernmental organizations (such as the UN Food and Agriculture Organization or the various regional fisheries bodies), several large and many small NGOs that work on the issue, businesses involved in private regulatory schemes like the Marine Stewardship Council, multistakeholder alliances like the International Coral Reef Initiative (which combines governments, NGOs, and businesses), or any number of national regulatory authorities.

## CONCLUSION

Two key findings emerge from this chapter. First, we have argued that scholars of global environmental politics have had a meaningful influence on the policy realm. Most of this influence can be categorized as "engagement influence": GEP scholars are actively involved in specific policymaking processes alongside government officials, NGOs, natural scientists, business groups, intergovernmental organizations, and other actors who shape environmental policy. We do not identify many instances of what we have termed causal influence, in which specific IR scholars or ideas have directly altered policy outcomes, and we suggest there are systematic reasons to expect this form of influence to be rare. Finally, we have found growing resonance between GEP scholarship and international environmental policymaking over time, which we term diffuse influence.

Much of the influence we observe in the GEP arena supports this book's overall argument that the nature or structure of the issue area strongly influences the extent of scholarly engagement, relevance, and influence. The emerging and scientific nature of global environmental issues produced opportunities for IR scholars to engage and influence policy and practitioners. Moreover, the porous nature of the global environmental arena created numerous opportunities for IR scholars to exercise engagement influence. The strong tradition of civil society involvement in the issue area, compared to the other issue areas examined in this volume, coupled with high levels of personal commitment to environmental protection, means that GEP scholars are more likely than IR scholars in many other subfields to produce relevant scholarship and to seek to engage and influence international and national practitioners.

Our second key finding echoes that of other scholars (Javeline 2014; Keohane 2014; Green and Hale 2017); the study of environmental politics has been undervalued in the discipline. As environmental policymaking becomes increasingly important to world politics, IR scholars, journals, and departments will need to increase their focus on environmental issues to remain relevant. At the same time, scholars studying primarily environmental issues could do more to frame their work for a broader IR audience.

Avey and Desch's analysis in chapter 16 suggests that efforts to engage the broader IR discipline could come at the expense of future policy engagement. As scholarship becomes less easily consumable (argument 3a) and as a subfield matures, producing increasingly specialized research for a disciplinary audience (argument 3b), its influence will likely wane. It is far from clear, however, that all issue areas evolve along a similar trajectory. Given the growing recognition of GEP's importance in the real world of international relations, this subfield is unlikely to follow the life cycle of the nuclear strategy subfield by becoming less policy relevant over time.

## ENDNOTES

We thank Peter Dauvergne, Kai Lee, Ron Mitchell, Marc Levy, and Stacy VanDeveer for comments on an earlier draft. We are grateful to Quentin Karpilow for his excellent research assistance.

1. Note that "the environment" was not listed as a secondary research area.
2. Even among accounts within IR, the contours of the discipline have been drawn differently. See, e.g., Zürn 1998; Mitchell 2002–16; Dauvergne 2005; Busby 2010; Paterson 2014; Stevis 2014.
3. Although some of the contributors had distinguished academic careers, none were part of mainstream IR discussions.
4. GEP scholars have created numerous typologies for characterizing environmental problems. See, e.g., O'Neill 2009; Mitchell 2010.
5. Mitchell's work has provided the empirical basis for work by a number of other scholars. See, e.g., Green 2014; Kim 2013.
6. Anticorruption was added later.

7. In the human rights realm, Ruggie also has developed a second policy effort, a set of Principles on Business and Human Rights, which were adopted by the member states of the UN Human Rights Council in 2011.
8. Haas (1989) is the seminal work on this topic, cited in our informal poll of leading scholars in the field as one of few works that has had extensive influence in IR beyond GEP.
9. Numbers of GEP scholars vary from 116 to 250 observations.
10. Authors' count of organizations listed on http://maindb.unfccc.int/public/ngo .pl?sort=const.og_name.

# 5

# THE LIMITS OF SCHOLARLY INFLUENCE ON GLOBAL ENVIRONMENTAL POLICY

Marc A. Levy

Jessica F. Green and Thomas Hale's provocative and interesting chapter, "The Study and Practice of Global Environmental Politics: Policy Influence through Participation," explores the role of IR scholars in the field of global environmental politics (GEP). The authors argue that IR scholars have had a more substantial role than a cursory examination would lead one to believe. They lay out three mechanisms of influence and assess the evidence for scholars' impact. They make good use of the Teaching, Research, and International Policy (TRIP) datasets to test their ideas. I agree with the core points in the chapter, but the question deserves a tougher take. In some ways Green and Hale's chapter reads a bit as an apologia for IR: we aren't really that irrelevant, give us a break. Like any good work, this chapter provides a useful service in raising new questions that ought to get more attention.

Green and Hale's argument relies heavily on the spectrum of influence model that varies across two factors, whether scholars intend to seek policy change and how decisive scholarly action is for a given policy outcome. This produces three types of influence (and one null set): causal influence, engagement, and diffuse influence. Green and Hale argue that the most common form of influence for GEP scholars is diffuse influence: scholarship influences policy, although the scholars who produced that work may not have intended to influence policy. That is a bit unsatisfying, however, because that mode of influence is difficult to measure directly. It just requires that IR scholars publish their ideas, which then "leak into policy discussions and, ultimately, policy" (Green and Hale, this volume, p58). What Green and Hale call "influence" could be called "noise" or even "policy tourism." Or it could simply be called "scholarship."

Green and Hale grant the IR community far too much leniency when they fail to call it to account for not doing more direct engagement. Lawyers do it all the time. Perhaps you could say that lawyers have an insider's advantage because they are trained in manipulating legalistic processes of the sort that characterizes most policy. But then how to excuse the comparison with economists, physicists, and biologists? Collectively, lawyers, economists, physicists, and biologists account for almost all of the academic engagement with GEP. It is not obvious why this should be so. And one could make a good case that their engagement is counterproductive. The Kyoto Protocol, for example, was conceived by lawyers, economists, and physicists for the most part. Political scientists were almost completely united in thinking that it was very poorly designed, and they turned out to be right, but they were not in the fray where they could have made a difference.

Green and Hale's historical discussion is interesting, as much for new questions it raises as for insights it provides. The discussion of the 1970s could have gone deeper. If you look back from the vantage point of the present to the early 1970s, then the questions posed by the Sprouts (1971) and the frameworks they elaborated to answer them have an enduring resonance. They were asking how territoriality interacted with modernization to alter political dynamics. They constitute a rare bridge between the timeless geopolitics that goes back to Thucydides and the new politics around globalization and environment. Yet they occupied this space almost entirely on their own; they had few disciples. Choucri and North (1975) highlight another road not taken: their lateral pressure theory was an attempt to modernize ideas about resource constraints as drivers of geopolitics, yet it remained marginal to the evolution of IR in the coming decades. What the practitioners of international politics increasingly focus on are precisely the things the Sprouts (1971) and Choucri and North (1975) were trying to get scholars to pay attention to: the scramble for control of Arctic resources, offshore minerals in the South China Sea, even the struggle to control how much carbon dioxide is in the atmosphere are all examples of their enduring relevance.

I agree with Green and Hale's conclusion that regime theory was largely a sedative in this context. The overwhelming focus on the question, "Do regimes matter?" killed many opportunities for meaningful engagement with practitioners. Can you imagine Clausewitz asking, "Do armies matter?" or Hirschman asking, "Does economics matter?"

The finding that, according to the TRIP data, GEP scholars are more committed to their cause than other scholars is weird. I believe the data; the observation fits my intuitive sense of the field. If I had to point to the single most important reason that IR scholars, especially political scientists, have had such limited impact on GEP, however, it is that we have largely stripped away all vestiges of the normative foundations that originally motivated the discipline.

We have evolved a form of scholarship in which we reproduce an inverse relationship between the scope and ambition of the questions we ask. We tolerate transformative scholarship only for narrow questions. If you want to do research on a coastal fishery in a single village, you may be as ambitious as you want with respect to transformative scholarship. But if you are asking how humans can avoid planetary catastrophe, you must scale back your ambition. We have legions of IR scholars playing small ball while the other disciplines are killing us with the big game. This point is relevant to a somewhat odd omission in the Green and Hale chapter, the work of Elinor Ostrom. Unlike the Sprouts (1971), Ostrom (1990) has legions of disciples.

The reasons for that difference are not hard to grasp, but the implications include one unfortunate unintended consequence. The style of scholarship that Ostrom and her followers embraced is one that does not lend itself to engaging the high-profile environmental challenges of the day. Ostrom tried to translate the implications of her work for policy issues, but these efforts did not have much of an effect as far as I know; she remained strongest when looking at small-scale matters.

As a result, we have no one occupying the space that someone like Thomas Schelling (1966) occupied regarding nuclear strategy. Schelling was deeply engaged in bringing about fundamental transformations in security policy. He made no effort to disguise his normative agenda; he wanted to avoid the destabilizing use of nuclear weapons. He aimed at high-level political processes.

The Global Compact is a clear and important exception, and I wish Green and Hale had spent more time with it. They do not do much with this example except to say Ruggie was at the right stage in his career to put time into it. However, that applies to almost all IR scholars at some point or another, so it does not adequately explain Ruggie's success.

In the end, when they conclude that IR scholars have had meaningful influence on global environmental politics, Green and Hale are not specific about what this influence was or what consequences have followed from it. The claim amounts to saying that IR scholars are doing things, but that is not quite the same as saying they are making a difference or that they are making a positive difference.

When I ask about political science and global environmental politics, I try to start from first principles rather than looking at what specific scholars are doing. Given the state of the global environmental agenda, what are the big-picture questions that our discipline should be able to address?

First among these are the politics of restraint. I mean restraint not just at the margin but larger scale. The decisions to relinquish authority over legitimate use of violence to the state, abandon slavery, and drastically reduce the use of international war are all relevant examples. If achieving progress in GEP requires a similarly ambitious form of restraint, perhaps in the form of abandoning a method of social organization that requires constant economic growth, then we should have a lot to say about how such dynamics play out. Yet we are barely even talking about it.

Equally important is the politics of creating shared visions of the future. The proposition that we have to make specific choices about what kind of future we want—otherwise we will end up with a future that is extremely unpleasant—is becoming more compelling. Sustainability scientists essentially argue that the global predicament is analogous to the situation faced by the American colonists who decided to break with England in 1776 and needed to design a new form of government: how they chose would determine their fate profoundly. Yet one looks in vain for the equivalent of the *Federalist Papers* seeking to guide us in this quest.

In this light, Arrow's theorem looms large. One formulation of the theorem is that all collective choice is inherently unstable; all winning coalitions can be defeated. Against the backdrop of growing complexity, globalization, and issue linkage, then, the difficulty in making collective choices about our future is clear. Among the most critical challenges facing the quest for sustainable development are broadening our repertoire of tools for coping with the practical problems of Arrow's theorem and acquiring an ability to apply such a repertoire to ever more difficult challenges.

I believe that Ruggie is instructive because I see what he did as facing these two fundamentals head-on. He chose to address directly the issue of how to restrain the actions of multinational corporations in order to make it the central question. Few political scientists were doing that. And he did so in a manner that took into account the problem of Arrow's theorem. He chose to make the specific solutions normative in character, slower perhaps to take root but more resilient down the line.

Finally, another fundamental issue that deserves more engagement from our discipline is the relationship between science and policy. If it is true that the modern world is becoming increasingly complex, and that because we are stressing environmental systems to unprecedented degrees with greater regularity, then it follows that we are increasingly dependent on constructing effective links between science and politics. In the United States we have relied largely on a cartoon model that says maintaining strict separation between science and politics is best. The organization of the National Academy of Sciences and the Intergovernmental Panel on Climate Change reflects this model. Europeans are more comfortable with other models in which science and politics are more intertwined. As time goes on, the US model looks less and less effective. The country that has taken the greatest pains to separate science from politics is the country where science is most politicized, and this is not a coincidence. But the question is not well understood, few people are working on it, and there is little active work on understanding what models would be fit for the purpose given the challenges we face.

So, I have a somewhat more pessimistic conclusion than Green and Hale. I believe that IR scholars are shying away from the most important questions and that this limits our relevance to the most important questions on the global environmental agenda. We appear not to have the courage of our convictions and are overly reticent when it comes to relating the full depth of our discipline's canon of knowledge to the most pressing problems of the day. The contrast to economics and physics is striking.

# 6

# MIND THE GAP?

*Links between Policy and*
*Academic Research of Foreign Aid*

Christina J. Schneider

espite the increasingly prominent position of foreign aid research in international relations (IR) and international political economy (IPE), few attempts have been made to assess opportunities for bridging the scholar-practitioner gap or describing existing patterns of collaboration between the practitioner and scholarly communities in the subfield of foreign aid.[1] To shed light on this question, I analyze the linkages between these communities on several dimensions. My analysis is based on the premise, supported by data from the 2011 and 2014 Teaching, Research, and International Policy (TRIP) surveys of IR scholars in the United States and nineteen other countries, that some demand for closer linkages exists, at least among academic researchers. As table 6.1 shows, across IR subfields almost 23 percent of scholars favor tighter links with the policy community, and only 1 percent of IR scholars prefer no involvement with the policy-making process.[2] Within the foreign aid subfield (respondents who identified development as their primary or secondary field of interest), 37 percent of scholars favor more links. The demand for linkages is greater in development than in the two major subfields, IPE (24.8 percent) and international security (31.7 percent). Almost 30 percent of foreign aid scholars believe that policy relevance and current events should primarily motivate research in the discipline, and more than 50 percent of respondents have changed their research topics in response to major events in world affairs in an effort to make their research more relevant to policymakers.[3]

Given scholars' desire for greater linkages between the policy and academic communities in the foreign aid subfield, one might expect the gap between scholars and practitioners to be relatively small. I analyze the extent of this gap from a historical perspective. Like other chapters in this volume that address areas of IPE research (e.g., Mansfield and Pevehouse; Pepinsky and Steinberg), I find that primarily economists occupy the nexus between scholars and policymakers in the foreign aid subfield. This dominance persists despite the fact that practitioners' changing interests have provided ample opportunities for political scientists to contribute to foreign aid policies and practices. I also find that political scientists have influenced development policies at least recently, especially relative to their colleagues in international trade and finance.

**TABLE 6.1.** Demand for links between policymakers and academia

|  | Overall (%) | Development (%) | Other IPE (%) | Security (%) |
|---|---|---|---|---|
| More links | 22.6 | 37.0 | 24.8 | 26.4 |
| No involvement | 1.1 | 0.8 | 1.6 | 0.7 |
| Policy relevance | 28.7 | 28.7 | 27.0 | 28.0 |
| Major world events | 54.0 | 58.0 | 51.0 | 61.0 |

*Source:* TRIP Faculty Surveys, 2011 and 2014

I discuss why this gap exists and may have narrowed in recent years. I make extensive use of the TRIP journal article database and the TRIP faculty surveys of 2011 and 2014 (Maliniak et al. 2012, 2014; TRIP 2017; Maliniak et al. 2018). I also analyze formal and informal networks and interactions between the policy and academic worlds in the foreign aid subfield and find that IR scholars have significant influence on development policies through these alternative channels. Finally, I trace the history of AidData—a research consortium that has provided new data on development finance and consciously attempted to increase the linkages between scholars and practitioners—as an illustration of some of the opportunities and challenges for scholars in development finance.

My findings are mixed. Whereas IR scholars increasingly use methods that are relevant for practitioners in foreign aid agencies—that is, opportunities for greater linkages abound—historically, economic research tends to inform broad policy choices. There are two explanations. First, political scientists nowadays use sophisticated methods in their foreign aid research, but they tend to be regarded as "economists light." Second, practitioners care little about the areas in which political scientists have a comparative advantage (i.e., the politics of foreign aid allocation, power relationships, and democratic governance). The closest links between IR scholars and the policy community occur when practitioners are interested in broad strategic questions—that is, why, how, and where aid should be provided and when foreign aid is effective—but less so when it comes to the basic operational questions. Finally, much of the existing gap can be explained by conflicting incentive structures and time constraints.

At the same time, I detect a recent trend toward increased involvement by IR scholars in development policy and practice. Most of these interactions originate from the increasing interest among practitioners in questions that concern the political dimension of development finance. This renewed interest in governance and the politics of development may have opened a niche for political scientists. I show that the utilization of similar datasets, as well as expanding formal and informal networks, have led to increasing interactions among practitioners and scientists. In practice, political scientists seem most relevant when they are part of an interdisciplinary epistemic community. AidData (and other federally funded labs) have played an important role in brokering these interactions. AidData's experience supports my findings: (a) consistent with argument 1b outlined in the introduction to this volume, where novel and highly technical methods are required to answer practical questions, linkages will increase because the policymakers and scholars' interests converge, both in terms of methods and research questions; (b) consistent with argument 2b, because development practitioners' traditional disciplinary partners have been economists, political scientists' influence is limited and often will be based on their potential methodological contributions (they sell themselves as quasi-economists); (c) the main obstacles to collaboration persist because academic incentives for career advancement differ from those in the policy world, as suggested by argument 3b about the effects of professionalization within a discipline; and (d) the AidData study provides support for a theme introduced by Zoellick (this volume), but not fully addressed in the introductory chapter, that interdisciplinary research teams are in greater demand among policymakers, and they are likely to have more influence than research groups composed solely of political scientists (see also Murdie and Green and Hale, this volume). Perhaps this should not be surprising. Real-world problems do not respect disciplinary boundaries, so why should their solutions?

## A BRIEF HISTORY OF FOREIGN AID IN THEORY AND PRACTICE

One of the most salient and controversial questions in development policy is whether and what type of foreign aid is effective in generating positive development outcomes in recipient countries. This question has received major attention in scholarly work and speaks to a central concern of those who make and implement foreign aid policy. The history of foreign aid is characterized by the adoption of various competing policy paradigms for promoting effective economic and social development. The absence of any clear scholarly consensus has helped to sustain academic interest for decades. Economists, who analyze the effect of foreign aid on economic growth, largely dominated this debate from the 1960s through the mid-2000s. The findings in this literature have been mixed, with some scholars seeing a positive relationship between foreign aid and economic growth, some finding no relationship, and some finding a negative relationship.[4] One of the implications of these findings is that foreign aid can be effective but that certain conditions limit that effectiveness. This realization, in turn, piqued policymakers' interest in the conditions under which foreign aid is effective.

Much of the early debate on this question focused on economic and political conditions in recipient countries.[5] The World Bank induced a paradigmatic shift in foreign aid policies and research with its 1998 report based on a study by Dollar and Pritchett (1998). The Bank report led to a seminal article by Burnside and Dollar (2000), which found that foreign aid could foster economic growth under the condition that recipient countries pursued "good" economic policies. As a consequence, an increasing number of donors announced they would make good governance a central consideration in their foreign aid policies. This meant allocating aid to those countries with sound institutions and policies in some cases (Hook 2008) and providing aid to help developing countries improve the quality of their governance in other cases (Kaufmann et al. 2009). Yet, despite practitioners' increasing efforts to focus foreign aid allocation on countries with good governance in hopes of fostering economic development, academic research has not unequivocally established that foreign aid is more effective in well-governed countries (e.g., Easterly et al. 2004).

The 2000s witnessed increasing calls to move development finance toward a partnership between donors and recipients. In the World Bank, the shift was evident with the 2005 Paris Declaration on Aid Effectiveness, in which the World Bank indicated the importance of a give-and-take approach to development. One of the strategies to implement this new approach emphasizes community-driven development (CDD). CDD is based on the notion that politicians sometimes exploit foreign aid to maximize their survival (e.g., Bueno de Mesquita and Smith 2007). They either capture foreign aid resources to conduct patronage spending (e.g., Golden 2003; Jablonski 2014; Dreher et al. 2019) or, if that is not possible, replace their local budget resources with foreign aid and use the local budget to spend for electoral purposes. The fungibility of foreign aid is particularly problematic because recipient governments tend to spend these resources for electoral purposes or shift them to other sectors that may inhibit economic growth (Collier and Hoeffler 2007). Cruz and Schneider (2017) note another troubling relationship: incumbents whose municipalities receive foreign aid projects are more likely to get reelected even if they had no influence over how the foreign aid or the local budget was allocated.

The political capture of foreign aid resources has become an important topic in discussions among practitioners. For example, World Bank research and policy focuses increasingly on the political capture of World Bank loans and grants (e.g., Platteau and Gaspart 2003; Hasnain and Matsuda 2011). CDD projects aim to establish ownership in order to overcome elite capture. CDD implies that foreign aid is given directly to communities in recipient countries. The communities participate in the development and management of the project to ensure that (a) the project is most appropriate for the actual development needs of the community and fits with local conditions, (b) local individuals monitor individual behavior and enforce the project rules, and (c) individual recipients take ownership of the projects, thereby making them self-sustainable in the long term (Platteau and Gaspart 2005). The World Bank has been at the forefront of the movement toward CDDs. It made CDDs an integral part of its comprehensive development framework (World Bank 2001), which led to an increase in CDD funding from about $325 million in 1996 to about $2 billion in 2003. This shift in strategy did not come without problems. CDD projects are more vulnerable to elite capture because local elites find it easier to collude and evade the control of national and international institutions. Local politicians are also more likely to use the poor-quality information environment to exploit the projects to ensure their political survival (Bardhan 2002). Platteau and Gaspart (2005) argue that CDD can only be effective in reaching its goals if local beneficiaries are empowered to prevent elite capture. This view is represented in many discussions of World Bank operational staff when deciding how to implement particular CDD projects on the local level.

In sum, looking at the broad strategic questions underlying foreign aid policies, practitioners and scholars' interests have correlated over time. In some cases, policy developments spurred research interest in certain topics. In other cases, new research findings changed the broad strategies that practitioners pursued. Arguably, the greatest impact that academic research has had on practitioners (including research conducted by academics in the policy world) has been the work on good governance and more generally the conditions under which foreign aid is effective. Scholars also started analyzing the micro-level aspects in addition to the macro-relationships of foreign aid, thereby renewing interest in questions of design, management, and effectiveness at the project level. Research in this area remains sparse, however, despite its importance to policymakers.

What about the impact that IR scholars have had on development policy and practice? At least over the last couple of decades, economists and political scientists have largely worked in concert in the field of development finance. In fact, much of the work builds on efforts in other disciplines; there are many interdisciplinary collaborations. The history of the foreign aid field builds on both disciplines, and relatively optimistic conclusions about the linkages between academia and the policy world result from these interrelationships. My conclusion about the existing linkages between academia and the policy world in IR is much less positive. Many of the linkages described previously have been between economists and practitioners. This is not surprising because foreign aid policy used to be an economic policy and practitioners rarely considered political factors. As I show in the following sections, many practitioners and academic consultants have academic degrees in economics or public policy. In addition, policymakers have been more interested in the questions that economists tend to address—for example, does aid lead to economic growth—than in the questions that political scientists tend to address—such as how is foreign aid allocated.[6] Nevertheless, my review suggests that political science has become more relevant over the last two decades. As the World Bank and other development institutions have become more concerned with the politics of development, opportunities for IR scholars have abounded. Political scientists have contributed a large number of well-known studies about the domestic politics of donor countries and foreign aid allocation, as well as the politics of international development institutions. Some of these have had direct implications for policymakers and practitioners charged with implementing aid policy.

# HAS IR RESEARCH BECOME MORE ATTRACTIVE TO PRACTITIONERS?

The historical trends suggest that economists traditionally have dominated policymaking (and they still do), but the increasing interest in questions of recipient governance and politics may have opened a niche for political scientists to contribute to the policy and practice of development. According to the results of the TRIP faculty survey, development research is on par with other IPE research in terms of its impact on foreign policy.[7] One important question is whether IR scholars use methodological approaches that make their work accessible to practitioners.

There is not much information about the methods that practitioners in development finance find most compelling, but most practitioners have an academic background in economics or public policy, so one assumes that they value positivist work. There is a large body of important qualitative work, but recently we have witnessed a move toward large-scale quantitative analyses and field experiments. The TRIP faculty survey finds that development scholars are more likely to believe that quantitative and qualitative research are useful to policy practitioners than are scholars in other fields, notably IPE, more generally, or international security scholars (see table 6.2).[8] In my interviews with AidData and USAID staff, I found that the greatest demand is for consultants to conduct quantitative and qualitative work. Interestingly, most controversies arise over the question of whether randomized controlled trials (RCTs) are valuable.

Table 6.2 further demonstrates that IR scholars still overwhelmingly use qualitative analysis in their research (60 percent).[9] Only 14 percent of foreign aid scholars use quantitative analyses, and only 0.6 percent conduct experiments.[10] Although I cannot compare whether the methodologies used by IR scholars coincide with practitioners' preferences, almost 80 percent of IR scholars apply methodological approaches that are frequently used by practitioners in foreign aid agencies.

**TABLE 6.2.** Methodological approaches in theory and practice

|  | Overall | Development | Other IPE | Security |
|---|---|---|---|---|
|  | Usefulness of IR research to policy practitioners (%) | | | |
| Quantitative | 70 | 83 | 76 | 71 |
| Qualitative | 91 | 94 | 89 | 92 |
|  | Research IR scholars primarily employ (%) | | | |
| Quantitative | 14 | 14 | 29 | 18 |
| Qualitative | 60 | 63 | 56 | 61 |
| Experiments | 0.6 | 0.6 | 0.2 | 0.4 |

*Source:* TRIP Faculty Survey 2014

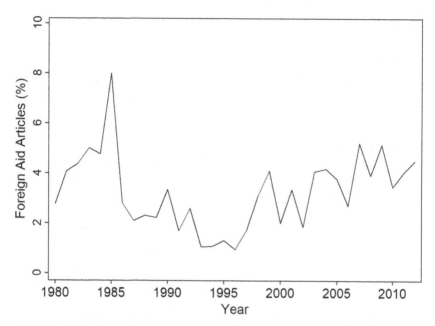

**FIGURE 6.1.** Foreign aid articles in international relations, 1980–2012

In addition to the data provided by the TRIP faculty survey, the TRIP journal database provides information on foreign aid research. Figure 6.1 is a graph of the share of aid articles published annually between 1980 and 2012. Whereas the raw data depict some trends (such as the increase in the relative number of foreign aid articles published in the early 1980s and the stark drop in 1986), with the exception of an increase in consistency with which foreign aid articles have been published in the last five years of the time series, these trends do not represent significant shifts in research on foreign aid.

Table 6.3 provides a closer look at the share of articles in important IR subfields (and IR in general) that use positivist epistemology, quantitative

**TABLE 6.3.** Methods in IR research

|  | All IR (%) | Foreign aid (%) | Other IPE (%) | Security (%) |
|---|---|---|---|---|
| Positive epistemology | 82 | 94 | 91 | 86 |
| Recent time frame | 62 | 88 | 75 | 58 |
| Qualitative | 34 | 36 | 42 | 34 |
| Quantitative | 37 | 60 | 46 | 37 |
| Experimental | 3 | 0.4 | 0.8 | 2 |
| Policy prescription | 9 | 9 | 3 | 1 |
| Policy analysis | 4 | 5 | 1 | 6 |

*Source:* TRIP Journal Article Database, Version 2.0

analyses, a contemporary time frame, qualitative analyses, experiments, policy prescriptions, and policy analyses.[11] With the exception of qualitative analyses, research on foreign aid differs from other IR research across all these variables. First, whereas a large percentage (82 percent) of IR research uses a positivist epistemology, articles that address questions of foreign aid are significantly more likely to employ a positivist epistemology (94 percent). This trumps other IR research. Foreign aid research is also more likely to employ a contemporary timeframe, qualitative and quantitative analyses, and policy analyses than other IR research. The largest difference between the foreign aid subfield and other IR subfields is the extent to which quantitative analyses are utilized. Whereas about 37 percent of non–foreign aid research uses quantitative analyses, in foreign aid research the percentage is about 60. This is particularly interesting given the significantly lower numbers in the TRIP faculty survey (only 14 percent of foreign aid scholars claim to use quantitative methods, but these may be the ones who get published in the top IR journals).

The research methods employed by foreign aid scholars is conducive to policy applications and in line with research conducted by practitioners, but much depends on the particular content of scholarly contributions. Whereas much of the political science and economics literatures (at least until recently) have focused on large-scale quantitative analyses at the national or international level, practitioners (especially those charged with implementing aid programs) are interested in the operational and technical aspects of development aid. Policy-based research focuses on particular countries, sectors, time periods, or even projects to analyze what has happened and what can be learned from particular interventions. Practitioners are particularly interested, too, in policy evaluation and prescription, and these are the fields where foreign aid research by IR scholars does not distinguish itself from other research. Only about 3 percent of articles in the top IR journals (0.4 percent in foreign aid articles) use experiments, only about 4 percent of articles analyze policies (5 percent in foreign aid research), and only about 9 percent of articles make policy prescriptions that follow from the article's analysis. Security research is much closer to what policymakers are interested in.[12]

## FORMAL AND INFORMAL INTERACTIONS

Next, I analyze the formal and informal interactions between academia and policy communities. First, many bilateral, regional, and multilateral donors have made their data accessible to researchers, thereby increasing both the likelihood that academics use data that are relevant to policymakers and the opportunities for linkages. One notable example is the Creditor Reporting System (CRS). To better monitor each donor's foreign aid allocations and progress toward the common aid goals, the Organization for Economic

Cooperation and Development (OECD) established a system to collect statistical data on aid spending. CRS provides a centralized database for foreign aid flows from its twenty-two member states, as well as a number of multilateral aid agencies, and it has provided data for many academic and policy studies on foreign aid.

Another important example is the World Bank's Open Data Initiative. Then World Bank President Robert Zoellick launched the initiative in 2010 to provide public access to seven thousand datasets that were previously unavailable or available only to governments and individual researchers (Strom 2011). The World Bank has moved toward greater transparency since the 2005 Paris Declaration on Aid Effectiveness. With the Open Data Initiative, the organization shifted from a "positive list" of limited materials available to a "negative list," in which all materials not on the list would be available to the public (Weaver and Peratsakis 2014). This policy shift was a radical step away from the Bank's reputation as a secretive, nontransparent organization. The Open Data Initiative includes the publication of data collected by the International Evaluation Group (IEG), which evaluates the activities of the institutions of the World Bank Group. The IEG has built a dataset that includes project-level performance evaluations across the history of the World Bank. Many academic researchers believe it will enable a substantially better understanding of foreign aid effectiveness. By 2012 the World Bank's documents and reports database was visited more than 4.5 million times and had more than 795,000 downloads (Weaver and Peratsakis 2014).

Second, there are increasing linkages between researchers in policy institutions, such as the World Bank or USAID, and researchers at academic institutions. A number of policy-based researchers have published in IR journals, and coauthorships between policy-based researchers and academic researchers are common. Researchers from both communities participate in common workshops and conferences, such as the Political Economy of International Organizations (PEIO) workshop. European and American economists and political scientists organize the PEIO workshop as an interdisciplinary event. I analyzed the PEIO programs going back to 2008 and found that the two-day workshop included at least three scholars from the policy community in each year (2014 is the exception, where only one World Bank researcher participated). In some years, the number of policy-based participants was as high as ten.[13]

Third, although the career switch from academia to policy, and vice versa, is not seamless, there are examples of such careers. An increasing number of academic researchers also seek and receive short-term consulting jobs at foreign aid institutions like USAID, the UK's Department for International Development, or the World Bank. Most consultancy jobs are still filled with economists (David Collier and Steven Radelet are two examples), but there is a trend toward hiring political scientists when political issues are concerned. James Robinson, a professor of government at Harvard University, has repeatedly consulted for the World Bank about the political economy of development. Nicholas Sambanis, a professor at Yale University, was previously hired as a consultant at the World Bank. Michael Doyle, well known for his work on the liberal democratic peace and professor of political science at Columbia University, was the chair of the United Nations (UN) Democracy Fund and a member of the External Research Advisory Committee of the UN High Commissioner for Refugees (UNHCR) and the Advisory Committee of the Lessons-Learned Unit of the Department of Peacekeeping Operations at the UN. Pippa Norris, lecturer in comparative politics at the Harvard Kennedy School, served as the director of Democratic Governance at the UN Development Programme (UNDP) and as a consultant to the UN, Organization for Security and Co-operation in Europe (OSCE), International Institute for Democracy and Electoral Assistance (IDEA), UN Educational, Scientific and Cultural Organization (UNESCO), the Council of Europe, National Endowment for Democracy (NED), and UNDP. Other prominent political scientists who have worked for the World Bank and other international organizations include Miles Kahler, Beth Simmons, Joseph Grieco, Ngaire Woods, and David Leblang.

It is difficult to get a complete list of such moonlighters and in-and-outers (see Parks and Stern 2013). According to the TRIP faculty survey, about 17 percent of IR scholars (23 percent of development scholars) have engaged in paid consultation with government agencies. The percentages are higher for unpaid consultation: 30.4 percent and 34.5 percent, respectively.

Donor agencies are becoming increasingly aware of the potential contribution of political scientists for development finance, at least when it comes to issues of democratic governance (see also my discussion of AidData in the next section). The Center for Democracy, Human Rights and Governance—which is a subdivision of the Bureau for Democracy, Human Rights, and Conflict at USAID—has an explicit mandate to increase the number of political scientists advising USAID. The Center focuses on independent and rigorous impact evaluations of USAID projects, using RCTs. The RCTs that are currently in the field for the Center involve a number of political scientists. In addition, the Bureau has given more resources for academic projects in political science.

The Center's mission seems promising, but the interest in hiring IR scholars at USAID is mainly limited to this Center. From my interviews with USAID staff, it appears that economists still dominate policy consultancy at the agency. The Bureau of Democracy, Human Rights and Conflict is small compared to other bureaus, such as the Bureau of Agriculture and Food or the Bureau of Education. In 2012 the Bureau for Democracy, Human Rights and Conflict had 502 staff, compared to 2,083 staff at the Bureau of Africa. The Center's budget is declining, due to the decreasing overall budget for USAID. The bureaus that operate within the President's Initiative program have a relatively steady budget, but the Center, which is not part of the initiative and therefore relies on discretionary funding, is more prone to budget fluctuation.

In sum, the formal and informal interactions between IR scholars and the policy community largely support my previous results. Opportunities for linkages exist, and IR scholars are likely to engage with the policy community as long as they study questions that practitioners find relevant to their foreign aid policies. These opportunities are still rare, however, because (a) policymakers have not embraced the importance of power relationships as well as domestic and international politics of foreign aid, and (b) IR scholars have not embraced the policy world's demand for particular research topics (and if they do, they fail to market them effectively). I will discuss some of the potential reasons for these differences in the following section, but first I want to elaborate on one other dimension on which the policy world has increased its linkages with IR scholars, arguably very successfully.

## THE AIDDATA INITIATIVE

The increasing trend toward analyzing particular aspects of foreign aid and the shortcomings in the existing system of recording and providing data on aid allocations have led a team of researchers at William & Mary to collect increasingly granular, data on development finance. I provide a detailed account of the AidData initiative to analyze how it has led to a shift in the way practitioners and IR scholars interact. The project's initial goal was to collect fine-grained data on the project level, increase the availability of data, and provide information on the functional sectors of the projects. Since then, however, AidData has expanded to include a large range of other data collection efforts that have increased links with the policy community. By now, many of AidData's projects are cofunded by development finance institutions, such as the World Bank, the Asian Development Bank, Germany's GiZ, and USAID, as well as by recipient governments in developing governments.[14]

The CRS database provides the foreign aid subfield a potential advantage over other subfields in terms of the gaps between the policy world and academia. Both sides have the opportunity to study similar questions with the same publicly available data, although the database is limited in many aspects. The sectoral-level data in the CRS database are incomplete, and the categorization into functional sectors is sometimes ambiguous and problematic for the research questions that academic researchers address. In addition, the CRS reports that foreign aid flows from traditional bilateral donors as well as a few regional and multilateral aid agencies. Overall, it reports a development finance value of $2.6 billion. AidData augments the CRS data by adding non-OECD donor states (e.g., China, Saudi Arabia, or Kuwait) and institutions. It further organizes the data on the project level, which allows a clear assignment of sector and activity codes. AidData expanded the OECD sector codes to 717 AidData purpose and activity codes.

The first release of the AidData database in 2008 (version 1.92) reported an overall value of development finance of $4.3 billion (like the CRS database, in constant 2000 US dollars); that is almost twice the amount reported by CRS (Tierney et al. 2011). With these data, AidData not only enhanced researchers and practitioners' knowledge about many specific aspects of development finance (the *who*, *what*, *when*, and *where* questions); it also provided new insights into questions that are at the heart of development (the *why* and *how* questions). The data are ever-expanding, with new projects and donors entering the database on an annual basis. Recent data collection and provision efforts include the geocoding of project-level data, as well as the collection of project-level data that allows researchers and practitioners to study the long-term impact of development efforts. Most of the recent data collection efforts aim to provide improved information to both practitioners and academic researchers who evaluate and test theories relevant to many development questions. With the inclusion of the new donors, for example, AidData allows both the academic and policy worlds to analyze the behavior of emerging new donors such as China or India (e.g., Dreher and Fuchs 2011; Strange et al. 2017). In addition, the collection of data on institutional development at the project level will provide policymakers the ability to study their projects' long-term impacts, a question that has not been studied in depth before.

Already, it is possible to see the fruits of this massive effort. An increasing number of researchers use the common datasets, making comparisons and applications across analyses easier. AidData encourages researchers to post their results in various formats such as policy briefs, articles and books, and research and working papers. There is no way to assess whether these publications influence foreign aid policies, but they reflect the marketing strategies that practitioners in the development field told me would be most effective (Knack et al. 2011; Easterly and Williamson 2011). Argument 3a in chapter 1 of this volume summarizes the assertion that research products need to be shorter, contain less jargon, and summarize their main findings so that the knowledge can be more easily consumed by busy practitioners who may not have advanced degrees in the social sciences.

The data collection project that has influenced linkages between academia and practitioners most significantly may be AidData's geocoding project. AidData provides geospatial data to enable the development community to target, coordinate, and evaluate aid more effectively. AidData works with USAID and other international development agencies and governments and encourages scholars "to conduct cutting-edge research on development issues that will support evidence-based policy and program decisions by practitioners."[15] Since launching this project in 2010, AidData has grown to more than forty full-time staff members who are active around the world in governments, think tanks, civil society organizations, and universities. In 2010 AidData started a partnership with the World Bank to geocode all project activities on a local level in an effort to improve targeting, coordination, and evaluation. Recipient governments quickly became interested in georeferencing foreign aid projects from a variety of sources in their countries. In an unusual move, the Malawi government gave AidData complete access to its nonpublic government aid management system, and AidData georeferenced all projects on the subnational level. The results have had a huge impact on the policy discussion about what constitutes effective coordination of development finance efforts. This led to the creation of a trust fund at the World Bank, the so-called Open Aid Partnership, to georeference local aid projects. Finance ministers in developing countries around the world expressed interest in participating, and AidData was able to secure commitments from these governments to provide access to their aid management systems, further increasing the transparency of foreign development finance. By 2019, AidData had geocoded aid projects in a large number of developing countries. The geocoding is successful, domestically and internationally, and demand is increasing in the developing world. Partly as a consequence, AidData has evolved from an initiative that was driven by academic researchers to an interdisciplinary powerhouse where researchers from various disciplines and subfields of political science work together with policy practitioners.

With the provision of the database and the initiatives summarized previously, AidData has made a substantial contribution toward a deeper engagement between foreign aid scholars and practitioners. AidData sees itself as a broker between researchers and members of the policy community who are interested in the type of data collection and analysis that AidData offers. The linkages between policy and academia exist on several dimensions, with varying strengths. First, AidData's greatest success in establishing linkages has been its ability to connect the policy world with academic researchers to help them address particular questions or problems. Second, AidData's success as an organization has allowed it to share some of its profits in the form of research funding for scholars using innovative methodologies to study development finance. Third, AidData is fixated less on any one academic discipline and more on developing methods to address real-world problems. It does not sell researchers as "economists" or "political scientists" but as scholars who are able to help solve particular problems—that is, those who have the necessary methodological skills to answer a particular question. The fact that AidData initiators have come from various subfields (including political science, economics, geography, and sociology) allows them to tap into different networks. Finally, AidData has had an indirect impact on the linkages between political scientists and practitioners because the two groups use similar data.

Many challenges remain. My interviews revealed that the basic challenges discussed previously persist even in this environment. AidData has made great strides in bringing practitioners and academics together, but interests and incentives diverge, and often both sides are dissatisfied. Political scientists are mainly interested in studying power relations—for example, who gets foreign aid and why—but policymakers are more interested in questions of coordination and effectiveness. The most successful partnerships tend to be those in which (a) the scholar does not have a rigid research agenda and is willing to listen to practitioners, or (b) the practitioner is open to questions or research methods that are overlooked in foreign aid agencies. Different incentive structures seem the most persistent obstacle (see, e.g., Parks and Stern 2013). The questions that interest policymakers are not necessarily the questions that allow tenure-track faculty to improve their chances for publication in top-tier journals.[16] To make matters worse, practitioners often have difficulty articulating researchable questions, which can frustrate scholars. Moreover, researchers need two to five years to provide high-quality research results, but policymakers need results in three to six months. Nevertheless, AidData has been successful, particularly when questions are aligned, and the growing relationships increased practitioners' interest in understanding questions of political economy in areas where political scientists can offer unique contributions.

## SUMMARY AND CHALLENGES

I paint a mixed picture of the interactions between the academic and policy worlds in the area of foreign aid. Linkages between IR scholars and the policy community are increasing. My analysis reveals that these positive developments appear to result from (a) the increasing transparency of foreign aid agencies coupled with AidData's data efforts, which have increased the usability of academic research for policy purposes; (b) the increasing use of methods by IR scholars that are useful to study the questions that policymakers want to answer; (c) practitioners' increasing acknowledgment that it is important to take politics and governance into account when designing effective development projects; and (d) IR scholars' increasing willingness to focus their research on questions that may be more relevant to practitioners, especially as a consequence of increased funding of this type of research by policy agencies.

My analysis still reveals a sizeable gap between IR scholars and development policymakers. In many areas, economists dominate the linkages between academia and the policy world, limiting the number and types of opportunities (argument 2a) available for IR scholars in this space. There is an increasing focus on quantitative and experimental work in IR, but the TRIP data on IR scholars and the published discipline do not reflect a dramatic increase in the use of these research methods. Two underlying obstacles to creating more linkages stand out. First, there have been significant overlaps and interdependencies in the broad questions addressed when analyzing foreign aid, but beyond that IR scholars' and practitioners' interests have varied substantially. Whereas policymakers are often concerned about the operational level of their foreign aid projects, as well as the evaluation of development impact, political scientists are primarily concerned with the broader strategic context and the international and domestic politics of foreign aid. The political environment is clearly important to understand why foreign aid projects sometimes fail to achieve their intended results, but many policymakers shy away from addressing these issues for practical reasons. From my own experience, World Bank staff are aware of the perverse political incentives that recipient country incumbents face when receiving foreign aid projects. Political scientists focus on the problems, but they do not provide many ready-made solutions to these problems.

To provide just one example of the practical challenges that aid agencies face, World Bank projects increasingly compete with Chinese foreign aid projects, and recipient country incumbents are less willing to accept a wide range of project conditions imposed by the World Bank. The increasing competition decreases the donors' ability to design projects that maximize effectiveness. Academic research can tell donors that projects will likely be unsuccessful if corruption is not circumvented, but academics have no answers to how aid agencies should deal with some of these practical challenges. The debate is whether to withdraw the project if all the conditions are not met or corruption is detected, or whether the project is still more likely to improve the situation as compared to a situation in which no foreign aid is allocated (or allocated by another donor with less stringent requirements). In addition, practitioners usually face much more serious time constraints, which reduce their ability to engage with the newest research on some of the broader questions (i.e., how to design projects to maximize effectiveness) even if they wanted to. The World Bank moved toward greater coordination of development projects within and across recipient countries, but the time constraints drastically limited the value of academic research for operational staff.[17]

Second, the policy and academic communities still face different incentive structures in respect to the timing of research activities and publication venues. Whereas policymakers often address crises that need immediate attention, typical research projects take several years from beginning to publication. The timing for academic research is justified by the value of valid and reliable results; however, it comes at the cost of not being timely enough to be of immediate value to practitioners. This also explains why the gap has been smallest when it comes to the broad strategies of how and where foreign aid is allocated, rather than questions about individual foreign aid projects. Many policymakers focus on particular regions and even projects, however, and are therefore interested in project-specific questions. To make an impact, IR scholars need to market their research more effectively through policy briefs and participation in think tanks. Such marketing would be likely to influence practitioners, but it also would put yet another time constraint on scholars, lowering incentives to engage with the policy community. Even if IR scholars were to translate their work into digestible blog posts or policy briefs, their influence would depend on their willingness to spend considerable time networking with the policy world.

# ENDNOTES

I am grateful for comments I received on an earlier version of this paper from participants at the TRIP conferences in Washington, DC, and Williamsburg, VA, and also from Steve Radelet, Mike Tierney, Brad Parks, Sue Peterson, and Samantha Custer.

1. According to the TRIP faculty survey (2014) and the TRIP journal article database, more than 10 percent of all IR research focuses on development and foreign aid, and the proportion of articles on aid has risen over time. Only international trade research has a larger share within IPE (see also Pepinsky and Steinberg, this volume).

2. Variables $fsqg\_924$ and $fsqg\_1110\_329$; TRIP faculty survey 2011.

3. Variable $fsqg\_621$; TRIP faculty survey 2011 (regarding the belief that policy relevance and current events should primarily motivate research). Variable $qg\_260$; TRIP Faculty Survey 2014 (regarding changing research topics in response to major events in world affairs in an effort to make research more relevant to policymakers).

4. For an overview of these debates, see, for example, Hansen and Tarp (2000); Clemens et al. (2004); Addison et al. (2005); Radelet (2006); Doucouliagos and Paldam (2008, 2009). Clemens et al. (2012) find that the studies with no results are often fragile to model specifications, and after some adjustments to model specification, the effect of foreign aid on economic growth becomes significant.

5. Other researchers have focused on the donor perspective. Many IR scholars have contributed to this body of research, but the debate is more prominent in academic circles and less prominent in policy circles, so I do not discuss it here in detail.

6. I have no conclusive evidence for why practitioners are less likely to use this research. One possible explanation is that practitioners are well aware of the political and strategic biases that foreign aid allocation exhibits. Even to the extent that they care about sustainable economic or social development, few political science studies provide guidance for how to use their results on the politics of foreign aid to improve development finance in practice. Whereas much of that literature is better suited for understanding why foreign aid is allocated in a certain way, more recent work (as discussed in the next section) focuses on topics and methods that are important to guide foreign aid practice and policy. The discussion of political capture is only one example of many. For another example, Dietrich et al. (2018) show how foreign aid projects can increase the legitimacy of donors, a highly relevant topic for practitioners.

7. Variable $qg\_421$; TRIP faculty survey 2014. About 10 percent of respondents believe that IPE and development are issue areas in which IR research had the largest impact on foreign policy (about 18 percent name the issue area of security).

8. Variable $qg\_159$; TRIP faculty survey 2014.

9. Variable $qg\_104$; TRIP faculty survey 2014.

10. Note that more recent work employs more experiments, so we may see a change in these numbers in the coming years.

11. Information about issue areas was only available for all IR, other IPE, and security. To identify foreign aid articles, I referred to another variable, the substantive focus of articles. In all data on IPE, I removed articles/scholars that are coded as foreign aid in order to avoid double counting.

12. Looking at some of the current research articles presented at IR workshops and conferences, one would expect to see more experimental publications in the future. A drawback of the current analysis is that the dataset focuses on the twelve leading IR journals. The database does not include journals where one would expect to see much more policy-focused work, such as *Foreign Affairs* or *World Development*.

13. PEIO may represent a special case. The participation of practitioners is much lower in pure political science conferences, such as the International Political Economy Society (IPES) conference.

14. I am grateful to Brad Parks, executive director of AidData; Samantha Custer, director of policy and communications at AidData; and Mike Tierney, cofounder of the AidData project for their willingness to answer my questions.

15. See AidData 2016. http://aiddata.org/aiddata-research-consortium (last accessed: July 2, 2016).

16. In addition to including different opinions about which questions are important, academic work often is difficult to digest for policymakers who have severe time constraints. It is not the aim of this chapter to provide a normative assessment of whether linkages are desired, but these differences, in my view, provide huge obstacles to closer linkages between the two communities. For a recent empirical study that attempts to assess IR scholars' actual and the normatively preferred value of peer-reviewed journal articles versus various types of policy publications in the tenure and promotion process, see Maliniak et al. (2018).

17. In my interviews with USAID staff, I also heard that some practitioners question the usefulness of theoretically informed research, arguing that the field missions are a decade ahead of academia in terms of programming. For the impact of aid competition from China on World Bank conditions, see Hernandez (2017).

# 7

# MAKING ACADEMIC RESEARCH ON FOREIGN AID MORE POLICY RELEVANT

Steven Radelet

C hristina Schneider's enlightening chapter explores the extent to which research conducted by international relations (IR) scholars is used and seen as relevant by policymakers and the extent to which the issues on policymakers' agendas are of interest to IR researchers. These are important issues; as someone who has worked in both the research and policy communities, I am regularly struck by the gaps between the two. As Schneider points out, policymakers are not always interested in academic research, and researchers are not always interested in the issues that are most important to policymakers.

There are many reasons for these gaps, but three stand out. The first is timing. Policymakers typically want answers within a few weeks, whereas good research often takes a year or more. The second is the incentive structure within academia. The types of articles that are accepted in top journals and that count heavily toward tenure and promotion typically have a heavy theoretical or methodological emphasis that is of less interest to policymakers who want to know answers to more practical questions in the messy real world. Third, even when researchers produce studies that should be of interest to policymakers, they often fail to communicate the findings effectively. Researchers often erroneously assume that once an article is published, somehow the results will magically find their way to the attention of policymakers, which of course they do not, thereby relegating relevant research into irrelevancy.

My comments come in three parts. First, I add to Schneider's literature review on aid effectiveness, which is missing some important pieces. Second, I comment on some promising topics for IR research and how these might be made relevant for policymakers. Third, I provide thoughts on more effectively disseminating this literature.

## THE AID "EFFECTIVENESS" LITERATURE

Most of the research on aid effectiveness has focused on the relationship between aid and growth. Although I have contributed to this literature, I think it is unfortunate that so much research has focused exclusively on growth because so much aid is aimed at other issues: health, education, clean water, governance, environment, emergency relief, and so on. These issues do not get the attention they deserve. Indeed, many people assume that "aid effectiveness" and "aid-growth effectiveness" are synonymous, and whatever we think we know about aid and growth is true for aid effectiveness more broadly. Of course, this is not true.

One reason for this problem is the dearth of reliable disaggregated data on the purposes of aid at the sector and project level. The project-level coding of aid introduced by AidData in 2008 is an important first step in addressing this issue. The detailed nature of the information in AidData—what aid projects are intended to do, where they are located, who is carrying them out, and so forth—substantially increases researchers' ability to explore a wider range of development outcomes. In the coming years, these data should add tremendously to our knowledge of what works with aid and why.

Even though this research is in its early stages, it is important to augment Schneider's literature review with some discussion of the effectiveness of aid in achieving other development goals. I focus on two issues relevant to IR researchers: health and democracy. I also provide additional comments on aid and growth.

## Aid and Health

There is widespread agreement that many aid programs have directly improved health and saved lives. Donor-financed programs have helped to increase the number of childhood vaccinations; eradicate smallpox and nearly eradicate polio; and reduce deaths from malaria, HIV/AIDS, tuberculosis, diarrhea, and other diseases. These programs have saved tens of millions of lives and rank among the world's greatest achievements in recent years. Yet they receive scant attention in the aid effectiveness literature, which contributes to some of the misleading negative views on aid.

Why should these health successes interest IR researchers? Because whereas aid was a big part of these achievements, they were not the product of aid alone: They required the combined efforts of aid agencies, international organizations, scientists, committed governments, nongovernmental organizations, church groups, and local actors all working in concert across borders and agencies. Why did these initiatives work so well? How were incentives aligned across agencies? What created the opportunities for large-scale cooperation? Are there implications for the design and implementation of education, water, environmental, or agricultural programs? Economists cannot answer these questions, nor can health experts. But IR scholars can help us understand how and why various groups worked together effectively and the possible implications for other programs. Policymakers would be very interested in better understanding these issues.

## Aid and Democracy

What is the relationship between aid and democracy? A common criticism of aid is that it keeps authoritarian governments in power and therefore undermines democracy. There was truth to this during the Cold War, when rich countries provided large sums to some of the world's nastiest dictators, and the objective actually *was* to keep the dictators in power. To some extent, the practice continues today with support for authoritarian governments that are fighting terrorism, combating drug trafficking, or are otherwise aligned with the priorities of rich-country governments. Ultimately, however, this issue is less about aid per se and more about rich countries using a wide array of tools to keep allies in power: diplomacy, trade preferences, military support, private investment guarantees, loans, information campaigns, and—yes—foreign aid. Like any other tool, aid can be used for good or ill, or for purposes other than development. Using these examples to suggest that aid is a failure makes no more sense than claiming diplomacy is a failure because it has been used to support authoritarian governments.

Newer research explores how aid affects democracy through two other channels: directly, by supporting civil society groups, election processes, judicial systems, and other institutions that undergird democracies; and indirectly by influencing other development outcomes (e.g., growth, health, education) where success can add to the legitimacy of democratically elected governments. Most of the recent studies have found a positive relationship between aid and democracy through both of these channels, especially since the end of the Cold War.

For example, Dunning (2004) found a positive effect of aid on democracy in Africa after the Cold War. Bermeo (2011) found that after 1992 foreign aid from democratic donors was associated with a greater likelihood of democratic transition (aid from nondemocratic donors, such as China, did not have this impact). Dietrich and Wright (2015) concluded that in Africa "economic aid increases the likelihood of transition to multiparty politics, while democracy aid furthers democratic consolidation by reducing the incidence of multiparty failure and electoral misconduct." In a well-known earlier study, Knack (2004) found no positive relationship between aid and democracy through 2000 but also found no evidence that aid undermined democracy or supported nondemocracies. These studies did not find support for the idea that aid undermines democracy or keeps autocrats in power. But the research is still thin; much more is needed so we can better understand the linkages and possible pitfalls of how aid influences democracy.

## Aid and Growth

Schneider's chapter devotes less than one paragraph to studies that find a positive relationship between aid and growth, juxtaposed against several paragraphs on why the relationship might not be positive. Unfortunately, this imbalance reinforces the popularly held (yet incorrect) view that most research finds either no relationship or a negative relationship between aid and growth.

In fact, the majority of recent studies have found a positive relationship between aid and growth. Arndt, Jones, and Tarp (2010) found that aid equivalent to 10 percent of gross domestic product added about 1 percentage point to growth rates over the long term. Brückner (2011) carefully controlled for reverse causality (faster growth can attract more aid) and found an almost identical result. Galiani, Knack, Xu, and Zou (2014) focused on thirty-five countries that had "graduated" from World Bank International Development Association (IDA) to International Bank for Reconstruction and Development (IBRD) eligibility, and therefore lost access to certain types of aid (because concessional IDA loans and grants count as foreign aid but IBRD loans do not), and these researchers found a significant positive impact of aid on growth.

Moreover, many of the prominent earlier studies that find no relationship between aid and growth are fragile and are based on dubious assumptions that often do not hold up under deeper scrutiny. In my own work with three colleagues (Clemens et al. 2012), we examined three of the best known earlier papers (Boone 1996; Burnside and Dollar 2000; Rajan and Subramanian 2008). We found that by making a few small, sensible, and consistent adjustments to their underlying assumptions, the results in each case were reversed and became positive.

After thoroughly examining the aid-growth research, Collier (2007) concluded that "A reasonable estimate is that over the last thirty years, aid has added around one percentage point to the annual growth rate of the bottom billion." Ravallion (2014) concluded that "the recent macro evidence is more consistent with the claim that sustained aid commitment to poor countries is good for their economic growth over the longer-term." It's time to move beyond the outdated claim that most research finds no relationship between aid and growth and recognize that, although not definitive, the preponderance of recent evidence favors the conclusion of a modestly sized positive relationship.

## SOME PROPOSALS FOR IR RESEARCH

How can IR research become more relevant for policymakers? I have already mentioned two issues that are ripe for more IR research: understanding the successful international initiatives in health and exploring the linkages between aid and democracy. There are several other questions that IR researchers are well suited to address.

1.  Does country ownership improve outcomes in aid programs? What does "country ownership" mean, especially in a world of coalition politics and interest groups? Does it have multiple meanings in different contexts? What are the implications for aid programs? Country ownership opens a set of issues that economists cannot deal with, much less health or education specialists, but IR experts can. IR researchers could create a taxonomy of definitions and characteristics of country ownership. Researchers could aim to develop practical ideas and relevant guidance on how aid agencies can garner the benefits of local participation without hopelessly complicating programs and projects. I suspect that these

approaches would differ significantly in democracies and nondemocracies because in democracies (at least to a greater extent) the government represents local interests. Untangling these issues and moving beyond simplistic platitudes require the expertise of political scientists to better understand whether the shift to country ownership is simply a slogan or has meaning in terms of effectiveness, and, if so, how and under what circumstances.

2.   Should aid be delivered differently in democracies than in nondemocracies? If so, how? It seems reasonable to believe that there is more scope to provide aid directly to governments and invest in institution building in democracies rather than dictatorships. Moreover, it seems reasonable that democratically elected governments better represent the wishes of their citizens than do nondemocracies. Aid agencies need to move beyond the "one-size-fits-all" approach and begin to provide aid differently in different contexts. For too long, aid agencies have been stuck with a binary choice of financing projects or budget support, when some creativity could lead to new approaches that might make particular sense in more open and accountable governments. For example, in Liberia, donors to the health sector combine their resources into a "pool fund" managed by an independent expert (not by any of the donors) who sits in the Ministry of Health. The idea is to segregate aid financing from government budgets while tightly integrating aid initiatives with the government's policies and programs. There is much scope for new ideas on how to manage aid-financed projects in democracies. Once again, IR researchers are well positioned to provide ideas, evidence, and guidance on these issues because of their expertise on the impact of political institutions on policy choices and outcomes.

3.   Do programs aimed at directly supporting democracy work? Although some research suggests that aid can support democracy (Carothers 2004; Finkel et al. 2007), we know surprisingly little about this question. Part of the difficulty is the lack of precision in defining democracy (or attributes of democracy), and part of it is that democracy (however defined) does not proceed in a linear fashion. Democratic "progress" is hard to measure. Even if we could clearly define the objective, it is difficult to make connections between particular efforts (like supporting civil society groups) and specific outcomes (like greater accountability). These difficulties do not mean we can simply avoid the question. If we expect taxpayers to fund programs that directly support democracy, and if we expect to be effective in supporting democracy, we need to develop new tools and methodologies to evaluate program effectiveness (however defined).

4.   How can we better understand the politics around aid in donor countries and how it influences aid effectiveness? In recent years, there has been a big focus on the politics of recipient countries (e.g., aid works better in well-governed countries). There is also a substantial body of research on how donors' strategic considerations affect aid distribution

(e.g., more aid goes to former colonies). But there is less understanding about how these pressures affect aid agencies. How do aid agencies deal with forces pushing to allocate aid on political considerations rather than development objectives? To what extent do the distortions in aid allocation caused by donor politics hinder or help aid effectiveness? What kinds of political or institutional reforms might insulate allocation from donor country politics?

5.  What strategies have been most effective in postconflict recovery? I was struck in my work in Liberia after the end of the civil war by how little useful research existed on postconflict recovery strategies. Better understanding the approaches that have been successful and why requires multidisciplinary research—IR scholars working with economists, security experts, health and education specialists, and others. One promising example of this type of research is the University of Maryland's multifaceted project "Aiding Resilience? The Impact of Foreign Assistance on the Dynamics of Intrastate Armed Conflict." IR scholars can contribute through a better understanding of coalition politics, interest groups, and key populations. They can also help understand the inherent tensions between the need to deliver quick results to build legitimacy and the need to make longer term investments to build effective institutions.

## GETTING THE WORD OUT

Let me conclude by shifting to research dissemination. Academic researchers, whatever their discipline, are tightly focused on publishing their research in journals, books, and book chapters. Doing so is all well and good, as far as it goes. But it doesn't go far enough. Academics tend to assume that if their research has been published, it will find its way to policy officials, and if it doesn't the fault lies with the policymaker's staff or with structural problems that are outside of their control.

Although there's some truth to this, I think the larger truth is that academics are lousy at marketing their policy-relevant research. Neither policymakers nor their staff have time to wade through forty-page papers that cover literature reviews, methodological approaches, data issues, and results. They just aren't going to do it.

Researchers who are more successful in getting their ideas to policymakers actively pursue strategies to make it as easy as possible for policymakers to learn about it and understand the core ideas. One way to do this is to write separate short briefs that distill the most important ideas for policymakers. These need to be written with a different tone, using different words and language, and with an eye toward focusing on the most important issues for policymakers, which are quite different from the most important issues for academics and journal referees. Once these briefs are written, researchers need to find different outlets for distribution, including blog posts, op-eds, and other mechanisms. In addition, they need to find policy-oriented panel discussions or other events where they can publicly discuss their research findings.

None of this happens automatically, especially if researchers are passive. Academic researchers need to learn the lessons from the most successful think tanks, such as the Brookings Institution, the Peterson Institute, and the Center for Global Development. These bodies excel at anticipating the issues that are most important to policymakers and then actively pursuing ways to communicate the messages to the right people. Academic researchers need to find these kinds of outlets, perhaps by affiliating with such think tanks or by establishing similar outlets within their own universities or through consortiums of other researchers. The AidData blog and newsletter are good starting points. In addition, researchers (perhaps working with AidData) should set up events in Washington, DC (e.g., panel discussions) that are easy for policymakers or their staff members to attend. In short, researchers need to do more than create a good product; they need a marketing strategy to get their good products to the right consumers. With these steps, we can begin to move from "mind the gap" to "close the gap."

# 8

# TRADE POLICY AND TRADE POLICY RESEARCH

Edward D. Mansfield and Jon C. W. Pevehouse

Over the past half century, international political economy (IPE) has emerged as one of the most vibrant and important subfields in political science. Much of the research in this subfield has focused on explaining aspects of international trade. In this chapter, we assess the linkages between academic research on the political economy of trade, on the one hand, and both the trade policies implemented by countries and broader developments in the international trading system on the other.

We begin by addressing the extent to which research on the political economy of trade is policy oriented. Based on an analysis of the TRIP data on journal articles and authors, we find that policy-oriented studies tend to be conducted by more senior scholars. This finding is consistent with explanations that focus on professional incentives of individual faculty members and is thus a distant cousin of argument 3b presented in chapter 1 of this volume, which suggests that as a subfield professionalizes, it will become less policy relevant. The finding may reflect either a generational divide among scholars in the value placed on such work or a tendency to establish academic credentials by initially conducting more theoretically driven work before turning to more policy-oriented work later in one's career. That scholars may focus on more traditional and theoretical work early in their careers is most consistent with argument 3b. After all, tenure and promotion are largely determined by publications in peer-reviewed outlets (Maliniak et al. 2018); thus, junior faculty are more constrained in the type of research products that will be rewarded. We also find strong evidence, consistent with argument 4 summarized in chapter 1, that quantitative work on trade is less likely to have an explicit policy orientation than nonquantitative work. Again, it is not clear what mechanism explains this result. Scholars conducting quantitative research on trade may be less interested in policy, they may assume that practitioners are less likely to read quantitative work than other types, or more technical work on the political economy of trade may be published in venues that discourage authors from focusing on policy implications or making policy recommendations.

Next, we analyze the linkages between trade policy and academic research on the political economy of trade. We argue that it is difficult to identify instances in which trade policy was directly affected by such research. That is not to say that work on the political economy of trade has played no role in shaping trade policy, but any impact of this work has been indirect and is difficult to uncover. This is hardly an ideal state of affairs. Consistent with argument 2 in chapter 1, we find that trade policy has been guided largely by research in economics and law rather than by political science. As the editors suggest, when "practitioners within a given issue area have an established working relationship with another epistemic/disciplinary community, then the opportunities for influence and engagement by international relations (IR) scholars will be more limited." It appears that there simply is not much intellectual space for IR scholars' work on trade. Economic and legal research on trade policy typically lacks an adequate theory of politics, however, which is a point emphasized by the policymakers who contributed to this volume (see Zoellick and Demekas, this volume). Although it is not clear how IPE research could directly contribute to the formulation of trade policy, government officials need to understand the ways in which politics influences trade policy.

Finally, we argue that whereas research on IPE and the political economy of trade has had little direct bearing on trade policy, developments in the international trading system—many of which have been driven by trade policy—have had a substantial impact on such research. We trace how these developments have influenced virtually every major body of research in this field over the past half century.

## WHAT DO IPE SCHOLARS THINK?

To what extent is academic research on the political economy of trade policy oriented, and which factors influence the policy orientation of such research? To address these questions, we draw on the TRIP journal article database to assess the policy content in studies published in the leading political science and IR journals. We also rely on five waves of the TRIP scholar survey, which were conducted in 2004, 2006, 2008, 2011, and 2014. We focus on the respondents who self-identify as IPE scholars.

One item in the TRIP journal database indicates whether the author makes "explicit policy prescriptions." Another item codes the substantive focus of the article, based on the dependent variable. This allows us to identify the 771 articles that focus on international trade in the database, which comprises 7,050 articles published in the four leading political science journals and eight top IR journals during the period from 1980 to 2012.

Not surprisingly, most of the articles on this topic are published in the leading IR journals: nearly 40 percent are published in *International Organization*, almost 20 percent are published in *International Studies Quarterly*, and 10 percent are published in *World Politics*. Of those articles that analyze trade, only about 5 percent are coded as making an explicit policy recommendation, whereas roughly 10 percent of the articles that do not examine trade make such recommendations. In part, this probably stems from the tendency for certain international security journals—most notably, *International Security*—to publish papers that will appeal to both academics and policymakers and to insist that authors address the policy implications of their research. There is no top journal in the IPE field with a similar focus or requirement. Consequently, articles on trade tend to be written for a scholarly audience and ignore policy implications. Consistent with this conjecture, articles on international security are more than four times as likely to make an explicit policy prescription as articles on IPE (15 percent compared to 3.5 percent).

Which factors influence whether articles on international trade include explicit policy recommendations? Our analysis reveals that the methodology used and the author's rank are most important. We estimated a set of logit models, where the observed value of the dependent variable is 1 if a trade article is coded as making policy prescriptions and 0 if the article does not make such prescriptions. Articles that use quantitative methods are less likely than other articles to make policy recommendations, and authors holding the rank of full professor are more likely than more junior authors to write articles that include such prescriptions. The effects of both methodology and author rank are both sizable and relatively strong, with the estimate of methodology statistically significant at the .05 level and the estimate of author rank statistically significant at the .10 level.

That policy-oriented papers tend to be written by more senior authors may reflect a generational divide in the value placed on such work. Younger scholars feel they must establish credentials as theoretically driven researchers in order to be awarded tenure and promotion. Later in their careers, scholars may decide that they have more freedom to pursue policy-oriented work or that they have developed more fully formed views on policy problems.

The tendency for quantitative work on trade to contain less of an explicit policy orientation than nonquantitative work is harder to explain. Perhaps scholars conducting quantitative work on trade are less interested in policy than their nonquantitative counterparts, although there is no obvious reason why this should be the case. Perhaps they assume that policymakers are less likely than other analysts to read quantitative work. Perhaps more technical work on the political economy of trade is published in journals that explicitly discourage authors from devoting much time to policy implications. Whatever the reason, this tendency strikes us as unfortunate.

Equally interesting are the factors that do not affect the extent to which policy issues are addressed in papers on trade. There is no evidence that the level of analysis at which the paper is cast (global, domestic, or the individual person), the regional focus or lack thereof, or the paradigm guiding the research influences whether studies of trade contain policy prescriptions. Nor does the author's gender or whether she or he works at a research university or a different type of institution have any strong bearing.

The TRIP scholar surveys do not provide information on whether scholars conduct research on trade, but they report whether scholars work on IPE.

In the 2011 scholar survey (the only year in which the question was asked), 26 percent of respondents indicate that "policy relevance or current events" should motivate research in their discipline, and 31 percent indicate that "policy relevance or current events" is an important feature of their own research. Thus, although the top IR journals do not publish much policy-oriented work, many IPE scholars believe that such work is important and report that they conduct it themselves.

Given the stark difference in the amount of policy-oriented work published by international security scholars and IPE scholars, it is noteworthy that these groups exhibit little difference in their views about the importance and desirability of such research. Approximately 29 percent of security scholars report that "policy relevance or current events" should motivate research in the discipline compared to 26 percent of IPE scholars, a difference that is not statistically significant. However, more than 42 percent of security scholars claim that "policy relevance or current events" motivates their research, compared to nearly 31 percent of IPE scholars, a difference that is statistically significant (at the .01 level). This latter result is somewhat surprising because there is no difference between what these sets of scholars feel *should* motivate research.

A similar question asked across all five waves of the survey addresses whether a scholar's work is "primarily basic," "primarily applied," or a mix of the two. Parallel to our previous findings, we find that scholars of security studies are more likely to report that their work is closer to the applied end of this spectrum compared to IPE scholars (a difference that is statistically significant at the .01 level).

Consistent with results from the article database, we find that IPE scholars who indicate that their research is primarily quantitative (more than 30 percent of IPE scholars who took the surveys) are much less likely to report that they do policy-relevant work or that policy issues should motivate research on IPE.

## TRADE RESEARCH AND TRADE POLICY

Having surveyed the extent to which research on the political economy of trade has a policy focus, we now turn to two related questions: has academic research on the political economy of trade influenced policymakers, and has trade policy affected work on the political economy of trade? It is difficult to uncover any direct evidence that research on the political economy of trade has had a bearing on policy. In this sense, it is similar to research on the political economy of money and finance (Pepinsky and Steinberg, this volume) and work on the politics of foreign aid (Schneider, this volume). However, we argue that developments in the global arena—many of which are driven by policy initiatives—are an impetus for much of the academic literature on the political economy of trade. We examine the evolution of this literature over the past half century and show that many key avenues of inquiry have been guided by events in the international trade system.

## The 1970s

The IPE field emerged as a coherent area of scholarly inquiry in the 1970s, spurred by interest in the end of the Bretton Woods agreement in 1971, the success of Europe and Japan in rebuilding after World War II, the oil embargoes of the 1970s, and the general decline in the economic health of the United States (Katzenstein et al. 1999, 15). These developments contributed to hegemonic stability theory and regime theory, both of which shaped IPE debates in the 1970s and 1980s. Hegemonic stability theory stressed that the existence of a hegemon—a state powerful enough and willing to lead the global economy—is necessary to promote an open, stable international trading system. A variant of this theory developed by Charles Kindleberger (1973) emphasized the need for public goods provision in the international political economy. The Great Depression, he argued, had deepened due to a lack of leadership in providing such goods: Great Britain was unable to lead and the United States was unwilling to do so. The result was the collapse of the international trading system, as well as the rest of the global economy. A second variant of hegemonic stability theory was advanced by Robert Gilpin (1975) and Stephen Krasner (1976), both of whom emphasized the incentives for a hegemon to establish a trading system that was consistent with its interests. These realist accounts stressed that hegemons promote international openness because they benefit from openness and are powerful enough to sanction any remaining states that increase trade barriers.

The 1950s and 1960s witnessed the establishment of a liberal trading system. The United States took the lead in setting up the Bretton Woods system. And although the International Trade Organization was stillborn, the General Agreement on Tariffs and Trade (GATT) succeeded in reducing tariffs and promoting trade among member states. The architects of hegemonic stability theory were guided in many ways by the events of these two decades.

Many observers viewed the 1970s as the end of US hegemony. The United States went off the gold standard in 1971 and suffered through nearly a decade of stagflation brought on by two oil shocks, the Vietnam War, and other factors. Equally, the European and Japanese economies grew stronger and their firms seemed poised to challenge US firms. From the standpoint of both strands of hegemonic stability theory, these developments augured poorly for the international trading system's stability and threatened to promote closure and protectionism.

Yet that is not what transpired. The Tokyo Round of the GATT was completed in 1979 and represented a significant milestone. In the face of declining American hegemony that was widely acknowledged throughout the negotiations, "[a]dvanced capitalist states virtually eliminated tariffs on most manufactured goods, and for the first time they extended multilateral regulations to cover many nontariff barriers to trade" (Lipson 1982, 236). To be sure, the global trading system continued to face significant challenges during the 1980s amid growing concern about the rise of "managed trade," industrial policy, the use of voluntary export restraints, dumping, and other related measures. Particular concern was expressed that Japan was poised to overtake the United States economically and that it was not committed to the liberal trade policies espoused by the United States (cf. Tyson 1993).

Despite the widespread view that the United States was in decline, the global trading system did not collapse. In many respects, it thrived. These developments led to a variety of important studies aiming to explain the system's resilience and stability. Some of the most influential research on this topic was contained in a seminal volume first published as a special issue of *International Organization* (Krasner 1982). One perspective, offered by Susan Strange (1982; see also Russett 1985), was that hegemony had not declined as much as was widely believed, if at all. The stability of the trading system, from this perspective, owed to the durability of American hegemony. A second perspective, which was advanced by various authors in the aforementioned project, was that such stability stemmed from the multilateral institutions and "regimes" that the United States had established in the wake of World War II, especially the GATT and its principle of most-favored-nation status (Finlayson and Zacher 1981; Keohane 1982; Lipson 1982; Ruggie 1982).

Robert Keohane (1984) crafted a particularly influential variant of this argument. He argued that US hegemony had been necessary for the establishment of the Bretton Woods system, including the multilateral trade regime. Nonetheless, this regime withstood the erosion of US hegemony because there was a demand for the regime's maintenance and a small group of actors (primarily the United States, Japan, and West Germany in combination with the European Economic Community [EEC]) cooperated to ensure that the GATT and other features of the regime did not falter. Keohane argued that it is possible to sustain a stable trading system after hegemony if a small group of countries band together to support the system. And they have every reason to do so because such stability is in their economic interests.

One reaction to the events of the 1970s and 1980s was to emphasize the role of international regimes in supporting the global trading system. Another reaction was to emphasize the role of domestic politics. During this period, American firms began facing greater foreign pressure, particularly from European and Japanese firms. There was concern that these foreign firms were benefiting from industrial policies and other government-led efforts to promote their competitiveness. For many years, the United States had tolerated these illiberal policies as a means to foster prosperity in political-military allies that were still recovering from World War II and were on the front lines in the effort to contain the Soviet Union. But as the American economy deteriorated during the 1970s, calls for protection increased in the

United States. These developments contributed to a number of different bodies of research.

One strand of research analyzed how downturns in the economy generate protectionist pressures (McKeown 1984). A second strand addressed the rise of "managed trade" and the "new protectionism," especially in industries such as textiles, semiconductors, automobiles, and computers (Milner and Yoffie 1989; Friman 1990; Richardson 1990). A third strand emphasized how the integration of countries in the global economy influences the preferences of domestic actors and trade policy outcomes. Helen Milner (1988), for example, conducted an influential study arguing that heightened economic interdependence in the 1970s created demands for openness on the part of export-oriented interests in various countries, providing a counterweight to protectionist interests and helping to sustain a relatively open trading system.

## The 1980s

As the economic crises of the 1970s subsided, new research programs began to emerge. One focused on economic sanctions and statecraft. The use of economic statecraft is virtually as old as international economic exchange itself. But during the post–World War II era, various observers asserted that such instruments were used with increasing frequency, both as a feature of Cold War politics and for other foreign policy aims. Gary Hufbauer, Jeffrey Schott, and Kimberly Ann Elliott (1990, 1) argued that two foreign policy actions by the United States during the early 1980s stimulated particular interest in sanctions: the US decision to embargo grain produced by the Soviet Union and the US attempt to block the Soviet-European gas pipeline. There is no doubt that the academic literature on sanctions and economic statecraft that emerged during the 1980s and 1990s was shaped in crucial ways by the foreign policy of the United States and other countries.

Various studies on this topic argued that sanctions rarely succeed, especially if their objectives are ambitious (Pape 1997). Such studies, for example, concluded that economic sanctions imposed on South Africa did little to end apartheid and that sanctions imposed on the Soviet Union had failed to stimulate improvements in its human rights record. Others agreed that sanctions are of limited utility in achieving ambitious aims and that their usefulness has declined over time but nonetheless argued that sanctions were useful tools of US foreign policy during the first few decades of the Cold War (Hufbauer et al. 1990). Still others pointed out that the experience of the Coordinating Committee for Multilateral Export Controls (COCOM) and other Cold War sanctions efforts demonstrated the importance of facilitating cooperation among the states imposing sanctions, if they were to harm a target state, and studied the conditions under which such cooperation emerged (Martin 1992; Mastanduno 1992).

Led by David Baldwin (1985), some scholars criticized the sanctions skeptics on the grounds that this debate had been cast too narrowly and had therefore arrived at a set of misleading conclusions. Why, many of these scholars asked, do economic sanctions and other aspects of economic state-craft continue to be used with such frequency if they are ineffective? The answer, in Baldwin's opinion, is that analysts tend to rely on overly restrictive definitions of effectiveness. Economic instruments of foreign policy, he maintains, can have purposes besides those explicitly articulated by the states imposing such instruments. These secondary and tertiary purposes might include signaling displeasure with a targeted state's behavior, demonstrating resolve to third parties, or satisfying demands for political action abroad by the sending government's core domestic constituents. Researchers often ignore these secondary and tertiary goals, Baldwin argues, but economic statecraft that achieves these goals is at least moderately effective.

## The 1990s

During the late 1980s and 1990s, two trends emerged in work on the political economy of trade: heightened interest in the domestic sources of trade policy, and growing interest in how political-military relations shape trade.

Research on the domestic sources of trade policy is hardly new. Eighty-five years ago, E. E. Schattschneider (1935) analyzed how interest groups influenced such policy in the United States. Since then, a wide variety of studies have been conducted on this topic. During the 1970s, various observers noted that the advanced industrial countries responded in different ways to that decade's severe economic downturn (Katzenstein 1978). During the 1980s, interest in the domestic sources of trade policy accelerated. Some of this work focused on the United States and much of it was in direct response to the contemporary state of international economic affairs (Stern 1987; Destler 1992). In the United States, concerns grew that the appreciation of the dollar was placing export-oriented and import-competing firms at a competitive disadvantage. But there were also worries that domestic politics in Japan and the European Community (EC) were inhibiting trade liberalization and threatening the stability of the multilateral trading system. As a result, a large body of research addressed how interest group pressures, domestic political institutions, and government-business relations affected trade policy.

In addition, the 1990s witnessed a rise in work on the links between political-military relations and trade. Again, interest in this topic was not new. Seminal contributions to it had been made decades earlier by Albert Hirschman (1945), Jacob Viner (1950), and others. Furthermore, this issue was closely linked to some of the early work on hegemonic stability theory.

During the late 1980s and early 1990s, however, research on this issue both gained momentum and shifted in focus. Some of this work centered on alliance politics and was a direct outgrowth of the concentration of trade within alliances during the Cold War (Gowa and Mansfield 1993; Gowa 1994). Such concentration stemmed in large part from trade policies implemented by both Western nations and states in the Soviet bloc. A related line of inquiry addressed how patterns of conflict and cooperation influenced trade (Pollins 1989). Studies of this topic concluded that "trade follows the flag" because interstate cooperation (conflict) encourages (discourages) foreign commerce. This finding suggested that firms responded to international political contexts when making decisions about where to do business. These studies started with simple economic models of trade and then added key political factors, helping them to demonstrate that spare economic models were incomplete. It also allowed them to account for important economic sources of trade in their political economy models.

Studies of the political influences on international trade during the 1990s also displayed the first signs of a growing convergence with research on the economics of trade, in terms of both methodology and ontology. Like economists, political scientists studying trade become more interested in explaining trade flows and trade policies. Furthermore, the 1990s also witnessed a growth in quantitative analysis in the field of IPE (Mansfield and Pevehouse 2008). Political scientists began conducting research that shared much in common with economic analysis of trade and finance, leading to a more technical turn in IPE research. Although this development has led to significant benefits in terms of generalizability, replicability, and reliability, it may have made research on the political economy of trade somewhat less accessible to portions of the policy community, as our previous analysis has indicated.

## The 2000s

The 1990s were marked by rising scholarly interest in international trade agreements and institutions. This stemmed from a variety of developments in the global economy. First, the protracted Uruguay Round of GATT negotiations led to widespread concern about the future of the multilateral trading system. In 1995 the GATT was replaced by the more institutionally muscular World Trade Organization (WTO), an event that many observers believed would reinvigorate the multilateral regime.

These developments prompted considerable interest among scholars after the turn of the millennium in the design features of international trade institutions and the efficacy of these institutions in guiding trade policy and trade flows (see also the response chapter in this volume by Demekas). Scholarship has focused on how the WTO contributes to the reduction of trade barriers by promoting reciprocity and nondiscrimination among member states (Bagwell and Staiger 2005; Goldstein et al. 2007). Research has also addressed the WTO's ability to monitor the behavior of contracting parties, resolve conflicts among them through its dispute settlement mechanism (DSM), and reduce the volatility of trade (Rosendorff 2005; Mansfield and Reinhardt 2008).

The GATT and WTO's DSM systems have attracted particular attention. Various studies have examined the timing of dispute settlement (Busch and

Reinhardt 2000), patterns of participation by member states (Bown 2005), the role of third parties in WTO disputes (Busch and Reinhardt 2006), and patterns of judicial appointments (Elsig and Pollack 2012). Increasingly, research is also turning to domestic political factors in investigating which states file disputes at the WTO (Bobick and Smith 2013).

Another strand of policy-focused work on the GATT and WTO examines whether certain states have advantages in the legal process. Early concerns by WTO observers suggested that developing states were at a disadvantage in the legal process due to the highly technical nature of the system and the resulting costs of litigation (Busch and Reinhardt 2003; Bown 2005). Although the findings are decidedly mixed, recent contributions suggest that even though developing states' legal capacity may have little bearing on their odds of victory, factors such as domestic regulatory quality may influence outcomes for developing states (Zeng 2013).

Scholarly interest in the GATT and the WTO has been driven by significant events involving these institutions. Whether it was the highly successful rounds early in the GATT's history, the protracted Uruguay Round negotiations, the moribund Doha Round, high-profile WTO disputes, or other episodes, research on trade policy and the trading system has been shaped by key events in the global economy.

In addition, the post–World War II era has been marked by a proliferation of preferential trade agreements (PTAs), a broad class of institutions that grant member states preferential access to the markets of other participating countries. Throughout the 1960s and 1970s, various studies addressed the EEC and the many attempts that developing countries made to promote growth and economic integration through such agreements. As many of these agreements flagged, so did scholarly interest in PTAs. But over the last few decades, there has been a substantial increase in the number of PTAs and states entering these agreements. Currently hundreds of them dot the international economy and virtually every country belongs to at least one (WTO 2011). This development has generated substantial interest in the effects of PTAs on state behavior (Mansfield and Pevehouse 2000; Haftel 2007) and the stability of the international trading system (Baldwin 2008). It has also prompted interest in the factors that give rise to PTAs (Mansfield 1998; Manger et al. 2012).

Almost all of the latter research examines why new PTAs form or why states elect to enter such arrangements. Among the factors shown to influence whether and when states enter PTAs are concerns about the stability of the multilateral trading system (Mansfield 1998), the regime type of countries (Mansfield et al. 2002), the number of "veto players" that can block policy change (Mansfield and Milner 2012), pressures from exporters (Milner 1988; Gilligan 1997), diffusion of PTAs throughout the global system (Pahre 2008), and competition among trade blocs (R. Baldwin 1993).

Other questions related to PTAs and economic regionalism also garnered significant attention in the 1990s and 2000s. Particular interest was expressed in the design of PTAs (Kucik 2012; Baccini et al. 2013), when the institutions expand by taking on additional members (Mansfield and Pevehouse 2013), and the effects of overlapping PTAs, a situation in which member-states belong to more than one agreement (Gomez-Mera and Molinari 2014).

IPE scholars have produced a large stream of recent research on the GATT/WTO system and PTAs. Most of this work has been shaped in crucial ways by developments in the global economy. There is very little evidence, however, that this research has had much direct bearing on trade policy. Various studies have found that PTA membership generates political and economic benefits. Perhaps the revelation of these gains contributed to the recent popularity of PTAs, especially among states like the US that have traditionally eschewed preferential trade groupings. However, there is no indication that IPE research on PTAs or the multilateral regime has contributed to foreign economic policy. Savvy rent-seeking politicians or their bureaucratic agents might well (personally) benefit from following the logic of such theories, but these real-world actors likely already knew of these gains, which helps to account for the scholarly appeal of such explanations. To demonstrate the impact (or lack thereof) of political economy research on policy decisions, we would need a different research design and more qualitative evidence on practitioners' knowledge and motives.

# The 2010s

Recently, changes in the structure of the global trading system have spurred a shift in focus for trade scholars. The rise of intraindustry trade networks and increased intrafirm trade have changed the landscape of the global trading system. The growing importance of intrafirm trade has made it harder to argue that states should be the exclusive focus of work on trade. Within economics, the turn to "new new" trade theory grew out of these changes (Melitz 2003). In political science, the last decade has brought a new turn to firm-level analysis.

For example, recent studies have argued that workers in importing industries hold different views of the threats from imports than workers in other industries (Owen and Quinn 2013). Further, Jensen et al. (2015) argue that the rise in vertical foreign direct investment to create production chains explains the decline in American antidumping (AD) filings. They argue that currency undervaluation is a potent impetus for AD filings; but because these filings could generate retaliation and trade hostilities, firms that engage in extensive trade with the offending country do not push to file. Their research shows that the likelihood of AD filings falls as intraindustry trade expands. Work thus continues to develop about how factors such as vertical integration and international supply chains influence the politics of international trade (cf. Peterson and Thies 2012).

Another significant motivation behind recent research in trade is the global financial crisis or the Great Recession of 2007–09. Whereas many countries are still wrestling with the fallout from that event, IPE scholars are wrestling with how the crisis influenced trade policy.

The received wisdom is that protectionism is countercyclical, rising during recessions and declining during expansions. Yet trade barriers did not grow substantially during the Great Recession. Various explanations have been offered for this outcome. Intraindustry trade may be less threatening to US workers because that trade is usually part of vertically integrated production networks that produce goods "at home" (Gawande et al. 2014). This creates a smaller incentive for firms to press governments for protection because trade disputes mean interrupted trade between branches of the firm, even in tough economic times. Kishore Gawande, Bernard Hoekman, and Yue Cui (2014) also show that the WTO constrained the use of tariffs during the Great Recession (see also Kee et al. 2013). Chad Bown and Meredith Crowley (2013) find that the US and the European Union (EU) largely refrained from resorting to temporary trade barriers during the Great Recession and that when barriers were erected, they targeted states less affected by the economic downturn. Christina Davis and Krysztof Pelc (2015) argue that US and EU strategic restraint arose out of the constraining effects of the WTO.[1]

Of course, it is possible that countries responded to the Great Recession by using financial and monetary instruments rather than trade policy. More specifically, instead of imposing protectionist policies during the recession, countries such as the United States may have used monetary policy (e.g., quantitative easing) to influence exchange rates, which then improved the terms of trade for US exporters. This has been one source of the inspiration for recent work attempting to link research in trade policy with work on the political economy of finance (Copelovitch and Pevehouse 2015).

Scholars have long realized that fluctuations in exchange rates can have substantial effects on domestic producers' competitiveness in world markets (Frieden and Broz 2001). All else equal, exporters and import-competing industries lose from currency appreciation, whereas the nontradable sector and domestic consumers gain (Frieden 1991). Yet the trade-related effects of exchange rates have largely gone unconsidered in both literatures.

This has begun to change as tension between the United States and China over the latter's undervalued exchange rate has become a more prominent political issue. In this context, Lawrence Broz and Seth Werfel (2014) maintain that several industry-specific characteristics determine the protectionist response to changes in the exchange rate, including the degree of exchange-rate pass-through, the level of import penetration, and the share of imported intermediate inputs in total industry inputs.

It is also likely that decision-makers consider these interactions between trade and exchange rates when they design policies in each area. For example, Mark Copelovitch and Jon Pevehouse (2013) argue that PTAs influence both a country's choice of exchange rate regime and the propensity to allow its currency to depreciate. They find that countries that have signed a PTA with their "base" country—the country most likely to be their anchor currency based on current and past experience with fixed exchange rates, regional proximity, and trade ties (Klein and Shambaugh 2006)—are less likely to adopt a fixed exchange rate and tend to have more depreciated currencies.

## CONCLUSIONS

There is ample evidence that the IPE field and research on the political economy of trade have been shaped in important ways by both developments in the international trading system and trade policy. But is anyone in the policy realm paying attention to this research? That is much more difficult to establish, yet early evidence suggests the answer is yes. Among respondents to the 2017 TRIP trade policymaker survey, 52 percent reported relating arguments and evidence from social science research into their work on a daily basis. An additional 35 percent reported doing so at least a few times a month, if not weekly. Of course, social science is composed of various disciplines, so it is difficult to determine whether respondents are referring to political science-based IPE work. As we have emphasized, research by economists seems to be much more influential. In this volume, Schneider as well as Steinberg and Pepinsky draw similar conclusions in their respective issue areas of foreign aid and finance policy. All three chapters speak to argument 2a from chapter 1: there are fewer opportunities for influence when practitioners already have established a working relationship with another disciplinary community.

Why are economists more influential than political scientists when, as we have argued, political variables drive important trade policy decisions? We suspect multiple factors are at play. First, becoming a staff member or bureaucrat making trade policy often requires a degree in economics. These individuals are thus far more familiar with the literature in economics and likely unfamiliar with the literature on the politics of trade.

Second, that economics has far fewer significant debates over research methods or theoretical approach leads to a core set of ideas and literatures shared by these staffers and bureaucrats. Thus, policymakers will be more familiar with the underlying ideas that drive the academic literature, and they will have the skills to reach back into the field of economics, rather than political science, if necessary.

In a similar vein, one traditional explanation for why political science has little traction with policymakers is that academic writing is too theoretical and technical (Nye 2008a). Yet the same critique could be made of economics research, which is more technical, on average, than published research in political science journals. Nonetheless, economists have more influence in the policy process. This suggests that neither theory nor methodological sophistication is necessarily a barrier to influence. Rather, having staffers or bureaucrats trained in that theory or method who can translate the work to others is important. In the 2017 TRIP trade policymaker survey, for example, 60 and 70 percent of respondents respectively replied that quantitative analysis and policy analysis methodologies were "very useful" in their work.

Finally, most of the "action" in international trade politics revolves less around tariffs and more around safeguard actions, antidumping, and countervailing duties. These policies are the purview of executive branch agencies, not national legislatures. This has two important implications. Most arguments in political science and economics traditionally establish the legislature (or legislator) as the target of trade politics (Rodrik 1995), but as this is less true today, it potentially limits the applicability of those arguments. Further, it means that the staffers in the offices of key decision-makers are much more likely to be technically oriented (i.e., economists) compared to staffers in the legislature, a conclusion supported by the educational backgrounds provided by respondents in the 2017 TRIP trade policymaker survey. This could further limit the influence of academic research on trade policy.

Like Schneider and Steinberg and Pepinsky (this volume), we argue that policymakers would be remiss to ignore what political science offers in terms of guiding trade policy. Understanding the interaction of institutions, preferences, and structure has been a comparative advantage of IPE research since its inception. As the literature we have discussed has shown, politics is more than simply a market imperfection—political institutions can condition and constrain how policymakers pursue their economic preferences.

In sum, we have argued that major waves of research in IPE concerning the politics of trade have corresponded to significant world events. Yet this has not been enough to carry this research from the ivory tower to the beltway. Our analysis of published articles in international relations and surveys of academics are also enlightening. Scholars are clearly responding to academic incentives, especially in the IPE field. Even scholars who believe research should be policy relevant rarely engage in that kind of scholarship. It is thus worth thinking about whether more policy-relevant scholarship should be viewed more favorably by tenure and promotion committees. Although this still will not guarantee that policymakers pay attention to the work, it certainly gives scholars more of an incentive to grab their attention.

## ENDNOTE

1. For a general argument on the constraining role of multilateral institutions during the recent financial crisis, see Drezner (2014b).

# 9

# MAKING INTERNATIONAL RELATIONS RESEARCH ON TRADE MORE RELEVANT TO POLICY OFFICIALS

Robert B. Zoellick

In their helpful chapter, Edward Mansfield and Jon Pevehouse assess the linkages between academic research and the political economy of trade, including the influence of research on both national trade policies and the international trading system. They acknowledge frankly that "it is difficult to identify instances in which trade policy was directly affected by such research." Instead, they explore the reverse proposition: that developments in the international trading system and trade policies "have had a substantial impact on such research." Their chapter offers an informative review of the connections between international events and trade policy scholarship from the 1970s until today. Mansfield and Pevehouse also examine variation in policy relevance among journal articles and authors, focusing specifically on the gap between quantitative political economy research and policy advice.

My response complements their contribution by (1) offering a methodological observation, (2) suggesting additional source material, (3) adding one more dimension to the authors' historical review of policy and scholarship, and (4) supplementing the Mansfield-Pevehouse approach by recommending possible policy topics that could guide future political economy research.

## ACADEMIC METHODOLOGY AND POLICYMAKING

Effective policymakers solve problems. They achieve results. As officials face issues, or develop strategies, they are unlikely to think in academic categories. In the lexicon of the academy, policymakers might be characterized as "multidisciplinary" students.

In making trade policy, practitioners draw from economics, law, and political science, as Mansfield and Pevehouse recognize, but also from history, psychology, science, studies of negotiating behavior and cultures, and other fields. Policymakers are interested in experience, analysis, effects, dynamics, organizational execution, and implementation.

The Mansfield and Pevehouse chapter implicitly recognizes the value of a particular realm of scholarship that is rarely mentioned but should be remembered: history. The work of the late diplomatic historian Ernest May edged toward a discipline of "applied history" to help decision-makers think of questions to ask or perspectives to add to their analyses (Neustadt and May 1986). More recently, Graham Allison and Niall Ferguson (2016) have advocated for an "applied history" research agenda. I. M. Destler's *American Trade Politics* (2005) represents an effort (sometimes flawed) to recognize the connections between trade policy history and current policy.

The economics profession took a wrong turn when it abandoned the heading of "political economy." Then, scholars of politics and institutions followed suit by proclaiming a "political science." But as German Chancellor Angela Merkel of Germany, a student of physics, once concluded after a small dinner in Berlin with the heads of international economic organizations, when this author was president of the World Bank, "Economic theories don't seem scientific to me."

To assist policymakers, or at least to make one's research most useful, scholars ought to think beyond disciplinary boundaries. Real-world problems are multidimensional; perhaps research could be more multidisciplinary. In seeking connections between political economy research and trade policy, one might also find evidence in references to trade policy works from related disciplines. At a minimum, scholars of international political economy (IPE) who wish to influence policy should consider how policymakers actually try to solve policy problems.

## OTHER SOURCE MATERIAL

Mansfield and Pevehouse state that the evidentiary connection between international political economy research and policy "has been indirect and is difficult to uncover" (p106). This is undoubtedly true, yet sources that scholars discount or overlook might reveal a fuller nexus between scholarship and policy.

A review of policy officials' speeches, congressional testimonies, statements by members of Congress, and advocacy points from executive departments and organizations such as the US Chamber of Commerce might well reveal, to paraphrase Lord Keynes, that "[p]ractical men, who believe themselves to be quite exempt from any intellectual influences, are usually the slave of some defunct [political] economist."[1]

These source materials may seem insubstantial to scholars, yet the policy community communicates through such media. Similarly, opinion pieces in newspapers or online may seem immaterial to scholars but are the proving grounds, test labs, and debate societies for many policy influentials. Indeed, consider the influence of an eminent forerunner, *The Federalist Papers*. Such writings can reveal intellectual connections. Articles in policy magazines, rather than academic journals, are also likely to help political economists to better understand whether or how their work influences policy.

Political economists may also wish to mine oral histories to trace the connectivity between research ideas and policymaking. Political economists could participate in this and similar projects to interview individuals active in making trade policy and other IPE topics; scholars might even ask interviewees about the use of findings or ideas associated with published studies.

Such primary source material is sometimes employed by historians; perhaps other scholars' interest in historical methods could provide future impetus for multidisciplinary work. These sources could supply evidence that would fill out the chronological narrative of policy research offered by Mansfield and Pevehouse.

# A HISTORICAL ADDENDUM

I enjoyed reading Mansfield and Pevehouse's concise review of the evolution of scholarly research in the light of changes in the world's political economy. I have only minor quibbles with their assessment of events, politics, and published learning. I would, however, suggest one addition that may add a perspective to scholarship.

Understandably, IPE scholars are drawn to analyze policies through prisms of organizations, institutions, regimes, or systems. Yet there may be times when political leaders resist and even block structures or systems that they believe are counterproductive. In doing so, transformative leaders can create the basis for new, or at least substantially revised, orders.

After the stagflation, oil shocks, and economic frustrations of the 1970s, some experts argued for more controls, regulation, and redistribution. Internationally, these causes were embodied in initiatives such as the New International Economic Order, New World Information Order, and the first Deep Seabed Mining Regime of the Law of the Sea Treaty. The United Nations and its related agencies, the Group of 77, and similar assemblies were the foremost progenitors of such schemes. In contrast, some economists and lawyers pressed for deregulation and policies grounded in a new "law and economics" movement. This deregulation scholarship influenced policies in the latter part of the Carter administration.

President Ronald Reagan and Prime Minister Margaret Thatcher wanted to revive their national economies by freeing their citizens of constraints on economic liberty. They adamantly opposed international orders that would choke their national efforts and, in their view, stymie international economic recovery too.

Once Reagan and Thatcher revitalized their domestic economies, other governments advanced bold, liberalizing plans for trade policy. (Analogous economic policy reforms were adopted in Australia, Canada, Germany, and Japan.) Especially in Reagan's second term, his administration pressed IPE designs for G–7 economic coordination, exchange rates and monetary policies, free trade, debt, and development; Reagan used this agenda to resist rising protectionism in the US Congress. Secretary of the Treasury James Baker and his deputy, Richard Darman, were influenced by the political economy work of Fred Bergsten at what today is the Peterson Institute for International Economics.

The policy point is that at times, perhaps especially in eras of flux, a strong political economy case can be made for resisting flawed international orders because of both the costs of the rules and the benefits of encouraging adjustment or transition to a new policy equilibrium. In the realm of economics, Friedrich Hayek referred to an analogous idea: the benefits of permitting markets to attain a "spontaneous order."

In 2018–19, we have witnessed a different type of transformation: the Trump administration, which has complained about the results of the rules-based trading order of the World Trade Organization (WTO) and the US Free Trade Agreements (FTAs), has ignored those disciplines in order to impose barriers while seeking transactions to address bilateral trade deficits.

# POLICY TOPICS FOR POLITICAL ECONOMY RESEARCH

In the spirit of Mansfield and Pevehouse's chapter, I suggest six areas for future political economy—or perhaps, multidisciplinary—research to assist those who make trade policy.

## The Role of the US Congress in Trade Policy

The US Constitution (Article I, Section 8) grants the Congress authority over commerce and trade. In the nineteenth and early twentieth centuries, tariff bills were among the signal items that defined Congresses, political parties, economic strategies, regions, the causes of the Great Depression, and even a secession crisis.

Beginning with the Reciprocal Trade Agreements Act of 1934, Congress created a new negotiating partnership with the president and the executive branch. That arrangement has evolved over time, including through the creation of the Office of the US Trade Representative (USTR) in the Executive Office of the President and delegations of authority under "fast track" and later "Trade Promotion Authority" (TPA) legislation.

Neither policymakers nor scholars can understand US trade policy without appreciating the powerful, and continually evolving, role of Congress. The principal committees making trade policy remain Finance in the Senate and Ways and Means in the House, but as trade topics have extended far beyond tariffs, many more committees have insisted on a role, as have their associated constituencies and interest groups.

The outside groups involved now extend far beyond a spectrum of businesses, farm groups, and labor unions. Environmentalists, human rights organizations, religious bodies, and lobbyists for counterpart countries are all engaged. With the expansion of interested congressional committees and groups, the congressional leadership must play a larger role in steering processes and preparing for votes.

Congress affects every aspect of US trade policy: negotiating priorities, objectives, packaging of topics, coalitions, defensive actions, trade-offs, foreign partners and foes, sequencing, process and timing, advocacy, issue presentation and communication, enforcement, litigation, respect for international rules and norms, and agency roles.

Other countries are aware of Congress's role in trade policy. Pascal Lamy, the former European Commission commissioner for trade and WTO director-general, spent many hours working with Congress on his visits. Twenty years ago, the Mexican government transformed its representation in the United States to support passage of the North American Free Trade Agreement (NAFTA). Embassy staffs in Washington that used to concentrate on relations with the State Department, and perhaps others in the executive branch, recognized the need for diplomacy with Congress.

President Trump's aggressive use of trade authority delegated by Congress—for example, "to protect national security"—has begun a new debate: whether Congress must constrain a protectionist president. Over the past seventy years, presidents' national perspective usually led them to counter Congress's inclination to protect local interests; President Trump's approach—as a self-described "tariff man"—has reversed the traditional institutional roles.

## The Role of an Energetic Executive in Trade Policy

Given the myriad complex issues presented by congressional involvement with trade, only an energetic executive can set a policy direction for the United States as a whole. Absent executive leadership, US trade policy devolves into a least common denominator mix of disparate actions that tend to increase barriers to trade by responding to domestic complaints about foreign competition.

The chief executive must design and implement a trade policy agenda that accounts for both international and domestic interests. The executive must negotiate at home and abroad at the same time. It must seek to reconcile differences, make tradeoffs, frame arguments, assemble coalitions, and even match interest across borders. As former USTR Robert Strauss once wisely counseled me, "Once you decide to make a trade, trade it as many times as you can."

If the president authorizes the USTR to lead this agenda, the USTR will face a rare fusion of domestic and international responsibilities, combining both policy substance and fundamental politics. USTRs need to learn the "economic geography" of America by state and even by congressional district.

## Bureaucratic Politics within the Executive

Presidential interest is a sine qua non of any US trade policy that seeks to open markets. The president may delegate considerable decision-making to others, but even cabinet or other top officials will be unable to marshal executive authority domestically or internationally without presidential backing.

Other parts of the executive branch can help or hurt. White House legislative staffs dislike the "heavy lift" of trade legislation or agreements. The Office of the USTR, a small staff in the Executive Office of the President, must coordinate with other US officials while cooperating with Congress, working with foreign counterparts, consulting diverse constituencies, and leading most international trade litigation. The behemoth Commerce Department creates trade policy through judgments on "unfair trade" practices (e.g., antidumping, countervailing duties, plus safeguards); Commerce also has links to many industry groups and with the appropriate leadership can influence Congress. The Department of Agriculture plays a similar role related to farm issues. Other departments—such as Labor, Homeland Security, Energy, Justice, and the Environmental Protection Agency—can add friction or expertise, policy support, and political weight. The Treasury and State Departments are senior players that traditionally have been oriented toward supporting open international trade—but the use of their standing and influence depends on whether their top leadership combines goodwill with actions—in the interagency process, with other governments, with Congress, and with outside groups.

## Understanding Trade Negotiations

The domestic politics of trade have led many negotiators to posture as if trade negotiations are like a poker game, where one hides a hand and plays cards with care, in a contest where one wins the pot and the other loses.

In reality, most trade negotiations are joint problem-solving exercises. Each participant needs to manage "offensive" and "defensive" interests in a way that enables negotiators to both achieve a good result and sell it back home. Good negotiators seek to understand their counterparts' sensitivities and help solve their problems in a win-win fashion. Negotiators help others provide explanations to use domestically. Even trade negotiators who recognize the economic benefits of reducing their own country's barriers or subsidies often need to manage the politics of such concessions.

Institutions and countries also embody different negotiating cultures and styles. During the 1990s, Rand and then the US Institute of Peace published an informative series of books on different national negotiating styles (see Solomon and Quincy 2010).

As political economists recognize, the institutional context for a negotiation can shape behaviors, assumptions, and interaction dynamics. For example, the WTO has struggled to prepare effective negotiating environments as the organization has added members, more members have become active, the relationships between Geneva staff and capitals have changed, and newer topics have filled the policy agenda.

## Trade and Foreign Policy

Surprisingly, commentators on foreign policy treat trade policy as a technocratic legal cousin of the esoteric family of economic policy—and, therefore, at best a very distant relation of the foreign policy tribe. Of course, trade, especially in its expanding jurisdiction, is an important dimension of micro-economics, structural reforms, productivity, investment, and growth. Yet as an assembly of international political economists knows well, trade, finance, and investment are vital components of international political and security orders. Moreover, the private parties and companies that trade, and now contribute to specialized logistical and supply chains, are among the most important transnational actors.

There is a storied intellectual history of the connection between trade and statecraft, although recognition of the bond has faded among US strategists. For many reasons, the intellectual bridges between IPE and foreign and security policies became rickety during the Cold War and the decades that followed. The introduction of "geoeconomics" in recent years has, so far, only contributed a few weak conceptual cables to reconnect trade and international economics to foreign policy.[2]

Most policy discussions of trade and security center on sanctions policies, military technologies, the management of the defense (and intelligence) budget, and perhaps the connection of resources to power. This agenda is much too narrow.

Possibilities for further study include the trade and economic bonds that support security alliances; effects of private, transnational links fostered by trade; relationships among open markets, open societies, and common values; the role of trade regimes in developing the rule of law and win-win exchange; how to facilitate trade while securing borders against terrorist or other transnational threats; trade and development, including not only economic efficiency but also institutions, governance, links to international partners, rising middle classes, anticorruption, transparency, and security; trade and development in postconflict or fragile states; trade facilitation, institutional development, and links to multinational enterprises and supply chains; and connections between international economic regimes with regimes to address other topics such as human rights and the environment.

US strategies for bilateral FTAs and regional FTAs are natural components of the United States' geopolitical interest in secure links with the western, eastern, and southern borders of the Eurasian continent. NAFTA should be the cornerstone of a strategy that recognizes North America as a continental economic, political, and security base for global policies, although President Trump has used Mexico's economic dependence to press on immigration and asylum policies. US FTAs in the Western Hemisphere could provide a foundation for US and Canadian cooperation with the Latin American countries of the Pacific Alliance so as to keep moving toward Western Hemispheric free trade and partnership among American democracies. The Trans-Pacific Partnership in effect sought to extend US FTAs with six countries into a regional FTA of twelve—although President Trump withdrew US participation.

# Systemic International Trade Issues

Mansfield and Pevehouse offer an excellent look back at the evolution of the international trade regime over the past half century. What about the future?

The Generalized Agreement on Tariffs and Trade (GATT)-WTO order is failing to facilitate successful liberalizing negotiations. There are many possible explanations; one is that the balance of rights and responsibilities, guided for decades by the "Trilateral" developed economies, must adapt to the rise of and competition from middle-income countries. The size of the WTO, especially given its governance principles of unanimity and most favored nation, also has made it harder to conclude deals. New arrangements based on coalitions of the willing that share extensive and exclusive rights and responsibilities will be necessary. This approach could look to past experience with "codes" under the Tokyo Round, one of which, for Government Procurement, retains its special status.

New issues also need to be discussed. Innovative approaches to these topics are most likely to be addressed through smaller assemblies, whether in FTAs or regional associations. The inclusion of labor and environmental issues in trade accords followed this course, as have cutting-edge economic and investment matters. For example, although the articles of both the International Monetary Fund and WTO/GATT address the possibility of exchange rate policies nullifying trade concessions, the two institutions (and their governing boards) have been unable to design acceptable practices for even considering such disputes. International pledges or commitments to limit carbon will also pose questions of the effects on trade competition. China's reliance on state-owned enterprises has prompted the United States and others to seek new disciplines to prevent unfair competition.

Political economists could usefully examine the effects of FTAs on regional and global trade liberalization. A few prominent trade economists have asserted, without political economy evidence, that FTAs are simply trade diverting and undermine global trade liberalization.[3] However, economic analyses have found evidence to the contrary in both Latin America and East Asia (Freund and Ornelas 2009; Calvo-Pardo et al. 2009; Estevadeordal et al. 2008).

From the perspective of political economy logic and practice, comprehensive FTAs would seem likely to support trade liberalization and liberalizers. The FTAs help reformers lower their national barriers, thereby supporting internal structural reforms and boosting competitiveness; often, these reforms enable governments to lower barriers to others, too. Many topics covered in comprehensive FTAs require legal steps (e.g., to ensure transparency, open regulatory practices, intellectual property right protections) that are then available to other countries and even local nationals. Successful FTA deal making can strengthen reformers within their own political systems. Comprehensive FTAs often cover cutting-edge topics that all WTO members will not or cannot address at the same time or stage of development. Furthermore, liberalizers are usually willing to work with liberalizers in other governments (as theorists of transnational politics would surmise) to push for freer trade bilaterally, regionally, and globally.

## Comparative Trade Politics

Most of these suggested topics have been centered on US policy and institutions, but the same issues arise in other countries. Negotiators need to understand the "authorizing environments" for one another's trade policies. Officials face disparate conditions within their executive authorities and coalition governments; with Parliaments and legislatures; across federal, confederal, and unitary systems; with a host of private and public sector constituencies; and amid democratic and authoritarian polities.

Furthermore, each negotiating partner brings a different political, and often negotiating, culture to the table. Trade has played varying roles in national political histories. For example, the Labour parties in the UK and Australia have been free traders, tracing their political logic back to Britain's 1846 repeal of the Corn Laws' protections against grain imports.[4] In contrast, US labor unions are adamantly protectionist and have pulled the Democratic Party in that direction.

European attitudes toward science have contributed to a "precautionary principle" that has been used to block innovations in agricultural and other technologies, impeding trade in these products and services. Rules on data privacy, security, and localization requirements will affect the cross-border use of "Big Data" services.

Researchers could provide immense benefits to trade policymakers by helping them understand the origins of these differences and suggesting possible ways to overcome, address, or accommodate them.

## CONCLUSION

I am greatly encouraged that the contributors to this book, and particularly Mansfield and Pevehouse, wish to expand the network of connections between scholars and policy practitioners.

During my public service, I hoped for frameworks, insights, ideas, data, and even questions that would contribute to both qualitative and quantitative analysis. Sometimes arguments were handy, too, because policymakers usually must be advocates. Yet I have been disappointed to watch the academy drift further and further away from policy-relevant topics.

Mansfield and Pevehouse point to one cause, the incentives that young scholars face. Quantitative work can be useful, but some scholars seem drawn to mathematical modeling for its own sake.

The Mansfield-Pevehouse survey revealed that many IPE scholars believe they should be seeking to influence policy, and they want to do so. I hope they do. Governments and citizens could gain from scholarly contributions.

# ENDNOTES

1. Indeed, some officials—or their staffs—may deliberately reference scholars' ideas. A reader of Secretary of the Treasury James Baker's speeches in the late 1980s on the international economy will find references to Charles Kindleberger, one of the "greats" cited by Mansfield and Pevehouse. My remarks as US trade representative and World Bank president drew on the ideas of Robert Keohane and Joseph Nye (both former teachers of mine), as well as other scholars cited by Mansfield and Pevehouse.
2. For an effort to stimulate thinking about the traditional, and very practical, connection between US international economic policy and security policy, see Zoellick (2012).
3. For example, Jagdish Bhagwati has been both outspoken and nonempirical.
4. The repeal of the Corn Laws lowered the cost of food for working people and reduced the economic prerogatives of the landed aristocracy.

# 10

# IS INTERNATIONAL RELATIONS RELEVANT FOR INTERNATIONAL MONEY AND FINANCE?

Thomas B. Pepinsky and David A. Steinberg

One of the most fundamental motivations for international relations (IR) scholarship is to contribute to policymaking. As a discipline, IR has had a deep and lasting imprint on foreign policy, providing concepts such as mutual assured destruction, balance of power, and the clash of civilizations that fundamentally affect the way that national policymakers conceive of the problems they face and how such problems might be solved. However, the policy relevance of scholarly contributions from IR research in the areas of international money and finance is more difficult to discern. In this chapter, we provide systematic evidence that research on international money and finance contributes less policy-focused research than do some other IR subfields. This is the case despite agreement among both policymakers and IR scholars that issues relating to international money and finance are some of the most important issues confronting policymakers today.

Using data from the Teaching, Research, and International Policy (TRIP) journal article database (TRIP 2017; Maliniak et al. 2018), we show that research on international money and finance remains a small minority of all published IR research in the leading peer-reviewed journals. At the same time, data from the TRIP policymaker survey (Avey and Desch 2014) reveal that even policymakers who work on security issues consider various aspects of global finance, such as financial regulation of the Global Financial Crisis, to be among the most important policy issues facing the world today. Further, we show that the overwhelming majority of IR articles focusing on international money and finance do not offer explicit policy recommendations, a trend that is especially pronounced in paradigmatic research on international money and finance.

This low level of policy relevance for international money and finance relative to other IR subfields is striking and demands explanation. We consider several possibilities. Perhaps there are simply no actionable policies that follow from IR research on money and finance. A related possibility, articulated as argument 4 in chapter 1, is that current research practices, such as stringent adherence to positivist and statistical methodologies, prevent IR scholars of money and finance from saying anything useful about important real-world events (see, e.g., Cohen 2009). Alternatively, as suggested by argument 2a in chapter 1, it could be that the discipline of economics provides more suitable analytical tools to guide policymakers, and those scholar-practitioner networks are already well-established among policy-makers who deal with monetary policy. Finally, it could be that IR scholars who focus on money and finance have chosen to focus disproportionately on disciplinary concerns—in particular, meta-theoretical and paradigmatic debates—rather than on the kind of middle-range theories and bounded explanations that contribute more readily to the types of questions that policymakers face. This last possibility follows from the "professionalization logic" articulated in argument 3b in chapter 1. All of these factors may be at play in various ways, but we find that the third and fourth explanations—the success of economics in providing the types of analytical tools that policymakers need and the disciplinary incentives that have emerged in much current research—provide the most compelling explanations for why IR scholarship on money and finance has proven comparatively less relevant to policymakers.

The paucity of policy-focused IR research on international money and finance is not a good thing, in our view. Nor is it a natural or unavoidable consequence of the nature of the subject matter. Quite the opposite; we believe that IR research can and should contribute to contemporary policy debates in international money and finance, just as in other IR subfields. IR scholars have the ability to offer monetary policymakers important insights about the potential political consequences of their policy options, and this information has the potential to improve the quality of international monetary policy-making. Given the dominance of academic and professional economists in financial and monetary policymaking, however, the ways that IR research can best contribute to policy will be necessarily different than in the cases of war, aid, or nuclear weapons proliferation. Instead of displacing economics, IR research can complement a more narrowly economic analysis of international financial and monetary policy by helping policymakers understand the potential political consequences of their policy options and advising governments on how best to achieve their policy goals. When confronting issues of global financial regulation, monetary integration, or Chinese demand for US debt, scholars of IR (and political science more generally) provide useful insights about the objective function that national governments maximize, the constraints that they face in doing so, and the political consequences of various policy choices, which may be more important than their economic consequences. The quality of international monetary policy might improve if policymakers paid greater attention to the insights that IR and political science research provides.

In the next section, we provide an overview of IR research on money and finance using evidence from the TRIP journal article database. The following section turns to a broader discussion of possible reasons for the relative paucity of published IR research on money and finance, and the relative exclusion of IR insights from contemporary policy debates. In the final section, we make the case that greater engagement between scholars and policymakers is both possible and desirable, and we outline ways in which IR scholars can provide useful policy influence.

## INTERNATIONAL RELATIONS RESEARCH ON MONEY AND FINANCE

We begin by situating research on monetary policy and international finance within the broader IR literature. From there, we turn to consider possible explanations for the relative paucity of research on money and finance in published IR research.

## The Importance of International Money and Finance in Theory and Reality

In table 10.1, we provide a breakdown of articles within the TRIP article database by their substantive focus or issue addressed.

The majority of published articles in the TRIP database focus on international security, followed by international political economy (IPE). But within the category of IPE articles, money and finance remain just a small minority, representing less than 3 percent of total IR articles and a smaller proportion than trade, aid, and economic interdependence.

Have money and finance always been rare in published IR research? We can answer this question by examining how the proportion of published

**TABLE 10.1.** IR articles by issue area

| Issue area | Articles on topic (%) |
|---|---|
| Security | 71.8 |
| Nonmonetary IPE | 29.0 |
| Monetary policy | 2.6 |
| Other IPE topics | |
| Trade | 11.4 |
| Regional integration | 1.3 |
| Migration | 1.3 |
| Economic interdependence | 8.9 |
| Foreign aid and lending | 3.3 |
| Development | 7.1 |

*Note:* This table shows the percentage of articles falling within each issue area in the TRIP journal article database. We use the term "issue area" here not to refer to the TRIP variable *issue area* but to the variable *substantive focus of the article*, which can take on multiple values if the article addresses multiple issues. The "Security" entry includes the following values from the *substantive focus* variable: alliances, balance of power, bargaining deterrence strategy, interstate crisis, interstate war, intrastate conflict, terrorism, weapon systems, and WMD proliferation. The "Nonmonetary IPE" entry includes the values migration, trade, regional integration, economic interdependence, foreign aid, and development.

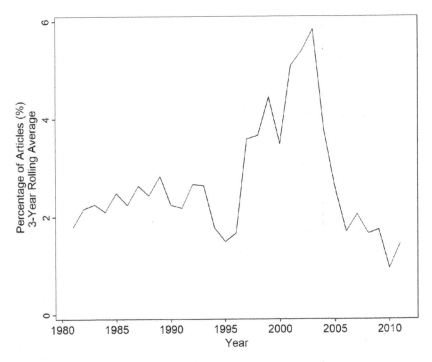

**FIGURE 10.1.**   Money articles over time
*Note:* This figure shows the three-year rolling average of the percentage of published articles in the TRIP article database that are coded as covering monetary policy.

articles covering money and finance has changed over time. In figure 10.1 we do just this, plotting a three-year rolling average of the percentage of articles in the TRIP database covering international money and finance between 1980 and 2012.

We learn two things from figure 10.1. First, the general downward trend reveals that research on money and finance is lower today than it was thirty years ago, but even in the 1980s research on money and finance occupied only a small minority of published IR articles. Second, the only real exception to this downward trend is a large spike in the early 2000s, which likely reflects an upsurge in research on money and finance following the late 1990s financial crises in Asia, Russia, and several other emerging economies. We might conclude from this spike that interest in international money and finance from IR scholars follows significant world events, but our data do not reveal any such spike following the Global Financial Crisis beginning in 2008. Of course, we cannot rule out the possibility that we would see more published research on international money and finance if we extended the dataset forward to 2014—and we are aware of several recent articles, such as Nelson and Katzenstein (2014) and Drezner (2014a)—but we are not the first to have identified a curious lack of published IR research on the Global Financial Crisis (see, e.g., Nexon 2011; Winecoff 2013).[1] Following the TRIP article database's coding criteria, between 2008 and 2012 only twenty-three of 1,403 IR articles—less than 2 percent—focused on monetary policy.

If international money and finance were unimportant policy issues, then the scarcity of published work on international finance would be un-problematic from the perspective of academic IR's policy relevance. How-ever, the TRIP survey of senior policymakers in the area of national security shows that policymakers find monetary issues to be some of the most press-ing foreign policy issues faced by the United States and the rest of the world. When respondents were asked what is the most important foreign policy issue facing the United States back in the fall of 2011, the Global Financial Crisis received the second most mentions after only the rising power of China. The data reveal that policymakers consider finance-related issues to be far more important than more widely discussed IPE topics such as trade negotiations, international cooperation, foreign aid, and regional integra-tion. Policymakers also consider finance-related issues to be more important than prominent security policy issues such as international terrorism and failed states.

The perceived importance of international monetary issues is not unique to policymakers or to the United States. Table 10.2 looks beyond the United States to the entire sample of *scholars* in the TRIP survey. It shows that IR scholars the world over think that money and finance are critically important policy issues facing their countries.

When asked what is the most important issue facing their country, re-spondents identified global financial regulation as the third most common response, followed closely by the global debt crisis. The decline of the dollar

**TABLE 10.2.** Foreign policy priorities

| Foreign policy issue[1] | Responses (%) |
|---|---|
| Global climate change | 24.18 |
| Rising power of China | 22.04 |
| *Global financial regulation* | *11.57* |
| Conflict in the Middle East | 10.90 |
| *Global debt crisis* | *10.87* |
| Global poverty | 9.83 |
| Global reliance on oil | 8.79 |
| *Decline of the US dollar as a reserve currency* | *8.59* |
| Failed states | 6.07 |
| Resource scarcity | 5.93 |

[1] Money and finance-related issues are in italics.

*Note:* This table shows the percentage of IR scholars in the 2011 TRIP faculty survey reporting that each option is one of the three most important foreign policy issues facing his or her country over the next ten years. The table lists the ten most commonly cited issues.

ranked eighth. Even though the community of IR scholars has devoted relatively little effort to the study of international monetary relations, IR scholars *themselves* believe that money and finance issues are two of the five most important policy issues facing their countries, and three of the top ten most important issues.

## Money and Finance as IR Topics

Our next step in making sense of the paucity of policy-relevant research on international money and finance in contemporary IR is to describe published research in more detail. We focus on five principles around which IR research is organized: epistemology, methodological orientation, materialist-ideational divide, levels of analysis, and paradigmatic orientation. We compare money and finance articles to those about other IPE topics, security topics, and all IR articles in the TRIP article database. The results appear in table 10.3.

We begin by looking at the articles' methodological and epistemological orientations. Published articles in monetary IPE are overwhelmingly

**TABLE 10.3.**   Five organizing principles in IR research

| | Issue area | | | |
|---|---|---|---|---|
| Epistemology | Monetary IPE | Other IPE | Security | All IR |
| Positivist | 92.8 | 88.3 | 82.5 | 80.9 |
| Methodology | | | | |
| Quantitative | 46.4 | 46.8 | 34.0 | 36.2 |
| Qualitative | 47.1 | 37.9 | 31.8 | 34.0 |
| Formal modeling | 13.8 | 10.2 | 15.5 | 11.4 |
| Ideas vs. interests | | | | |
| Material | 97.8 | 97.8 | 96.3 | 92.9 |
| Ideational | 18.8 | 29.5 | 37.4 | 42.8 |
| Level of analysis | | | | |
| Third | 69.6 | 73.2 | 70.8 | 61.6 |
| Second | 87.7 | 77.1 | 59.1 | 64.9 |
| First | 4.3 | 6.3 | 13.5 | 13.1 |
| None | 0.7 | 1.1 | 5.6 | 6.2 |
| Paradigm | | | | |
| Atheoretic/none | 2.9 | 5.8 | 15.9 | 12.6 |
| Constructivist | 5.1 | 5.3 | 5.4 | 7.5 |
| Liberal | 55.1 | 35.9 | 15.4 | 18.8 |
| Nonparadigmatic | 34.1 | 44.0 | 49.7 | 51.7 |
| Realist | 2.2 | 3.9 | 13.2 | 7.7 |

*Note:* Each entry contains the percentage of articles in the TRIP article database that are coded as falling into each category. "Other IPE" and "Security" were determined as in table 10.1. Columns do not sum to 100 percent within groups because many articles use multiple methods, use more than one level of analysis, paradigm, and so forth.

positivist, significantly more so than in IR as a field ($\chi^2(1) = 20.1, p < .001$). They are also significantly more likely to use both quantitative and qualitative methods. The common use of quantitative methodologies is representative of all IR research, but articles on money and finance are significantly more likely than other IPE articles to employ *qualitative* methods as well ($\chi^2(1) = 8.7, p = .003$). Policy analysis is rare for money and finance: only 2.2 percent of monetary IPE articles fall into this category, which is less than the 4.4 percent for IR as a whole, but this difference is not statistically significant ($\chi^2(1) = 2.14, p = .14$).

Turning to the substantive content of published articles, we learn that the overwhelming majority of published IR articles on money and finance involve materialist explanations for their phenomena of interest. This is wholly consistent with general patterns in nonmonetary IPE, security, and, indeed, IR as a whole. Where monetary issues stand out is in their reliance on ideational explanations: relative to both all IR articles and nonmonetary IPE articles, ideational explanations are significantly less common in published articles in the TRIP database on money and finance ($\chi^2(1) = 44.1$, $p < .001$ for all IR articles; $\chi^2(1) = 6.7, p = .01$ for nonmonetary IPE articles). Published IR research on money and finance in the TRIP database is also more likely to employ second-level (i.e., domestic level) analyses ($\chi^2(1) = 42.7, p < .001$), and less likely to employ first-level (i.e., individual level) analyses ($\chi^2(1) = 13.3, p < .001$), than IR research as a whole. Finally, most published research on money and finance either falls into the liberal paradigm or is nonparadigmatic in nature. This parallels the paradigmatic orientations of IPE research more generally, which is significantly more likely than security or IR in general to follow a liberal paradigm. But perhaps surprisingly, published articles on money and finance are much more likely than the rest of IPE research to fall into the liberal paradigm ($\chi^2(1) = 90.3, p < .001$).[2]

Broadly, the results in table 10.3 show that most IR research on money and finance in the TRIP database is positivist, strictly materialist, and focused on domestic-level explanations for international monetary phenomena. As such, it tends to be liberal or nonparadigmatic in orientation.

## The Policy Relevance of IR Research on Money and Finance

The final step in this analysis is to examine how frequently published articles in the TRIP database make policy prescriptions. Policy prescriptions are generally uncommon in published research in the TRIP database, appearing in about one in ten articles. But even relative to this low baseline, and even given the overall paucity of money and finance articles in the dataset, articles on money and finance are *still* less likely to make policy prescriptions than are other articles in the database: policy prescriptions are provided in just 5.1 percent of articles on monetary IPE ($\chi^2(1) = 3.2, p = .06$).

Part of the explanation for this may relate to the lack of overlap between those IR journals that tend to include policy recommendations and those that publish articles related to monetary policy. Among IR journals in the TRIP database, *International Security* is by far the most likely to contain policy prescriptions, but it includes precisely zero articles on international money and finance between 1980 and 2012.[3]

Paradigmatic debates are another factor that seems to reduce the policy relevance of IR research on money and finance. Only 6.4 percent of articles on international monetary relations that advance a theoretical paradigm present clear policy prescriptions. Although one must be cautious, given the small sample size, the fact that similar patterns are found when comparing all IR articles, instead of just those focused on monetary policy, makes us more confident that scholarship focused on paradigmatic debates tends to be less likely to provide clear policy prescriptions.[4] Thus, scholars on international monetary relations (and IR more generally) seem to face a trade-off between paradigmatic debate and policy relevance.[5] We return to this issue again in the conclusion when discussing strategies for shrinking the gap between IR theory and practice in international monetary affairs.

## CRITICISMS AND CAVEATS

For scholars and policymakers looking to strengthen ties between the monetary policy and academic IR worlds, the view from the TRIP article data is decidedly negative. IR research on money and finance is scarce, narrow, and even more unwilling to engage with policymakers' priorities than is most of the IR scholarship that appears in the best journals. We believe that these are appropriate conclusions, but before moving on, it is worth considering three important caveats to what we have learned from the TRIP article data.

First, it may be particularly difficult for projects such as the TRIP article survey to detect scholarship on money and finance and code it appropriately. This type of coding exercise is inherently difficult, and measurement error is inevitable. It is especially challenging to code articles about monetary policy because the international politics of money is so often bound up in broader discussions of power, foreign policy, and interdependence, and as a result, this issue area may be subject to larger-than-average measurement error. The example of Drezner (2009)—coded as being about economic interdependence, trade, foreign policy, and the balance of power even though its central concern is Chinese purchases of US Treasuries—neatly illustrates this point.[6] Altogether, despite the TRIP article database's generous coding rules for topic area, such examples suggest that the existing data may understate the prevalence of IR research on money and finance.

We probed the extent of this problem by using a simple keyword search, looking for several terms from the article titles in the TRIP article database.[7] This procedure produced seventy more articles than had appeared in the original coding, raising the percentage of articles on money from 2.6 percent to 3.5 percent. Using this alternative coding, the vast majority of articles on international monetary affairs continue to be positivist (94 percent) and materialist (98 percent); a similar share of articles use the liberal paradigm (48 percent) and focus on the second level of analysis (83 percent); the use of quantitative methods (49 percent) and qualitative methods (45 percent) changes little; and the same percentage of articles provides policy prescriptions (4.4 percent). So, even though we find that this (still imperfect) exercise can expand the list of articles on money and finance, it does not change our substantive conclusions appreciably.

The second reaction that many scholars of international money and finance will have to this survey of published IR research is that the dataset omits the journals in which research on monetary affairs is published. The most notable omission is probably the *Review of International Political Economy (RIPE)*.[8] IR research on money and finance also appears in subfield journals, such as *Review of International Organizations*; generalist international studies journals, such as *Review of International Studies*; journals focused on the subfield of comparative politics, such as *Comparative Political Studies*; and in political economy journals, such as *Economics and Politics*.

To shed light on the prominence of research on money in these other journals, we analyzed data collected by Catherine Weaver and Jason Sharman in collaboration with the TRIP project on all *RIPE* articles between 2000 and 2010. Of the 375 articles coded, fifty are coded as being focused on monetary policy. The percentage of articles about international money and finance (13 percent) is much higher than for the main TRIP article database, but this largely reflects the narrower scope of this journal. As a share of IPE articles, monetary policy is only modestly more prominent in *RIPE* than it is in the larger article database, where 8 percent of IPE articles examine this issue area. As in other venues, articles published in *RIPE* were more likely to focus on trade (22 percent) or development (21 percent) than on monetary policy. This implies that an exclusive focus on the TRIP database may understate the total amount of IR research on international finance, although incorporating additional journals is not likely to substantially alter the *relative* prominence of this subfield.

It is also useful to examine how research published in *RIPE* differs from that published in other journals. Compared to the articles in the TRIP database, articles in *RIPE* are much less likely to be positivist, are less reliant on quantitative methods, are less likely to focus on second-level arguments or to be based on a liberal paradigm, and are more likely to invoke ideational explanations. At the same time, although *RIPE* articles on money and finance are different in approach from articles in other journals, articles on money and finance remain more positivist, less focused on ideas, and more likely to use second-level analyses and liberal approaches than the IR field as a whole. Articles on money and finance in *RIPE* also present policy prescriptions less frequently (2 percent) than the journal as a whole (4.8 percent). These data give some credence to the view that IR research appearing in the TRIP article database is not broadly representative of scholarship in the field.

A final necessary caveat to the TRIP article data is that it omits books. There is undoubtedly a great deal of prominent research by IR scholars working on money and finance that appears in books. Taking into account the research that appears in books would make IR research on money and finance more visible in an absolute sense. However, taking book publications into account hardly alters the relative prominence of the field of international monetary relations. In the TRIP book database, which codes a stratified random sample of approximately one thousand books that were published by five major presses (Cambridge, Cornell, Oxford, Princeton, and Routledge) between 2000 and 2010, the share of books on money and finance is about the same as in the article database. Thirty of the 1,004 books in the sample—less than 3 percent—focus on money and finance.

Does excluding books affect our understanding of what IR research on money and finance looks like? The distinctively positivist, materialist, second-level analysis of money and finance that is characteristic of the TRIP articles can be found in a number of books (e.g., Frieden 1991; Simmons 1994; Pepinsky 2009; Walter 2013; Steinberg 2015), but there are also many prominent examples of realist and/or systemic analyses (e.g., Helleiner 1994; Kirshner 1995; Cohen 1998; Gray 2013) and books that focus on the role of ideas in monetary policy (e.g., McNamara 1999; Chwieroth 2010). The TRIP data confirm that books and articles tend to be homes to different styles of IR scholarship. Compared to IR articles in the TRIP database, IR books are substantially less likely to be positivist, less likely to use quantitative methods, less liberal in orientation, less focused on second-level analysis, more likely to incorporate the role of ideas, and more likely to offer policy prescriptions. IR books on monetary policy track most of these broad trends, although they remain more positivist and less focused on ideational explanations than books on other aspects of IR.[9]

These three caveats notwithstanding, we emphasize that, broadly speaking, the TRIP article data accord with our perceptions of the state of research on money in IR. IR scholarship on money and finance is less prominent than its perceived importance among scholars and policymakers would suggest. Moreover, even though academic IR is generally not receptive to offering policy prescriptions, IR scholarship on money and finance is a particular offender.

## POLICY RELEVANCE: INDIVIDUALS AND IDEAS

Our analysis thus far has shown that published IR research on money and finance is relatively rare and that policy recommendations rarely appear in such research. We now consider the policy relevance of IR research on money and finance more expansively, motivated by the experiences of those IR scholars whose research and policy work *have* put them at the center of the policymaking community.[10] The following is a more speculative discussion of how IR research on money and finance might become more relevant.

There are many, many examples of IR scholars whose academic expertise has translated into high-level policy positions in national governments or influential positions in international organizations. A hopelessly incomplete list includes Robert Cox, Michael Doyle, Peter Feaver, Henry Kissinger, Harold Koh, Stephen Krasner, Hans Morgenthau, Joseph Nye, Condoleeza Rice, John Ruggie, and Anne Marie Slaughter, among many others. Others have had primarily academic careers but nevertheless have played important roles as consultants and thought leaders. These include scholars such as Samuel Huntington, Robert Jervis, Kathryn Sikkink, John Mearsheimer, Thomas Schelling, Stephen Walt, and Kenneth Waltz, again among many others.

When we ask ourselves who would be the closest analogue to these IR scholars on topics related to money and finance, few names spring to mind. The closest example at present is probably Daniel Drezner, whose recent scholarship has focused on money and finance (Drezner 2009, 2014a, 2014b).[11] It is perhaps not a coincidence that Drezner, unlike many other leading scholars of international monetary relations, has also written on a wide range of other IPE topics.

Even if few IR scholars have played a direct role in making monetary policy, a few prominent scholars within this subfield have become increasingly prominent public intellectuals, and in recent years have participated in public debates over international monetary and financial policy. Jeffry Frieden, for example, has written two mass-market books on international finance that draw on the insights of IR scholarship (Frieden 2006; Chinn and Frieden 2011). He has also contributed articles on this topic to venues that are widely read by the policy community, including *Foreign Policy*, *New York Times*, and voxeu.org. Mark Blyth has published a mass-market book (Blyth 2013) as well as policy-oriented articles in venues with wide audiences (e.g., *Foreign Affairs* and *Fortune*). Prominent political scientists have also been engaging more directly with the policy community through conferences and other meetings: Eric Helleiner participated in a conference organized by the Center for Financial Stability that featured former heads of state and finance ministers; several IR scholars, including Jeffry Frieden, Lawrence Broz, and Benjamin Cohen, have presented their research at the Federal Reserve Bank of Dallas; and David Leblang has organized conferences featuring top monetary policymakers. Leblang has also engaged with policymakers by serving as a consultant to the International Monetary Fund (IMF) and the Directorate of Finance and Economics of the European Commission. Kevin Gallagher has provided another avenue through which IR scholars can engage with the policy community: he has coauthored reports on Chinese international financial policy with prominent government officials from that country (Gallagher et al. 2014).

These accomplishments of IR scholars are notable and impressive, and they confirm that IR scholars can indeed contribute to policymaking. But the overall impact of the IR and political science disciplines on international financial policy remains limited—both compared to the contributions of economists in this issue area and relative to IR scholars' contributions to other aspects of foreign policy (see, e.g., chapter 12 by Kreps and Weeks and chapter 6 by Schneider).

Most of the policymakers with academic backgrounds who hold prominent positions on international monetary relations are trained as economists. It is for this reason that a well-known strategy to document the rise of neoliberal economic ideas is simply to count the number of US-trained economists who serve as central bank governors or finance ministers (Chwieroth 2007; Nelson 2014). The United States is unique in this regard, with all Treasury secretaries in recent years having backgrounds as bankers or lawyers (including former movie producer and investment banker Steven Mnuchin). However, we can look to the position of undersecretary of the Treasury for International Affairs to see evidence of academics in high-ranking positions in international monetary affairs, and without exception those academics hold economics degrees. The Board of Governors of the Federal Reserve also draws heavily on academic economists, most of whom hold advanced degrees in economics and are currently or formerly employed in economics departments (see, e.g., Fligstein et al. 2014).

Beyond the role of key individuals, IR theory—especially as it pertains to grand strategy and national security—remains influential among policymakers. This impression is supported by the data in the TRIP policymaker survey (Avey and Desch 2014), which asked security and defense policymakers about their familiarity with several important theoretical insights drawn from IR scholarship (see chapter 12 by Kreps and Weeks).

The Avey and Desch policymaker survey demonstrates two things. First, it shows that a substantial number of policymakers included in their survey are familiar with prominent theoretical insights derived from IR scholarship. Second, it reveals something about IR scholarship on money and finance (and IPE more generally) by *what it does not ask*. None of the items covers IPE, much less any theoretical or conceptual insights drawn from IR scholarship on money and finance.[12]

This is not a criticism of the TRIP policymaker survey, for we ourselves cannot think of such a policy-relevant theoretical insight on money and finance from IR either. What we are looking for is something like mutual assured destruction or population-centered counterinsurgency, a framework that emerges from an IR literature and that fundamentally orients how policymakers conceptualize their own policy choices or makes recommendations for policy action. Note that we are *not* arguing that there is a dearth of important or theoretically sophisticated research in IR scholarship on money and finance (in addition to the many works cited previously, we might add

Cohen 1977 and Strange 1988). We are simply arguing that whatever the merits of this research, it has not generated a body of research that fundamentally shapes the way that policymakers think and act.

Again, academic economics has a much more influential role in shaping the policy agenda.[13] We can use the academic and policy debate over monetary integration in Europe to illustrate. This is a debate in which academic research has played a large role, dating at least to Mundell's (1961) "A Theory of Optimum Currency Areas." Politics, of course, also shaped decisions regarding European monetary integration (see, e.g., Eichengreen and Frieden 2000), but economic theories were utilized extensively to justify policy positions for or against the euro. By contrast, to our knowledge, theories of international monetary relations drawn from the IR discipline had little, if any, impact on policy debates over joining the euro. In addition, since the onset of the Global Financial Crisis reignited debates about the costs and benefits of European monetary integration, economists such as Paul Krugman, Barry Eichengreen, and Paul de Grauwe have dominated the public discussion. Our sense is that this is also true "behind closed doors," as policy choices are debated within governments and international institutions. Much the same was true in the late 1990s during the Asian Financial Crisis. Scholars of politics and IR were eager to join many others in lambasting the IMF for what they perceived to be inappropriate adjustment strategies, but the anti-IMF policy prescriptions that actually had traction among national governments came from economists such as Paul Krugman and Steve Hanke.

## CONCLUSION: STRENGTHENING THE LINKS BETWEEN IR SCHOLARS AND MONETARY POLICYMAKERS

Economic theory provides many useful insights about the conduct of international monetary and financial policy, but IR scholarship also has much to offer monetary policymakers. Policymakers have increasingly recognized that a country's financial well-being depends as much on a nation's politics as on its economics. For example, in his recent book on the Global Financial Crisis, Raghuram Rajan (2010, 19), an economist and the former central bank governor of India, points out that "good economics cannot be divorced from good politics." Similarly, former IMF chief economist Simon Johnson observes that "[f]inancial crises, at least in emerging markets, have political roots" (Johnson and Kwak 2010, 48). There is clearly a need for sophisticated understandings of how politics shapes international monetary and financial policy, a need recognized by many policymakers and economists. This is an area where IR scholars have a strong comparative advantage over economists and are capable of providing policy-relevant insights.

How, exactly, can IR scholars contribute to international monetary and financial policy? Displacing economists is neither likely nor desirable.

Economists will always be needed to help governments make informed decisions about international monetary policy, and pragmatic governments have little choice but to consult with economists on international monetary affairs; it could hardly be otherwise.

Note what this point does not imply: that economics is a settled discipline, that welfare analysis maps cleanly onto policy choices, that intertemporal maximization is self-evidently appropriate for representing mass behavior, or that economists are nonideological. We suspect that there are many disciplinary trends—the insistence upon individual microfoundations in macroeconomics, in particular—that have impeded good policymaking, and that ideology both divides economists and at least partially determines the course of research paradigms (see Terviö 2011; Klein et al. 2013). Yet such failings are not unique to economics: no discipline is free from ideology, disciplinary tunnel vision, or academic turf wars (see, e.g., Monroe 2005; Shapiro 2007; Rathbun 2011).

We do, however, insist that other disciplines can contribute to the making of economic policy and that an exclusive focus on one approach to policymaking is dangerous. IR scholars can play two important roles when it comes to the practice of international monetary and financial policy. First, political scientists have a unique body of knowledge that can help governments select international monetary policy. Second, political scientists, to an even greater degree than economists, can help with policy implementation—that is, ensure that governments are able to implement their preferred policies and achieve their objectives. We discuss each potential contribution in turn.

How might political scientists help governments choose their international financial policies? Most economics research in the fields of international money and finance asks what financial policies are best for aggregate welfare.[14] However, in the last half century, economics as a discipline has tended to downplay distributional questions (see Piketty 2014), and this is equally true of economic research on international money and finance. As in other areas of political science, however, political science scholarship on international money and finance naturally pays considerable attention to distributional issues because the distributional consequences of policy choices generate a distributional politics of policy choice (Frieden 1991; Pepinsky 2008; Broz and Werfel 2014; Steinberg 2015). Political scientists also have more sophisticated understanding of how political institutions mediate distributional interests (see, e.g., Bearce 2014). Greater familiarity with IR theories that focus on the distributional consequences of international financial policies has the potential to help governments make more informed choices about which policies they would like to adopt.

IR scholarship also can help policymakers understand some of the international political consequences of their policy choices. The analysis of power falls squarely within the ambit of political science and IR and is relevant because greater awareness of how international financial policies influence global power dynamics might shape governments' evaluations of a policy's desirability. European monetary integration provides a useful illustration.[15] Prior to forming a common currency with Germany, it is likely that many national governments on Europe's periphery underappreciated the degree to which Germany would dominate the eurozone and failed to realize how little weight would be placed on their national economic interests.[16] IR scholars of international monetary relations might have forecast such an outcome, and these insights would have been useful to governments contemplating this policy. China's accumulation of US Treasury securities provides another example of how greater awareness of the political consequences of financial policy might lead to better policy decisions. Since the 2008 crisis, the Chinese government has been frustrated that their prior accumulation of dollar-denominated assets, such as US Treasury bonds, has left them vulnerable to US monetary policies (Drezner 2009; see also Schweller and Pu 2011). China may well have taken a different course earlier had it been more aware of these risks, and it is IR scholars, not economists, who are best placed to characterize the problem of monetary interdependence in the context of a potential power transition.

Turning to the question of policy implementation, consider, for example, the problem of currency crises. Political science research has documented how certain types of institutional structures and political coalitions discourage governments from implementing policies that prevent currency crises and make it more difficult for them to respond adequately when those crises hit (Leblang and Satyanath 2008; Pepinsky 2009; Walter 2013; Steinberg et al. 2015). Awareness of these findings could help policymakers to understand some of the political obstacles that may limit their ability to prevent currency crises. IR scholars can facilitate this by serving as thought leaders, identifying opportunities for policy coalition building, or providing evidence-based support for particular policy choices. We are, of course, acutely aware that academic political science and IR are limited in their ability to affect policy. Nevertheless, scholars working in both international and comparative politics have long accepted that "ideas matter" (see, e.g., Hall 1989; Goldstein and Keohane 1993), and the same argument that economic ideas can have political power justifies a belief that ideas drawn from other disciplines can have political power.

In addition to helping government implement domestic policy, IR scholarship can also help states to achieve their preferred outcomes at the international level. Consider the example of the conflict between the United States and China over the "undervaluation" of the Chinese renminbi. Since 2003 the US government has been pressuring China to revalue its exchange rate, but the evidence suggests that American efforts have either had no impact on Chinese exchange rate policy (Liu and Pauwels 2012) or have reduced China's willingness to revalue (Ramírez 2013). IR scholars with a strong understanding of Chinese politics do not find this surprising. As Foot and Walter (2011, 119) point out, "public demands from the United States . . . make it more rather than less difficult for China's government to fall into line, lest it be seen by domestic nationalists as overly deferential to foreigners."

Narrowing the gap between IR theory and policy in the area of money and finance requires two changes: the policy community must have some "demand" for political science insights, and IR scholars must do more to "supply" policy-relevant insights. We have already given some reasons why policymakers could benefit from IR scholarship—in other words, why they should seek the advice of IR scholars. But IR scholars must do a better job, too. Compared to other IR topics, money and finance remain understudied in the discipline's most prominent outlets, and what research does exist pays little attention to developing policy prescriptions that can be of use to policymakers. Those journals, such as *International Security*, that do publish policy-relevant scholarship rarely include research on money and finance. Increasing the prominence and the policy relevance of IR research on money and finance should, in turn, help to convince policymakers of the utility of IR research for financial policymaking—a greater supply of IR research on money and finance might itself create a greater demand for IR research on money and finance.

## ENDNOTES

We gratefully acknowledge the helpful feedback we received on an earlier version of this paper from participants at the TRIP conferences in Washington, DC, and Williamsburg, VA, and also from Jonathan Kirshner, Dan Maliniak, Thomas Oatley, and Jon Pevehouse. We also thank Patrick Van Orden for his research assistance.

1. Oatley et al. (2013) and Pepinsky (2014) are two additional articles, but they fall outside the range of journals included in the TRIP article database.
2. We suspect that the differences between articles on monetary policy and those on other aspects of IPE are largely due to the idiosyncratic intellectual history of the field of monetary politics, such as the fact that some of the early leaders in this field were strong proponents of particular theoretical approaches. This accords with Cohen's (2008) analysis that the trajectory of the IPE field was heavily influenced by a small group of prominent scholars.
3. This observation gave us pause, given the prominence of one particular article (Drezner 2009) that we consider an ideal example of policy-relevant IR research on international money and finance. The TRIP article database codes this as a 1 for the variables *balanceofpower, economicinterdependence, foreignpolicy*, and *trade*. We return to this point in the next subsection.
4. Overall, 12 percent of nonparadigmatic articles and 7 percent of paradigmatic articles in the TRIP database provide policy prescriptions ($\chi^2(1) = 33.7, p < .001$).
5. We also investigated whether policy prescriptions are more frequent when articles on monetary relations use qualitative vs. quantitative methods or across different levels of analysis, but we found limited differences in both cases. This suggests that a reduced emphasis on quantification or statistical testing is unlikely to improve the usefulness of IR scholarship on money and finance.
6. This error has been corrected in the database.

7. We searched for the following strings: exchange rate, exchange-rate, capital account, capital control, monetary, money, debt, finance, currency, IMF, and EMU (the abbreviation of European Monetary Union).
8. The TRIP article database selected journals for inclusion based on their impact ranking in Garand and Giles (2003). *RIPE* fell just below the threshold in Garand and Giles's (2003) study: it was ranked seventy-sixth, just below *European Journal of International Relations* in seventy-fifth place.
9. These two differences are statistically significant. However, some of the differences between research on monetary policy and research on other aspects of IR that we observed in the article database are not present in the book database. For example, within the TRIP book database, books on monetary policy were not significantly more likely to use quantitative methods or provide liberal explanations than other IR books.
10. We focus here primarily on the United States, as it is the case with which we are most familiar.
11. Drezner's books cover issues ranging from economic sanctions (Drezner 1999) to trade policy (Drezner 2006), not to mention zombies (Drezner 2011)!
12. That the survey covered security and defense policymakers probably explains why money and finance topics were not included in the questionnaire.
13. Economists seem to play an even more prominent role in monetary policymaking than in other areas of economic policy, such as trade policy. This difference likely stems from the stronger reliance on technocrats to implement monetary policy, which is in turn driven in part by a prominent strain of economic thought that emphasizes the need to grant independence to monetary policymakers.
14. Posed this way, there is surprisingly strong consensus among economists on certain facets of financial policy. For example, most economists agree that the Federal Reserve's response to the 2008 crisis was beneficial in aggregate welfare terms. There is also strong agreement that the US should not adopt a gold standard–like fixed exchange rate system today. See IGM Forum (2012), (2014).
15. We are grateful to Thomas Oatley for suggesting this example.
16. German interests had an oversized influence on the creation and structure of the common currency (Moravcsik 1998), and Germany has been one of the greatest beneficiaries of the common currency (Vermeiren 2013).

# 11

# IS INTERNATIONAL RELATIONS RELEVANT FOR INTERNATIONAL MONETARY AND FINANCIAL POLICY?
*Reflections of an Economist*

Dimitri G. Demekas

## WHERE ECONOMISTS ROAM

Thomas B. Pepinsky and David A. Steinberg have written an honest, insightful, and meticulously researched paper about their discipline. They examine the influence of international relations (IR) research on the conduct of monetary and financial policies and, on the face of the evidence, conclude that it is negligible: economists dominate the field of monetary and financial policy.

This finding should not really come as a surprise. Consider the biggest monetary and financial policy issues of the last half century: tackling stagflation in the advanced economies in the 1970s, managing recurring balance of payments and debt crises in Latin America in the 1980s, debating the role of monetary policy in deflating asset price bubbles around the turn of the twenty-first century, dealing with the Global Financial Crisis in 2008. You would be hard-pressed to detect a trace of influence from IR literature in all this. The canon that shapes the thinking of monetary and financial policymakers today is written in graduate economics departments.

To be sure, most of the policy decisions are taken by politicians, not academic economists. Regardless of who is the ultimate decision-maker, however, the theory behind these decisions is provided almost exclusively by economics. This is what Alan Blinder, whose career spans both academia and policymaking (as a member of the Council of Economic Advisers and then vice chairman of the board of governors of the Federal Reserve System in the 1990s), meant when he wrote: "Having looked at monetary policy from both sides now, I can testify that central banking is as much art as science. Nonetheless, while practicing this dark art, I have always found the science quite useful" (Blinder 1997).

# IS THIS REALLY A PROBLEM?

This finding may not be particularly cheerful for IR scholars, but is it a problem? Is there evidence that monetary and financial policymaking is suboptimal or somehow deficient because it is dominated by economists?

Before going further, it is useful to define "monetary and financial policies." For the purposes of this discussion, monetary and financial policies are the strategies and actions of central banks, financial supervisory agencies, and governments to control money supply and safeguard the orderly functioning of the financial system, with the ultimate goal of ensuring monetary and financial stability. This also encompasses actions policymakers in individual countries take to coordinate policies across borders.

Economists have a strong historical claim to "own" monetary and financial policies. The modern theory of money originated in the work of Thomas Joplin and Walter Bagehot in the nineteenth century and evolved through contributions by economists such as Georg Knapp, John Maynard Keynes, Friedrich Hayek, Milton Friedman, and Harry Johnson, among others, in the twentieth century (O'Brien 2007). Finance theory, which underpins our understanding of how financial markets work, is a more recent creation: it was built with tools developed in probability and optimization theory and stochastic calculus and came of age in the 1960s and 1970s through the contributions of Harry Markowitz, Franco Modigliani, Merton Miller, William Sharpe, Eugene Fama, and Robert Merton (Robert Merton's [1997] Nobel lecture provides a brief but excellent genealogy). The award of several Nobel prizes in economics to finance theorists have placed finance theory squarely within the domain of economics. This long academic pedigree means that, by now, a broadly accepted intellectual framework in economics has emerged, within which monetary and financial policy successes and failures can be analyzed, lessons drawn, and adjustments made.

One possible criticism is that this intellectual framework may be too narrow. Monetary and financial policies have important political dimensions and distributional consequences. Doesn't this mean that such policies should be formulated under a variety of disciplinary perspectives in addition to economics?

The fact is, however, that the theoretical framework provided by economics has proved quite flexible. Economists have been able to extend in different directions to capture these aspects without much help from other disciplines. For example,

- Empirical research in the United States in the 1970s focusing on the political nature of economic fluctuations, an idea going back to Schumpeter, provided the foundation for the political business cycle theory, which explains movements in economic variables as a result of the electoral cycle (see the overview in Drazen 2000).

- This theory has been extended to explore the interaction of the political business cycle with independent central banks' monetary policy decisions (Drazen 2005).
- The impact of economic policies on income distribution has been a long-standing topic in economics (Bourguignon et al. 2003). The impact of monetary and financial policies, in particular, on income distribution has been, and continues to be, extensively studied (e.g., Bernanke 2015).

So the dominance of economists over monetary and financial policies at the expense of experts from IR (or other disciplines) does not seem to be a problem. Or does it?

# THE UTILITY OF BROADER PERSPECTIVES: THE ARCHITECTURE FOR INTERNATIONAL POLICY COOPERATION

There is (at least) one area where perspectives from political theory and international relations could enhance real-world policymaking: the architecture for international cooperation and coordination of monetary and financial policies. This encompasses established international institutions, formal cooperation mechanisms, and informal arrangements and has changed substantially over the last seventy years. A short historical detour may be useful here.

## International Monetary and Financial Policy Cooperation since World War II

Although the architecture for international cooperation in the area of monetary and financial policies has evolved continuously in line with changes in the world economy and the global political power balance, one could distinguish four different periods.

### *The Bretton Woods Period (1945–1973)*

Following World War II, the Western powers' priorities included financing reconstruction, restarting growth, and avoiding the trade wars of the 1930s. To achieve this, they put in place a new international monetary system, the Bretton Woods system, based on fixed exchange rates and anchored on the US dollar, whose value was in turn fixed to gold. To safeguard this system, they created an institutional framework—an architecture—with three pillars: the World Bank to finance reconstruction and development; the International Monetary Fund (IMF) to police the international monetary system and its members' fiscal, monetary, and exchange rate policies; and the

International Trade Organization, to promote orderly trade. Of these pillars, the first two were established immediately. Because of a lack of US support for the third, the informal General Agreement on Trade and Tariffs (GATT) was created instead, which was eventually transformed into a fully fledged entity, the World Trade Organization (WTO), in 1995.

The three pillars of this architecture are treaty-based international organizations, with independent staff, and explicit internal governance and decision-making arrangements. Membership is open to all countries. These organizations are governed by boards representing their member countries, albeit not on an equal footing.

## The World of Gs (1973–1997)

The collapse of the fixed exchange rate system in 1973 required some repurposing of the surveillance or "policing" function of the IMF but otherwise left the three pillars of the postwar architecture untouched. However, a new structure emerged and quickly gained prominence as the locus for monetary and exchange rate policy coordination among the major economies: the G-groups. These were meetings of finance ministers of the major economies to discuss their economic policies, especially their exchange rate policies. The G5 (US, UK, Germany, France, and Japan) started meeting in 1974; it was expanded to G7 (the original five plus Italy and Canada) in 1976; and to G8 in 1997, with the addition of Russia—although this was mostly a political move.

The Gs are informal political groupings, with closed, self-selecting membership, no legal or institutional status, no staff, and no formal decision-making rules. Their decisions are not binding for their members. The key advantages of this new structure are informality, flexibility, and discretion. The creation of the G-groups could be seen as a new kind of multilateralism, favoring informal, self-selected groups of the biggest players over the treaty-based, open, relatively transparent, and globally representative Bretton Woods institutions.

## The Expansion of Transnational Regulatory Networks (1997–2008)

Contrary to previous crises, which were largely macroeconomic in nature, the Southeast Asian crisis in 1997 originated in the financial sectors of these countries, partly reflecting deep-seated problems of governance and corruption. The international community reacted in a number of ways, including adjustments to the architecture for economic policy cooperation. The most noteworthy of these was the emergence of transnational regulatory networks (TRNs).

TRNs are groupings of national financial regulatory agencies that appeared in the 1970s as the financial industry became more globalized, in order to promote a level regulatory playing field for large global firms. The Basel

Committee on Banking Supervision was created in 1974 and included central banks or bank regulators from twelve countries (the G7 plus Luxembourg, Switzerland, Belgium, the Netherlands, and Sweden). It was followed by the International Organization of Securities Commissions in 1983, the International Association of Insurance Supervisors in 1994, and others. The TRNs' role in the global architecture became central after 1997, when the G7 asked them to codify best practice standards for financial supervision in their respective areas, and used the IMF and the World Bank to promote compliance with these standards globally, regardless of whether or not a particular country had a say in their formulation.

TRNs share some similarities with the G-groups: they are self-selecting, informal, without clear decision-making rules, and their decisions, including the standards they promulgate, are not binding. Unlike the G-groups, which are constituted by representatives of governments that are, in principle, subject to some democratic accountability at home, TRNs are made up of representatives of independent regulatory agencies and central banks and are not subject to any clear accountability mechanisms.

## Today's World (2008–Present)

The most recent global financial crisis brought further adaptations in the architecture for policy cooperation. First, it triggered big reforms in IMF governance (increasing the representation of emerging market and developing countries). Second, it pushed a new G-group, the G20, to center stage (the G20 includes the G7 plus Australia, Mexico, Russia, China, South Africa, Turkey, Brazil, Argentina, Korea, Indonesia, Saudi Arabia, India, and the European Union), replacing the G7 as the preeminent economic forum. Third, a new "super-TRN" emerged to coordinate the work of all the others and report to the G20: the Financial Stability Board (FSB).

The FSB is a peculiar organization. Its membership is a mixed bag, including representatives from finance ministries, central banks, and financial regulatory agencies from twenty-five constituencies (all G20 plus Hong Kong, Spain, the Netherlands, Switzerland, and Singapore), as well as four international organizations (Bank for International Settlements, IMF, Organization for Economic Cooperation and Development, and World Bank) and six TRNs. Although it has its own charter and legal personality, it is not a treaty-based international organization and has no transparent decision-making rules. It has a small secretariat, but its activities are largely supported by staff of the constituent agencies, whose duty of loyalty is to their agency. The FSB has been tasked by the G20 to coordinate financial sector reforms globally, including in nonmember countries, although its decisions are not legally binding even on its own members: instead, it was designed to spur a voluntary "race to the top" in financial regulation through monitoring, greater transparency, and "naming and shaming" the laggards. The FSB was described by then US Treasury Secretary Tim Geithner (2009) as the "fourth pillar" of the postwar global architecture.

# The Silence of Economists

This brief detour into the evolution of the architecture for international economic and financial policy cooperation suggests a number of patterns, each of which could provide a rich seam for research. Here, I highlight just a few.

First, the architecture has evolved from crisis to crisis, and successive changes tended to add to, rather than replace, existing arrangements. Some would argue that it is inevitable: like all institutional constructs, the architecture for global policy cooperation is subject to historical path dependence, where the original design constrains future evolution. Because we are always condemned to fighting the last war, the best we can do is to learn the lessons quickly and plug the holes we discover. But is this process of gradual, backward-looking adaptation really the best we can do?

Second, the architecture for policy cooperation is characterized by a diversity of arrangements, spanning broad, treaty-based international organizations; small, informal intergovernmental groupings; and TRNs. One way to think about this diversity is in terms of the tradeoff between efficiency and legitimacy. Forms of cooperation that emphasize limited, self-selecting membership, informality, and discretion facilitate rapid decision-making but lack legitimacy. Broad-based, inclusive, transparent, and representative institutions have legitimacy but are more cumbersome. Is this a productive way to analyze the diversity of organizational arrangements? If so, is there an optimal point along this continuum?

Another way to think about the observed variation of organizational arrangements is in terms of the policy areas to which they correspond. There seems to be a revealed preference for informal arrangements, such as TRNs and the FSB, promoting best practice standards and encouraging voluntary adherence—in other words, producing "soft law"—for global cooperation in financial regulation. In contrast, in the areas of trade and exchange rate policies, there are treaty-based institutions with well-defined rules and the authority to impose sanctions—in other words, "hard law." Does this reflect a fundamental difference in the nature of these policies, or are other factors at play?

Given the importance of getting international economic and financial policy cooperation right, these questions are crucial. It is therefore surprising how little attention they have attracted among economists.

To be sure, the silence of economists is not complete; the rise of the G20 and the establishment of the FSB have attracted some attention. However, most contributions by my colleagues take the current state of the architecture as given and examine its implications for monetary and financial policy coordination (see, e.g., Griffith-Jones et al. 2010; Aizenman et al. 2010; Eichengreen 2013); there is no attempt to explain the provenance of the particular institutional arrangements or explore alternatives. One notable exception is Raman et al. (2016), who use an analytical framework based on game theory to explain the choice of different policy coordination mechanisms.

The reluctance among economists to engage with these questions is somewhat puzzling. After all, economists have studied the optimum institutional design for policy effectiveness in other areas—for example, the importance of central bank independence for monetary policy, or the role of fiscal councils for budgetary policy. However, at the international level, where the policy goal—international policy cooperation—depends crucially on the institutional arrangements, they have been (mostly) silent.

In contrast, these questions have attracted considerable attention among political scientists and IR theorists, such as Helleiner (1994), Germain (2001), Singer (2007), Beeson and Bell (2009), Cooper and Bradford (2010), Hampson and Heinbecker (2011), to name just a few. Many of these contributions, however, seem preoccupied with abstruse theoretical controversies that are distant from policymakers' concerns: what Pepinsky and Steinberg (this volume) call "meta-theoretical and paradigmatic debates" (p130). It is hard to imagine ministers or senior officials at a G20 meeting debating whether the G20 should be seen as an instrument of "collectivist cooperation" or "hegemonic incorporation," a question that has apparently attracted quite a lot of attention among IR theorists. Indeed, legal scholars have made more policy-relevant contributions than IR theorists: for example, Kelly and Karmel (2009), who reviewed the evolution of "soft law" in securities regulation; Verdier (2013), who explored several hypotheses that could explain the cooperation arrangements that have emerged over time; and Gadinis (2015), who distinguished between the role of private, regulator, and government networks in creating and promoting global financial standards.

So, here is one important aspect of monetary and financial policy that economists have so far been unable or unwilling to explore and where insights from non-economists, including IR scholars, could be useful.

How we should go about bridging this gap lies beyond the scope of this chapter. But it is clear that it should be bridged from both sides. Economists should accept the limitations of their discipline in addressing these questions and be open to approaches that are conceptually and methodologically different from the established paradigm of neoclassical economics. Political scientists and IR theorists, on the other hand, should focus on the policymakers' real-world priorities and, in Pepinsky and Steinberg's words, do a better job in supplying policy-relevant and operationally actionable insights.

## ENDNOTE

The views expressed here are those of the author and not necessarily of the Bank of England or the International Monetary Fund.

# 12

# LOST IN TRANSLATION
## Academics, Policymakers, and Research about Interstate Conflict

Sarah Kreps and Jessica Weeks

P olicymakers have long lamented that the academy does not produce more policy-relevant scholarship. Paul Nitze, a high-level policymaker who later became president of Johns Hopkins University's School of Advanced and International Studies, once categorically derided the academy's contributions by saying that "most of what has been written and taught under the heading of 'political science' by Americans since World War II . . . has been of limited value, if not counterproductive as a guide to the conduct of actual policy" (quoted in Walt 2005, 24). In his analysis of the academic-policymaker gap, Walt quotes another policymaker who criticized scholarship as being "locked within the circle of esoteric scholarly discussion" (Walt 2005, 24). Perhaps most emblematic of academic shortcomings was that all major theories failed to predict the end of the Cold War (Gaddis 1992), but the criticism that academic theories are inaccessible and of limited value has continued unabated (Kristof 2014).

This chapter takes stock of those criticisms and poses several questions about the gap between policymakers and academics in understanding the causes of interstate war. Which theories, if any, do policymakers know about? Which theories do policymakers find most useful and influential? To what extent do the theories that are seen as useful or influential reflect prevailing academic views? For international relations (IR) scholars who want their research to affect real-world outcomes, knowing how policymakers currently learn about, and regard, academic scholarship is crucial. Only by understanding how ideas from the ivory tower currently make their way into the policy world can scholars learn to maximize the likelihood that policymakers will incorporate academic research into their policy work in the future. To that end, we focus on understanding how policymakers' views of important IR theories compare to the view from academia.[1]

One of the central challenges in answering questions of this type is how to gather the appropriate data. How do we know what "policymakers" and "academics" think about IR theories? For information on policymakers, we draw on a unique survey of senior members of the United States national security establishment, the 2011 Teaching and Research in International Politics (TRIP) survey (Avey and Desch 2013a). The survey allows us to examine policymakers' knowledge of and attitudes about four core theories related to interstate conflict. To gather evidence about academics' exposure to and attitudes about these theories, we combine data such as citation counts, syllabi, and TRIP faculty surveys with our qualitative assessment of the view from academia. By comparing policymaker and academic perspectives on the same theories, we can shed light on our core question of how scholars can increase practitioners' exposure to academic findings.

We draw several conclusions from our analysis. First, we find that there are significant gaps between academic evaluations, at least of these four theories, and policymakers' exposure and perceptions. Second, we find that to the extent that policymakers are aware of theories, they profess them to be useful for their work. Third, and relatedly, we find that the extent to which policymakers are attuned to scholarship and find it useful varies greatly by topic.

In short, Nitze's categorical statement hides some nuance. Our analysis suggests that the largest academic-policymaker divide does not come from policymakers finding the theories they know about to be of little value. Rather, it comes from practitioners (a) not being exposed to theories that have received extensive attention in the academic literature, and (b) valuing theories that academics do not value. For example, whereas the vast majority of policymakers are familiar with the "clash of civilizations" (CoC) and many find it useful, academics appear to have largely discredited the argument and do not assign it on their syllabi. In 2004, moreover, when TRIP researchers asked IR scholars what they considered the least productive controversies or research programs in recent years, 29 percent of respondents chose CoC. Only one option received a higher percentage of responses.

Many of the empirical chapters in this volume explore reasons for the relative influence of IR scholarship on policy and practitioners. In this chapter we address a prior problem, accurately assessing the extent to which academic ideas on interstate war have permeated policy circles. We are, in short, more concerned with measuring the gap than explaining it. At the same time, our analysis provides at least indirect support for the supply-side argument, 3a, described in chapter 1; academic ideas that are presented in formats that are not easily consumable will not resonate with or influence policymakers. In particular, we find that policymakers are far more likely to report that they read about IR concepts and theories in opinion pieces or policy journals than in more traditional academic outlets. This exposure to academic theories matters; across all four topics we discuss, when policymakers are more familiar with an academic theory—that is, they have been exposed to it via an op-ed or policy article—they are more likely to report that they find the scholarly argument useful to their work.

The rest of the chapter proceeds as follows. First, we outline our methodological approach, focusing on how we evaluated policymaker views and compared them with academic views. Second, we turn to the evidence, discussing each of the four theoretical arguments/approaches for which we were able to gather systematic data. The last section concludes with implications and suggestions for follow-on research.

## RESEARCH APPROACH

Although scholars have long grappled with the notion of an academic-policy gap, they more recently have sought to go beyond early anecdotal evidence to capture the precise nature of the problem. In a disheartening finding, a 2011 TRIP survey showed that American IR scholars had little engagement with the policy community (Maliniak et al. 2012), and Avey and Desch (2014) similarly found disenchantment among policymakers with academic methods. Some observers have sought to counter this pessimistic picture by citing instances in which the policy world has demanded IR research, such as through the Department of Defense's Minerva Initiative, which funds policy-relevant security research (Weaver 2014), or by showing that academics have become more effective in making their work accessible to policymakers (Horowitz 2015). Indeed, we need not look any further than policymakers' assertions that democracies do not attack each other to see evidence that the democratic peace (DP) theory has infused the policy process (Owen 1994).

Each useful in its own right, these approaches generally focus on either the "supply" or "demand" side but not the strategic interaction between the two. Those that look at the point where supply meets demand—indeed, where policymakers have been in conversation with academic research—are often anecdotal. To gain purchase on the question of an academic-policy divide especially when it comes to attitudes about interstate war, we therefore sought to evaluate the question systematically by evaluating the degree to which policymakers' views mesh with those among IR scholars.

For evidence on policymakers' views, we turn to the 2011 TRIP survey, a unique and innovative survey that queried senior members of the US national security establishment. As Avey and Desch (2014, 229) describe in more detail, the respondents were members of the following departments or agencies: Defense, Homeland Security, State, Central Intelligence Agency, National Security Council, Office of the Director of National Intelligence, and Arms Control and Disarmament Agency. Respondents were asked about four main areas related to interstate relations: Huntington's CoC, Waltzian realism, democratic peace theory, and Bruce Bueno de Mesquita's expected utility approach. In particular, the survey prompted individuals about their familiarity with the particular argument, how they learned about it, and the degree to which they find it useful and influential. Respondents also answered questions about their educational background—whether they studied economics, international affairs, area studies, law, or public policy as their highest degree, for example—and level of educational attainment.

Our analysis of these data, which are to our knowledge the only data of their kind, comes with the caveat that the surveys were not conducted with the express goal of comparing policymakers' views to those of academics, so in some cases there is not a perfect correspondence between the question wording and the underlying concept we would like to measure. We therefore point out where and how specific question wordings could affect the conclusions that we draw.

Having evaluated policymakers' familiarity with IR theories, as well as how they learned about those theories and how they evaluated them, the next step establishes how scholars think about these same themes of interstate warfare. In the absence of such comparable survey questions, we rely on three forms of evidence to establish how academics view the four main arguments we consider.

First, we offer a qualitative assessment of trends in IR. We rely on our reading of the literature, conversations with colleagues, and identification of major scholarly contributions that had either built on or critiqued the particular theories in question. Given that this is a necessarily subjective exercise, however, this cannot be the sole source of evidence.

Second, we examine syllabi from the institutions listed as the top twenty for IR in the 2014 TRIP survey. We supplement our own syllabus data with data from an independent research effort by Jeff Colgan at Brown University, who in 2014 collected data on assigned readings for the core IR theory course for PhD students from forty-two universities (Colgan 2016).

Third, we examine bibliographic data from Google Scholar and the Social Sciences Citation Index (SSCI). Google Scholar accesses what it calculates is a scholarly source and assesses the number of times that source has been cited, although Google has not disclosed its ranking algorithm. Even though both of these citation indices are imperfect (e.g., generating many non–peer-reviewed hits, such as conference papers, and ranking more on title than keyword and therefore perhaps missing research using clever but nondescriptive titles), we consider this a useful metric for comparing relative scholarly influence.[2] For each section that follows, we explain in greater detail which queries we conducted and how we interpret them.

We also use the SSCI as an alternative measure. As with Google Scholar, it includes outlets that are not peer reviewed, but it limits those outlets to journals such as *Foreign Affairs* and *Washington Quarterly*, which solicit articles; it does not include conference papers. Perhaps most important, the SSCI can filter the citations according to discipline, restricting its count to, for example, just political science and IR journals. Unfortunately, the SSCI excludes books before 2005. Moreover, it only considers research where the topic is included in the title, abstract, or keywords, which means that it does not include research that mentions in passing a topic such as the CoC.

Taken together, this brief comparison of citation sources suggests that for the same article, the SSCI will tend to reflect lower citation counts than Google Scholar, which includes any paper or book from any discipline. By including both measures, we can have more confidence in the impact of research relative to both policymakers and to the other topics in IR. To do so, we assess the frequency with which particular articles, authors, or ideas were cited, focusing on the twenty-five years leading up to the 2011 policymaker survey (1986–2011) when possible.[3]

# ANALYSIS OF FINDINGS

A comparison of policymaker and academic views points to a number of discrepancies and similarities in the approaches each group finds useful. As we discuss in the following sections, the disjunctures do not always result from academics believing an argument is more useful than policymakers do; in fact, in the case of Huntington's CoC hypothesis, the reverse is true. Moreover, the alleged policymaker-academic divide does not hold uniformly; rather, both camps value some of the other three approaches similarly, conditional on exposure and varying by topic. We analyze the divergences and convergences in the following section.

## The Clash of Civilizations

We begin by focusing on differences between policymakers and academics when it comes to the CoC.

### Policymakers

Table 12.1 summarizes our analysis of policymaker perceptions of four academic theories. It shows awareness of and confidence in these theories both among policymakers in general and then in the subset of those who are familiar with the theories. As we detail below, policymakers are most aware of the CoC but are least confident in its accuracy and inclination for it to influence their work in government.

Table 12.1 indicates that, of the IR topics related to interstate war, policymakers proclaim the most familiarity with the CoC hypothesis. The top left of the table summarizes policy respondents' familiarity with the CoC argument according to the Avey and Desch data. A startling 90 percent of policymakers report that they are familiar with the thesis. The majority of respondents who knew about the theory (69 percent) indicate that they encountered the argument in *Foreign Affairs*, compared to those who heard about it from colleagues (51 percent).

The survey then asked those who said they were familiar with the thesis whether they believed that "civilizations, not states, are likely to be the most important actors in the future of world politics." The responses elicited an apparent paradox. Only 32 percent of all policymakers were somewhat or very confident in the accuracy of the thesis, although 59 percent of all policymakers expressed the view that the hypothesis is somewhat or very useful. (Among those who did proclaim familiarity with the thesis, 69 percent said it was somewhat or very useful.) Yet only 27 percent of policymakers overall

**TABLE 12.1.** Policymaker perceptions of four IR theories

| | Clash of civilizations | | Waltzian realism | | Democratic peace theory | | Expected utility theory | |
|---|---|---|---|---|---|---|---|---|
| Familiar with...? | 90% | | 69% | | 56% | | 21% | |
| | If familiar | All | If familiar | All | If familiar | All | If familiar | All |
| Read academic source? | 39% | 34% | 61% | 42% | 42% | 23% | 33% | 7% |
| Read nonacademic source? | 69% | 60% | 59% | 41% | 76% | 42% | 69% | 14% |
| Learned about from colleague? | 51% | 44% | 54% | 37% | 44% | 24% | 51% | 10% |
| Somewhat or very confident in accuracy? | 37% | 32% | 52% | 35% | 63% | 35% | 56% | 11% |
| Somewhat or very useful for policymakers? | 69% | 59% | 70% | 47% | 65% | 36% | 60% | 12% |
| Influence your own work for government? | 32% | 27% | 54% | 36% | 47% | 26% | 45% | 9% |
| | $N \approx 202$ | $N \approx 234$ | $N \approx 152$ | $N \approx 222$ | $N \approx 123$ | $N \approx 224$ | $N \approx 45$ | $N \approx 220$ |

indicated that the thesis influences their work in the government (compared to 32 percent who knew about the thesis).

Perhaps one reason for the paradox that policymakers are aware of the CoC and find it useful but they do not agree that it is influential in their work may be the nature of respondents, who are drawn from the departments of Defense, Homeland Security, State, Central Intelligence, and National Intelligence. At the time the survey was taken (2011), the United States was in the midst of a withdrawal from Iraq, a surge in Afghanistan, a UN-sanctioned war in Libya, and a counterterrorism campaign in Pakistan. Against this backdrop, it is not clear that insights about civilizational differences are particularly salient. Perhaps those insights might have seemed more salient in a context such as the Balkans, where historical enmities between and among groups may have been seen as the basis for both conflict and conflict resolution. Indeed, Huntington (1993, 31) himself points to events in the Balkans as an illustrative, motivating case: "As the events in Yugoslavia show, it is not only a line of difference, it is also at times a line of bloody conflict."

## Academics

That policymakers are aware of the thesis and that a third of them find it convincing is surprising because CoC is regarded very differently among academics. Not only is it considered empirically and conceptually wrong, it has also—perhaps as a result—not had much sway in the scholarly discourse or even in the classroom. Indeed, scholars have generally cast a skeptical eye on the CoC. In a representative treatment, Russett, Oneal, and Cox (2000, 583) show that realist and liberal factors—such as contiguity, alliances, and regime type—"provide a much better account of interstate conflict" than "pairs of states split across civilizational boundaries." Henderson and Tucker (2001, 317) disaggregate by time period and find that in the period where Huntington's thesis should be most operative, 1989–92, civilizational differences had no effect on interstate conflict onset. Chiozza (2002, 711) initially appears to be more complimentary, referring to the "intellectual shock waves" that Huntington's work sent "through the academic and policy communities." He notes that previous studies only analyze conflict until 1992; however, the results may have been confounded by the Cold War, during which intercivilizational conflicts were less likely, and the studies did not consider whether civilizational status intensifies conflicts even if this status does not actually cause them. By extending the analysis five additional years and testing for the possibility that civilizational dynamics indirectly affect geographical and regime type factors that influence conflict onset, Chiozza (2002, 713) concludes that civilizational divides do not generate a "conflict syndrome."

These empirical studies are consistent with other measures that suggest skepticism within academe about the CoC thesis. Evaluating IR field syllabi for the top-twenty PhD-granting departments suggests that the topic has had little enduring impact pedagogically. The syllabus of only one seminar (Georgetown) among the fourteen we collected assigns Huntington's work on civilizations.[4] Colgan (2016) similarly finds that among the forty-two universities for which he collected syllabi, only two taught anything with the phrase "clash of civilizations" in the title.

Perhaps unsurprisingly, an analysis of citations of the CoC reveals that scholars of political science in general and IR in particular have largely disengaged from the CoC argument. Using SSCI to search for "clash of civilizations" as a topic from 1993 to 2011 within the fields of political science and IR, we found that Huntington's work in 1993 was the seminal piece, which caused an initial surge of interest in the late 1990s, with twelve articles dealing with the CoC in 1997, fourteen in 1998, and only five in 1999. Overall, taking into account research about the CoC—where the term appeared in the title, abstract, or keywords—just eighty-seven published pieces engaged the topic in IR or political science more generally. SSCI further reports that 383 pieces cited the 1993 article through 2011. (No data are available for the 1996 book.)[5]

Google Scholar citations are more generous toward the CoC, reporting that 19,800 pieces referencing the term "clash of civilizations" were published between 1993, when the *Foreign Affairs* piece was published, and 2011. Even though this may sound impressive, a qualitative search of these citations suggests that much of this research is not about interstate conflict but rather questions of religion (Fox and Sandler 2004), culture (Axelrod 1997), peacekeeping (Autesserre 2010), and secessionist conflict (Saideman 1997). Moreover, some of the most influential pieces citing the article are direct critiques (e.g., Henderson and Tucker 2001).

Taken together, our analysis points to an academic-policy gap on the CoC argument but one in which policymakers regard the argument more favorably than political scientists, who have generally been skeptical on both theoretical and empirical grounds. To the extent that bridging the gap is valuable, alerting policymakers to some of the ways the CoC has been discredited could be desirable.

## Realist Theory

We now compare policymaker and academic views on a second body of theory, structural realism.

### *Policymakers*

On the 2011 TRIP survey a large majority (69 percent) of policymakers reported that they are "familiar with Kenneth Waltz's 'realist thesis' of state behavior."[6] Compared with those who are familiar with the CoC, those familiar with structural realism were more likely to have learned about it from academic sources. More than half (61 percent) report that they have read either *Theory of International Politics* or a related academic article. Fifty-nine percent report that they read about structural theories from a nonacademic source such as an op-ed or article in the *National Interest*. More than half of respondents who were familiar with the theory (54 percent) learned about it secondhand from colleagues.

Of those familiar with Waltzian realism, more than half (52 percent) were very or somewhat confident that it is an accurate reflection of what motivates state behavior; only 35 percent of respondents overall expressed such confidence. However, whereas policymakers indicated that they had confidence in the CoC but that it did not affect their work, the dynamic was reversed for realism; respondents were more skeptical about realism's utility, but most of those who were aware of it (70 percent) found it to be useful for their work. Of those who were aware of realism, 54 percent went as far as to say that it influences how they do their work, which is more of an endorsement of both utility and influence than for Huntington's thesis. Nonetheless, when one takes policymakers' knowledge into account, the figure for *overall* confidence in the accuracy of Waltzian realism is more similar to that for the CoC.

As with the analysis of the CoC, responses about familiarity with realism introduced some intriguing puzzles. In particular, respondents seem to suggest that the arguments are neither accurate nor influential but that they are nonetheless useful. One reason for this finding may have to do with policymakers' position within a country that has had unipolar status in the post–Cold War period. American policymakers have cited their "indispensable nation" status since the 1990s (Friedman 2012), suggesting why policymakers may see balance-of-power factors as a useful way to think about foreign policy decisions.

## Academics

Policymakers may find the distribution of power to be a useful thesis, but academic views appear to be more mixed. Waltzian realism remains well cited in the literature, with the book generating 10,900 citations in Google Scholar in the twenty-five years before the TRIP survey. Using SSCI to examine the influence of the *Theory of International Politics* is impossible because the index is unable to access the impact of books from 1979. Searching on "structural realism" as a "topic" generates forty-nine articles or books (just IR or political science) between 1986 and 2011, and 135 for the topic "neorealism." Our inability to search for citations of the book means we may be underestimating the true level of scholarly engagement with this text.

Further evidence of neorealism's impact is its presence on IR graduate syllabi. Our own syllabus collection of the top TRIP institutions indicated that Waltzian realism appeared on *every* syllabus in our sample; instructors often used it as the point of departure for the remainder of the course, giving it pride of place as a focal point for the subsequent theoretical discussions.[7] Indeed, Waltzian realism became the fulcrum—or rather usually the foil—for many theories in the 1980s and 1990s. For example, two major theoretical contributions, one from each of those two decades (Keohane 1986; D. Baldwin 1993), engaged Waltzian realism by offering a series of revisions or rebuttals. They each offer criticisms, but the fact that they felt the need to engage Waltzian realism is a testimony to its influence.

Despite having a remarkable presence, at least pedagogically, and spending two decades as the point of departure for almost any theoretical contribution, Kenneth Waltz (2000, 5) acknowledges the onslaught of criticism that structural realism came under in the post–Cold War period. "[S]ome students of international politics believe that realism is obsolete. They argue that, although realism's concepts of anarchy, self-help, and power balancing may have been appropriate to a bygone era, they have been displaced by changed conditions and eclipsed by better ideas."

Indeed, throughout the 1990s scholars questioned whether realism was able to explain the end of the Cold War (Lebow 1994) because bipolarity was thought to be a stable distribution of power. Moreover, the so-called "end of history" had given the illusion that regime type mattered more than structural realism would acknowledge, with leaders like President Clinton embarking on major foreign policy shifts of "engagement and enlargement" intended to expand the North Atlantic Treaty Organization (NATO) and democratic governments around the world in the belief that democracies were more peaceful and law-abiding than nondemocracies (Slaughter 1992). The editors at the *Review of International Studies (RIS)* (2003, 401–2) added that neorealism was unable to explain the rise of nonstate actors and attention to ethics and human rights in the post–Cold War world. Wagner joined the chorus of criticisms, citing realist theories (2007, 12–13) as "collections of bad answers to important questions." Nonetheless, the same *RIS* editorial also declared that "realism remains the dominant approach in America to international relations."

Despite Waltz's defense of structural realism, and a series of rebuttals to the *RIS* critique (Glaser 2003; Desch 2003), few major theoretical contributions of the last two decades have engaged neorealist principles. One exception is the unipolarity literature, which emerged in the late 1990s as a way of showing, first, unipolar status and the stability of a unipolar world (Wohlforth 1999). The next phase of the research provided an interlude, with questions about whether unipolarity might produce fewer international checks and more recklessness than bipolarity and whether, in this case, states were beginning to balance against the United States as a consequence of unilateral actions such as the Iraq War (e.g., Ikenberry 2003; Kreps 2011). The most recent phase of the research has debated the distribution of power in the context of China's rise: whether the United States retains its preponderance of power (Brooks and Wohlforth 2008; Monteiro 2014) or whether China is a contender and, if so, what the transition of power might look like (Buzan and Cox 2013).

To the extent that realism has enduring traction in IR, it is not structuralism but variants of realism that incorporate domestic political variables. First, neoclassical realism has attracted attention in part because it can explain foreign policy decisions in ways that Waltz conceded his theory could not (Rose 1998). As Schweller puts it (1998, 3), "system structure neither determines specific outcomes nor dictates actions, and so it cannot tell us why a particular event occurred at a particular time." As such, he concludes that balance-of-power theory is "not very useful." Structural realism cannot explain puzzles about why states underbalance, for example. The distribution of power might create constraints, but how states deal with those constraints—and whether they balance—is a function of whether states are satisfied states, in which case they "join the status quo coalition, even when it is the stronger side," or dissatisfied, in which case they tend to be driven by profit rather than security, triggering an impulse to bandwagon with a rising power (Schweller 1998, 22).

Second, some scholars are returning to richer, less parsimonious versions of realism in the spirit of classical realists like E. H. Carr, Hans Morgenthau, and Robert Gilpin. Most germane to the criticisms of structural realism, classical realism incorporates "the role of things like ideas, norms, and legitimacy; politics that structural realism rejects, and concepts that it dismisses at most as solely instrumental of power" (Kirshner 2012, 56). As Kirshner points out, whereas structural realists diminish the role of domestic-level factors such as regime type, classical realists like Thucydides privileged such factors as type of government and bureaucratic politics. Gilpin, for his part, emphasized prestige.

In sum, the data suggest some congruence between the influence of Waltzian realism in the academy and among policymakers. Policymakers profess to be aware of structural realist theory, which is consistent with the prominent place it has held in the academy. That they find it useful, however, is somewhat at odds with the skepticism that structural arguments have met in the post–Cold War environment relative to arguments that accommodate domestic-level factors.

# The Democratic Peace

The third set of theories we investigate is democratic peace theory, or the proposition that democracies are particularly unlikely to fight wars against each other.

## *Policymakers*

We begin with policymakers. The Avey and Desch survey first asked whether policymakers were "familiar with the democratic peace thesis." The wording of the question asks about a somewhat technical term and does not define the term, meaning that the survey may underestimate familiarity with DP theory, the idea that democracies tend not to fight each other (although it is possible that some individuals who were not familiar with the precise term inferred its meaning). About 56 percent of respondents said they were familiar with the DP thesis. Of these, 42 percent said they learned about it from an academic source, 76 percent from a nonacademic source, and 44 percent from a colleague.

Next, how confident were policymakers about the DP thesis? The survey asked those who said they were familiar with the term whether they were confident that "because two countries are democracies, they are not likely to wage war against each other." Of those who knew about the DP, 63 percent were somewhat or very confident in its accuracy. Of the total set of policymakers, including those who professed no familiarity with the DP, 35 percent expressed at least some confidence.

Relatedly, the survey assessed policymakers' perceptions of usefulness and influence. Of those who had heard of the DP, 65 percent said it was somewhat or very useful for policymakers, and 47 percent said it influenced the work they did for the US government. Of policymakers as a whole, including those who did not claim knowledge of the DP, 36 percent said it was somewhat or very useful, and 26 percent said it influenced their work. Evidence of its utility has been manifested in a number of policies since the end of the Cold War, particularly the promotion of democracy in the 1990s, the attempt to democratize Iraq, and NATO and European Union expansion, the premise being that democracies tend to be more peacefully governed and do not fight each other (Moreland 2017). Thus, even if policymakers report that they have not heard about the "democratic peace thesis," they nonetheless may believe that fellow democracies are less threatening and implicitly draw on the mountain of studies mentioned in the next section positing that war between democracies is extremely unlikely.

## Academics

The view from the ivory tower is different from that of policymakers. In fact, a massive literature has shown a robust correlation between shared democracy and peace. Scholars have attributed this correlation to various causal mechanisms. Some have argued that norms and institutions reduce perceptions of threat and increase the prospects for peaceful mediation (e.g., Doyle 1986; Maoz and Russett 1993; Owen 1994; Risse-Kappen 1995). Others have argued that the mechanism driving peace among democracies is more akin to deterrence; for example, Lake (1992), Reiter and Stam (2002), and Bueno de Mesquita et al. (1999) argue that democracies avoid wars with fellow democracies because they expect democracies to make formidable opponents. Finally, some have attributed the DP to citizens' and elites' moral qualms about using violence to subvert policies that have been freely chosen by citizens of another country (e.g., Tomz and Weeks 2013). Although the existing scholarship disagrees about the precise pathways through which shared democracy leads to peace, a vast body of work concludes that at least some of the observed correlation between joint liberalism and peace is caused by shared democracy. The strength of the correlation does not prove causation, but scholars have yet to convincingly demonstrate that the relationship between democracy and peace does **not** have some causal element.

An examination of citation counts further indicates that whether or not one believes the DP thesis is accurate, DP articles are among the most widely cited in the discipline. In Google Scholar, 15,300 pieces referring to the term "democratic peace" were published from 1986 to 2011, the twenty-five years prior to the 2011 policymaker survey.[8] Michael Doyle's 1986 article "Liberalism and World Politics" was cited 1,520 times during that time period, according to the same search engine; Bruce Russett's 1993 book *Grasping the Democratic Peace* garnered 2,200 citations. Maoz and Russett's 1993 article "Normative and Structural Causes of the Democratic Peace, 1946–1986" was cited 1,210 times. Even though these numbers are individually less than Waltz's seminal *Theory of International Politics*, as discussed previously, they are massive citation counts overall.

A similar pattern emerges from the 2011 TRIP faculty survey. One question asks faculty to list four scholars who have "had the greatest influence on the field of IR in the past 20 years." Even though much of the seminal work on the DP was done either outside the twenty-year limit posed in the question or close to the beginning of that time period, DP proponents such as Bruce Bueno de Mesquita and Bruce Russett make the list.

Finally, we turn to our two data sources on IR graduate syllabi. Among the syllabi we were able to locate, *every single institution* assigned material about the DP. Many, if not most, syllabi devoted entire weeks of instruction to the topic.[9] Colgan's data (2016) indicate that of the forty-two institutions he surveyed, twenty-nine assigned at least one reading with "democratic peace" in the title; this likely undercounts the concept's importance because it does not catch readings like Doyle's (1986). Nonetheless, even this narrow measure suggests that DP is covered in the core IR graduate courses in nearly 70 percent of the universities in Colgan's sample.

Although the readings about the DP are abundant on syllabi and reams of data document a correlation between democracy and peace, some skeptics do not accept the causal relationship between the two. Some critics have attributed the correlation to shared interests that happened to coincide with democracy, especially during the Cold War (e.g., Farber and Gowa 1995; Gartzke 1998). Alternatively, the peace among democracies might be due to capitalism (Gartzke 2007; McDonald 2009).[10] Others have suggested that the absence of war among democracies is a historically contingent consequence of American hegemony after World War II (Rosato 2003; McDonald 2015). To a (vocal) minority of scholars, the DP is a historical accident rather than a robust "empirical law," as Levy (1989) has famously described it. Dafoe (2011), however, shows that it is extremely difficult to overturn the correlation between democracy and peace even when taking into account other possible causes of peace highlighted by skeptics.

In sum, although debate continues about causal mechanisms and an outspoken minority doubts whether the correlation between democracy and peace is causal, the DP has been one of the most dominant research programs in political science. Absent a survey of academics, it is difficult to quantify the percentage of scholars who believe that the DP represents a causal relationship, but we can say with some confidence that it would be difficult to find an IR scholar who is not familiar with the basic tenets of DP theory.

At the same time, only 56 percent of the security policymakers surveyed by Avey and Desch were familiar with DP theory. Moreover, of the US policymakers who were familiar with the DP, 65 percent deemed it to be somewhat or very useful for policymakers. Thus, it appears that many policymakers are not getting state-of-the art knowledge that they themselves deem useful.

Putting these facts together, the gap appears to be more about *exposure* than it is about the interpretation of the evidence, again suggesting that the more consumable and readily available academic ideas are, the more likely they are to be used by policymakers. The question in this particular instance is, therefore, how can scholars who wish to bridge the divide between theory and policy expose policymakers to this major debate in the field. And why has this not happened to date?

One potential source of insight is informative about where those who knew about the DP thesis learned about it. Respondents in the policymaker survey who said they were familiar with the DP were asked how they learned about it and were given four answer choices that were not mutually exclusive. Table 12.1 indicates that of those who knew about the DP, about 42 percent said they read scholarly works such as Kant's *Perpetual Peace* or articles and books by the scholars Michael Doyle and Bruce Russett. Thirty-seven percent said they read about the thesis in the 1994 and 2002 *National Security Strategies*, which did not mention "the democratic peace" explicitly but repeatedly referred to shared democracy as a factor promoting peace abroad (Office of the White House 1994, 2002). A whopping 76 percent said they read about the thesis in opinion pieces or other nonacademic sources, and 44 percent said they heard about it from colleagues.

Another way to look at the data is to look at policymakers as a whole, including the 46 percent of policymakers who said they were not familiar with the DP thesis. Of the *entire* set of policymakers, 23 percent said they read scholarly works. Forty-two percent said they read about the thesis in nonacademic sources, such as opinion pieces or *National Security Strategies*, and 24 percent said they heard about it from colleagues.

Thus, as a whole, it appears that the vast majority of national security practitioners are not reading scholarly journals frequently enough to learn about one of the most widely discussed theories in contemporary IR scholarship. This suggests two conclusions consistent with arguments developed in chapter 1: scholars wishing to publicize their findings need to write op-eds early and often, and they need to phrase their findings in a way that allows for hallway conversations or pithy descriptions in meetings.[11] That is, they need to make their work easier to consume—more accessible more quickly and in more digestible formats—if they want to influence policy and policymakers.

Together, the data suggest that the people we would expect to know about the DP do tend to be familiar with it, although at levels that are slightly lower than one might think given the idea's ubiquity in IR syllabi and its prominence in the academic literature. Moreover, policymakers are not reading political science journals with any frequency. Of all policymakers, only 23 percent said they had read an academic book or article about the DP.

## Expected Utility Theory

Finally, we turn to Bruce Bueno de Mesquita's "expected utility" approach to IR and foreign policy.

### Policymakers

We first analyze whether policymakers said they are "familiar with Bueno de Mesquita's 'expected utility' approach to international relations and foreign policy." This academic approach relies heavily on game theory, a tool that, according to Avey and Desch (2014), is unpopular with policymakers.

Given the characteristics of the "expected utility approach"—both its level of abstraction and its reliance on game-theoretic models—it is perhaps not surprising that table 12.1 shows that only 21 percent of policymakers are familiar with Bueno de Mesquita's approach. A tiny minority (7 percent) of all policymakers had read an academic article or book by Bueno de Mesquita (among those few policymakers familiar with the theory, the figure is 33 percent). Sixty-nine percent of those who were familiar with the approach say they read about it in a nonacademic source such as *Foreign Affairs*, and 51 percent learned about it from a colleague.

In a familiar pattern, however, those who *were* exposed to the approach tended to deem it useful. Of those who answered "yes" to the familiarity question, 56 percent said they are somewhat or very confident "that states or political leaders make cost/benefit calculations of their interests and act rationally upon them in their foreign policy behavior," 60 percent thought the approach was useful for policymakers, and 45 percent believed it influenced their own work. These numbers all hovered around 9–12 percent among the sample of policymakers as a whole because most respondents were not familiar with the approach.

We add a caveat to these conclusions. It is hard to know whether policymakers are actually familiar with Bueno de Mesquita's work or rather the economic concept of expected utility theory. If the latter, then the aforementioned data may overestimate policymakers' true familiarity with Bueno de Mesquita's specific approach.

## Academics

As with many of the topics broached in this chapter, it is difficult to quantify academics' familiarity specifically with Bueno de Mesquita's work. It is also difficult to know whether to fold Bueno de Mesquita's work in with equally prominent work in the same vein, such as that of James Fearon (1995, among others) or Robert Powell (2006). Given the wording of the Avey and Desch question, however, we focus on knowledge of Bueno de Mesquita's work specifically.

Citation counts suggest that Bueno de Mesquita's work has been enormously influential in the IR field. His Google Scholar profile indicates that his body of work garnered approximately 10,835 citations from 1986 to 2011. Among the works explicitly named in Avey and Desch's policymaker survey, *The War Trap* (Bueno de Mesquita 1981) had 1,190 citations in that time period; *War and Reason* (Bueno de Mesquita 1992) had 989; *The Logic of Political Survival* (Bueno de Mesquita et al. 2003) had 1,540; and "An Institutional Explanation for the Democratic Peace" (Bueno de Mesquita et al. 1999) had 765. By any metric, this is an impressive citation count.

Another indicator of exposure is appearance on syllabi. Of the fifteen institutions for which we gathered at least one relevant syllabus, nine assigned at least one reading by Bueno de Mesquita (although in a couple of cases the reference was to "further reading" rather than the core assigned material). Of the twelve top US IR programs for which we gathered data, the figure was 67 percent. (Two of the British syllabi in our sample omitted references to Bueno de Mesquita's work.) The Colgan data tell a similar story; of forty-two institutions surveyed, twenty-nine, or nearly 70 percent, had a core IR theory course that assigned a reading by Bruce Bueno de Mesquita. These data are not a perfect match with the survey question; future analysis could assess whether instructors assign the readings mentioned in the TRIP survey specifically. In the meantime, our tentative conclusions from this limited data suggest that exposure to Bueno de Mesquita's work is significantly lower than the near universality of Waltzian realism and DP theory, although it is far from trivial.

Finally, it is worth looking at the TRIP faculty survey, which asked about the four scholars who have had the greatest influence on the IR field in the past twenty years. Bueno de Mesquita ranked eleventh among the twenty most often mentioned scholars. Again, the view from the academy appears to be quite different from that among policymakers.

## DISCUSSION AND CONCLUSIONS

In this chapter we sought to measure the gap between policymakers and scholars by assessing each group's knowledge of and commitment to four different scholarly arguments about the causes of interstate war. Our findings show that some of the pessimism regarding the academic-policymaker divide is misguided, at least in the context of theories about interstate relations. In one case, that of realism, policymakers and academics both hold the argument in high regard. In the three other cases, however—the CoC, the DP, and expected utility—significant gaps exist, although for different reasons.

In the case of Huntington's argument, policymakers were overwhelmingly aware of the argument and found it to be a useful way of thinking about the world, a view that contrasts starkly with the view of academics, who have jettisoned the argument as simplistic and empirically inaccurate. In the case of the DP, the way each camp values the argument is inverted. Whereas policymakers appear to be less familiar with the argument, it has occupied a central position in IR scholarship, with academics generally finding the correlation convincing and studying the mechanisms that underlie the relationship. Finally, few policymakers are aware of Bueno de Mesquita's expected utility approach, although our findings here are more tentative given that the question was asked about a single strand of work by a single author.

What do these findings suggest for scholars who want to bridge the IR academic-policy divide and disseminate their findings within the policy community? Perhaps our preferred answer would be to staff the government with individuals with PhDs in political science or international affairs, whose knowledge of and confidence in the theories studied here most closely match the views from the ivory tower. We find this to be an unlikely solution, however, and humbly admit that academic political scientists often lack other crucial skill sets.

One clear finding from our analyses is that exposure matters. *Conditional on being familiar with a theory*, policymakers said across the board that they believed the theory to be somewhat or very useful for policymakers. Of course, it could be that policymakers primarily seek out theories to which they are predisposed, but the data nonetheless suggest that exposure is key. In short, our findings are consistent with the argument, outlined in chapter 1, that the way scholars package their research matters; scholarship that is presented in lengthy, jargon-laden academic articles and books that may take years to appear in print will be less influential than academic ideas that are published in more accessible, timely formats.

How does one increase exposure to prominent academic ideas? Across the four approaches, policymakers professed that op-eds and articles in *Foreign Affairs* were the most significant source of direct information (information from colleagues also ranked high but is less direct; the survey did not ask about other venues, such as *Foreign Policy*). The obvious implication is that scholars need to publish in these outlets using language that will resonate with those who are *not* trained in political science or law. The linking of the *Monkey Cage* blog to the *Washington Post* appears to have encouraged political scientists to write blog posts that are featured on the *Washington Post* website and therefore draw more mainstream readership. Other blogs such as *Political Violence at a Glance* also attempt to translate complex models from political science into simple insights about political violence, including interstate conflict, and provide useful bridges between the two communities. It would also be beneficial to generate greater connection between academics and practitioners. On their end, universities could organize more workshops and conferences where academics and policymakers can interact and practitioners can become more familiar with recent research; this would require a different model of presenting research, in which academics focus less on the technical details and more on their big picture findings. Practitioners, on the other hand, might find more ways to invite academics to share their perspectives on policy issues of the day. Academics would certainly benefit from learning more about policymakers' practical needs, while policymakers might learn what ideas have been discredited and why.

Another clear implication of our findings, when combined with Avey and Desch's (2014) findings, is that the messenger matters. IR scholars view James Fearon (whose work is similar in flavor to Bruce Bueno de Mesquita's) as producing some of the best and most influential work in the field, but Fearon is not even mentioned on the list of policymakers' rankings of most influential scholars (Avey and Desch 2014, 236). In fact, the overlap on the two lists includes only four scholars: Joseph Nye, Kenneth Waltz, Robert Jervis, and Samuel Huntington, and some of these scholars are eclipsed by figures such as Henry Kissinger, Francis Fukuyama, and Zbigniew Brzezinski, whose work has been far less influential (at least in recent years) in the academy.

Thus, "unknown" scholars may need to partner with and coauthor articles with luminaries whose name will get the attention of policymakers.[12]

To be clear, we are not arguing that influencing policy should be the primary objective of political science research. Indeed, we see intrinsic value in IR scholars conducting basic scientific research. Insofar as research dealing with the political process and in particular relations between states is well suited to being policy relevant, however, it is useful to think about the ways in which is it more likely to be conducted so that it actually reaches those who are engaged in the policy process.

Although we have offered some suggestions on how scholars might meaningfully engage the process through their work, these recommendations are based on our preliminary research on the academic-policymaker gap in understanding the causes of interstate conflict. We close by suggesting fertile areas for future research and presumably other avenues for influence. Our analysis exploited survey data that had already been collected, but doing so created limitations in terms of the issue areas studied and the nature of the evidence. We first suggest that it would be worthwhile to expand the analysis to other areas of interstate conflict—for example, bargaining theories of war or audience costs. Both topics have had considerable influence in recent IR scholarship, so examining whether these ideas have traction in policy circles would address the possibility that the four theories we studied were outdated in policymakers' minds or that more contemporary researchers have been more attuned to the question of policy engagement. Second, one should consider forms of evidence other than the existing survey data on policymakers, whether through interviews or other qualitative evidence. Nonetheless, we consider this a valuable first step in understanding and, we hope, bridging the academic-policymaker gap on interstate conflict.

## ENDNOTES

1. This is different from Avey and Desch's (2013a) analytical approach of focusing solely on policymakers' views; by comparing policymakers' and academics' views, we can learn how research has been disseminated historically and uncover misperceptions among scholars about what practitioners want.
2. One example would be "All Mortis, No Rigor" (Zagare 1999), which addresses the question of whether formal theory has utility for international relations but would not be identified with that topic based on title alone.
3. Our tallies were calculated in June 2019.
4. Ideally we would conduct a historical analysis of syllabi, a task that currently seems infeasible.
5. One difference in these two measurements is that searching by topic sets a higher bar for engaging the CoC, requiring that titles, keywords, or abstracts include some reference to the CoC. Citation of the "clash of civilizations" sets a lower bar because it means that an article or book need only have cited Huntington's work, even if just in passing, with the research actually dealing with topics ranging from European integration or the politics of secularism.

6. The survey later elaborates on realism as "the influence of international factors like the distribution of power rather than the nature of their domestic politics," but this description was not included in the first question gauging familiarity with the thesis.

7. Colgan's data indicate that *Theory of International Politics* was assigned in the core IR theory seminars at twenty-five of the forty-two universities surveyed; other versions of Waltzian realism may have been assigned as well.

8. Google Scholar citation counts can be inflated because they can include unpublished papers and nonscholarly commentaries; at the same time, the SSCI/Web of Science citation counts do not include book citations.

9. Unfortunately the 2011 TRIP faculty survey does not speak directly to this question.

10. Although, see Russett (2010) and Dafoe (2011).

11. It is worth mentioning that much (although certainly not all) of the work on the DP has employed quantitative methods, an approach that policymakers in the national security space tend not to embrace (Avey and Desch 2014).

12. We recognize the catch-22 in terms of these unknown scholars attracting the eye of luminaries, which may require first that they become known.

# 13

# REFLECTIONS FROM AN ERSTWHILE POLICYMAKER

Peter D. Feaver

f I were back on the National Security Council and assigned to lead a "deep dive" for the president on interstate war, how would I prepare and what would I want to cover? I would probably build the agenda by combining the results of two different thought processes: one academic oriented and one policy oriented.

The academic-oriented line of thinking would ask, "What important scholarship have I seen or heard about that might help the president set his particular interstate-conflict–related challenges in broader perspective?" Informed by Kreps and Weeks (and others), I might list a few big empirical findings/debates:

- In historical terms, are we in a period of high, medium, or low rates of interstate conflict?
- How do interstate wars break down by motive?
- What proportion of wars end in negotiated settlement, victory, stalemate, and so forth? How do the ends of war correlate with the recurrence of conflict?

The policy-oriented line of thinking would be driven by several specific problems:

- Putinism on the Fritz:
  - How can we lower the likelihood that Vladimir Putin will do to another country what he has done to Ukraine at a price acceptable to the United States?
  - How best can we mitigate the unintended effects of the administration's uneven rhetoric about our allies and partners?
- Xi Who Must Be Obeyed:
  - What mechanisms are available to tamp down security spirals in Northeast and Southeast Asia?
  - How do trade wars exacerbate security conflicts?
  - How much hedging and pushing back against Chinese adventurism can we do before we have crossed irrevocably into containment and a new Cold War?

- Beating the Rap on Reputation
  - Did the mostly successful campaign against Islamic State in Iraq and Syria (ISIS) sufficiently restore the confidence in American coercive power that was lost by the rise of ISIS? Has a premature declaration of victory led to a power vacuum that will simply repeat the problem suffered under the previous administration?
  - How do reversals in one theater affect our strategies in another?
  - Can we retreat in the Middle East without it undermining our position in Asia?[1]

In preparing this deep dive, I would probably not have the president read the policy prescriptions sections that usually get tacked on to the end of the readings I selected from the academic-oriented line of thinking. In general, the self-identified policy prescriptions tend to be overstated. For instance, an academic article might rightly conclude that external interventions in civil wars since 1816 have produced "success" (as coded by the researcher) less than half the time, but that hardly settles the policy question of whether the United States should arm the opposition in Venezuela. The policy question is always about "compared to other tools" and "compared to the costs of doing nothing." Many academics tend to count only the costs of action and ignore the costs of inaction.

Note how few of those academic readings that suggest themselves when you approach the "deep dive" really do much more than set in context the policy challenges generated by the policy-oriented line of thinking. For instance, aside from a throwaway line or two in a speech, it is not likely that a policymaker would learn that "incidences of interstate conflict have dropped" and conclude, "Good, then I don't need to pay attention to national security, let's go hit the links."

The reason why a policymaker who has to work in the real (read: political) world might respond this way is clearer if you consider a similar fact from a separate sphere: political economy. People in the bottom quintile in socioeconomic status (SES) in the United States today are vastly better off than were the poor wretches in the global bottom SES quintile one hundred, five hundred, or one thousand years ago. Today they are better fed, have access to better medicine, are less likely to die from predators, and have better access to education and entertainment than their earlier counterparts. Of course, political leaders remain seized with the issue of poverty, and indeed the wealth gap is arguably more politically salient today than it was two hundred years ago, when the gap may have been narrower but the misery greater.

Consider another example. As Christopher Gelpi, Jason Reifler, and I have shown (Gelpi et al. 2009), there is an underlying logic that explains how rising casualties affect public support for war. The public is not casualty phobic so much as it is defeat phobic; the public will tolerate casualties that are necessary to achieve victory. We trace this logic through a variety of wars over the past sixty years but also note another phenomenon: the same shifts in public support emerge today from casualty rates that are an order of magnitude lower than they were in Vietnam, let alone World War II. Changes in technology and the American way of war have changed expectations about how high the human toll of war "needs" to be in order to achieve a given outcome. A casualty rate that was deemed horrible but acceptable in World War II would be deemed totally unacceptable in a contemporary US intervention. So, telling a policymaker that public opinion shifted only so many points after four thousand US casualties suffered in World War II would be misleading without also explaining how expectations have shifted. It is fine to provide the larger context for the policymaker, but that context is unlikely to shift the policy frame as dramatically as the academic might expect.

As should be evident by now, the agenda I would suggest would also not spend much time on the academic literature that was the subject of the Kreps and Weeks chapter: the grand theory debates surrounding clash of civilizations, neorealism, democratic peace, and expected utility theory. That is not a criticism of the Kreps and Weeks chapter. Their focus flowed very logically and naturally from their assignment, which was to analyze the Teaching, Research, and International Policy (TRIP) data to determine what they tell us about the academy-policy gap in the area of interstate conflict. My point is that if you were preparing a deep dive for the president with, by policy standards, a broad horizon (a year to a couple of years), then you would probably not spend any time on the grand theory debates of academic international relations (IR).

This is not to say that theory is irrelevant to policy, or that we should take at face value a policymaker's subjective assessment of the extent to which he or she relies on theory (which is precisely what the TRIP study measures). On the contrary, a policymaker cannot "do" policy without relying on theory, at least implicitly (Feaver 1999). The policy-academy gap on theory is not about the existence of theory so much as it is about the awareness of theory. Good academics are explicit about the role of theory in their arguments. Good policymakers do not need to be explicit and so sometimes are unaware of the role theory plays in their policy debates. Substitute *method* for *theory* in the previous sentences and the paragraph is equally true.

Kreps and Weeks do a convincing job mining the data for insights. But I think their answer boils down to "The TRIP data do not tell us a great deal about the gap in this area." The data show pretty convincingly that sizable fractions of the midlevel policymakers who responded to the survey have some vague familiarity with some of the most prominent IR theory debates of the 1980s and 1990s, but they consider these theory debates to be only somewhat useful, and they do not have the details so readily at their fingertips that they could answer fact-based questions about it on a survey.

Even if experts in the debates were to compile the concrete policy implications that derive from the literature, there are not many that could be listed that would move the needle much past "somewhat useful." If clash of civilizations is correct, it means that religious/cultural identity markers will be more important in driving conflict in the present/future than it was in the past; "Okay," President Trump might say to me, "I already knew that [or believed that] but my real concern is what can I do about that?" If Waltzian neorealism is correct, it means that eventually other states or groups of states will seek to balance against US unipolarity; okay, but what should I do about that? If democratic peace theory is correct, it means that the spread of democracy will, eventually, lead to a more peaceful world; okay, Americans have long cheered the spread of democracy, so this nicely reaffirms American values, but I also know that the process of democratization is messy and can backfire on me, so I remain wary. If expected utility theory is correct, it means that the vast majority of what the government analysts do is sound (at least as a point of departure) because they are engaged in a daily effort to determine the interests and strategic cost-benefit calculations of other states. Fine, so what follows?

The counterfactual doesn't change much either. If any or all of those theories are conclusively false (so conclusively that no enterprising next generation of scholars could ever revive them in slightly modified form), what would or should policymakers do or have done differently? Admittedly, the counterfactual is itself implausible, and that may be part of the explanation itself for why policymakers do not follow academic debates as closely as some academics would like; policymakers know that what IR theorists "know" today may not be what they "know" tomorrow, but there is a decent chance they will "know" it again the day after that.

Even if what is known endures, at best it will be probabilistic knowledge. It is helpful for policymakers to know what the literature considers to be general probabilities, but the business of policy is figuring out whether the next case in your inbox is following the central tendency or is one of the outliers. Even more, the business of policy is figuring out what answer would be the best one for the United States and then doing what you can to make that more likely to be true.

The limitation is also inherent in the original exercise. We know that the theory that scores the worst in the TRIP survey of policymakers—expected utility theory—in reality has one of the strongest policy links of any IR academic theory. The *ne plus ultra* of "policy relevance" would be if the US government were to use its scarce resources to hire you to use your theory to provide bespoke answers to questions, and then to have those answers go more or less directly into analytical products that reach the highest levels of government. And all of this must not merely be "wise academic opining on the subject" but "theorist churning the levers and wheels of his theory to produce the answer." The policy practitioners surveyed by TRIP may not realize that Bruce Bueno De Mesquita long ago reached that level, but we do (Lerner and Hill 2007).

I suspect that the TRIP survey understates the degree to which policy arguments inside the government are shaped by concepts and findings that originate (or at least are themselves shaped) inside the academy. A survey aimed at the strata of officials whose job is to prepare "the boss" for interagency meetings—the staffers who are writing the background papers and related meeting memos—and worded in such a way so as to not require bibliographic memory (let alone a recall of the paradigmatic pedigree) might reveal that such officials are paying attention to what at least some academics are saying. To be sure, it is doubtful that many of those officials have read the latest peer-reviewed journals, but it is just as doubtful that they have not read the policy-oriented summaries of those academic debates, at least the ones that land in popular outlets like the major newspaper opinion pages and leading foreign policy and national security websites. And if those officials have not read such work themselves, in my experience the people those officials do read—the journalists and major columnists—have read that work.

Even with these limitations, these data are the best we have right now. That said, I hope there are additional rounds of surveying and, if there are, I wonder if a question like this asked of the policymakers might yield even more interesting results: "What specific questions regarding international conflict [or other prompts] do you wish academics addressed [more extensively] in their research?" An open-ended question like that would produce a range of interesting research suggestions, and there may well be gaps between what they say and what the TRIP academic respondents say to that question. Or the policymakers may ask for research that is already being done and just needs to be brought to their attention more effectively. Either way, we would learn interesting things about how to strengthen the links between the academy and the policy world.

Which brings me to Kreps and Weeks' recommendations. I actually like best the one they offer and then retract as "unlikely": expand the number of in-and-outers, folks who are card-carrying academics but who work in government. There are more of those than one might think, and one of the great strengths of US strategic culture is that there are more of those here than in other countries. Let's have even more of them. I also agree that outlets like *Monkey Cage* that explicitly translate cutting-edge academic research into policy pieces are excellent. I know for a fact that well-placed advisors in both the Obama and Trump administrations have made use of *Monkey Cage*, and I expect that to continue as long as the quality of the outlet, and others like it, remains high.

In the end, I concur wholeheartedly with what I take to be Kreps and Weeks' net assessment of how constructively IR research on interstate conflict is informing policymakers: not as good as it might be, but not as bad as is feared.

# ENDNOTE

1. This question taps into one of the more interesting policy-academy gaps: different estimates about the utility of reputation as a factor affecting international behavior. Most policymakers understand that reputation is an important resource that is difficult to cultivate but valuable if used carefully. Some academic literature (Hopf 1995; Mercer 1996; Press 2007) has emphasized how difficult it is to cultivate reputation and raised doubts about the naïve version of reputation theory—namely, that reputation translates into effectiveness in an easy one-to-one conversion. Even though few policymakers believe this naïve version of reputation theory, some prominent academics and pundits have made a cottage industry lambasting policymakers for emphasizing reputation at all, given the cautionary findings of the older academic literature (Walt 2015a; Fisher 2016). Enter the next generation of academics (Crescenzi 2007; Tomz 2007; Cochran 2011; Lupton 2014: Yarhi-Milo 2014; Yarhi-Milo and Weisiger 2015), who show that the skepticism of the older literature was overstated and that the policymakers have had it more or less right all along.

# 14

# THE WEAKEST LINK?
## Scholarship and Policy on Intrastate Conflict

Michael G. Findley and Joseph K. Young

How do theory and practice interact in the critical domain of intrastate conflict? When events, such as the Syrian civil war, spiral for years, do policymakers consult academics for their ideas? Do academics respond to such events by trying to explain why these intrastate conflicts start or end? Should this interplay between policy and academia occur? If and when it does, how will we know? When thinking about strengthening the links between the policy and academic worlds, these are but a few questions to consider. A central task in this chapter is to examine various Teaching, Research, and International Policy (TRIP) datasets to learn about the role of intrastate conflict in the study of international relations (IR) and to relate this to the role scholars have played in the policy process.

Our core argument is that scholarly work has had modest direct influence on policy and likely small, although difficult-to-detect, indirect influences. Much of the intrastate conflict occurring in the world has taken place in geographic areas where policymakers have historically paid little attention. Africa, for example, represents about 15 percent of the global population. In the TRIP article database, however, only 5 percent of all articles are related to Africa, and only 5.5 percent of faculty in the thirty-two countries included in the 2014 TRIP faculty survey select Africa as their primary focus. Although violence in Africa may be of less concern to policymakers than violence in other parts of the world, 17 percent of the intrastate conflict articles in the TRIP database have an Africa focus. That said, Africa has experienced the largest share of the world's intrastate conflict, at least since World War II.

Even during the Cold War, much of the violence in Africa and Asia drew relatively little attention. Intrastate conflict has become more important in the academy over the last ten to fifteen years, and that interest has largely been fueled by an increase in analysis of large-N databases. Political science (comparative politics, specifically) has a somewhat longer tradition of studying revolution, but there have been few conflict studies groups to propel its research into the mainstream of political science, much less the policy world. Thus it would be unrealistic to expect that the intrastate war literature would have a strong effect on policy. Finally, what little covariance appears to exist comes from the literature on insurgency and development, although it is unclear how much scholarly work drives policy as opposed to the two co-occurring with no obvious causal link.

Turning to the question of whether the policy world has had an impact on scholars, we argue that scholarly work has integrated few insights from the policy community. It is far from clear that scholars pay attention to the decision calculus of policymakers in the United States, other western countries, or international organizations when developing their research claims. Growing numbers of collaborations between academics and practitioners, however, have led to greater insights in the peacebuilding and other literatures.

That said, scholars are often influenced by current events and study contemporary conflict processes. In the 2014 TRIP faculty survey, 62 percent of respondents answered in the affirmative when asked if they have increased their research related to a critical event, such as September 11, 2001. In fact, 54 percent of faculty answered "yes" when asked if they have responded to a major world event by seeking to make their work more relevant to policy practitioners. Unsurprisingly, of all major world events listed, 9/11 had the biggest impact on scholars' research, with about 42 percent of respondents citing this incident. The Arab Spring and the fall of communism were ranked next highest at 25 percent and 23.45 percent, respectively.

In this chapter we first describe the scope of the intrastate conflict issue area and employ qualitative evidence to describe the evolution of this subfield. Second, we introduce various TRIP datasets and discuss their strengths and weaknesses in further describing the evolution of this subfield and its relationship to the policy community. Third, we evaluate several arguments that are described in chapter 1. We find suggestive evidence that is consistent with the arguments that emerging issues (argument 1a) and more technical issues (argument 1b) provide greater opportunities for IR scholars to influence policy than do more long-standing and less technical issues. The demand for applied scholarship on terrorism and intrastate conflict increased dramatically after 9/11, when policymakers were desperate for more/better evidence and for more sophisticated models that would help them forecast conflict events at the subnational level. We also present evidence that speaks to two additional arguments presented in chapter 1: first, that the opportunities for scholarly engagement and influence will be more limited in issue areas in which another epistemic or disciplinary community already has an established working relationship with practitioners than in issue areas in which no such relationship exists (argument 2a) and, second, that IR scholars are more likely to directly influence policy in issue areas in which policy decisions are made frequently and at relatively low levels (argument 2b).

In the post-9/11 environment, policy implementers sought insights from new multidisciplinary teams of researchers when they lacked in-house expertise. Large contracts were awarded to IR scholars to conduct research on a weekly or daily basis for combatant commanders who were tasked with implementing policy. These were not consultations with the secretary of state but frequent forecasts for practitioners tasked with making tactical decisions or providing intelligence assessments.

Finally, we discuss the type of data collection efforts and research designs that would be helpful in pursuing a second generation of empirical research on the relationship between IR scholars and policy practitioners. Although the evidence collected for this book provides a strong foundation, and the tentative explanations advanced herein provide a plausible starting point, we all have more work in front of us if we are to take this research agenda on the theory-practice nexus as seriously as we take our individual substantive research agendas.

## STATE OF THE FIELD

For the past few decades, events such as the Rwandan genocide, the 9/11 attacks, and the Arab Spring have pushed the study of conflict beyond traditional areas of great power disputes and militarized interstate conflicts. After the end of the Cold War, events such as the crisis in Somalia and the breakdown of Yugoslavia drew scholars into studying substate processes. This development was further enhanced in the late 1990s by the upsurge of quantitative *civil war* research, which encouraged even more work in this area.

A tabulation of the *intrastate conflict* variable in the TRIP article database shows that 602 of the 5,306 articles coded have a substantive focus on intrastate conflict, amounting to about 11 percent of the articles. Figure 14.1 illustrates the percentage of all articles in the database that are devoted to intrastate conflict

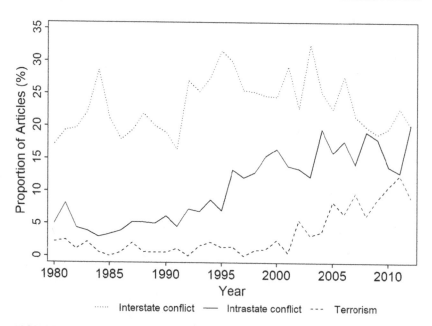

**FIGURE 14.1.** Plot of the percentage of all articles in the TRIP journal database on the topics of intrastate and interstate conflict and terrorism

over time as well as other types of conflict. The graph illustrates the dramatic growth in studies of intrastate conflict in the wake of the end of the Cold War. It is remarkable that from about the mid to late 1990s, around 15 percent of the articles published in the major IR journals were on intrastate conflict.[1]

What is intrastate conflict? Why is it different than interstate war? More directly, why are these distinct concepts worthy of their own investigation? Relatedly, is this form of violence a topic for IR? Comparative politics? Both? The standard definition of war that emanated from the Correlates of War (COW) Project defined interstate war as a dispute between two internationally recognized states that leads to battle deaths exceeding a one thousand–person threshold.[2] Early investigators used a similar definition for civil war, which was influenced by COW: civil war is an intrastate conflict between a state and a nonstate actor exceeding one thousand battle deaths. Some attributes vary, but most definitions are similar.

Thus, war within a state might seem like a topic for comparative politics. In the TRIP article database, however, 68 percent of the intrastate conflict articles are coded as IR. By contrast, 32 percent of the articles on intrastate conflict are coded as comparative. The blending of IR and comparative politics is fairly evident in the study of intrastate conflict.

Young (2013) suggests a deceptively simple, but critical, addendum to defining intrastate war. At its core, this violence is between state and nonstate actors, but it is conflict that *builds* up to and beyond a given threshold. Rather than large-scale violence simply breaking out or immediately crossing a large threshold, civil war is a point on a continuum of conflict processes that emerges from state-dissident interaction. This insight differentiates civil war from other forms of violence, but it also recognizes that civil war is part of the larger conflict repertoire available to states and nonstate actors. This point bridges some of the work in sociology and comparative politics by pioneers like Charles Tilly with civil war studies by IR scholars and economists.

This insight and some of the sociological work suggest that civil war is connected to these other kinds of violence because these forms of conflict build to civil war. These other forms of violence also may make civil war last longer, or they might even occur after civil war as a residual effect (Sambanis 2008; Findley and Young 2012). Terrorism is another common form of violence, which by contrast often lacks a death or violence threshold and is even more contentious to define than civil war (Hoffman 2006). We offer a fairly common definition: violence or threats of violence against a target used to persuade a third actor in pursuance of a goal.[3] This definition is agnostic to whether violence occurs within or across states, but empirically we witness most terrorism within states (Enders et al. 2011).

Scholars have attempted to speak to the issues of the day and often base their research on critical events. The TRIP article database includes thirty-five articles on terrorism published before 9/11. After 9/11, there were 164 terrorism articles published.[4] Interestingly, few articles about terrorism are in the comparative politics domain (only 3.6 percent of the comparative politics articles in the TRIP journal database). A smaller fraction, thirty-two of 5,306 articles, is listed as intrastate conflict *and* terrorism. Even though a majority of terrorist attacks are domestic or intrastate in nature (Sánchez-Cuenca and De la Calle 2009), it seems scholars see terrorism as more of an IR than a comparative politics topic. Whereas civil war, terrorism, and other intrastate conflict have been studied as "islands of inquiry" (Most and Starr 1984), more recent work is connecting these islands by recognizing the overlap and affinities among the types of violent contention (Findley and Young 2012; Thomas 2014; Fortna 2015).[5]

Some scholars focus primarily on stages of a conflict and ask questions about onset, duration, recurrence, or whether outside actors are involved. A different way of approaching intrastate conflict dynamics takes an actor-centric approach and considers the political or humanitarian reasons why third parties intervene (Findley and Teo 2006; Gent 2007). From the perspective of policy influence, the humanitarian approach is more relevant. Indeed, the scholarly literature on civil wars seems to be less connected to policy discussions relative to the peace studies literature.

What we are calling the *peace studies literature* examines a number of dimensions including peacekeeping, peacemaking, peace building, and peace enforcement. All of these peace operations are on the menu of options for countries such as the United States in thinking about how to get involved in intrastate conflicts abroad. Complete discussion of each type of peace intervention is beyond the scope of this chapter, but we note here that these different types of peace operations require different levels of material and time commitments ranging from short-term peacekeeping to long-term peace-building. They could be conducted by international organizations or by states. When conducted by states, however, there is often skepticism about how biased they are. The Russian aid convoy into Ukraine in 2014 is a prime example.

Peace operations have been criticized heavily, but there is evidence that they often may be effective (Doyle and Sambanis 2006). And even though the organizations that conduct peace operations lag behind development organizations, even many United Nations (UN) agencies are interested in learning and trying to adopt the more rigorous evaluation standards that scholars have applied. One of us recently completed an impact evaluation of the UN Peacebuilding Fund's (PBF) operations in Burundi (Campbell et al. 2014), conducted the PBF's first quasi-experimental evaluation, and had follow-up conversations with the PBF's monitoring and evaluation specialists, who are now requiring more rigorous evaluations.

## SCOPE CONDITIONS

In chapter 1, the editors identify a number of scope conditions, including what is a policy prescription, who are the key actors in the policy world, and how one would recognize policy influence. We will not rehash their arguments, but we provide a few additional thoughts here.

We begin with an anecdote that we fear may generalize: one of us received a revise-and-resubmit decision on a paper early in our career in which a reviewer, signaling some irritation, asked why there were no policy prescriptions in the conclusion of the paper. The reviewer said that the prescriptions must be there in order to endorse publication. The reviewer's instructions (paraphrased): two paragraphs would be sufficient, and the authors should simply communicate to "the policymakers" how they should redirect the country's activities based on the research findings.

The flawed logic suggests that scholars write an academic paper, fill it full of jargon, add some stars and bolded numbers, publish it in a gated venue, and put two paragraphs at the end of a long, oddly structured article that explain how policies should be changed. And the "policymakers"—presumably a Hillary Clinton or Mike Pompeo—will be paying attention and change things.[6] The standard academic policy prescription that we caricature is obviously insufficient. However, this sort of hastily provided policy prescription may be what we are seeing in the academic work we share with each other. The notion of offering policy prescriptions in academic articles is curious on multiple levels, which would be worthy of a discussion in itself. We wonder in particular whether the scholars who are least engaged are the ones who offer blunt policy prescriptions in articles, whereas those who are more engaged find much more subtle yet effective ways to communicate lessons learned. This is consistent with Parks and Stern's (2013) finding that IR scholars who take time during their careers to work full-time in a policy position return to academia with a new outlook; they devote more time to publishing in policy journals such as *Foreign Affairs* and *Foreign Policy*. In this case, attempts to learn about academic-policy connections from policy prescriptions in academic articles could give us precisely the opposite impressions about what is actually happening.

We also wonder how closely the policy prescriptions actually follow the empirical work discussed. We surmise, given that academics do not receive training in policy analysis, that policy prescriptions embedded within articles do not track closely with authors' empirical evidence. After all, if only a few other academics will read the paper, it is costless to give some advice to a Putin or a Merkel. Moreover, scholars may not have the appropriate skills or experience to derive a prescription that appropriately speaks to the policy world. A more in-depth qualitative review of policy prescriptions might be an important next step for researchers interested in the policy-academic nexus.

As discussed in chapter 1, some academics have taken to blogs, op-eds, policy briefs, and numerous other media to share lessons from their work. In our own area, *Political Violence at a Glance*, for which one of the authors is a contributor, may be the most prominent blog forum for disseminating academic work on intrastate conflict. Because policymakers, staff, or advocates can weigh in on such discussion through online fora, these approaches may provide different, and potentially more relevant, policy engagement.

However, similar questions apply: to what extent does this work offer policy advice rooted in strong evidence?[7]

Whether academics are clueless or savvy, influence could occur either way. In chapter 1 the editors identify a useful spectrum of policy influence, although we would point out (and do not think the editors would disagree) that the spectrum is something more of a heuristic for identifying relative impact that academics might make. How would we then measure this impact? Would we count the number of times a person or article is cited in congressional testimony? Would we count and weight the strength and duration of engagement with the policy world by taking into account formal versus informal advising, number of meetings, how close to the top of the organization the person is involved, or any number of other ways?

At American University, especially within the School for International Service and the School of Public Affairs, faculty and leadership have had related discussions as engagement with the policy world is an explicit goal of the university and thus something that figures into merit and promotion. The scale described previously provides guidance in thinking about these rankings. Exact measurement is more complicated and would likely need to be worked out more completely. A mention in congressional testimony, for example, is better evidence of impact than, say, a citation in a think tank report. For intelligence analysts, a mention in the President's Daily Brief is the highest honor (similar to an *American Political Science Review* article in political science).[8] In the intelligence world, at least, there is a parallel system where impact is considered and used for promotion and advancement.

Most important, and overlooked until now, how do interactions between academics and policymakers lead to reasonably informed policy? As Mack (2002) argues, policymakers need to understand that a few examples do not falsify a theory. Most academic theories are probabilistic and thus need to be supported or refuted based on the weight of evidence.[9] Academics need to do a better job communicating the strengths and limitations of their work. For instance, quantitative scholars need to share their material in a way that is digestible and makes clear to policymakers that their work is often complementary, not a substitute, for area studies knowledge (Mack 2002).

These issues give rise to the one with which we began: measurement of policy impact is difficult. If an academic speaks to some policy staff or advocates in Washington, DC, or Geneva, and then we observe some policy change, can we infer that academic work was responsible? What if, for example, the change was going to occur anyway, and an organization simply brought in some academics to speak to the issue? We could continue this exercise with many possible counterfactuals; suffice it to say that we need to be cautious about what we conclude.

We examined the 2011 and 2014 TRIP surveys (Maliniak et al. 2012, 2014), as well as the TRIP journal data, to understand various dimensions of the academic-policy nexus. Compared to other issue domains, the data are relatively sparse on intrastate conflict.

## THE TRIP JOURNAL DATA

We conducted several analyses with the journal data. Figure 14.1 examined patterns across articles for which the substantive focus variable has been coded as intrastate conflict, as well as the terrorism substantive focus variable to which we now turn. We also combined the two and conducted other subgroup analyses on whether the literature incorporates policy prescriptions.

The category of substantive focus, terrorism, could pick up a type of intrastate conflict. A tabulation of the *terrorism* variable shows that 213, or about 4 percent, of the 5,306 articles coded are substantively focused on terrorism. Figure 14.1 also illustrates the percentage plotted over time. Consistent with what many expect, there appears to be a significant increase in studies of terrorism after 9/11 (Young and Findley 2011).[10] We note that the articles coded for terrorism could be picking up terrorism internationally or domestically. Thus, to separate types of violence for the scope of this chapter, further work would need to explore whether the terrorism captured in these articles refers to intrastate conflict. A quick cross-tabulation shows that thirty-two of the 213 terrorism articles are also coded as intrastate conflict, perhaps reflecting the discipline's emphasis on transnational terrorism until recently.

Because terrorism is often a strategy used in intrastate conflict (Findley and Young 2012), we also pooled the two to show the percentage of all articles in the database on terrorism and intrastate conflict. Strikingly, in 2011 more than 25 percent of all articles are on one of these two topics. Whether the academic studies translate into policy influence is another matter, but at least there is sufficient emphasis on these topics to provide opportunity for policy impact.

To provide another point of comparison, we plotted intrastate conflict studies and terrorism studies relative to studies of interstate war. Figure 14.1 shows the results for academic studies over time. As expected, studies of interstate war dominate intrastate conflict and terrorism (separately). Although this is expected, it is curious that studies of interstate conflict continued to dominate until at least 2011, when so much emphasis in recent years has been placed on the empirical regularity that interstate wars rarely occur whereas intrastate conflict is rife. If the increased attention to intrastate conflict has led to an increase in studies, which the graph shows, there nonetheless appears to be a substantial lag in academic studies.

We now turn to a consideration of different methods in the study of intrastate conflict and terrorism. Figure 14.2 illustrates methods used over time, limiting the methods just to the categories, quantitative, qualitative, and formal modeling. Although there is substantial variation prior to the year 2000, with qualitative methods sometimes the most common, quantitative methods are now used much more extensively than other methods to study intrastate conflict. The trends for terrorism are less pronounced,

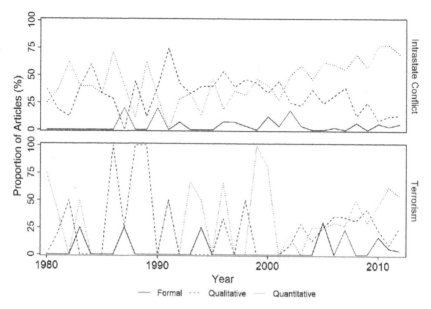

FIGURE 14.2. Plot of the percentage of all intrastate conflict and terrorism articles in the TRIP journal database by three methods

although quantitative studies also appear to dominate especially recently. This reflects larger trends toward the increasing use of quantitative methods in political science.

Finally, we examined what percentage of intrastate conflict and terrorism studies offer policy prescriptions. Figure 14.3 shows that the percentage varies widely; however, it does not provide any weighting for the number of articles per year. Thus, the low percentages in the late 2000s represent far more articles with policy prescriptions than the higher percentages in the early 1990s. The spikes in the early 1990s were likely driven by the end of the Cold War. Although the pattern is somewhat erratic, in raw percentages there may be a decline in policy prescriptions offered. Combined with the data on methods, this suggests that qualitative studies may be more amenable than quantitative approaches to policy prescriptions.

## THE TRIP SURVEY DATA

Despite excluding much of the substantive focus on intrastate conflict, the TRIP survey data contain some questions that are suggestive for our area. As with the journal article data, terrorism receives significant attention in the survey; it is a possible category for teaching and research interests. Scholars are also asked whether 9/11 influenced their teaching and research interests.

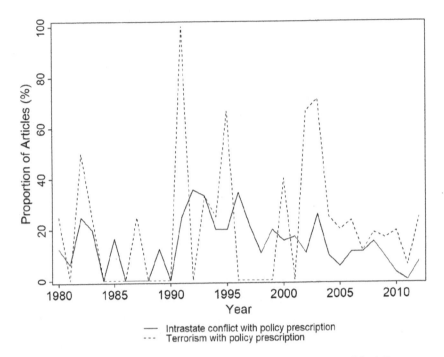

**FIGURE 14.3.** Plot of the percentage of all terrorism or intrastate war articles in the TRIP journal database that offer a policy prescription

According to the 2006 survey, 9/11 dramatically changed the issue areas covered in class. Less so, it also changed the geographical focus and theoretical approaches. Eighty-five percent of the respondents said that 9/11 significantly or somewhat changed the issue areas that respondents covered in at least one of their courses. Fifty-seven percent report significantly or somewhat changing geographic focus, and 40 percent report significantly or somewhat changing theoretical focus.

In addition to the questions about terrorism, the survey also asks about the most pressing foreign policy issues facing a given country. In these questions, a number of possibilities relate to intrastate conflicts in other countries, such as "Ethnic Conflict," "Genocide in Sudan," "Failed States," and "Arab Spring." Interestingly, for 2011 the most pressing foreign policy issues ranged from the Global Debt Crisis to Global Climate Change, but Arab Spring ranked second overall. Other traditionally intrastate issues, such as ethnic conflict, ranked much lower.

We also considered the descriptive data from the 2008 TRIP survey question asking respondents to "list four scholars whose work has most influenced your own research." Among the top forty scholars listed, only four had done significant work on intrastate conflict: James Fearon (no. 7),

David Lake (no. 25), Charles Tilly (no. 29), and J. David Singer (no. 37). Although at least three of these scholars have worked extensively on intrastate conflict, they are better known for their contributions to the interstate war literature.

We also considered the individuals listed as having the greatest influence on US foreign policy in the past twenty years. The list is similarly short on intrastate war scholars, with Michael Doyle moving up the list and the others mentioned previously moving down. It is possible that intrastate war scholars are not influential in the academy or in policy arenas, but it could also be the case that the area has only garnered more attention in the last twenty years. It is probably some combination of these and other factors.

## DISCUSSION OF THE TRIP DATA

There are some notable challenges in using TRIP datasets to describe the subfield of intrastate conflict or to analyze the relationship between research and policy practitioners. Some weaknesses may be partially addressed through keyword searching and/or automated text analysis. These empirical approaches certainly merit greater attention moving forward. A key limitation with the current TRIP data is that almost no attention is given to the peace(-making, -keeping, -building) literature. If one were to think about policy decisions the United States or other countries consider on a regular basis, many (most?) of them involve peace operations. Libya, Syria, Ukraine, and Iraq, to name a few, all had peace operations at stake. Indeed, for most developed countries, interstate wars are highly uncommon; yet many of these countries are active in peace operations worldwide.

Perhaps the greatest challenge is to connect the various types of data in ways that allow credible identification of the impact of scholarly work on policymaking or implementation. We venture that at this stage it may be impossible to identify precise causal effects in any completely satisfactory way. Instead, we may be limited to identifying patterns of covariation in academic ideas and policy impact through both TRIP data and case evidence. However, beginning the process of addressing the causal questions, even if piecemeal, is vital, especially given the tremendous pressure on political science to justify its relevance (see Jaschik 2013).

Accordingly, we ask: why not supplement the study of large-N correlations and anecdotes with randomized experiments in much narrower but perhaps more manageable domains? If carefully designed, an experiment might allow comparison as well as specifically designed interventions and outcomes, which could facilitate the identification of causal effects. With some careful consideration, interventions could be designed that could uncover causal mechanisms as well. In the event that the experimental evidence is consistent with the larger observational trends, it would add further validity to the findings. Such experiments are promising and one of us is engaged in a set of experiments that offer a model for moving forward in this regard (Brigham et al. 2013; Findley et al. 2014).

# STATE OF ACADEMIC AND POLICY ENGAGEMENT

Over the past fifty years most intrastate violence has occurred in areas of Africa and Asia (Uppsala Conflict Data Program 2018), where the United States and many other countries have had little strategic interest. Thus, even if academics and policymakers were speaking openly and consistently, there has been relatively little policy interest in the regions experiencing intrastate conflict. Brief forays into areas such as Somalia demonstrated how few benefits there were for third-party states to get involved. Even UN peace operations during the Cold War and immediate post–Cold War years were learning valuable, although painful, lessons about intervention in these areas.

At the same time that policy interest in intrastate conflict has increased, academic interest in the topic also increased. Yet, unfortunately, the two progressed along different paths. Scholars turned toward increasingly sophisticated quantitative methods to analyze large databases (for average effects) of various causes on war onset or dynamics. Few scholars expressed interest in serious engagement about specific cases with policymakers or practitioners. For their part, policy-minded individuals made little attempt to understand the pitfalls or potential promise of quantitative approaches.

There is thus little reason to expect that academics and policymakers should be having a healthy dialogue that produces real-world impact. Yet there appear to be at least some influential initiatives in which both policy influence and engagement have occurred, which we now discuss.

## From Academy to Policy

From the 1960s to the 1980s, the study of intrastate conflict was carried out primarily as examinations of revolution and rebellion. The work in these years is most commonly associated with scholars such as Davies (1962), Moore (1966), Gurr (1970), Tilly (1978), and Skocpol (1979). A related area, although not exclusively focused on intrastate war, is the study of counterinsurgency strategy, much of this associated with practitioner-scholars such as Galula (1964), who was also a military officer prior to publishing his scholarly work, and Leites and Wolf (1970) at the Rand Corporation. Neither the revolutions literature nor the counterinsurgency literature was particularly pervasive in public policy discussions, although the latter featured more prominently, if indirectly, in US strategy in Vietnam. Gurr's work was noticed and led to a 1968 appointment to the National Commission on the Causes and Prevention of Violence, a short-lived (by design) commission put into place following the assassinations of Martin Luther King Jr. and Robert F. Kennedy.

More prominently, Gurr helped found the State Failure Task Force (later renamed the Political Instability Task Force [PITF] in the mid-1990s). The PITF, which began under the Clinton administration and was housed within the CIA, has routinely engaged academics for help in providing its estimates of instability. Academics such as Jay Ulfelder, Erica Chenoweth, Monty Marshall, and Jeremy Weinstein have been involved to varying degrees. Other academics with regional or topical expertise have been invited on a more ad hoc basis. The Task Force's discussions are secret, making it difficult to assess just how much of the advice offered is actually implemented in some way by policymakers in the intelligence community or security industry.

The Integrated Crisis Early Warning System (ICEWS) is another example of scholarly input into policy arenas, specifically the military, and it provides suggestive evidence for the idea that when policymakers need cutting edge research methods (see argument 1b in chapter 1), this may provide opportunities for scholars to develop new knowledge and provide it to policy practitioners (in this case, policy implementers rather than policymakers). Academics have been involved with the program for years. In 2007, the Defense Advanced Research Projects Agency started ICEWS as a tournament to see which models could provide the best forecasts of crises around the globe. Since 2011, ICEWS has been an Office of Naval Research project. In comparison to PITF, ICEWS uses subnational event data at a granular temporal and spatial level. Mike Ward at Duke, Phil Schrodt formerly at Penn State, Ian Lustick at Penn, and Steve Shellman at William & Mary are all academics who are involved in the project. Again, many of the activities in the ICEWS project are not public, thus making it difficult to assess any impact. We do know that the US government is paying tens of millions of dollars to specific IR scholars and US universities to generate these event data and use them to forecast violent political events.

The Good Judgment Project, which works with the US Intelligence Advanced Research Projects Activity, is another initiative that has turned to crowdsourcing information to forecast world events, including intrastate conflict. The Good Judgment Project claims to be surprisingly successful at prediction—better even than intelligence analysts with classified information—and the question will now be to what extent the predictions they make transfer over to the policy community. This project is the result of a multidisciplinary collaboration that combines insights from political science and psychology to generate predictions but also to train forecasters how to make better predictions.

Academics have worked directly within various organizations either on a temporary or permanent basis; whole centers or institutes at places such as the World Bank or USAID are devoted to policy-relevant scholarly research. In fact, some influential work from scholars—such as Paul Collier, Nicholas Sambanis, Anke Hoeffler, and Michael Doyle—began or advanced while these scholars were embedded in policy organizations such as the UN or World Bank. In the area of intrastate conflict, one of the most visible impacts of academic work was the 2011 World Development Report devoted to the connection between armed conflict and international development (World Bank 2011). A number of noted development and conflict scholars contributed background papers and otherwise helped author the report, which is frequently cited by policymakers within the World Bank and member governments when they explain aid allocation decisions and design interventions.

In a similar vein, one of the fastest growing trends in recent years is policy-relevant experimental work. The Jameel Poverty Action Lab, Innovations for Poverty Action, Experiments in Governance and Politics, and other projects have actively conducted randomized controlled trials in a variety of developing countries on topics ranging from sex education interventions in schools to the administration of hundreds of millions of dollars for food distribution in violence-affected communities. Many of these experiments are formal academic-policy partnerships in which implementing partners explicitly commit to following academic design mandates. Christina Schneider makes a similar observation in chapter 6 and links such collaborations to the need for practitioners to draw on academic researchers when cutting-edge methods are required (argument 1b).

Over the past fifteen years many scholars and policymakers have slowly converged on examining and addressing intrastate conflict through the lens of development and governance policy. The UN Peacebuilding Architecture was established in the past decade with the mandate to work through other UN implementers to build peace through development and humanitarian-type assistance. USAID has devoted many resources to implement development projects in the context of war-to-peace transitions. The World Bank, UK's Department for International Development, and others also participate in this business. In a variety of direct and indirect ways, scholars have contributed to the implementation of development strategies in these contexts.

Academic, policy-relevant work is occurring, but it is unclear whether we have a solid understanding of just how much, in what form, or how consequential it is. And we may never know; as in the following discussion, it may be wiser to try to understand the precise conditions under which practitioners (policymakers, policy staff, and policy advocates) pay attention to academic research, even if it occurs in narrow settings but ones in which we can establish sufficient control to identify such effects.

## From Policy to Academy

Observing policy influence on academics (Ribar 2016) is ostensibly simpler than detecting the influence of academics on policy. There is a known set of academics whose work is tracked via journal articles and conference submissions and whose opinions can be solicited via surveys. Thus, the TRIP article database and scholar surveys provide useful tools to examine, for example, numbers of terrorism articles pre- and post-9/11. Indeed, surveys of this nature exist.

Some published work and other anecdotal evidence suggest that the impact does occur. In just two examples, Diehl (2002) wrote that scholars of war often "chase the headlines," and Young and Findley (2011) demonstrate this trend in the terrorism literature.

Certainly, funding availability has shaped the agendas of many researchers. In the field of international security, the Department of Defense Minerva Initiative has spawned large and important research activities in a wide variety of contexts and has attracted some of the most promising security scholars to use the funding. The United States Institute of Peace, Smith Richardson Foundation, and other funders conduct similarly motivated research.

Although we like to think of influence as positive, this is not always the case. Indeed, the improvements in impact evaluation in recent years were motivated by policy practices that were not sound. Thus, the policy world influenced the academy, but not necessarily by design. Scholars observed subpar practices and then began conducting research that would improve such practices. If the result is improved outcomes, however, the motivation for influence may be less consequential.

## Academy to Policy and Back Again

We are aware of some academics who have left their academic posts to work in governments, intergovernmental organizations (IGOs), or nongovernmental organizations (NGOs). Jeremy Weinstein (Stanford), as mentioned previously, served as deputy and chief of staff for Samantha Power, the US Ambassador to the United Nations, before returning to Stanford University. Michael Doyle left his academic posts to serve as assistant secretary-general and special advisor to Kofi Annan. Michael Horowitz returned to the University of Pennsylvania after a year working in the Department of Defense. Scholar-practitioners, including Stephen Stedman and William Zartman, also spent considerable time in high-level conflict resolution activities while also producing scholarly research at academic institutions. Other examples could be provided. That said, the vast majority of political scientists who begin work in the academy simply stay in the academy. And those who begin in the policy world typically stay there.

Academics and practitioners work together in other ways, however. Experimental field research, much of it on development and conflict, relies on close academic-policy collaborations. NGOs or IGOs seek to carry out large-scale projects but need assistance from scholars who have expertise in designing proper interventions. Thus, numerous partnerships are born, with examples ranging from USAID to the International Rescue Committee to small NGOs such as Deniva in Uganda. Thus, there are most likely many different models that would facilitate cross-fertilization of ideas.

# CONCLUSION

A broader examination of the TRIP data and discussion of the policy and scholarly nexus lead us to some final points. First, and to summarize this chapter, data on trends in scholarly and policy work for intrastate conflict are spotty. Much remains to be done and will require substantial attention from the academic and policy communities. We feel the data and this paper are an opening salvo, but we do not think that sufficient progress has been made to reach definitive conclusions or make credible recommendations.

Second, we understand that lines have to be drawn somewhere and that for this book those lines surround political scientists. But to fully understand the relationship between scholarship and policy on intrastate conflict, one would need to trespass across disciplinary borders (see also chapters 1 and 9 on this point). Other academics—such as economists, psychologists, lawyers, anthropologists, global health scholars, sociologists, mathematicians, and physicists—are working on intrastate conflict and are contributing to policy discussions. One of the most famous, John Yoo, who worked in the US Department of Justice, authored some of the detention and interrogation policies in the George W. Bush administration while on leave from his faculty position at the University of California, Berkeley.

Third, although intrastate conflict is clearly the dominant form of conflict in the world and has been for a long time, scholars and policymakers remain predominantly focused on interstate war. The empirical observation about trends in intrastate and interstate conflict is not novel (see Moore 2006). We were nonetheless surprised that the TRIP survey and more general disciplinary attention continue to lag behind the empirical dynamics of conflict in the world. These findings are sadly consistent with the expectations of argument 3b, presented in chapter 1; as a discipline matures and professionalizes, its scholarship may become less relevant to practitioners as new generations of scholars are incentivized to write for an increasingly institutionalized discipline.

Fourth, in our race to strengthen the links, it may be important to ask ourselves whether such strengthening could do damage. Clearly, there is tremendous variation in the quality of scholarship that makes it into the public domain. Do we need to set standards for what constitutes a credible evidence base for policymaking? Such standards may not be possible in today's climate, but the practicalities do not invalidate the question. We would be concerned about a significant portion of academic work making it into the policy sphere without passing significant validity, reliability, and identification checks.

Fifth, there is a large censoring problem that makes the task of understanding difficult. Many ideas are spawned but never written, or papers are written but never presented, or written/presented but never published, or published but never read. In the realm of teaching, most public course descriptions are brief, many syllabi still gated, most lecture notes not distributed, and so forth. We will not expand here, but academic incentives, university bureaucracy, and the publication system in the academy provide numerous challenges that would need to be accounted for to fully address impact.

Finally, we wish to draw attention to the sticky issues of demonstrating a causal effect of scholarly work on policy activity. There are many ways that the observational analyses in this book could understate or overstate the impacts, and it is conceivable that our inferences could be completely wrong. We hope that scholars will think creatively about how to prioritize strategies for stronger causal inference in international relations (Findley et al. 2013; Hyde 2015).

## ENDNOTES

1. The TRIP journal data has an *issue area* variable, which captures a higher level of aggregation than the *substantive focus* variable. The most relevant issue area for us is International Security, but this variable does not allow us to distinguish intrastate from interstate or other types of conflict.
2. See Moore (2006) for a discussion on the "dark side" of this definition.
3. See Hoffman (2006) and Young and Findley (2011) for a more complete discussion of defining terrorism.
4. This despite the fact that the dataset covers twenty-one years before 9/11 and only thirteen years after that date. Using a simple chi-square test, this difference is statistically significant at the $p < .05$ level.
5. Findley, Piazza, and Young (2012) and Conrad (2011) also connect the study of interstate war with transnational terrorism.
6. The editors' useful discussion of types of policy actors is important here and draws attention to the policy staff and advocates who are more likely users of policy prescriptions.
7. Of course, a policy prescription does not need to be expressly identified as such. Any work could fall into the hands of the policy community, who could draw lessons from this (or not).
8. We thank Tricia Bacon, American University faculty member and former member of the intelligence community, for this insight.
9. Some rigorous qualitative work, such as Skocpol (1979), outlines necessary and sufficient conditions where a single case could undermine the claim. These arguments are rarer among empirical scholars.
10. Many of these additional articles are in the quantitative tradition (Young 2019).

# 15

# ON THE CHALLENGE OF ASSESSING SCHOLARLY INFLUENCE ON INTRASTATE CONFLICT POLICY

Scott Edwards

In their assessment of the relationship between scholarship and policy on intrastate conflict, Michael G. Findley and Joseph K. Young characterize scholarship's influence over policy as modest and, above all else, difficult to detect. On this latter point, especially, we agree.

As good scholars do, the authors identify the challenge of inferring a causal effect of scholarship on policy based on the best available observational data (Teaching, Research, and International Policy [TRIP] survey), and they refrain from drawing any strong conclusions. They are, however, able to draw credible inferences about the effect of policy on scholarship (or rather, the effect of current events on the perceived policy relevance of studying certain topics, such as terrorism).

The mundane challenges to inferring scholarly impact on policy are the result of natural censoring. We should expect natural censoring as a product of the strategic nature of policy on intrastate conflict; information about an agency's rationale—whether informed by scholarship or not—has value as private information, even assuming that agency personnel are not trying to signal to other domestic or international actors. That is, unlike other areas of policymaking concerned with, for instance, the environment, economics, or technocratic areas of public life, policymakers dealing with matters of statecraft and conflict are incentivized to hold logics private. There is little demand, and thus little incentive, for policymakers affecting the course of conflict dynamics to justify their actions based on science.

The most significant challenge to the inference of scholarly influence on policy is an epistemological one. The complex and often opaque data-generating processes that lead to policy outcomes are the very things under examination by scholars studying intrastate conflict. We can still potentially map some scholarly insight on policymaking, and maybe even infer the occasional causal arrow, but the act of measuring something one is simultaneously attempting to act upon is difficult at best.

Leaving the challenges of inference aside, the endeavor to assess the academic influence on policy processes is at least partially predicated on the assumption that the world would be a better place if policymakers made use of academic insights. Yet it is not hard to imagine a scenario in which scholarly work is used to advance agendas with normative dimensions that might make scholars complicit in harm.

As an example, take as given that in this new digital world, information has diffuse but dramatic impact on all matter of social and political events. The challenges of coordination and mobilization among pro-democracy or government opposition groups are challenges primarily defined by the collection, sharing, and spread of information. As I write these words, the transitional government in Sudan—facing persistent coordinated action for civilian rule—has shut down the internet in the whole of the country. This has the effect of making coordination by opposition activists harder. It also has the effect of slowing the efforts of monitors and investigators seeking to document violence and human rights abuses by elements of the security forces.

Are we witnessing the knowing use of the insights of political science by the military government in Sudan to frustrate collective action? To minimize both domestic and international audience costs of violence against peaceful protestors? To mask agency slippage represented by roving bands of former Janjaweed responsible for much of the harm in Darfur now violently policing Khartoum? If so, this would certainly qualify as scholarly impact on real-world events, as well as an example of value conflict between scholar and policymaker.

Or—as I suspect—are we simply witnessing phenomena manifest and unfold as the academy would tend to predict: the decision-makers in Khartoum blissfully unaware that their tactics could have readily been devised by a malevolent political scientist? In this instance, the academic researcher working on information and collective action in the course of intrastate conflict may prefer to have had no impact on real-world events.

Notwithstanding the challenges of detecting academic influence, what explains Findley and Young's assessment of the modest impact of scholarship on policymaking in intrastate conflict? One likely answer, which the authors touch on, is the creation of units or the bounding of events that serves scientific inquiry well but may map poorly on policy processes. Take a hypothetical increase in repression in a given country. There is excellent scholarly work on dissent-repression dynamics, human rights compliance, and related dynamics. Now, assume that this country devolves into armed civil conflict. How reasonable is it to assume that the State Department desk officer for this country, or even the assistant secretary of state who manages a region as a matter of daily work, is going to consult an unfamiliar literature on intrastate conflict? The needs of the scholar to bound and categorize phenomena—crucial to the scholarly endeavor—does not necessarily map well on policy workflow.

The probabilistic nature of scholarly insights is itself problematic, and unless specifically crafted for decision support is not readily incorporated into policymaking. The hypothetical State Department actors likely perceive themselves as better able to predict whether their country of interest will devolve into intrastate conflict; they have access to classified information that scholars do not. In fact, they likely *are* better able to predict, not because of access to private information but because the predictive task at hand is not restricted by parsimony, theory, or a culture of ingraining the importance of "scholarly relevance" in their assessments and policy responses.

As Findley and Young point out, intrastate conflict is part of a continuum of conflict processes. In fact, the difference between the outbreak of intrastate conflict and the state of affairs immediately prior to outbreak is only meaningful based on the observer's motivation. These motivations differ between the academic and policy worlds. The difference between pre-outbreak and outbreak states is relevant to the scholar because they must define the phenomenon of intrastate conflict in order to study it, and it is relevant to the policymaker because of the normative importance of a shift to conflict through violence. Findley and Young note similar mapping disjunctures, especially with regard to terrorism, and these disjunctures are likely contributing causes of both a lack of scholarly influence on policymaking and difficulties in observing or inferring such influence.

As Findley and Young also note, there are areas of policy, most notably development, that in my experience appear to be heavily influenced by scholarship. Why is development practice more heavily influenced by scholarship than intrastate conflict policy is influenced by conflict research? It may be that there are fewer value conflicts. Policy decisions and deliberations of all magnitudes, especially as they relate to intrastate conflict, represent choices that are inextricably linked to values, normative aspirations, and often competing imperatives. In the case of development, scholars know well the motivations of their policymaking audience; in the case of intrastate conflict, in which actors with the greatest agency are inherently political, the priorities of the policy audience are less certain.

My own experience as a practitioner in the field of human rights and international humanitarian law—but one who was rigorously trained as a political scientist—may be instructive, if biased. Over the last decade, I have regularly applied theory to effect some outcome or policy objective, most often using strategic interaction modeling approaches to compel or dissuade certain behaviors by conflict actors. If this experience is more universal, and my sense is that it is, the influence of scholarship on policymakers may involve the application of models (or at least frames) by policymakers who assist in scenario mapping and decision-support modeling.

Indeed, some of the more visible instances of direct scholarly influence on policy cited by Findley and Young (e.g., the Political Instability Task Force and the Integrated Conflict Early Warning System) qualify as decision-support systems. I consulted on early warning systems for UN agencies and other monitoring mechanisms for political violence for nongovernmental entities over the years, marking my transition from academic to practitioner.

These initiatives were directly integrated into the policymaking process; they thus represent the ultimate policy relevance of scholarly work. Similar initiatives (increasingly relying on the mining of "big" data) in conflict, human security, and other related fields will continue to drive the demand for scholarly research outputs that inform decision-support mechanisms. This provides a fruitful area for scholarly impact and an avenue to monitor the potentially pernicious effects of biases in decision-support systems that process large volumes of data.

Like Findley and Young, I think that determining the influence of scholarship on policymaking in the area of intrastate conflict is challenging, even with the best data on hand; one should expect that direct observation of influence over policymaking in this domain would be highly censored. If influence is absent, the reasons may be many. Importantly, however, one should question, as the authors do, what we would want that influence to look like.

Based on my experience, the most effective pathway for the academy to influence the course of events related to intrastate conflict is *not* by persuading high-level policymakers of the applicability of scientific insights to a given problem. In the course of scientific inquiry, pains are taken to establish the policy relevance of a particular piece of research. To the extent that policymakers do not heed the lessons or seize upon the insights of political science in the context of intrastate violence, it is tempting to assume the problem is one of communication: the agents are simply not aware of how the academy can help. And although this may be the case, I suggest that the solution is not more engagement with policymakers, who are already attempting to satisfy multiple principals and audiences; policymakers, who, if we are honest with ourselves, may have priorities that are fundamentally incompatible with the normative aspirations of many political scientists.

In my role at Amnesty International, I have formulated and put into writing dozens of discrete policy recommendations (and occasionally policy "demands") for governments, armed opposition, and a range of other nonstate and intergovernmental actors. Any investigative report or paper released by a human rights or conflict watchdog will necessarily have policy recommendations attached to them. Although these watchdogs may have different mandates, and the normative underpinnings of their ethos may differ, it is safe to assume that none would be in stark contrast to the values of researchers working on conflict mitigation. As in the field of development, these actors—practitioners who serve as the strongest link between ground conditions and agents in government capitals—are the best-placed vehicles for integrating academy insights into practical effect. Unlike agents of governments or international bodies, these actors have a simpler rational calculus defined by mandate, few patrons, and comparatively limited concern with audience costs.

How do we ensure that these actors with the greatest influence over policymakers use the insights of the academy to generate policy demands?

As Findley and Young point out, individual academics moving into the practical realm have measurable effect. Consortia around discrete problems (e.g., forced displacement, sexual violence in conflict, environmental drivers of violence) can serve to directly bring academic insights into thematic policy work. Likewise, engagements between watchdogs and academics through geographic or state-level problem-solving groups—effectively "task forces"—can drive refinement and tailoring of policy proscriptions made by advocacy organizations, drawing on the best political science has to offer. Finally, there are volumes such as this: longer term engagements that require both academic and practitioner to evaluate their impact on real-world events and the rigor behind the rationale for their policy aims.

# 16

# THE BUMPY ROAD TO A "SCIENCE" OF NUCLEAR STRATEGY

Paul C. Avey and Michael C. Desch

International security has long been among the most policy-relevant sub-fields of academic international relations (IR) (Jervis 2004, 101; Schelling 2004, 137; also see Kaplan 1983, 336). This is still true today, at least as measured by the relative willingness of authors in top IR journals to offer explicit policy recommendations. There is a significant difference, as Teaching, Research, and International Policy (TRIP) data (Maliniak et al. 2011) show, between articles published since 1980 dealing with security issues and those dealing with other issue areas in the field. As figure 16.1 shows, however, the willingness of IR scholars to offer policy recommendations has declined in absolute terms since 1980, and this drop may have to do with the professionalization of the discipline of political science. Of course, the full story of the growing estrangement of scholars from policy also would have to include discussion of changes in government, public opinion, and the upper reaches of academic administration. However, in this chapter we focus on those changes that have taken place in disciplines and among individual scholars. Together, the chapters in this book highlight the nature or structure of the issue area under consideration and the changing incentives of scholars as explanations of scholars' policy engagement, relevance, and influence. Most chapters in this book focus on the structural sources of scholarly involvement in the policy world, but in this chapter we shine a light on the "supply side" of this equation—on the professional incentives of scholars and on features of the academy that moderate (or exacerbate) the effects of structural constraints.

The professionalization of a discipline, and its increasing irrelevance to policy issues, is neither historically nor logically inevitable, but there nonetheless seems to be an elective affinity between these two trends. First, the increasing emphasis on quantitative research has led to narrower research questions that are often too abstruse or narrow to be relevant to policy (Mearsheimer and Walt 2013). Second, many proponents of the scientific study of politics believe that advocacy of particular policies is incompatible with scientific objectivity and so avoid it (Proctor 1991, 3–5). Third, many pressing policy questions are not readily amenable to social scientists' preferred methodological tools; works that employ abstract theory or

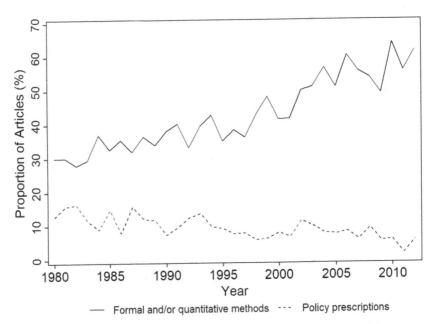

**FIGURE 16.1.**   Quantitative or formal methods and policy prescriptions in top IR journals, 1980–2012

quantitative and formal methods are less relevant to and have less influence on policy and practitioners than scholarship that uses qualitative approaches. Finally, even when the results of these approaches are relevant to policy questions, they are often not presented in an accessible way for policymakers or the broader public. (On this and the previous point, see Avey and Desch 2014; Desch 2015.) When scholarship is not presented in an easily consumable format, it will not resonate within or influence the practitioner community. The more "scientific" approaches to IR scholarship seem to be the least relevant, at least as measured by quantitative and formal scholars' willingness to offer policy recommendations, as figure 16.1 indicates. The problem is not so much that "scientific" approaches to national security policy are irrelevant by definition; rather, their current dominance within academic IR is a symptom of a larger trend among the social sciences to privilege method and theory over substance, with a resulting decline in policy relevance. This is because a methods-driven research agenda tends to privilege technique over substance, at best resulting in only "accidental relevance" (Waltz 1959, 76). Conversely, problem-driven research is more conducive to methodological pluralism, employing the most appropriate method for a given question, which is initially chosen based on its substantive importance.

In the area of nuclear strategy, it was not always so. Many believe nuclear strategy first opened the door for the civilian Cold War "Wizards of

Armageddon," as journalist Fred Kaplan (1983) dubbed these civilian strategists, to shape nuclear strategy, and it remains among the most relevant fields today. For this reason, we believe the nuclear issue area is a good one in which to explore the conditions under which academic IR influences policy. "Academic strategists" (Kraft 1962, 103) such as Bernard Brodie, Albert Wohlstetter, Herman Kahn, and especially Thomas Schelling reputedly exercised such influence that the period between 1945 and 1961 is regarded as the "golden age" of academic national security studies (Schelling 1978, 2). What is striking, for good and ill, is the relative paucity of political scientists among this group.

To be sure, not everyone is convinced that there really was a golden age in which social science actually influenced US national security policy. Pointing to the divergence between US nuclear declaratory policy (in which defense intellectuals apparently had influence through the theory of mutual assured destruction [MAD]) and operational doctrine and war plans (where in his view they did not), historian Bruce Kuklick (2006, 6, 15–16, 143–44, 150, 223–30; also see Gavin 2012, 4) presents the most sustained critique of the conventional wisdom: "[T]he men who actually made decisions were least concerned with *scientific* ideas of any sort" and the ideas of strategists had "little causal impact," save perhaps as *ex post facto* rationalizations for policymakers' decisions. In his view, "none of the critical aspects of decision making had much to do with the prevalent model of American social science—'whispering in the ear of princes'—the middle-range generalizations supposedly necessary to benign policy and learned in a Ph.D. course." Deborah Larson (1995, 88–89) agrees that even the dean of civilian nuclear strategists, Bernard Brodie, actually had little impact on the government or the wider public.

This debate about the extent of the influence of academic social scientists on nuclear strategy matters for several reasons. First, if civilian academic strategists had no influence on nuclear thinking during the early Cold War, there is little reason to expect them to have any today. Second, if there is no variation in their influence, this case can tell us little about when and under what conditions academics have influence (see King et al. 1994, 129). Finally, the nuclear case speaks to the larger question, in the words of a National Research Council study, whether there is any "relationship between basic [social science] research . . . and programmatically useful results" (Advisory Committee 1971, xii).

To answer this question, we explore the changing relationship between academia and national security policy during the so-called golden age of cooperation between the two realms, roughly 1945 to 1965, focusing on nuclear strategy. (This draws from Desch 2019a, chap. 6.) We aim to establish the academic strategists' actual influence (the value of the dependent variable) as well as to explain their changing role in nuclear strategy (identifying the independent variable). Using this history we develop criteria for when scholarship can influence policy. We further demonstrate the plausibility of this

framework by using it to explain why the first post–Cold War wave of nuclear studies struggled to be relevant.[1] We then employ these criteria to determine when and how the current generation of academics working on nuclear
issues might influence policy much as political scientist Robert Gilpin did
for the role of natural scientists in US nuclear weapons policy (Gilpin 1962,
300; also see 7).

Briefly, we agree with Jervis that the golden age theorists' "influence
may be greater than Kuklick portrays," (Jervis 2006, 9) but show that it
waxed and waned during the Cold War. It did so even before the Vietnam
War, the most common explanation for the end of the golden age, eventually
reaching an intellectual dead end. By this, we mean that intellectual developments within social science—the privileging of method and theory over substantive issues—reduced the relevance of many academics' work. What led
to diminished relevance, we suggest, was scholars' growing embrace of economic approaches to nuclear strategy. The increasingly abstract character of
late golden age theories would eventually disconnect them from real-world
policy concerns by pushing nuclear strategy beyond MAD. The end of the
golden age is thus a cautionary tale for today's generation of nuclear scholars,
many of whom in their effort to recreate a "science" of strategy seem again to
be emulating the economic methods and approaches that brought academic
nuclear strategy to a dead end.[2]

This chapter proceeds in three sections. We begin by tracing and explaining the waxing and waning of the golden age of academic nuclear
strategy to develop criteria for influence. Next, we apply these insights to
post–Cold War nuclear theorizing, including the optimist-pessimist debate and the purported "renaissance" in nuclear studies. We conclude with
some recommendations for how to balance rigor with relevance so that the
current wave of academic nuclear theorizing can avoid another intellectual
cul-de-sac.

## THE WAXING AND WANING OF THE GOLDEN AGE OF ACADEMIC NUCLEAR STRATEGISTS

Because there is debate about the actual influence of golden age civilian nuclear strategists, our first task is to establish whether they in fact affected
policy. After establishing that they did, at least early on, we consider two explanations for the waning of their influence. Conventional wisdom suggests
that academic influence ended as a result of the Vietnam War, which dele-
gitimized collaboration with the US government among academics. There is
some truth in that view, but we suggest that it was the increasing influence
of economic approaches that further undermined the relevance of academic
strategy by privileging internal disciplinary concerns such as theoretical elo-
quence and the use of sophisticated methods over addressing concrete policy
problems.

# Four Criteria for Influence

Ascertaining whether academic nuclear strategists had influence on policy practitioners is challenging for two reasons. As political scientist John Kingdon warns, the influence of academics on policy debates is often "hidden," and the secrecy surrounding national security decision-making makes their role in nuclear strategy even more opaque (Kingdon 2003, 199). Moreover, such an exercise involves the more general challenge of tracing the influence of ideas, the currency of academics, on policy outcomes (see Legro 2000; Adler and Hass 1992; and especially Kingdon 2003, 2–3). Given that, our expectations for the influence of those ideas need to be reasonable. On occasion, we see clear evidence of their direct impact in instances when scholars consult for or work in government for an extended period of time.[3] Often, however, it is the indirect effect of ideas in which they provide the mental maps that frame how policymakers and the public think about strategy (Latham 1998, 205–6) that are the most important. The history of the golden age shows that some of these ideas about the effects of nuclear weapons on statecraft, particularly the unique deterrent effects embodied in the MAD concept, had real impact on presidential crisis decision-making even if they did not shape operational plans and doctrine.

Based on our examination of the decline of the early Cold War golden age, we propose four criteria for influence First, academic work should deal with "important" topics and pressing problems that practitioners—senior policymakers and their staffs—and members of the general public care about. Second, scholarship should focus on variables that government policy can manipulate. Third, it should make explicit policy recommendations about how to do so in both general classes of cases and specific instances on the policy agenda. Finally, scholarship needs to offer clear, consistent findings about the effect of specific variables (e.g., Van Evera 1997, 97).

## Academic Influence during the Early Cold War

Two related events at the end of World War II set the stage for the longest peacetime period of national security cooperation between the academy and the US government. These were the invention and use of the atomic bomb against Japan in the last weeks of the war and the outbreak of the Cold War two years later. For much of history, in political scientist Bernard Brodie's view, the use of military force had been a viable instrument of statecraft. With the advent of nuclear weapons, only the threat of the use of force remained available to statesmen because the actual use of nuclear weapons would be mutually catastrophic (Herken 1985, xi–xii). Brodie foresaw that the development of the H-bomb would tilt the cost/benefit ratio against war permanently (Steiner 1991, 134). These ideas crystallized in a volume of essays Brodie edited for Yale's Institute for International Studies titled *The Absolute Weapon*, which established the contributors as the country's leading experts on nuclear strategy, their services much in demand in government and the military (Trachtenberg 1991, 11).[4]

However, lack of enthusiasm among universities for policy-relevant national security research encouraged policy practitioners to seek alternative means for marshalling academic resources to fight the Cold War (Lyons and Morton 1965, 130–34). As journalist Joseph Kraft put it, "a main part of [the US Air Force's Project RAND's] job was to bridge the ancient gulf between scholars and soldiers" (Kraft 1960, 69).

RAND's most important national security research involved how the United States ought to think about nuclear strategy once the Soviet Union developed its nuclear capability. A number of RAND analysts studied this issue, but the most influential was Albert Wohlstetter, later a professor of political science at the University of Chicago (Kuklick 2006, 63). Wohlstetter's first project for RAND was his famous "basing study," which explored how the Strategic Air Command's dependence on a small number of air bases might make it vulnerable to a Soviet first strike. Although Wohlstetter struggled to get SAC to concede this vulnerability, in the end Wohlstetter's study "finally led SAC to reduce its dependency on elaborate overseas bases. . . . There is no question that the Wohlstetter study helped reduce this reliance" (Kaplan 1983, 110).

Wohlstetter's second contribution to US nuclear strategy was the research that led to his famous January 1959 *Foreign Affairs* article, "The Delicate Balance of Terror," in which he argued that the United States could not assume the continuing invulnerability of its nuclear deterrent (Wohlstetter 1959; Kaplan 1983, 108–10). Wohlstetter's analysis of the vulnerability of US intercontinental ballistic missiles overcame Air Force skepticism that "hardening" them in concrete silos would serve to mitigate their vulnerability (Herken 1985, 156). It bolstered Democratic critics of Eisenhower's massive retaliation strategy (Kaplan 1983, 171–73; Herken 1985, 124).

A number of academics, including Henry Kissinger and Robert Osgood, were skeptical of massive retaliation, but the most trenchant critic of the strategy, which relied solely on nuclear weapons to deter a conventional Soviet attack, was Princeton University political scientist William Kaufmann (Freedman 1983, 100–102). His Princeton Center for International Studies report "The Requirements of Deterrence" landed the "critical blow" in the public debate about whether to rely exclusively on the threat of nuclear retaliation to deter a Soviet conventional attack on Western Europe (Kaplan 1983, 186–89). It attracted the attention of Hans Speir, the new head of the RAND social science division, for whom Kaufmann began doing summer consulting. His recommendation that the United States engage in a buildup of its conventional forces not only appealed to the US Army's bureaucratic interest but also became a major plank in John F. Kennedy's campaign platform (Herken 1985, 99).

Kaufmann's work also spurred interest in the use of strategic nuclear forces to limit damage from the Soviets' nuclear arsenal. "Counterforce" was a response to the growing problem of the credibility of the United States' extended deterrent in Europe, but it also represented a possible means for limiting damage and avoiding bloody "counter value" exchanges against cities and population centers (Kaplan 1983, 201–19; Kuklick 2006, 107–8). Kaufmann's work was influential not only among defense intellectuals but also in the US Air Force, where it was viewed as a potent bureaucratic weapon in the war against the US Navy, whose Submarine Launched Ballistic Missiles were not yet accurate enough to conduct such strikes (Kaplan 1983, 245). Kaufmann's influence peaked in 1962 when Secretary of Defense Robert McNamara announced his "no cities" doctrine in two speeches in Athens, Greece, and Ann Arbor, Michigan (Kaplan 1983, 283–85; Herken 1985, 79, 151; Shapley 1993, 139–40, 193).

Ironically, given the president's dislike of civilian strategists, the Eisenhower administration had started the trend of relying on outside experts in strategic affairs, but the Kennedy administration was the high water mark for the influence of academic defense intellectuals (Herken 1985, 133). Throughout the 1950s a group of Harvard and Massachusetts Institute of Technology (MIT) faculty played an increasingly public role in the debate about US defense policy, including as members of the academic advisory group during the 1960 presidential campaign (Kaplan 1983, 195). Its members were a who's who of academic luminaries, including Kissinger, John Kenneth Galbraith, Carl Kaysen, Paul Samuelson, Richard Neustadt, and Arthur Schlesinger Jr. A young Harvard graduate student named Daniel Ellsberg, who was working at Rand while finishing his PhD, served as a back channel to the campaign for staffers like Wohlstetter, Enthoven, Harry Rowen, and Fred Hoffman (Wells 2001, 157).

Kennedy drew liberally on universities throughout his administration, but the appointment of Ford Motor Company President (and former Harvard Business School professor) Robert McNamara as secretary of defense opened wide the Pentagon doors to civilian defense intellectuals. The social scientists whom McNamara recruited to the Pentagon were collectively referred to as the "Whiz Kids" in recognition of their brilliance and youth. Their ranks included political scientists like Kaufmann, who had left Rand and was then teaching at MIT, and economists like Enthoven, Harvard's Thomas Schelling, and former Oxford don and then current director of the economics division at Rand Charles Hitch (Kuklick 2006, 34–36).[5]

Kuklick minimizes the influence of these Whiz Kids in the Kennedy administration, noting that civilian theories of the nuclear revolution and MAD were not reflected in the military's actual war plans and operational doctrine. However, this argument hardly constitutes proof that academic ideas were irrelevant. Some writings by defense intellectuals like Wohlstetter did have a direct impact on operations. Although others did not directly shape military war plans, civilian nuclear theories also influenced other levels of US government, particularly presidential decision-making during nuclear crises (Smith 1966, 230). Jervis (1989, 8–9), for example, concedes that "most of the history of American doctrine and war planning has been the attempt to design substitutes for damage limitation . . ." He goes on to suggest that "the influence of the fear of war on political leaders is not sensitive to the details of doctrine and war planning that preoccupy the specialists . . . [because] mutual vulnerability exists and casts an enormous shadow. This condition is not subtle nor does it depend on the details of the strategic balance or targeting that may loom large to academics or war planners; such details are dwarfed in the eyes of decision makers by the danger of overwhelming destruction" (Jervis 1989, 98).[6]

Confirming Jervis's intuition, even President Eisenhower, the architect of massive retaliation, did not really believe that the United States could fight a nuclear war, remarking that "you can't have this kind of war. There just aren't enough bulldozers to scrape the bodies off the streets." Endorsing a version of MAD, Eisenhower was confident that, "until an enemy [has] enough operational capability to destroy most of our bases simultaneously and thus prevent retaliation by us, our deterrence remains effective" (quoted in Ghamari-Tabrizi 2005, 192).

This view continued into the Kennedy and Johnson administrations. Kennedy flirted with counterforce warfighting strategies but ultimately reverted to MAD. Former Kennedy White House staffer Marcus Raskin attests that "most of the people who actually made high policy thought that planning for nuclear war was merely an exercise in the theory of annihilation, that it could have no practical consequences" (Raskin 1963). Secretary of Defense Robert McNamara (quoted in Gavin 2012, 36) informed Paul Nitze in 1962 that "[t]he concept of a 'worsened relative military position after a general nuclear war' is not a meaningful one to me when each side has the capacity to destroy each other's civilization." In other words, there is good evidence that MAD provided the mental map that guided policymakers through the early days of the nuclear age.

## Vietnam and the End of the Golden Age

There is no doubt that the golden age ended roughly coincident with the Vietnam War (Trachtenberg 1991, 3). Many believe that this was no coincidence. Journalist Fred Kaplan (1983, 329), for instance, links the two, arguing that America's "Vietnam strategy was essentially a conventional-war version of the counterforce/no cities theory—using force as an instrument of coercion, withholding a larger force that could kill the hostage of the enemy's cities if he didn't back down." Kaufmann's (1956, 34) critique of massive retaliation connected a limited war in Vietnam to the larger struggle with the Soviet Union through the need to maintain US credibility. Schelling's work on bargaining in trade negotiations also seemed readily transferable to strategic interaction, especially reinforcing the importance of holding off Communism in South Vietnam to maintain America's reputation as a stalwart ally and determined foe (Larson 1995, 100). Finally, Schelling suggested that the limited use of force could "signal" US resolve to stand by its South

Vietnamese ally through a graduated bombing campaign against the North (Nacht 1980; Shapley 1993, 322–23).[7]

Attesting to the deteriorating intellectual climate for policy-relevant national security research, Kaufmann and Schelling argued that the unrest caused by the Vietnam War in Cambridge nearly put an end to the academic study and teaching of national security (Herken 1985, 220–21). As Schelling explained his post-Vietnam intellectual reorientation away from security studies, "I lost the access, I lost the audience, and I lost the motivation" (quoted in Herken 1985, 313). Indeed, some major universities such as Columbia, MIT, Chicago, Princeton, Stanford, Berkeley, and Case Western Reserve had institutional connections with other federally funded research and development centers (FFRDCs) aside from Rand. These connections became particularly controversial during the height of the antiwar movement, and most were severed (see Bell 1968).

By the early 1970s, there was a marked change in campus attitudes about academics engaging in national security policymaking. Many still did as individuals (e.g., Kissinger and Zbigniew Brzezinski), but the bridge from the Ivory Tower to the Beltway increasingly became a one-way street, with most of those taking it to Washington never returning to academe (Kuklick 2006, 182–203). To be sure, there were a handful of senior scholars who managed to go back and forth—people like Samuel Huntington, Joseph Nye, and Jervis—but as time went on, they became more the exception than the rule among leading scholars (Avey and Desch 2014).

## Following Economics to an Intellectual Dead End

Was Vietnam the only, or even the most important, reason for the estrangement of academics from policy-relevant work on nuclear strategy? There was evidence of increasing intellectual tensions between academia and government well before Vietnam. Indeed, the establishment of Rand and other FFRDCs was a response to the growing difficulty of working with universities directly. The root of this difficulty was the increasing influence of the economic approach to strategy. As historian Marc Trachtenberg (1991, 15, 13; see also Herken 1985, 49, 75–76) explains, "there was an intellectual vacuum in the whole national security area. The economists, and people heavily influenced by their style of thinking, were for a variety of reasons drawn to this vacuum. What they had was something very general, a way of approaching issues, rather than anything that in itself suggested substantive answers that went right to the heart of the strategic problem." "What was new," Eliot Cohen (1982) agrees, "was not the use of numbers or equations to help solve military problems but rather the coronation of one social science—[e]conomics—as the rightful queen of war-planning and strategy."

Brodie (quoted in Steiner 1991, 42) initially believed that strategy could become a "science" and economics provided the model for it: "the strategy of strategic bombing is very largely a matter of target selection, where the economist (possibly also the psychologist) has at least as much to offer as the military specialist." But in a letter to James Holland of the Army War College, Brodie later confessed that he had become a "trifle uneasy" about his early call to make strategy a science modelled on the methods of economics: "I must tell you that I am not so disposed today as I was then to toss so many bouquets to the economists. It is not the substance of what I say in that paper that bothers me so much as the tone. I am concerned with the fact that the relevant political issues tend to be automatically de-emphasized by giving so much emphasis to the comparability of strategy with economics" (Brodie 1966). The problem was that by the mid-1960s the economic approach to strategic thought in the United States had reached something of an intellectual dead end. This was the result, in Trachtenberg's (1991, 44) view, of the fact that "the most basic issues were [at that point] analyzed on a very abstract level. One could work out in general terms the argument for 'strategic stability' or for various nuclear war–fighting strategies. But at this level of abstraction there were no final answers—at this highly abstract level of conceptualization the most basic intellectual tensions could not be resolved."

As they fell for the seduction of theoretical elegance and method, the golden age nuclear strategists lost touch with the practical concerns of policymakers (Betts 1987, 195). Typical of policymakers' responses to this increasingly economic approach, Harvard Dean and Kennedy National Security Advisor McGeorge Bundy (1964, 9) lamented that "there is enough, and perhaps too much, analysis aimed at scholarly rigor and scientific validity. There is enough and perhaps too much system-building in which models of this or that political process are constructed. There is enough, and perhaps too much, detailed historical recording of political phenomena. What there is not enough of yet, and what I come to praise, is the kind of academic work which proceeds from the same center of concern as that of the man who is himself committed to an active part in government." Their "center of concern" was the concrete policy problems they faced.

There were limits to the influence of civilian strategists, particularly when their increasingly arcane theories led them beyond MAD. Bundy (quoted in Freedman 1983, 361) notes that

> There is an enormous gulf between what political leaders really think about nuclear weapons and what is assumed in complex calculations of relative "advantage" in simulated strategic warfare. Think Tank analysts can set levels of "acceptable" damage well up in the tens of millions of lives. They can assume that the loss of dozens of great cities is somehow a real choice for sane men. They are in an unreal world. In the real world of political leaders . . . a decision that would bring even one hydrogen bomb on one city of one's own country would be recognized in advance as a catastrophic blunder . . . [8]

In other words, MAD was not only a fact, it was also de facto policy despite civilian strategists' increasing rejection of it (Freedman 1983, 399; also see Gavin 2012, 4).

The initial golden age of academic theorizing provided policymakers grappling with the problems of new technologies (the atomic bomb) in a new security environment (the Cold War) with a new way of thinking.[9] By contrast, as economic approaches came to dominate nuclear theorizing, the scholarship seemed increasingly divorced from the problems that policymakers actually encountered. The basic MAD logic provided a framework for policymakers to guide behavior in nuclear crises. The economic approaches gave stylized interpretations of how actors might behave but little discussion of how historical and political circumstances would lead specific actors to behave.

Wohlstetter's influential basing study nicely illustrates our four criteria outlined at the beginning of this chapter. The study dealt with an important, problem-driven issue, how to keep the US deterrent effective as Soviet capabilities increased. Wohlstetter identified a policy that the US government could enact and made a clear recommendation: diversify basing and platforms. Finally, most strategists accept the basic argument that nuclear weapons must be survivable to effectively deter even if they differ on the precise number of weapons necessary to meet that requirement.

This is also why, in the final analysis, it was the more eclectic political scientist Brodie, rather than the economist Thomas Schelling, whose ideas had the most influence on actual nuclear statecraft (Jervis 1989, 49). Already in 1946, the former had set the "basic axioms of the nuclear age"—the absence of any meaningful defense against nuclear attack, the inevitable mutual vulnerability of each side's population, and the need for secure second-strike capability—which were the enduring facts of the nuclear age that policymakers recognized they had to grapple with (Freedman 1983, 44). Brodie's views directly influenced Secretary of Defense Robert McNamara's thinking on the subject (Steiner 1991, 21–22). The reason he did, in Lawrence Freedman's judgment, was that he "was not a formal strategist in that he lacked confidence in conclusions derived from 'war gaming' or rigorous but abstracted analysis, isolated from the real world" (Freedman 1983, 300).

Schelling, conversely, is the more highly esteemed in scholarly circles these days, having won the 2005 Nobel Prize in Economics. His work is also assigned more frequently in undergraduate and graduate courses and is more highly cited. He undoubtedly made "an original (and very important) contribution to the study of strategy," although it was largely derivative, applying concepts from economics to the world of strategy (Ayson 2004, 113). But after reviewing Schelling's contributions to strategy, his intellectual biographer Robert Ayson (2004, 200) concluded that Schelling ultimately fell "victim to the sense of unreality which afflicts aspects of nuclear strategy." Or as P. M. S. Blackett (Blackett 1961, 16) put it, Schelling's approach, and that of other game theorists like John von Neumann and Oskar Morgenstern, ultimately failed because it did not "clothe the skeleton conflicts of the theory of games with the complex flesh and blood attributes of real nations; hence the bizarre nature of some of their practical conclusions." Schelling himself eventually acknowledged the limits of using domestic bargaining analogies to analyze international conflict between states in the nuclear age. By 1964, well before the Vietnam War had begun to poison Ivory Tower/Beltway relations, he began to move away from strategic studies, perhaps a tacit admission that his economic approach to strategy had in fact reached a dead end (Ayson 2004, 152–53, 35).

In sum, the end of the golden age was not only, or even primarily, driven by real-world events like Vietnam; it was largely the result of the effort to make strategy a "science" that led it to an intellectual dead end. The increasing influence of economics led to a growing preoccupation with theory and method over substance.

## A CONTEMPORARY RENAISSANCE IN POLICY-RELEVANT RESEARCH?

Given the major changes in the world since 1989, the field of national security affairs ought to be ripe for a new golden age of theorizing about the influence of nuclear weapons on statecraft.[10] Some observers argue that we are living in a "second nuclear age," whereas others point to technological changes that may upend the basic MAD logic (Lieber and Press 2006a; Bracken 2012). Surveys indicate nuclear issues remain a top concern for the public and policymakers (Avey and Desch 2013b, 40–41; Smeltz et al. 2014, 21–22).

To the extent that there is an efflorescence of scholarship on nuclear weapons, it developed slowly. At least as judged by the number of articles engaging with these issues, academic social science failed to fully exploit any window of opportunity in the immediate post–Cold War world. The trend of articles dealing with weapons of mass destruction (WMD) and arms control in top IR journals was decidedly downward from approximately 9 percent of the articles published in the 1980s to less than 1 percent from 2010 to 2012 (figure 16.2). Although the data we used end in 2012, the trend may have abated, with a small uptick in the number of WMD and arms control articles published in these journals in 2013–14. It remains to be seen whether this interest can be sustained, although there are a number of pressing nuclear-related policy debates that scholars can usefully address. Within this smaller pool of articles, there is also a decline in the percentage of WMD and arms control articles offering policy prescriptions (figure 16.2). Consistent with these trends in the published discipline for most of this period, Paul Bracken (2012, 217) lamented that "the quality of thinking about nuclear weapons has reached a dangerously low level, in Washington and in the country. . . . In universities there is little knowledge of nuclear matters" (see also Nichols 2013, 5–6).

A closer examination of the two broad waves of post–Cold War political science scholarship on nuclear strategy reinforces this conclusion. In the rest of this section we assess each wave using our four criteria for influence. We are not judging the importance or findings of the works; indeed, we find

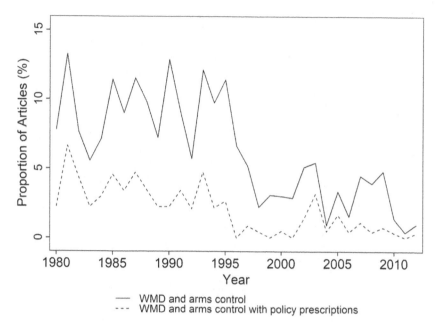

FIGURE 16.2. WMD and arms control articles in top IR journals, 1980–2012

much of the theory and evidence compelling and have learned much from these debates. Rather, we focus on the narrower question of what will be most relevant to policymakers and thus have the greatest likelihood of influencing them. We first examine the 1990s optimist-pessimist debate, which followed a pattern similar to the Cold War scholarship with the result that it eventually hit something of an intellectual dead end. Next, we examine the second wave, which began in the late 2000s and which Scott Sagan (2014) characterizes as a "renaissance" in nuclear security studies.

## The 1990s Proliferation Optimism-Pessimism Debate

The first wave crested in the wake of the Cold War and drew its lessons from the superpower experience.[11] To be sure, scholars marshaled evidence from emerging nuclear states, but the core of the historical evidence was US and Soviet behavior. Yet by the end of the 1990s the debate tapered off with little resolution. "As lively and consequential as the exchange was," writes David Karl (2011, 620), "it quickly approached the point of diminishing returns." No single work better epitomizes this scholarship than Scott Sagan and Kenneth Waltz's (2013) widely cited *The Spread of Nuclear Weapons*. An examination of this work is therefore useful in assessing why this important scholarly debate had little noticeable influence on policymakers.

Practitioners in Washington flatly rejected the optimist prescription. Former Clinton and George W. Bush National Security Council staffer Peter Feaver (1995, 770) writes that "regardless of how persuasive Waltz and the nuclear optimists may be in an academic setting, it is doubtful they would ever be persuasive in a US policy setting." Policymakers adopted the pessimist prescription against proliferation, but they did not do so by following the pessimists' logic. US policy had opposed proliferation since at least the 1960s, so more recent scholarship could not have influenced it (Gavin 2015). The reason had less to do with specific pessimist concerns and more to do with an underlying strategic logic: if other countries acquired nuclear weapons it would constrain US freedom of action. As Les Aspin, then chairman of the House Armed Services Committee, put it in 1992, "A world without nuclear weapons would not be disadvantageous to the United States. In fact, a world without nuclear weapons would actually be better. Nuclear weapons are still the big equalizer, but now the United States is not the equalizer but the equalizee" (quoted in Sagan and Waltz 2013, 107).[12] Additionally, proliferation could increase the odds that nonstate actors might acquire nuclear weapons, a concern that grew more salient in 2001 after the high point of the optimist-pessimist debate.

The lack of influence of the optimist-pessimist debate stemmed from its inability to meet the four criteria for relevance outlined previously. Most important, the debate moved away from a focus on problem-driven scholarship. Instead, it privileged deductive theory or generalizing from the US-Soviet Cold War experience to establish the superiority of one theory. Important new problems went unaddressed. For example, neither side examined in depth how regional politics might influence deterrence or how those states would conceptualize and integrate nuclear weapons into their defense. In addition, there was no sustained discussion of how to link nuclear strategy to foreign policy objectives in the environment. This was particularly problematic given the ongoing public confusion surrounding the 1994 Nuclear Posture Review, repeated in 2002 and 2010 (Nichols 2013).

Neither Waltz nor Sagan consistently identified manipulable policy levers that US officials could pull to realize their desired outcomes. In fact, Waltz offered few if any specific proposals, in part because his primary objective was analytical, not prescriptive. Sagan did more on this front, although as he and others noted, there was a tension between an aversion to proliferation and solutions that involved transferring technology and operational knowledge that could encourage proliferation (Seng 1997, 89–90; Sagan and Waltz 2013, 80).

The emphasis on deductive theory and generalizing from the US-Soviet experience also came at the expense of making recommendations for specific situations. This was particularly noticeable on the optimist side, as Waltz made little effort to identify how certain cases might deviate from general trends. Finally, there was little cumulativity in the debate, as evidenced by the fact that both authors maintained their initial positions in the most recent iteration of their edited volume.

Different concerns among scholars and practitioners compounded the lack of relevance. As Feaver (1993, 162) notes, a finding that nuclear deterrence works 99.5 percent of the time would be in the "social science theory hall of fame, but it would not make nuclear proliferation trivial" in government circles. How much risk to accept and the nature of US interests are political judgments that social science is hard pressed to adjudicate. In sum, the inability to meet more criteria for relevance lessened the chance that the debate would exert influence in the face of discrete policy interests.

## Prospects for a Contemporary Nuclear Studies Renaissance?

The second post–Cold War wave of nuclear studies builds on past debates to assess the broader political effects of nuclear weapons. There is some cause for optimism regarding its increased relevance. Public and policy interest in nuclear issues remains high, and there is no shortage of nuclear-related challenges. These studies are therefore tackling an important and timely set of issues. In addition, several authors have communicated their findings in policy-accessible outlets. At the same time, there is cause for concern that this renaissance may, like the Cold War golden age, end up in an intellectual dead end as method- and theory-driven research crowd out problem-driven work.

Several recent studies are relevant for policy debates, and their authors engage the policy process even if the extent of their influence is debatable. For instance, Matthew Kroenig (2013b, 141–71) utilizes formal and quantitative methods to argue that nuclear superiority conveys bargaining advantages. Byman and Kroenig (2016, 315–16) report that the research was specifically mentioned by US Senator Jon Kyl and featured in interagency debates on the 2010 Nuclear Posture Review. Keir Lieber and Daryl Press (2017, 2006a, 2006b) employ a number of sophisticated models to examine how revolutionary qualitative advances in the US nuclear arsenal may upend MAD. Building on this work, they highlight the implications of technological changes for US policy toward specific adversaries and likely responses. The work drew responses from US officials as well as reportedly influencing debates in other countries (Blank 2008; Farley 2007; Flory et al. 2006).

These works exhibit a number of factors consistent with our argument. Each presents its findings in accessible outlets and briefs various officials. Both sets of works address important ongoing policy debates, highlight at least somewhat manipulable variables—qualitative and quantitative aspects of the US nuclear arsenal—and offer a variety of explicit policy recommendations. Similarly, a number of other studies in the most recent wave of nuclear scholarship utilize a variety of methodological approaches to address ongoing debates and specific policy options. These range across such issues as the danger of nuclear conflict with China (Talmadge 2017), regional nuclear postures (Narang 2014), the limits of deterrence and compellence (Sechser and Fuhrmann 2017; Avey 2019), the durability of MAD (Lieber and Press 2006a;

Green and Long 2017), and nonproliferation approaches (Whitlark 2017; Miller 2018; Lanoszka 2018; Mehta 2019).

The "renaissance" risks following the Cold War and immediate post–Cold War era paths of privileging theory and technique over substance, however. Figure 16.3 shows that within the TRIP journal article dataset the percentage of nuclear articles employing formal and quantitative approaches to these questions has increased (see also Gartzke and Kroenig 2016).[13] At the same time, policy analysis has declined. To be sure, if new methods and data better answer a problem, then social scientists should use the new tools. The problem for relevance arises when the ability to apply a new technique or develop a new deductive insight, independent of any particular policy concern, drives research. Moreover, as figure 16.3 suggests, the more econometric approaches tend to be less associated with a willingness to make explicit policy recommendations.

To that end, a number of analysts have questioned the applicability of advanced econometric methods to the issues under discussion and what new insights have been gained (see H-Diplo 2014; Gavin 2014). As Yale political scientist Alexandre Debs cautions, "The new wave of quantitative [nuclear] studies has not lived up to its promise because it has focused too much on questions of methodologies" (Debs 2014; Nichols 2014). Abstract theory and methods also struggle to provide what Alexander George (1993, 120)

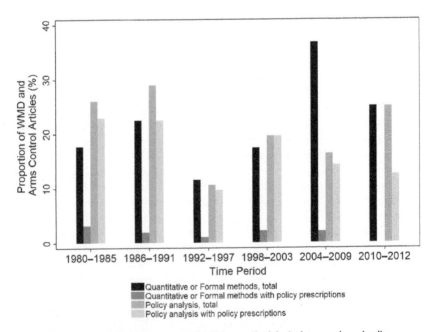

**FIGURE 16.3.** WMD and arms control articles, methodological approach, and policy prescriptions, 1980–2012

called "conditional generalizations" that identify specific patterns that lead to success or failure rather than "a probabilistic relationship . . . between two variables." Colin Kahl, a political scientist and former national security advisor to Vice President Joe Biden, notes that Washington must worry about factors of specific cases rather than generalizations typical of statistical models (Kahl 2014). Much of the recent wave of scholarship—both quantitative and qualitative—has failed to take the next steps to better understand magnitude, situational, and threshold effects which aid in making specific recommendations.

Finally, these studies have not produced clear and consistent findings. This is not to argue that scholars should strive for false consensus; academic debate is central to the advancement of knowledge. Yet important recent debates, such as the lively disagreement between Kroenig and Sechser and Fuhrmann on the utility of nuclear superiority and compellence, turn heavily on coding decisions and model specification.[14] These debates are a necessary and to some extent unavoidable component of scholarship; and the scholarly and policy enterprises overlap but are also distinct. One should not, therefore, expect the relationship to be perfectly seamless. Still, the authors of the most recent wave of nuclear studies would be advised to recognize the tensions between the two realms and seek ways to balance them.

In sum, reports of a "renaissance" in academic nuclear strategy may not translate to greater relevance in the long term. As the TRIP data show, academic IR in general is becoming less policy relevant, at least in terms of offering explicit policy recommendations. The trends among articles looking specifically at nuclear issues are similar: even with the recent uptick in nuclear studies fewer scholars explore these issues than in the past, and their willingness to offer policy advice varies widely. The explanation for this seems to be that as more "scientific" approaches become dominant in the field, scholars' willingness to do policy-relevant work declines.

## CONCLUSIONS AND RECOMMENDATIONS

What are the lessons of the golden age? Academic strategy did have important effects on policy. At times this was direct, as with Wohlstetter's basing study. More often it was indirect, providing the intellectual frameworks and mental roadmaps that shaped presidents' thinking about the utility of nuclear weapons during confrontations with other states, rather than formulating doctrine or drafting operational plans. Despite bureaucratic dynamics within the US military that led the services to adopt nuclear warfighting doctrines and force postures, in the heat of crises, presidents spoke and behaved as if Brodie's assessment of the "nuclear revolution" was correct that the absolute weapon was of use only for deterring an adversary from using one. In other words, MAD was not only a fact, it was also a policy at the highest level.

The history of the golden age also tells a cautionary tale: Intellectual dynamics within universities and even among social scientists working at places like Rand can, under certain circumstances, lead nuclear strategists into intellectual dead ends when internal disciplinary incentives privilege sophisticated methods and theoretical elegance over real-world problems. This is by no means an across-the-board indictment of sophisticated social science methods, but it is a caution about their limits and their tendency to lead scholars to favor technique over substance. For example, the highly quantitative approach of operations research proved extremely useful to military planners during the Second World War but the mathematical tools of Systems Analysis proved useless, if not counterproductive, as a basis for formulating higher level US national security policy during the Cold War (Schlesinger 1963, 298).[15] One of Robert McNamara's Kennedy administration colleagues tartly observed of the former Whiz Kids' approach to strategy, "management is accounting and McNamara is the best accountant I've ever seen. He may turn out to be the best Secretary of Defense too, but when it comes to international politics statistics are not enough" (quoted in Hilsman 1967, 43). The golden age provides many examples of the compatibility of cutting-edge social science and policy relevance but it also shows that the quest to completely make strategy a "science" is quixotic.

To avoid following the golden age into an intellectual cul-de-sac, and to realize a true renaissance in policy-relevant academic strategy, the current generation of nuclear scholars ought to embrace the sort of problem-driven approach that characterized the early years of the nuclear age. Method-driven or purely theoretical scholarship is likely to lead us back into a dead end.

The most common examples of methods-driven research tend to use quantitative approaches, but there is no logical reason that such approaches cannot be policy relevant. As our golden age history shows, many of the leading figures in nuclear strategy employed cutting-edge social science techniques and developed elegant theories along the way. The problem is not so much the technique or the effort to employ theory as the privileging of them over practical problems. As Henry Kissinger (1959, 34) observed in another context, "The difficulty arises not from the analytic method but from the failure to relate it to the problems of the policymaker." Indeed, we worry that the growing preoccupation with certain qualitative and experimental methods, if taken too far, could lead to an intellectual dead end.

Much of this recent scholarship could be relevant, but scholars must work harder to translate their general findings into specific policy recommendations. Moreover, many questions are amenable to the type of careful historical analysis policymakers tend to find appealing (Avey and Desch 2014, 231–32). However scholars choose to address nuclear-related questions, it is clear that if the findings of the most recent wave of nuclear scholarship are going to have an influence on the policy debate, scholars must address broadly important problems, present clear findings, focus on factors that policy can influence, and make explicit recommendations. Our criteria for relevance increase the likelihood for influence, but they do not guarantee it. Policymakers may choose to ignore, dismiss, or may simply be unaware of the findings of a relevant study for any number of reasons. But as the history of the golden age of nuclear strategy shows, studies that fail to meet these criteria are unlikely to influence practitioners.

## ENDNOTES

We thank the participants in the "Strengthening the Links" conferences for helpful comments, especially Susan Peterson and John Harvey, our discussants, and Dr. Ji Hye Shin for data support.

1. In a sense we are "testing" the theory against new data. See King et al. (1994, 21–23, 30, 46).
2. This reflects a larger disciplinary trend in political science. See Hirschman (1970); Tullock (1972).
3. See Green and Hale, this volume, chap. 4.
4. Consistent with arguments 1a and 1b in chapter 1, the development of nuclear weapons during the early Cold War is a classic case in which practitioners were operating in an environment of high uncertainty; thus, demand for new ideas from the scholarly community was high.
5. For a contemporary discussion of the role of "defense intellectuals" in "thinking the unthinkable," see Alsop (1962).
6. This observation about the macro influence of big organizing ideas runs counter to the emphasis of other chapters in this book, which find academic influence at the operational level, where policies are being implemented, rather than at the strategic level, where broad policy is conceived and made. For example, see the Findley and Young, Schneider, and Murdie chapters, as well as argument 2b in chapter 1, which claims that when policy decisions are made at a lower (operational) level, scholars will have greater opportunity for influence.
7. For a caution against attributing too much influence to Schelling, see Trachtenberg (1991, 43). The failure of these policies, so this conventional wisdom holds, discredited the whole academic defense intellectual enterprise (Shapley 1993, 407; Halberstam 1993, 218).
8. Bundy made a similar statement while in office (see Editorial Note, *Foreign Relations of the United States 1961–1963*, Vol. 8, 463–464).
9. This observation and our interpretation of the golden age is a quintessential illustration of argument 1a from chapter 1. When policymakers confronted an emerging issue on which the level of uncertainty was high, scholars had an opportunity to influence the policymaking process. But once the issue became more well understood, and many of the initial insights of scholars were internalized by policymakers and bureaucrats, factors internal to universities, and particularly the discipline of political science, became more important in explaining the nature of the gap between scholars and policy practitioners.
10. Consistent with argument 1a from chapter 1, the radical change in the international system created a number of emerging issues and opportunities for relevance and potential influence.
11. For general histories of the optimist-pessimist debate demonstrating that it predated the end of the Cold War, see Lavoy (1995); Kroenig (2015).

12. Sagan (1995, 809) recognizes this source for Washington's nonproliferation proclivities. See also Kroenig (2009).
13. There were two WMD and arms control articles coded as both policy analysis and quantitative or formal. Both articles offered a policy prescription. We included these in both categories in figure 16.3; removing them did not substantively alter the findings.
14. See especially their four-part exchange at the *Duck of Minerva* (Kroenig 2013a).
15. For similar sentiments from a war-time practitioner of highly quantitative operations analysis, see Blackett (1961, 9).

# 17

# ACADEMIA'S INFLUENCE ON NATIONAL SECURITY POLICY
## What Works and What Doesn't?
John R. Harvey

I n their chapter, Paul Avey and Michael Desch explore trends in the policy impact of social scientists' work on international security with a focus on nuclear weapons strategy. They raise important questions, bring data to bear in answering those questions, and identify four criteria for academic research to maximize its policy relevance. Avey and Desch are on the mark in their assessment of the rise and fall of the "golden age of nuclear strategy" and the ebb and flow of later "waves" of policy influence. Reading their analysis caused me to reflect on my days at Stanford's Center for International Security and Arms Control (CISAC), where a major focus was research and writing with the goal of influencing national security policy. That experience relates to, and extends, a key point made by the two authors—that strict adherence to disciplinary boundaries and methods limit the academy's policy relevance. I comment on key points in the paper, including their four criteria for policy influence, and conclude with a list of additional questions that, as a (former) policymaker, I would like to see social scientists address.

## STANFORD EXPERIENCE

As a physical scientist, my initiation to the academic world of social science—particularly international relations (IR) theory—was forged during five well-spent years (1989–94) at the Stanford CISAC. I had been working on nuclear weapons at Lawrence Livermore and was recruited to Palo Alto by Bill Perry, who later became secretary of defense. Before I joined CISAC, a "meltdown" occurred at the Center involving Sid Drell's failure to secure faculty status for Ted Postol, a nuclear engineer subsequently hired by MIT, and Sally Ride, a physicist and astronaut later hired in 1989 as professor of physics at the University of California San Diego and director of the California Space Institute. Drell subsequently resigned as codirector, and Postol and Ride left Stanford. John Lewis, the other codirector, CISAC founder, and political science professor, strongly pressed Perry to replace Drell as codirector and help pick up the pieces. Perry asked me to backfill Postol and head up the science/technology and national security effort at the Center. Prior to joining CISAC,

I had participated in its research efforts while a physicist at the Lawrence Livermore National Laboratory (LLNL) across the Bay, and I had cochaired with Ride a joint Stanford-LLNL study on proposed monitoring limits on sea-launched cruise missiles under the Strategic Arms Reduction Treaty.

Why did Postol and Ride fail to achieve faculty status? There were a number of factors but, most important, neither of them were doing work that neatly fit into one of Stanford's departments. They were working on multidisciplinary studies that involved national security. They were not doing the traditional business of academia (i.e., abstract knowledge production advancing a narrow field of study); they were working on *real-world* problems.

Drell, Lewis, and Perry saw the Center as a national resource for conducting multidisciplinary research with a strong technical component and the intention to influence national security policy. Indeed, Perry made it clear that my job was to lead research efforts doing precisely that; our focus would be Washington defense policy circles, not academic seminars in Palo Alto. At the same time, it became clear to me that the larger Stanford academic community—outside CISAC and the Hoover Institution—had low regard for such work.

How did this tension manifest at CISAC? It was not easy to convince young social scientists and regional specialists to devote a portion of their time to policy-relevant research when prospective employers looked down on it. The predoctoral researchers at the Center were solidly focused on their PhD theses. The postdoctoral researchers and junior faculty were trying to get jobs or tenure. All the signals they received from the job markets and tenure process discouraged multidisciplinary, policy-relevant work. The idea of working with multiple authors on a paper often produced a reaction along the lines of, "My prospective employer will think that others did the work, not me." If you were an assistant professor in political science at Stanford, a department with a strong and growing "rational choice" faculty, you were taking a huge risk on tenure if you applied your skills to policy-relevant work rather than focusing on advancing IR theory with what Avey and Desch call "economic" methods. Only tenured faculty had flexibility to join in the work that so many of us saw as essential for the nation. I became convinced that the tenure process stunted, rather than enabled, academic freedom.

Regardless, we made do. The midcareer CISAC science fellows provided the team core. We coerced a graduate student/postdoctoral researcher here, a resident senior research associate there, secured important contributions from more senior faculty and, through Perry, acquired pro bono outside help from the legal and defense industry in the San Francisco Bay Area. We did some important, path-breaking work on ballistic missile proliferation, Trident nuclear weapons safety, threat reduction and arms control, shared early warning, export controls, and defense conversion in the former Soviet Union (FSU). Not all of this work was published in academic journals; still, it helped to shape national security policy in these areas.

## RESPONSE TO AVEY AND DESCH

Avey and Desch pose two important questions: How do we explain the ebb and flow in policy-relevant work carried out by social scientists in areas related to nuclear strategy, and why have declining trends led eventually to intellectual dead ends?

Their chapter examines the "golden age" from 1945 to 1965, when social scientists like Albert Wohlstetter, Bernard Brodie, Herman Kahn, Thomas Schelling, Henry Kissinger, and others shaped the nation's nuclear strategy (if not necessarily its operational plans). But what explains the sharp falloff in influential work at the end of this period? Avey and Desch contend that the emerging penchant of scholars to apply a quantitative approach to strategy, with a focus on theory and methods rather than substance, pushed out less formal, more historical approaches to defense analysis. This abstract quantitative work may not have been made intentionally opaque to the nonspecialist, but that sometimes was the case. A paper's accessibility to policymakers did not seem to be a priority for many authors. Moreover, this work rarely produced meaningful choices between alternative courses of action. Strategic warfare exchange models based on game theory may generate an optimal outcome based on esoteric metrics but not necessarily an outcome that is meaningful to national leaders.

What explains the trend toward a more abstract and quantitative approach to knowledge production that eventually led to policy irrelevance? From my Stanford experience, a major culprit is the rigidity of academic departments and associated university power structures that enforce an orthodoxy that discourages young scholars from exploring different research methods, taking on cross-disciplinary problems, or otherwise finding their own way. Unfortunately, too many of my academic colleagues note that this is no less true today.

## INFLUENCING NATIONAL SECURITY POLICY

In concluding their chapter, Avey and Desch develop criteria to guide scholars in maximizing the policy relevance of their work. Specifically, scholarship should:

- Deal with topics that policymakers and the public care about;
- Focus on variables that government policy can manipulate;
- Make explicit policy recommendations; and
- Offer clear and consistent findings about the effect of specific variables.

These criteria form a basic frame to guide policy-relevant academic work. I would add two insights based on my perspective as a former policymaker.

First, recognize that government service depletes, but rarely provides opportunities to replenish, the intellectual capital of many political appointees. Politicals often come into government with a set of ideas, work to implement them as best they can, and then go back to academia or think tanks to develop new ideas. Career bureaucrats rarely have this advantage. That said, both types of officials, if they are doing their jobs, are continuously on the lookout for good ideas. Even so, government officials do not have much time to hear new ideas, much less absorb them; they are often too busy implementing the old ones.

This reality provides both a problem and an opportunity. Government officials will generally take a meeting to discuss your ideas, but you have to be succinct and crystal clear about the basic elements of what you propose. Do not think that you will write a book, throw it over the transom to key officials, and wait for the call to come to Washington to help put your ideas into action. No one in government reads books unless they're on vacation. You need to write the one- to two-page paper that lays out the idea, states why it solves an important problem, and suggests the initial approach the official should take to get the idea in play. Moreover, you must be persistent when your idea does not "take" the first time it is offered.

There will always be obstacles. Knowledge of the way government does (or does not) function is invaluable; it is almost impossible to understand the bureaucratic process without having spent some time living it.

Second, the timing of an idea is critical. Near the time of the breakup of the Soviet Union, Bill Perry invited me into his office at Stanford to discuss plutonium. He and Ash Carter had an idea that they wanted to run by two senators named Sam Nunn and Richard Lugar. Within a year or so, Perry and Carter were in place in the Pentagon implementing the Cooperative Threat Reduction Program to secure warheads and fissile materials in the FSU and to eliminate launchers of nuclear delivery systems. This is probably one of the best examples of having the right idea at the right time with people who understood the mechanics of implementation.

Here is another example about timing: When at Stanford, we worried about degradation of the Russian ballistic missile early warning system. Russia's radars and launch detection satellites were not being kept up, causing concern that Russia could mischaracterize as threatening benign launches of space-launch vehicles and sounding rockets. We developed ideas for sharing early warning data that would benefit both sides. Shortly after that, Perry and Carter brought me to the Pentagon, and I wound up leading a team that negotiated and concluded an agreement for US-Russia shared early warnings. Later disputes over ballistic missile defense (and the rise of Putin) prevented this agreement from entering force.

We did apply some of these ideas to extend US early warning to allies, however. Good timing was once again a factor. During Desert Storm, when Israel came under fire from Iraqi Scud missiles, a kluge system was established on the fly whereby, once our satellites detected a launch, a phone call from North American Aerospace Defense Command (NORAD) in Colorado Springs alerted the Israeli command center and relayed where it was headed. After the war, we sought to shorten notification timelines by providing launch data to Israel electronically; indeed, a few extra tens of seconds of warning saves lives. This idea, however, was not an easy lift because of sensitivities that such data could help Israel prosecute offensive strikes on missile launchers. The idea was tabled until higher-ups decided to give a boost to Shimon Peres, who was in a close election campaign. The Israel desk in the Pentagon asked me to dust off the early warning idea. Within a few weeks an agreement was concluded providing Israel with rapid electronic data on regional launches. It did not get Peres elected, but the system was put in place and Israel's citizens are more secure as a result.

## WHAT "HARD" QUESTIONS IN INTERNATIONAL SECURITY CAN IR SCHOLARS HELP TO ANSWER?

I would be remiss if I did not highlight a few questions the answers to which would be of great interest to me, the national security community, and, very likely, the next president who reviews US nuclear posture early on in his or her first term:

1. What plausible geopolitical threats might the United States encounter in the next two decades, and how might related conflict start and evolve over time?

2. How can the United States prevent an adversary, early in a conflict, from the limited first use of nuclear weapons intended to solidify gains from an initial attack, discourage the United States from coming to the defense of allies involved in the fight, or end a conflict short of regime demise?

3. How will the challenge of assuring allies of US commitments to their defense evolve over the next two decades? What are the implications for needed strategic capabilities, nuclear employment policy, declaratory policy, and allied cooperation?

4. What is the impact of US nuclear modernization on the willingness of other countries to either forgo their own nuclear weapons or cooperate with US efforts to strengthen the nonproliferation regime?

5. Comparable technical barriers for producing nuclear weapons (e.g., uranium enrichment, spent fuel reprocessing) do not exist for bioweapons. Other than the failed Aum Shinrikyo experience with anthrax, why have we not experienced more bioterrorism?

## NEXT GENERATION

I conclude with a comment about the important role of academia in training the next generation of national security experts. As Linton Brooks, former head of the National Nuclear Security Administration, explained at a meeting I attended a few years ago: "As I look around the table today, I see the same folks talking about nuclear policy that sat around other tables in 1985 discussing those same issues!"

Excellence in teaching and training is essential in growing that next generation, including academic researchers, policymakers, specialists in nuclear arms control and threat reduction, technical stewards of our warheads and delivery systems, and the young men and women who operate nuclear forces. Budgets are tight, and entry-level positions in nuclear fields are shrinking even as our need for new talent increases. As a generation of baby boomers retires, we must think creatively about the best way to teach, grow, and sustain that next generation. It will require new initiatives by our government and also by our universities.

# 18

# SUPPLY- AND DEMAND-SIDE EXPLANATIONS FOR THE THEORY-PRACTICE DIVIDE

Daniel Maliniak, Susan Peterson, Ryan Powers, and Michael J. Tierney

In this book we address a set of recurring questions about the relevance, influence, and engagement of international relations (IR) scholars in the policy process. We use new data to test a number of existing arguments about the role that professional incentives within the academy play in affecting the willingness of scholars to supply their expertise to policymakers. At the same time, we develop and test a new demand-side theory of the theory-practice divide that highlights the effect of structural features of a problem on policymakers' demand for scholarly expertise. Our new demand-side argument focuses on two factors that powerfully affect the ability of IR scholars to engage practitioners and shape policy outcomes: (1) the level of uncertainty surrounding the policy problem and its potential solutions, and (2) the level of access that scholars have to the policy process. We also explore the effects of two supply-side factors: (1) scholars' ability to communicate their research to practitioners, and (2) their professional incentives to employ theory and methods that may not be useful or familiar to practitioners.

To investigate our arguments, we segmented the IR field into eight substantive issue areas and asked academic experts in these subfields to use new quantitative and qualitative evidence to describe and explain the relationship between IR scholars and practitioners over time. We also asked veteran practitioners in each issue area to respond to these chapters with criticisms and insights based on their policy experiences. The result is a first-of-its-kind, empirically grounded, and theoretically motivated investigation of the theory-practice divide in IR across different issue areas. Because the contributors rely, at least in part, on a common set of measures, this effort yields systematic insights into how the theory-practice divide manifests across issue areas and over time.

Unlike much of the past work on the theory-practice divide, which focuses on the supply side, we argue that a large portion of the variation we observe in IR scholars' ability to influence policy over time and across issue areas can be explained with reference to the two demand-side variables that we highlight. The level of uncertainty—about both the scope and nature of international policy problems and the likely effects of specific policy choices—is a particularly important determinant of the impact of academic knowledge on international policy. As the contributors to this book document, uncertainty varies over time and across issue area. We conclude that emerging and complex policy problems provide greater opportunities for scholars to shape policy, whereas less complex and more mature problems with which policymakers and practitioners are more familiar have the opposite effect. Similarly, we argue that variation in the level of access that scholars have to key decision-makers and policy implementers has important implications for the ability of IR scholars to shape policy debates and outcomes. That influence also varies with the frequency of decisions and the level at which those decisions are taken and revised. This variation in access stems from the structure of the policy problems; high-stakes policies that are revised only infrequently (e.g., nuclear strategy) provide few opportunities for scholarly input, whereas those issue areas in which policy decisions are taken on a weekly or daily basis and/or at relatively low levels (e.g., foreign aid allocation) provide scholars greater access and opportunities for influence.

Although the empirical chapters in this book highlight the significant influence of uncertainty and access on variation in academic engagement, relevance, and influence, we also explore more conventional supply-side arguments about the role of academic incentives and practices in opening and perpetuating the academic-practitioner divide. The empirical analyses in this book also confirm some of the conventional wisdom related to the supply side. For example, scholarship presented in a consumable format and in ungated venues has a greater likelihood of influencing practitioners and practice. Similarly, some of our contributors find that as a subfield matures and develops professional norms and standards—in this case, increasing the importance of peer-reviewed publications for tenure—its scholarship will be less relevant and influential beyond the discipline. Finally, we find limited and mixed support for the argument that the increasing use of quantitative approaches within some IR subfields hinders scholarly relevance and influence.

The remainder of this chapter summarizes patterns and findings across the book's chapters and briefly addresses the question of why the IR field is not more policy relevant. In short, we reflect on why IR scholars across the subfields do not produce more relevant knowledge, engage in the policy process at higher rates, or exert greater influence on the content of international and foreign policy. We then discuss the limits of our evidence for studying the theory-practice divide. Next, we briefly explore avenues for future research. Finally, we discuss the implications of this project for the normative debate over whether IR scholars should try to influence policy at all.

## RELEVANCE, ENGAGEMENT, AND INFLUENCE ACROSS IR SUBFIELDS

The contributors to this book report that IR scholars and scholarship have limited influence on the policies of government agencies and international organizations or the behavior of policy practitioners, and what influence they do have has generally been decreasing over time. Our theory of the theory-practice divide is premised on the argument that variation in uncertainty and access drives both the size and nature of the gap. To the extent that these factors vary systematically over time and across issue area, we should observe differences in the size and nature of the theory-practice divide. This is precisely what we observe.

As we noted in chapter 1 and as reflected in the subsequent empirical chapters, variation in the theory-practice divide across issue areas is implicit in the conventional wisdom about the relationship between the academic and policy communities of IR. This conventional wisdom suggests that the security subfield is more policy relevant than other subfields and that security scholars are more engaged and influential in the policy process.[1] Consistent with this conventional wisdom, articles published in leading peer-reviewed journals that focus on the security and foreign policy subfields are more likely to contain policy prescriptions than articles focused on other subfields. Twenty percent of security articles and 15 percent of articles that focus on foreign policy contain prescriptions, but less than 4 percent of international political economy (IPE) articles include specific advice to policy practitioners. Less than 11 percent of human rights scholars' publications contain explicit policy prescriptions, and only 5 percent of environmental articles do. Of course, this may be because human rights and environmental scholars disproportionately publish their applied research in policy journals and other outlets not captured in our journal article database, which only covers the twelve leading peer-reviewed journals. Combined, international security and US foreign policy constitute more than 70 percent of the total policy prescriptions in journal articles over the past thirty years in the twelve leading peer-reviewed journals, despite the fact that they represent just over 32 percent of all articles published.[2]

Nevertheless, results from the Teaching, Research, and International Policy (TRIP) faculty survey also show that scholars working in several smaller IR subfields are more likely to describe their research as "applied" than their counterparts who study security and foreign policy. Nearly 47 percent of development experts and 57 percent of global environmental politics scholars report having specific policy issues in mind when conducting research. Both of these subfields have higher rates of applied research than the security subfield, where only 35 percent report that their research is mainly applied.

The substantive chapters in this book contain many other measures of variation across issue areas in the levels of relevance, influence, and engagement. For example, contributing authors explore the extent to which scholars engage in paid or unpaid consulting for governments, intergovernmental organizations (IGOs), or nongovernmental organizations (NGOs), and whether they receive funding from such agencies, as well as other measures. Rather than rehash these measures here, however, we simply note that the chapters document significant variation across a range of variables. We turn now to an explanation of these patterns.

What explains variation across issue areas and, more generally, the relevance, engagement, and influence of IR scholars and scholarship? Our contributing authors provide evidence supporting many of the arguments presented in chapter 1 about the factors that vary across IR subfields and influence the willingness and ability of IR scholars to produce policy-relevant research that shapes practitioners' thinking and behavior. In the rest of this section, we organize our substantive findings around the arguments outlined in chapter 1. These findings show that both the demand-side factors highlighted—the level of policy uncertainty and porousness of the policy process—and the supply-side factors—the style of academic communication, professionalization of the IR discipline (including incentives for promotion and tenure), and the increasing use of sophisticated methods—help explain the existence and size of the gap between scholars and practitioners.

## Level of Policy Uncertainty, Emerging Issues, and Cutting-Edge Methods

To explain issue area variation in the relevance, engagement, and influence of IR scholars, half of the substantive chapters in this book highlight the role of uncertainty among policymakers when confronting a new issue (argument 1a from chapter 1) or the need for new or more technical methods to tackle a policy problem (argument 1b). The four chapters that shed the most light on these phenomena span a wide range of issue areas (nuclear strategy, intrastate conflict, environment, and development), but all four suggest that the immediate demand by policy practitioners for input from the academy may be short lived. Once an issue becomes well understood by practitioners, or when analysts within the government acquire the substantive knowledge or methodological expertise pioneered within the academy, then demand for external scholarly expertise declines. The two quintessential examples of a new policy issue driving demand are the dawn of the nuclear age, as Avey and Desch show in chapter 16, and the scientific discovery of the anthropogenic sources of climate change, as Green and Hale discuss in chapter 4. In both cases, external academic experts were central to developing policy responses to new problems, but as policy issues matured, the need (and opportunities) for scholarly input declined.

In the development and intrastate conflict issue areas, a need to help policy implementers better target their preparations and interventions, rather than the discovery of a novel and real-world problem (argument 1a), drives scholarly input. Both war fighters in various US combatant commands and intelligence officers required better forecasts of violent events in foreign countries so that they could redeploy forces more effectively based on likely threats. As Findley and Young show in chapter 14, these policy implementers relied on IR scholars working in US universities who had the substantive and methodological expertise to deploy new web-scraping methods, text analysis tools, and machine-learning algorithms to gather and analyze data that provided insights and forecasts that practitioners could not generate using traditional methods and government analysts. Similarly, Schneider shows in chapter 6 that a need to evaluate the effectiveness of aid interventions (driven by demands from political principals) provided an opportunity for IR scholars to sell new datasets and evaluation methods to practitioners who needed to demonstrate the effectiveness of different aid interventions. In the case of nuclear policy and environmental policy, however, as these tools became better understood by government practitioners and contractors in private corporations/think tanks, the demand for expertise from the university sector declined.

So, as long as there are truly novel real-world problems, or policymakers demand cutting-edge methods to address existing policy problems, there will be high demand for those academics who are willing to apply their expertise to these problems. As issues (and new methods) become well understood or institutionalized in policy shops, however, the demand for external engagement with the scholarly community on those issues will decline.

## Porousness of Policy Process, Preexisting Networks, and Frequency/Level of Decision

A second "demand-side" factor shaping the relevance, influence, and engagement of IR scholars in the policy world focuses on how porous the policymaking or implementation process is within a given issue area at a particular time. More of our authors focus on this demand-side factor than any other. Six of the eight chapters in which contributing scholars survey the ability of academics to shape policy within a specific issue area examine the access to policymakers or implementers within that issue area. One factor that shapes access is the degree to which the field is already crowded with other analysts who are providing the evidence, methods, and ideas demanded by practitioners (argument 2a). This seems especially relevant in the areas of trade (Mansfield and Pevehouse, chapter 8) and finance (Pepinsky and Steinberg, chapter 10), in which economists have long maintained a monopolistic position as disciplinary providers of knowledge and analysis. As Pepinsky and Steinberg explain in chapter 10, "the success of economics in providing the types of analytical tools that policymakers need" helps to explain the lack of demand for engagement with IR scholars in this issue area.

Surprisingly, perhaps, IR scholars have had significantly greater influence in another issue area in which economists are well established: aid and development. As Schneider shows in chapter 6, policy implementers in this area have been receptive to ideas from IR scholars and have helped to promote multidisciplinary collaborations on data collection, data transparency, and project evaluation. In fact, as Murdie argues in chapter 3, the cross-disciplinary nature of some issue areas may create space for IR scholars to have a seat at the table when policy is made and/or a voice in the process as that policy is implemented. Although IR scholars were relative latecomers to the human rights field, the cross-disciplinary and inclusive nature of that field has allowed these scholars to make a significant contribution to the academic literature and human rights policy and practice.

A second factor that shapes access to relevant decision-makers is the level at which policy decisions are taken (argument 2b). When discretion is delegated to lower levels of the government and when policy and/or operational decisions are taken on a monthly or even daily basis, the opportunities for scholarly influence and engagement increase. This logic is illustrated in chapter 2 where Murdie identifies multiple targets of IR research including governmental agencies, formal IGOs, NGOs, and even domestic and international courts. Human rights policy is not made solely in the National Security Council or the West Wing of the White House. Multiple actors with various delegated authorities make decisions on a daily basis, and these actors become targets for, and even partners in, research by IR scholars (see Murdie; Findley and Young; Mendelson; and Edwards, this volume). Both Schneider in chapter 6 and Green and Hale in chapter 4 make similar arguments about access points that are open to IR scholars doing research on development and the environment.[3]

## Supply-Side Factors

The primary focus of the arguments we present in this book is on the demand side, but we do not claim that more rehearsed supply-side factors, which highlight incentives within the academy, are unimportant. In chapter 1 we reviewed in detail the vast literature on the supply-side reasons for the theory-practice divide. The substantive chapters suggest that two, and perhaps three, such factors are particularly important in explaining varying levels of relevance and influence of scholarly research across issue areas.

First, research findings are likely to have greater resonance in the policy community if they are communicated in a format that is easy for busy practitioners to consume (argument 3a). Five of the eight chapters that examine the role of academic research in shaping policy and practice argue that this supply-side factor matters in their issue area, and six of the eight response chapters by practitioners make the same point.[4] In chapter 12, on interstate war, for example, Kreps and Weeks find that when policy officials are familiar with scholarly arguments, they are much more likely to find those ideas useful to their work. Moreover, policymakers are most likely to be exposed to such ideas in op-eds and policy journals like *Foreign Affairs*. Nevertheless, as Zoellick reminds us in chapter 9, scholars often underestimate the weight that the policy community places on op-eds and other commentary: "[O]pinion pieces in newspapers or online may seem immaterial to scholars but are the proving grounds, test labs, and debate societies for many policy influentials."

Second, three chapters in this volume—those on trade, finance, and nuclear strategy—highlight the importance of "academic incentives" that drive scholars to write for a disciplinary audience in peer-reviewed journals (argument 3b). Other chapters describe the flip side of this same coin; that is, "newer" and "less professionalized" subfields such as environmental governance, development, and human rights all value, draw on, and contribute to research in interdisciplinary journals or journals in other disciplines. Many of the chapters in this book written by policy practitioners conclude that it is no surprise that the more interdisciplinary the research the more useful it is to policymakers (see especially chapters by Zoellick, Harvey, and Radelet).

Finally, the empirical chapters in this book address the argument that as research methods become more technical and quantitative in a given issue area, the research will become less accessible to practitioners and, potentially, less relevant/influential. In chapter 16, Avey and Desch make this case explicitly about the nuclear strategy issue area. Mansfield and Pevehouse share a related finding in chapter 8: IPE scholars who primarily do quantitative research are less likely than their qualitatively oriented colleagues to say that they do policy-relevant work or that they believe that policy issues should motivate IPE research. Nevertheless, all three chapters that review "economically oriented" policy areas (Schneider on aid, Mansfield and Pevehouse on trade, and Pepinsky and Steinberg on finance) also assess but ultimately reject the hypothesis that as research in an issue area becomes more quantitative it becomes less relevant. Each author bases this argument in part on the fact that economists, who have significantly greater influence than IR scholars in these issue areas, rely on the same technical quantitative methods that quantitatively oriented IR scholars use. In chapter 6, moreover, Schneider specifically argues that the increasing use of quantitative methods by political scientists makes her subfield, aid and development, more relevant. It is possible, although we do not present evidence for this argument here, that the practitioners who populate a given issue area ask for different things in different issue areas. Because policymakers in the areas of trade and development are likely to be trained in more quantitative methods, they may be more numerate than their colleagues in other branches of the US foreign policy bureaucracy.[5] We also note that sophisticated formal models or quantitative analyses need not mechanistically lead to a decrease in relevance even if policymakers lack training to digest these outputs directly. For example, scholars might distill the conclusions of their work into a format that is readily consumable by someone with less specialized training for publication as an op-ed, blog post, policy report, or a support tool designed for policy implementers. This is an increasingly popular model, and there is robust evidence suggesting that both scholars and university administrators believe that such outputs should be more valued in the tenure/promotion process than they are currently (Maliniak et al. 2019).

## WHY ISN'T THE INTERNATIONAL RELATIONS DISCIPLINE MORE RELEVANT, ENGAGED, AND INFLUENTIAL?

Many distinguished members of the discipline believe that lack of attention to contemporary policy issues within the IR professoriate have created a "cult of the irrelevant" (Walt 2009; Nye 2009; Gallucci 2012; Campbell and Desch 2013).[6] They lament, in other words, that the entire IR discipline, like political science more generally, fails to effectively address policy problems and engage the policy process. In this book, we have not directly compared IR to other fields, such as economics or history. Nevertheless, in this section, we speculate about how the primary argument advanced in this book—that structural factors like the level of policy uncertainty and porousness of the policy process affect scholars' ability to influence foreign policy—helps explain why the field as a whole is not better able to shape policy or why its members may be less influential than those in other disciplines.

We have argued throughout this book that disciplinary incentives are less important than conventional wisdom suggests in driving the theory-practice divide. Most existing explanations of the gap between the academic and policy communities of IR blame academic culture and professional incentives for the existence and size of the gap (i.e., Walt 2005; Nau 2008; Nye 2009; Gallucci 2012; Kristof 2014). We do not dismiss the role that professional incentives play, and it is easy to see why many critics of the gap start the discussion there. Some of the changes to the field over time, whether viewed as a functional evolution and maturing of the discipline or a mistaken foray into scientism, do vary over time in a way that is observationally consistent with the idea that academic incentives explain the decline in IR scholars' influence on policy. These incentives are largely discipline-wide, however, and as such they cannot easily explain the variation by issue area illustrated by both the scholar-authors' and practitioners' accounts in the preceding chapters.

At the same time, however, such supply-side factors might help explain why IR is less relevant and influential, and its scholars seemingly less engaged, than those in other disciplines, such as economics. If the IR discipline were more mature and professionalized than other fields, for instance, supply-side arguments would lead us to expect it to have less influence in policy circles. In fact, however, IR is a relatively young discipline, compared with economics. The two academic fields are similar in their tenure and promotion standards, which tend to discourage interdisciplinary and policy work. Similarly, IR has made the move to formal and quantitative methods far more recently than its more influential neighbor, economics. A close (or even cursory) reading of leading economics journals demonstrates that economists who publish there are no more successful at making academic research accessible to policy practitioners and the general public. Rather, we are confident in saying that research published in economics journals is less accessible than that published in IR and political science journals. One important distinction between the fields, however, is that the younger IR discipline, having more recently adopted quantitative methods, is actually less likely to find a receptive audience among relevant practitioners.[7]

Some of the structural issues highlighted by our contributing authors help to explain the lack of policy influence by IR scholars relative to those in some other disciplines. For example, policy practitioners who work in diplomacy, intelligence, counterterrorism, and security policy sit in organizations that are typically less porous than those in economic policy areas. Therefore, IR scholars who study these issues may have less access to key decision-makers and implementers, on average, than do economists who tend to work in policy areas such as trade, finance, money, and development. IR scholars who bemoan their discipline's relative lack of influence in policy circles, the plurality of whom study security issues, often measure that influence by asking whether policy leaders at the top levels of government have relied on their data and analysis or have implemented prescriptions based on their ideas. Because life-and-death issues related to nuclear strategy, interstate war, and high-level diplomacy are made at the highest levels of government and changes in these policies occur infrequently, it is unsurprising that scholars who study these issues have limited access to or influence over the policy process. Scholars who study nonsecurity issues have had greater influence than the conventional wisdom suggests. This influence occurs at lower levels of the decision-making process, including working groups, IGOs and NGOs, and transnational networks (i.e., Hale and Green; Murdie, this volume) as more authority is delegated down to these levels to make frequent policy decisions. Future research might compare the relative gaps in influence on policy implementation between IR and economics scholars by focusing attention on these lower levels of decision making and, especially, to the implementation process in order to better understand whether the IR arena truly is less porous and accessible than the economics arena.

Finally, as several contributors to this volume (i.e., Mansfield and Pevehouse; Pepinsky and Steinberg; Schneider) note, much of the decision-making and intellectual space in fields like trade, finance, and development is already occupied by experts from another discipline: economics. In these issue areas, and potentially in the policy counterparts to other IR subfields, such as human rights (Murdie, this volume) and environmental governance (Green and Hale, this volume) populated by lawyers, scientists, and other experts, IR scholars may not always be recognized as experts or at least not as the most important or useful experts to consult. This crowding could be compounded by the fact that the IR academic profession has no exact counterpart within the policy world. Prominent economists serving in government and IGO circles are generally trained in economic theory and methods, but foreign and international policymakers within most national governments and IGOs are generally not formally trained as IR scholars and therefore may be less familiar with and receptive to IR theory and methods. Again, however, these remarks are largely speculative, and future research should compare the policy relevance, engagement, and influence of IR scholars with those in other fields such as law, economics, and climate science.

## THE LIMITS OF OUR EVIDENCE

The chapters in this book offer significant insight into the nature and structure of the theory-practice divide, but the image of the gap that we are able to construct is necessarily incomplete. We lack the granular and multifaceted data that would allow comprehensive tests of our theory of the theory-practice divide. Because of limitations in the type of evidence used by the authors in this project, some types of policy-relevant or influential research simply are not visible; that is, not all scholarly attempts to engage practitioners show up in academic publications or survey responses, and some types of policy relevance are not measured. The data we use here, for example, are largely blind to a number of ways in which IR scholars might engage with the policy process: we have no systematic means of capturing when IR scholars testify before Congress, provide confidential briefings to staff, evaluate World Bank projects, coauthor think tank reports, create datasets that are used by the UN Framework Convention on Climate Change, or engage in myriad other activities. Future researchers might offer measures of some of these activities (e.g., Congressional testimony), but other activities are harder or even impossible to systematically observe (e.g., informal consultations with members of the US intelligence community).

The contributions to this book rely heavily on a series of datasets compiled by the TRIP Project during the last fifteen years. To those data, a number of contributors add their own original evidence in the form of surveys, interviews, and bibliometric data. Together, they provide a rich picture and arguably the most complete depictions available of their subfields' relationships to the policy community. Nevertheless, we still lack the kind of data needed to rigorously address many key questions posed in this book and the discipline more broadly.

A recurring lament in some of the preceding chapters focuses on the fact that the written discipline of IR is substantially larger than the top twelve journals studied by TRIP researchers and includes dozens of other peer-reviewed journals, as well as books.[8] In addition to these traditional academic outlets, scholars also frequently write for a policy audience in other venues, including but not limited to policy journals, policy reports, newspaper op-eds, blog posts, private/confidential memos, and personal briefings to lawmakers and practitioners. None of these products or activities, which are informed by scholarly research, are captured by the data used by the contributors to this book in large part because the data do not yet exist. To remedy this omission, individual contributors included rich case study evidence from both primary and secondary sources. In addition, the conversations at our conferences spurred several new research efforts to collect data on many of the activities and research products named in this paragraph.

Many of the chapters in this book advance the notion that both policy-relevant research and active engagement by scholars in the policy process are likely necessary conditions for policy influence, when influence is defined as academic ideas or findings that "change practitioners' behavior, whether in the formulation or implementation of policy" (chapter 1). Because the TRIP data contain better measures of policy engagement than of policy relevance or influence, the contributors to this volume tend to focus on engagement and sometimes lament the fact that variation in scholarly influence is more difficult to assess empirically.

Despite the difficulties of measuring scholarly influence on policy, however, most previous discussions of gaps between scholars and officials have focused on (the lack of) influence that scholars and scholarship have in the policy process. At the same time that we recognize the limitations of the TRIP data, particularly in measuring influence, these data provide a wealth of information about the discipline, including an important measure of policy relevance—whether academic articles contain explicit policy prescriptions. These and other TRIP data, combined with the original data gathered by our contributors, allow us to take a significant step in advancing our understanding of the relevance of our discipline, the engagement of IR scholars in various policy circles, and the influence of academics and their ideas, data, and methods.

## AREAS FOR FUTURE RESEARCH

What might future efforts to expand on this work look like? One key issue we did not explore was cross-country variation in the relevance, engagement, and influence of IR scholars. We focused in this book largely on the role of the US academy in addressing foreign and international policy problems. The TRIP Project collects data from many other countries, however, and the governments of these countries vary in their foreign policy goals, engagement with academic experts, and roles in the international system. The scholarly journals and presses included in TRIP surveys are predominantly American, although some are based in other countries and most are highly regarded throughout the world (Maliniak et al. 2018). Future studies of the theory-practice divide might use TRIP and other data to compare the relationship between the academic and policy communities across different countries.

The structural factors we examine in this book vary in systematic ways across countries. The level of policy uncertainty is likely to be higher in developing and newly developed countries. Similarly, the level of access enjoyed by nonstate actors varies systematically depending on the structure of the state and state-society relations within a given issue area, and these structures vary considerably by country (i.e., Risse-Kappen 1991). At a more granular level, the links between the state and academic researchers also vary dramatically. On average, moreover, universities in most other countries have tighter links to the national government than in the United States, both in terms of funding and control over curricula and expectations that faculty consult for the national government (Horsburgh et al. 2014; Turton 2015; Maliniak et al. 2018).

Nuclear policy provides a useful example of an issue area in which variation by state in the structural variables identified here may affect scholars' ability to influence the policy process. US scholars of nuclear strategy may lack the influence they would like or that they once enjoyed, but the argument in this book suggests that this is due in part to the current stage in the lifecycle of nuclear policy. The United States was an early adopter of nuclear technology, so the level of uncertainty in this issue area has declined precipitously in this country compared to other non-nuclear states. Decision-making authority over nuclear policy remains relatively concentrated in the United States compared to other issue areas, but such authority is still far more dispersed than it would be in a military dictatorship or other authoritarian regime. The variation over time in the influence of US scholars on US nuclear policy is consistent with our theory's predictions, but so too would be higher levels of academic involvement in India, Pakistan, Israel, Iran, and other countries in which access and uncertainty skew in favor of more influence than in the United States.

Second, we are likely to see substantial variation in scholarly engagement, relevance, and influence, not simply across IR subfields but also at the university, department, and individual level. The academy comprises multiple units with different identities all competing for authority to function inside and outside the university setting. Political science departments do not teach the same courses or produce the same types of research as Schools of Public Policy, Schools of Foreign Affairs, or academic research institutes, yet all these units exist within the university and they all house IR scholars. Even comparing only political science departments would reveal wide variation in the degree to which policy-relevant research is conducted, rewarded, and promoted (Campbell and Desch 2013; Maliniak et al. 2018).

A final area for future research would explore the role of public opinion, advocacy groups, and/or the media as potential conduits for academic ideas in the policy process. The chapters in this book focus on scholars' direct influence on policy and practitioners—in other words, on what is likely the most efficient way for scholars to interact with practitioners in order to affect policy. As the contributors to this book discuss, however, there are important instances in which such options are closed to scholars. In those cases, scholars may influence policy and practitioners by further engaging the public. This, in turn, may pressure political leaders to heed the expert academic advice. This is especially likely when IR scholars come to an epistemic consensus about a particular policy issue and believe that they are shut out of the normal lines of communication with policymakers. Of course, the degree to which the public (or elites in the media or in advocacy groups) will shift their views or advocate for policy change based on a consensus among IR experts is an empirical question that has not been well researched to date.

## CHALLENGING ASSUMPTIONS: IS A GAP BETWEEN THEORY AND PRACTICE NECESSARILY BAD?

We should not end this book without interrogating the assumption made by many observers of the theory-practice divide that such a gap is bad for the academy and for foreign and international policy. We start by reminding readers that this is not a book about *how* to build better bridges between the scholarly and practitioner communities, although anyone interested in such an effort would be wise to start with a clear understanding of the structural factors that explain the gap. Rather, we seek to understand the conditions under which scholars are more or less likely to produce policy-relevant research, engage with the practitioner community, and exercise influence within practitioner circles. At the same time, we recognize that not all students of international relations want to build these bridges. In this section, we describe three distinct, if not always mutually exclusive, approaches to the theory-practice divide.

First, for a variety of reasons, some scholars wish to protect the sanctity of academic life and its associated institutions and practices. According to these "gap minders," the only way scholars can objectively evaluate the world around them, or prevent themselves from becoming tools of the state, is to ensure that they are separate from the policy world and not driven by the dictates of those in power. As Adam Elkus (2015) explains, "If we accept that politicians and policymakers are the best judges of whether or not research in political science is useful, then do not be surprised if the research questions and methods are dictated 'from above' by political actors. Also do not be surprised if notions of peer review [are] replaced by review from the standpoint of whether a particular piece of political science research is efficacious or useful to a particular political elite group." In a similar vein, Ido Oren (2015, 395) claims that we should strive to "increase the distance between political science and policymakers rather than narrow the gap between them," lest the concerns of US government officials dictate our research questions and the methods we use to address them. Elizabeth DeSombre (2011, 142) similarly argues for the value of critical scholarship on global environmental issues and concludes, "Rather than being less important because of that disconnect with policy, it is more important." Even Stephen Krasner, who has worked at the highest levels within the IR academy and the US Department of State, warns scholars of the danger of cooptation and ultimately the futility of efforts to bridge the gap. According to Krasner, his most recent experience in government "only reinforced my conviction that the 'gap' between academia and the policy world is unbridgeable" (Krasner et al. 2009, 116).[9]

Such gap minders constitute a minority of IR scholars in the United States, where 92 percent of respondents to the 2011 TRIP survey agreed with the statement, "There should be a larger number of links between the academic and policy communities." Further, in our own review of the literature on the "theory-policy divide," we find such gap minders to be a distinct minority. Of the 110 books, articles, and blog posts we identified on this topic, only six made an explicit and consistent normative argument to "mind the gap," and seventy-three made consistent arguments to bridge the gap between the academy and the policy community.[10]

Second, and far more commonly, IR scholars, as well as some practitioners and foundation officers, seek to build bridges that foster collaboration between the ivory tower and the policy community by inviting practitioners into the academy and scholars to venture outside and interact with practitioners. In 2008 former Secretary of Defense Robert Gates (US Department of Defense 2008) explained that the Minerva Initiative "seeks to increase the Department's intellectual capital in the social sciences and improve its ability to address future challenges and build bridges between the Department and the social science community." From the academic side, Erik Gartzke (2011) argues that there is enough space within the IR academic community for some scholars to pursue basic research, whereas others offer evidence, insights, or justifications to the policy community. Among private foundations and think tanks, the Council on Foreign Relations has long sponsored and recently expanded a fellowship program that temporarily places young scholars in various agencies of the US government in the hope that this "in-and-out" experience will bring academic insights into the policy process and a concern for "real-world" issues back into the ivory tower. Similarly, the Carnegie Corporation of New York has been at the forefront of several significant efforts to establish stronger links between scholars and practitioners. In addition to supporting this book, the conferences that brought scholars and practitioners together, and the larger TRIP Project, Carnegie has funded the Bridging the Gap initiative housed at American University, which trains graduate students and junior faculty to conduct policy-relevant research on international issues and provides professional development opportunities for scholars engaged in policy-relevant research. Carnegie also has funded the Cambridge-based Tobin Project, which brings together social science scholars to address policy-relevant issues and engage policymakers.

A third and often overlapping set of voices on the relationship between the academic and policy communities of IR seeks to remake the professoriate from within. In addition to opening the door between the academic and policy communities, these individuals seek to change the discipline so that policy work is respected within the academy and counts toward tenure and promotion. In a call to arms along these lines, Notre Dame professor Michael Desch launched the first meeting of a Carnegie-funded conference at the University of Texas in February 2009 by declaring, "We are here to figure out why our field has become policy irrelevant and then launch a series of political efforts to make our discipline more relevant to the practitioners of international relations." Desch and others (Campbell and Desch 2013; Van Evera 2015; Desch 2019a) seek to institutionalize incentives for scholars to help improve policymaking and policy implementation.

Some, but not all, of the bridge builders in the second category described previously also fall into the third category—that is, they locate the root cause of the gap between the theory and practice of international relations within the academy and seek to remake the academy to make it more relevant to the major international issues of our day. The evidence we present in this book is consistent with the notion that professional incentives are important to understanding the theory-practice divide. At the same time, however, we show that the nature and structure of policy problems and the policy process crucially affect the ability of scholars to influence that process.

# A FINAL WORD

The relationship between the academic and practitioner communities of IR is often described and analyzed as if it were a relationship between two homogeneous and distinct groups. In this view, one group lives in an ivory tower addressing abstract questions with esoteric analyses and the other deals with pressing real-world problems. Those adopting this picture of the theory-practice divide often lament a lost golden era of mutual engagement. This portrait of the earlier relationship between the academy and the policy world suggests that those who lived in the ivory tower cared a great deal about pressing real-world problems and ventured outside the walls frequently and with useful insights to help develop policy solutions. Belief in some version of this mythologized golden era is widely shared among IR scholars. The TRIP surveys reveal that huge majorities of scholars both believe that the theory-practice divide has grown and that it should be smaller. There is no doubt a kernel of truth in the myth of the golden era of engagement. We believe, however, that the preceding chapters have clearly demonstrated that the myth obscures as much or more than it reveals. We have documented substantial variation over time and across issue areas with respect to this divide and believe that more work is needed to understand the conditions under which IR scholars and scholarship can and should be policy relevant, engaged, and influential.

Macro-claims about the influence of IR scholars and scholarship often hide important differences among subfields. The contributions to this book move beyond the usual focus on international security. By disaggregating the security subfield into nuclear strategy, interstate war, and civil conflict and terrorism, and by widening our focus to include international trade, finance, the environment, human rights, and development, we have highlighted important differences today and historically across subfields in levels of scholarly engagement, policy relevance, and influence. More important, we have expanded on the conventional wisdom that most of the explanation of and responsibility for the theory-practice divide resides in the academy—its tenure and promotion standards and its reliance on abstract theory and quantitative research methods—to highlight the importance of structural factors, including the level of policy uncertainty and access to different parts of the policy process. We do not seek to exonerate academics for their role in opening and widening the theory-practice divide, but we do seek to understand the structural causes of that gap and variations in the divide across different IR subfields.

None of the answers provided in the preceding chapters to recurring questions about the policy relevance, influence, and engagement of IR scholars and scholarship represent the final word on the subject. Instead, all the contributors to this book provide plausible answers to these persistent questions with systematic, if limited, evidence from a variety of TRIP datasets and with additional evidence from their own original research. The answers advanced in this book are provisional, therefore, and some of the preceding chapters raise more questions than they answer. We believe this book provides a novel theoretical explanation for the gap and new evidence that can be employed to test this and other arguments. But we are most excited about the possibility that this book will help to launch a new generation of studies that collect more and better data on both the supply of academic knowledge and training that comes from the university and the demand for those knowledge products and tools among practitioners. As in any field of inquiry, more and better data are often necessary for making progress on any research agenda. When it comes to gathering systematic evidence about the IR field and the use of this knowledge by practitioners, we are closer to the start of this research agenda than its conclusion.

## ENDNOTES

1. See the works cited by Avey and Desch in chapter 1.
2. This finding is largely driven by the editorial policies of a single journal, *International Security*, which strongly encourages authors to articulate the policy implications of their research. If we limit the analysis to the other eleven journals in the TRIP journal article database, the differences between subfields are greatly diminished. See Hoagland et al. (2017).
3. For similar empirical illustrations of influence by scholars on development practitioners and development policy, see Hook (2008) and Honig (2018).
4. For a similar argument from other practitioners for reduced jargon and greater understanding of the immediate context within which policy is made, see Nussle and Orszag (2015).

5. In the TRIP 2017 US policymakers survey, we find that demand for research using quantitative methods is much higher among trade and development practitioners than among their counterparts who work on security issues. See Avey et al. (2019).
6. The term "cult of the irrelevant" has been popularized by Van Evera (2015); Desch (2019a, 2019b).
7. Unlike their economist counterparts in government, as we discuss in the following section, foreign policy officials who work in the areas of diplomacy and security policy are less likely to be trained in the modern academic field of IR and its methods of analysis.
8. For recent efforts to systematically measure the content of IR scholarship beyond the top twelve journals, see Sharman and Weaver (2013); Weaver and Sharman (2013); Turton (2016); Hendrix and Vreede (2019).
9. For additional examples of "gap-minder" arguments, see Oren (2004); Krasner et al. (2009); Turton (2015).
10. Many studies either did not address this normative question or advanced arguments both for and against policy relevance as a criterion that might guide scholarly research or teaching, which explains why these numbers do not add to 100 percent. See Campbell et al. (2015).

# REFERENCES

Abbott, Kenneth W., Philipp Genschel, Duncan Snidal, and Bernhard Zangl. 2014. *International Organizations as Orchestrators.* Cambridge: Cambridge University Press.

Abbott, Kenneth W., and Duncan Snidal. 2009. "The Governance Triangle: Regulatory Standards Institutions and the Shadow of the State." In *The Politics of Global Regulation,* edited by Walter Mattli and Ngaire Woods, 44–88. Princeton, NJ: Princeton University Press.

Addison, Tony, George Mavrotas, and Mark McGillivray. 2005. "Development Assistance and Development Finance: Evidence and Global Policy Agendas." *Journal of International Development* 17, no. 6: 819–36.

Adler, Emanuel. 1992. "The Emergence of Cooperation: National Epistemic Communities and the International Evolution of the Idea of Nuclear Arms Control." *International Organization* 46, no. 1: 101–45.

Adler, Emanuel, and Peter M. Haas. 1992. "Conclusion: Epistemic Communities, World Order, and the Creation of a Reflective Research Program." *International Organization* 46, no. 1: 367–90.

Advisory Committee on the Management of Behavioral Science Research in the Department of Defense. 1971. *Behavioral and Social Research in the Department of Defense: A Framework for Management.* Division of Behavioral Sciences, National Research Council. Washington DC: National Academy of Science.

African Manager. 2014. "Qatar 'Most Peaceful Nation' in Mena Region." June 23, 2014.

AidData. 2016. "AidData Research Consortium." Accessed June 30, 2019. Available at www.aiddata.org/people#ARC.

Aizenman, Joshua, Menzie D. Chinn, and Hiro Ito. 2010. "The Emerging Global Financial Architecture: Tracing and Evaluating New Patterns of Trilemma Configuration." *Journal of International Money and Finance* 29, no. 4: 615–41.

Allan, Bentley B. 2017. "Producing the Climate: States, Scientists, and the Constitution of Global Governance Objects." *International Organization* 71, no. 1: 131–62.

Allison, Graham, and Niall Ferguson. 2016. "Applied History Manifesto." Applied History Project, Belfer Center for Science and International Affairs. www.belfercenter.org/project/applied-history-project#!manifesto.

Alsop, Stewart. 1962. "Our New Strategy: The Alternatives to Total War." *The Saturday Evening Post,* December 1, 1962, 14–18.

Andonova, Liliana B. 2017. *Governance Entrepreneurs: International Organizations and the Rise of Global Public-Private Partnerships.* Cambridge: Cambridge University Press.

Andonova, Liliana B., and Ronald B. Mitchell. 2010. "The Rescaling of Global Environmental Politics." *Annual Review of Environment and Resources* 35, no. 1: 255–82.

Arndt, Channing, Same Jones, and Finn Tarp. 2010. "Aid, Growth and Development: Have We Come Full Circle?" *Journal of Globalization and Development* 1, no. 2.

Auld, Graeme. 2014. *Constructing Private Governance: The Rise and Evolution of Forest, Coffee, and Fisheries Certification.* New Haven, CT: Yale University Press.

Auld, Graeme, Lars Gulbrandsen, and Constance McDermott. 2008. "Certification Schemes and the Impacts on Forests and Forestry." *Annual Review of Environment and Resources* 33: 1–25.

Autesserre, Séverine. 2010. *Trouble with the Congo: Local Violence and the Failure of International Peacebuilding.* Cambridge: Cambridge University Press.

Avey, Paul C. 2019. *Tempting Fate: Why Nonnuclear States Confront Nuclear Opponents.* Ithaca, NY: Cornell University Press.

Avey, Paul C., and Michael C. Desch. 2013a. "2011 Policymaker Survey." *Notre Dame International Security Program.* Manuscript: University of Notre Dame.

——. 2013b. "Survey Results Book" online. Available at https://carnrank.nd.edu /files-that-pertain-to-the-above-project/policy-makers-survey/.

——. 2014. "What Do Policymakers Want from Us? Results of a Survey of Current and Former National Security Decision Makers." *International Studies Quarterly* 58, no. 4: 227–46.

Avey, Paul C., Michael C. Desch, Susan Peterson, Ryan Powers, and Michael J. Tierney. 2019. "(How) Do Policymakers Use Academic Knowledge and Data? Results of a Survey of Current and Former National Security, International Trade, and Development Policy Officials." Working paper.

Axelrod, Robert. 1997. "The Dissemination of Culture: A Model with Local Convergence and Global Polarization." *Journal of Conflict Resolution* 41, no. 2: 203–26.

Ayson, Robert. 2004. *Thomas Schelling and the Nuclear Age.* New York: Routledge.

Baccini, Leonardo, Andreas Dür, and Manfred Elsig. 2013. "Preferential Trade Agreements: Design Matters!" *VoxEU, CEPR Policy Portal, Centre for Economic Policy Research.* November 24, 2013. https://voxeu.org/article/design-preferential -trade-agreements.

Bagwell, Kyle, and Robert W. Staiger. 2005. "Enforcement, Private Political Pressure, and the General Agreement on Tariffs and Trade/World Trade Organization Escape Clause." *The Journal of Legal Studies* 34, no. 2: 471–513.

Baldwin, David A. 1985. *Economic Statecraft.* Princeton, NJ: Princeton University Press.

——. 1993. *Neorealism and Neoliberalism: The Contemporary Debate.* New York: Columbia University Press.

Baldwin, Richard. 1993. "A Domino Theory of Regionalism." In *Expanding Membership of the European Union*, edited by Richard Baldwin, Pertti Haaparanta, and Jaakko Kiander, 25–53. Cambridge: Cambridge University Press.

——. 2008. "Big Think Regionalism: A Critical Survey." In *The Regional Rules in the Global Trading System*, edited by Antoni Estevadeordal and Kati Suominen, 17–95. New York: Cambridge University Press.

Banks, Nicola, David Hulme, and Michael Edwards. 2015. "NGOs, States, and Donors Revisited. Still Too Close for Comfort?" *World Development* 66: 707–18.

Bano, Masooda. 2008. "Dangerous Correlations: Aid's Impact on NGOs' Performance and Ability to Mobilize Members in Pakistan." *World Development* 35, no. 11: 2297–313.

Bardhan, Pranab. 2002. "Decentralization of Governance and Development." *Journal of Economic Perspectives* 16, no. 4: 185–205.

Barkenbaus, Jack N. 1977. "The Politics of Ocean Resource Exploitation." *International Studies Quarterly* 21, no. 4: 675–700.

Barnett, Michael. 2006. "In Need of Nuance: What the Academy Can Teach." *Harvard International Review* 28, no. 2: 48–52.

Barrett, Scott. 1994. "Self-Enforcing International Environmental Agreements." *Oxford Economic Papers* 46: 878–94.

Bayefsky, Anne, ed. 2001. *United Nations Human Rights Treaty System: Universality at the Crossroads.* Boston, MA: Martinus Nijhoff.

Bearce, David H. 2014. "A Political Explanation for Exchange-Rate Regime Gaps." *Journal of Politics* 76, no. 1: 58–72.

Beeson, Mark, and Stephen Bell. 2009. "The G-20 and International Economic Governance: Hegemony, Collectivism, or Both?" *Global Governance* 5, no. 1: 67–86.

Bell, Daniel. 1968. "Columbia and the New Left." *The Public Interest* 13: 61–101.

Bell, Sam R., David Cingranelli, Amanda Murdie, and Alper Caglayan. 2013. "Coercion, Capacity, and Coordination: Predictors of Political Violence." *Conflict Management and Peace Science* 30, no. 3: 240–62.

Bennett, Andrew, and G. John Ikenberry. 2006. "The Review's Evolving Relevance for U.S. Foreign Policy 1906–2006." *American Political Science Review* 100, no. 4: 651–58.

Bermeo, Sarah. 2011. "Foreign Aid and Regime Change: A Role for Donor Intent." *World Development* 39, no. 11: 2021–31.

Bernanke, Ben S. 2015. "Monetary Policy and Inequality." *Brookings Blog.* June 1, 2015. www.brookings.edu/blog/ben-bernanke/2015/06/01/monetary-policy-and-inequality.

Betsill, Michele M., and Harriet Bulkeley. 2006. "Cities and the Multilevel Governance of Global Climate Change." *Global Governance* 12, no. 2: 141–59.

Betsill, Michele M., and Elisabeth Correll. 2008. *NGO Diplomacy: The Influence of Nongovernmental Organizations in International Environmental Negotiations.* Cambridge, MA: MIT Press.

Betts, Richard K. 1987. *Nuclear Blackmail and Nuclear Balance.* Washington, DC: Brookings Institution Press.

Blackett, Patrick M. S. 1961. "Critique of Some Contemporary Defense Thinking." *Encounter* 16, no. 4: 9–17.

Blank, Stephen J. 2008. *Towards a New Russia Policy.* Carlisle Barracks, PA: Strategic Studies Institute.

Blinder, Alan S. 1997. "What Central Bankers Can Learn from Academics—and Vice Versa." *Journal of Economic Perspectives* 11, no. 2: 3–19.

Blyth, Mark. 2013. *Austerity: The History of a Dangerous Idea.* New York: Oxford University Press.

Boardman, Robert. 1981. *International Organizations and the Conservation of Nature.* London: Palgrave Macmillan.

Bob, Clifford. 2002. "Merchants of Morality." *Foreign Policy* no. 129: 36–45.

———. 2005. *The Marketing of Rebellion: Insurgents, Media, and International Activism.* New York: Cambridge University Press.

Bobbio, Norberto. 1996. *The Age of Rights.* Cambridge: Polity Press.

Bobick, Talya, and Alastair Smith. 2013. "The Impact of Leader Turnover on the Onset and the Resolution of WTO Dispute." *Review of International Organizations* 8, no. 4: 423–45.

Bobrow, Davis, Robert Kudrle, and Dennis Pirages. 1977. "Contrived Scarcity: The Short-Term Consequences of Expensive Oil." *International Studies Quarterly* 21, no. 4: 619–45.

Boone, Peter. 1996. "Politics and the Effectiveness of Foreign Aid." *European Economic Review* 40, no. 2: 289–329.

Boswell, Christina. 2009. *The Political Uses of Expert Knowledge.* New York: Cambridge University Press.

Bourguignon, François, Maurizio Bussolo, and Luiz A. Pereira da Silva, eds. 2003. *The Impact of Economic Policies on Poverty and Income Distribution.* New York: The World Bank and Palgrave Macmillan.

Bown, Chad P. 2005. "Participation in WTO Dispute Settlement: Complainants, Interested Parties, and Free Riders." *World Bank Economic Review* 19, no. 2: 287–310.

Bown, Chad P., and Meredith A. Crowley. 2013. "Import Protection, Business Cycles, and Exchange Rates: Evidence from the Great Recession." *Journal of International Economics* 90, no. 1: 50–64.

Bracken, Paul. 2012. *The Second Nuclear Age: Strategy, Danger, and the New Power Politics.* New York: Times Books.

Breitmeier, Helmut, Oran R. Young, and Michael Zürn. 2006. *International Environmental Regimes.* Cambridge, MA: MIT Press.

Brigham, Matthew R., Michael G. Findley, William T. Matthias, Chase M. Petrey, and Daniel L. Nielson. 2013. "Aversion to Learning in Development? A Global Field Experiment on Microfinance Institutions." Unpublished manuscript. Brigham Young University.

Brodie, Bernard. 1966. "Brodie to Holland." Brodie Papers, Box 5, folder "Army War College." UCLA Library Manuscripts Room. July 13, 1966. (We thank Marc Trachtenberg for this source.)

Brooks, Stephen, and William C. Wohlforth. 2008. *World Out of Balance: International Relations and the Challenge of American Primacy.* Princeton, NJ: Princeton University Press.

Broz, J. Lawrence, and Seth H. Werfel. 2014. "Exchange Rates and Industry Demands for Trade Protection." *International Organization* 68, no. 2: 393–416.

Brückner, Markus. 2011. "On the Simultaneity Problem in the Aid and Growth Debate." *Journal of Applied Econometrics* 28, no. 1: 126–50.

Bueno de Mesquita, Bruce. 1981. *The War Trap.* New Haven, CT: Yale University Press.

———. 1992. *War and Reason: Domestic and International Imperatives.* New Haven, CT: Yale University Press.

Bueno de Mesquita, Bruce, James D. Morrow, Randolph M. Siverson, and Alastair Smith. 1999. "An Institutional Explanation of the Democratic Peace." *American Political Science Review* 93, no. 4: 791–807.

Bueno de Mesquita, Bruce, and Alastair Smith. 2007. "Foreign Aid and Policy Concessions." *Journal of Conflict Resolution* 63, no. 2: 309–40.

Bueno de Mesquita, Bruce, Alastair Smith, Randolph M. Siverson, and James D. Morrow. 2003. *The Logic of Political Survival.* Cambridge, MA: MIT Press.

Bulkeley, Harriet, Liliana Andonova, Karin Bäckstrand, Michele Betsill, Daniel Compagnon, Rosaleen Duffy, Ans Kolk, Matthew Hoffman, David Levy, Peter Newell, Tori Milledge, Matthew Paterson, Philipp Pattberg, and Stacy VanDeveer. 2012. "Governing Climate Change Transnationally: Assessing the Evidence from a Database of Sixty Initiatives." *Environment and Planning C: Government and Policy* 30, no. 4: 591–612.

Bundy, McGeorge. 1964. "The Battlefields of Power and the Searchlights of the Academy." In *The Dimensions of Diplomacy*, edited by Edgar A. J. Johnson, 1–15. Baltimore, MD: Johns Hopkins University Press.

Burnside, Craig, and David Dollar. 2000. "Aid, Policies, and Growth." *American Economic Review* 90, no. 4: 847–68.

Busby, Joshua W. 2007. *Climate Change and National Security: An Agenda for Action*. New York: Council on Foreign Relations.

———. 2008. "Who Cares about the Weather? Climate Change and U.S. National Security." *Security Studies* 17, no. 3: 468–504.

———. 2010. *Moral Movements and Foreign Policy*. New York: Cambridge University Press.

Busch, Marc L., and Eric Reinhardt. 2000. "Geography, International Trade, and Political Mobilization in U.S. Industry." *American Journal of Political Science* 44, no. 4: 720–32.

———. 2003. "Developing Countries and General Agreement on Tariffs and Trade/World Trade Organization Dispute Settlement." *Journal of World Trade* 37, no. 4: 719–35.

———. 2006. "Three's a Crowd: Third Parties and WTO Dispute Settlement." *World Politics* 58, no. 3: 446–77.

Buzan, Barry, and Michael Cox. 2013. "China and the US: Comparable Cases of 'Peaceful Rise'?" *The Chinese Journal of International Politics* 6, no. 2: 109–32.

Byman, Daniel, and Matthew Kroenig. 2016. "Reaching Beyond the Ivory Tower: A 'How To' Manual." *Security Studies* 25, no. 2: 289–319.

Caldwell, Lynton K. 1972. *In Defense of Earth: International Protection of the Biosphere*. Bloomington: Indiana University Press.

Calvo-Pardo, Hector, Caroline Freund, and Emanuel Ornelas. 2009. "The ASEAN Free Trade Agreement Impact on Trade Flows & External Trade Barriers." Policy Research Working Papers Series, World Bank Group, June 2009.

Campbell, Michael, Daniel Maliniak, Connor McCann, Susan Peterson, Ryan Powers, and Michael Tierney. 2015. "The Theory-Practice Gap in International Relations: An Annotated Bibliography." Teaching, Research, and International Policy Project, Institute for the Theory and Practice of International Relations, Williamsburg, VA.

Campbell, Peter, and Michael C. Desch. "Rank Irrelevance: How Academia Lost Its Way." *Foreign Affairs*, September 15, 2013. www.foreignaffairs.com/articles/united-states/2013-09-15/rank-irrelevance.

Campbell, Susanna, Tracy Dexter, Michael Findley, Stephanie Hofmann, Josiah Marineau, and Daniel Walker. 2014. "Independent External Evaluation: UN Peacebuilding Fund Project Portfolio in Burundi, 2007–2013." Centre on Conflict, Development and Peacebuilding. Graduate Institute of Geneva.

Carey, Sabine C., and Steven C. Poe. 2004. *Understanding Human Rights Violations: New Systematic Studies*. New York: Ashgate.

Carothers, Thomas. 2004. *Critical Mission: Essays on Democracy Promotion*. Washington, DC: Carnegie Endowment for International Peace.

Carothers, Thomas, and Saskia Brechenmacher. 2014. *Closing Space: Democracy and Human Rights under Fire.* Washington, DC: Carnegie Endowment for International Peace.

Carpenter, R. Charli. 2007. "Setting the Advocacy Agenda: Theorizing Issue Emergence and Nonemergence in Transnational Advocacy Networks." *International Studies Quarterly* 51, no. 1: 99–120.

Carson, Rachel. 1962. *Silent Spring.* New York: Houghton Mifflin.

Cashore, Benjamin, Graeme Auld, and Deanna Newsom. 2004. *Governing Through Markets: Forest Certification and the Emergence of Non-state Authority.* New Haven, CT: Yale University Press.

Castro, Joao Augusto de Araujo. 1972. "Environment and Development: The Case of the Developing Countries." *International Organization* 26, no. 2: 401–16.

Center for Strategic & International Studies. n.d. "iCon Team." *The International Consortium on Closing Civil Space (iCON).* Available at www.csis.org/programs /international-consortium-closing-civic-space-icon/icon-team.

Chevron Corporation v. Salazar, 11 Civ. 3718 (LAK) (JCF) (S.D.N.Y. Aug. 3, 2011).

Chinn, Menzie, and Jeffry Frieden. 2011. *Lost Decades: The Making of America's Debt Crisis and the Long Recovery.* New York: W. W. Norton.

Chiozza, Giacomo. 2002. "Is There a Clash of Civilizations? Evidence from Patterns of International Conflict Involvement, 1946–97." *Journal of Peace Research* 39, no. 6: 711–34.

Choucri, Nazli, and Robert C. North. 1975. *Nations in Conflict: National Growth and International Violence.* San Francisco: W.H. Freeman.

Christensen, Darin, and Jeremy M. Weinstein. 2013. "Defunding Dissent: Restrictions on Aid to NGOs." *Journal of Democracy* 24, no. 2: 77–91.

Chwieroth, Jeffrey. 2007. "Neoliberal Economists and Capital Account Liberalization in Emerging Markets." *International Organization* 61, no. 2: 443–63.

———. 2010. *Capital Ideas: The IMF and the Rise of Financial Liberalization.* Princeton, NJ: Princeton University Press.

Cingranelli, David L., David L. Richards, and K. Chad Clay. 2014. "The CIRI Human Rights Dataset." Version 2014.04.14. www.humanrightsdata.com.

CIVICUS. 2013. "State of Civil Society 2013: Creating an Enabling Environment: The Synthesis Report." CIVICUS Global Alliance.

*Civicus* (blog). 2014. "An Open Letter to our Fellow Activists Across the Globe: Building From Below and Beyond Borders." August 6, 2014. www.civicus.org /index.php/media-center/news/civicus-blog/2353-an-open-letter-to-our-fellow -activists-across-the-globe-building-from-below-and-beyond-borders.

Clapp, Jennifer, and Peter Dauvergne. 2011. *Paths to a Green World: The Political Economy of the Global Environment.* Cambridge, MA: MIT Press.

Clark, John. 2011. "Civil Society in the Age of Crisis." *Journal of Civil Society* 7, no. 3: 241–63.

Claude, Richard P., and Burns H. Weston, eds. 2006. *Human Rights in the World Community: Issues and Action*, Philadelphia: University of Pennsylvania Press.

Clemens, Michael A., Steven Radelet, and Rikhil R. Bhavnani. 2004. "Counting Chickens When They Hatch: The Short-term Effect of Aid on Growth." Working paper 44. Center for Global Development.

Clemens, Michael A., Steven Radelet, Rikhil R. Bhavnani, and Samuel Bazzi. 2012. "Counting Chickens When They Hatch: Timing and the Effects of Aid on Growth." *The Economic Journal* 122, no. 561: 590–617.

CNNMexico. 2014. "11 metas en derechos humanos que Peña Nieto fijó para su Mandato." 25 June. http://mexico.cnn.com/nacional/2014/06/25/11-metas-en -derechos-humanos-que-pena-nieto-fijo-para-su-mandato.

Cochran, Kathryn McNabb. 2011. "Strong Horse or Paper Tiger? Assessing the Reputational Effects of War Fighting." PhD diss., Duke University.

Cohen, Benjamin J. 1977. *Organizing the World's Money: The Political Economy of International Monetary Relations*. New York: Basic Books.

———. 1998. *The Geography of Money*. Ithaca, NY: Cornell University Press.

———. 2008. *International Political Economy: An Intellectual History*. Princeton, NJ: Princeton University Press.

———. 2009. "A Grave Case of Myopia." *International Interactions* 35, no. 4: 436–44.

Cohen, Eliot A. 1982. "Guessing Game: A Reappraisal of Systems Analysis." In *The Strategic Imperative: New Policies for American Security*, edited by Samuel P. Huntington, 163–91. Cambridge: Ballinger.

Colgan, Jeff D. 2016. "Where Is International Relations Going? Evidence from Graduate Training." *International Studies Quarterly* 60, no. 3: 486–98.

College of Arts & Sciences. 2015. "Social Practice of Human Rights." University of Dayton Human Rights Center. https://udayton.edu/artssciences/ctr/hrc/sphr /sphr-15.php.

Collier, Paul. 2007. *The Bottom Billion: Why the Poorest Countries Are Failing and What Can Be Done About It*. New York: Oxford University Press.

Collier, Paul, and Anke Hoeffler. 2007. "Unintended Consequences: Does Aid Promote Arms Races?" *Oxford Bulletin of Economics and Statistics* 69, no. 1: 1–27.

Commoner, Barry. 1972. "The Environmental Cost of Economic Growth." *Population, Resources, and the Environment*, edited by Ronald G. Ridker, 339–58. Washington, DC: US Government Printing Office.

Conrad, Justin. 2011. "Interstate Rivalry and Terrorism an Unprobed Link." *Journal of Conflict Resolution* 55, no. 4: 529–55.

Cooley, Alexander, and Matthew Schaaf. 2017. "Grounding the Backlash: Regional Security treaties, Counternorms and Human Rights in Eurasia." In *Human Rights Futures*, edited by Stephen Hopgood, Jack Snyder, and Leslie Vinjamuri, 159–188. Cambridge: Cambridge University Press.

Cooper, Andrew F., and Colin I. Bradford Jr. 2010. "The G-20 and the Post-Crisis Economic Order." *CIGI G-20 Papers*, no. 3. Waterloo: Center for International Governance Innovation.

Copelovitch, Mark S., and Jon C. W. Pevehouse. 2013. "Ties that Bind? Preferential Trade Agreements and Exchange Rate Policy Choices." *International Studies Quarterly* 57, no. 2: 385–99.

———. 2015. "Bridging the Silos: Trade and Exchange Rates in International Political Economy." In *Oxford Handbook of The Political Economy of International Trade*, edited by Lisa Martin, 457–75. Oxford: Oxford University Press.

Cortell, Andrew P. 2005. *Mediating Globalization: Domestic Institutions and Industrial Policies in the United States and Britain*. New York: SUNY Press.

Crescenzi, Mark J. C. 2007. "Reputation and Interstate Conflict." *American Journal of Political Science* 51, no. 2: 382–96.

Cross, Mai'a K. D. 2011. *Security Integration in Europe: How Knowledge-based Networks Are Transforming the European Union*. Ann Arbor: University of Michigan Press.

Cruz, Cesi, and Christina J. Schneider. 2017. "Foreign Aid and Undeserved Credit-Claiming." *American Journal of Political Science* 61, no. 2: 396–408.

Dafoe, Allan. 2011. "Statistical Critiques of the Democratic Peace: Caveat Emptor." *American Journal of Political Science* 55, no. 2: 247–62.

Dauvergne, Peter. 2005. "Research in Global Environmental Politics: History and Trends." In *Handbook of Global Environmental Politics*, edited by Peter Dauvergne, 8–34. Northampton: Edward Elgar Publishing.

Davenport, Christian. 2007. "State Repression and Political Order." *Annual Review of Political Science* 10, 1–23.

Davenport, Christian, and Patrick Ball. 2002. "Views to a Kill: Exploring the Implications of Source Selection in the Case of Guatemalan State Terror, 1977–1995." *Journal of Conflict Resolution* 46, no. 3: 427–50.

Davenport, Deborah S. 2005. "An Alternative Explanation for the Failure of the UNCED Forest Negotiations." *Global Environmental Politics* 5, no. 1: 105–30.

Davies, James. 1962. "Toward a Theory of Revolution." *American Sociological Review* 27, no. 1: 5–19.

Davis, Christina L., and Krzysztof J. Pelc. 2013. "Cooperation in Hard Times: Self-Restraint of Trade Protection." *Journal of Conflict Resolution* 61, no. 2: 398–429.

Davis, David R., Amanda Murdie, and Coty G. Steinmetz. 2012. "'Makers and Shapers': Human Rights INGOs and Public Opinion." *Human Rights Quarterly* 34, no. 1: 199–224.

Debs, Alexandre. 2014. "The Curious Case of Nuclear Studies." *The Monkey Cage* (blog). July 10, 2014. www.washingtonpost.com/news/monkey-cage/wp/2014/07/10/the-curious-case-of-nuclear-studies/.

Desch, Michael C. 2003. "It Is Kind to Be Cruel: The Humanity of American Realism." *Review of International Studies* 29, no. 3: 415–26.

———. 2015. "Technique Trumps Relevance: The Professionalization of Political Science and the Marginalization of Security Studies." *Perspectives on Politics* 13, no. 2: 377–93.

———. 2019a. *Cult of the Irrelevant: The Waning Influence of Social Science on National Security*. Princeton, NJ: Princeton University Press.

———. 2019b. "How Political Science Became Irrelevant." *The Chronicle of Higher Education*. February 27. www.chronicle.com/article/How-Political-Science-Became/245777.

DeSombre, Elizabeth R. 2011. "Studying and Protecting the Global Environment: Protecting the Trees but Sometimes Missing the Forest." *International Studies Review* 13, no. 1: 133–43.

Destler, I. M. 1992. *American Trade Politics*. 2nd ed. Washington, DC: Institute for International Economics.

———. 2005. *American Trade Politics*. 4th ed. Washington, DC: Institute for International Economics.

Diamond, Larry. 2002. "What Political Science Owes the World." *PS: Political Science & Politics Online Forum*, 113–27.

Diehl, Paul F. 2002. "Chasing the Headlines: Setting the Research Agenda on War." *Conflict Management and Peace Studies* 9, no. 1: 5–26.

Dietrich, Simone, Minhaj Mahmud, and Matthew S. Winters. 2018. "Foreign Aid, Foreign Policy, and Domestic Government Legitimacy: Experimental Evidence from Bangladesh." *Journal of Politics* 80, no. 1: 133–48.

Dietrich, Simone, and Joseph Wright. 2015. "Foreign Aid Allocation Tactics and Democratic Change in Africa." *Journal of Politics* 77, no. 1: 216–34.

Dimitrov, Rado. 2002. "Confronting Nonregimes: Science and International Coral Reef Policy." *The Journal of Environment & Development* 11, no. 1: 53–78.

———. 2003. "Knowledge, Power, and Interests in Environmental Regime Formation." *International Studies Quarterly* 47, no. 1: 123–50.

Dingwerth, Klaus, and Philipp Pattberg. 2009. "World Politics and Organizational Fields: The Case of Transnational Sustainability Governance." *European Journal of International Relations* 15, no. 4: 707–43.

Dollar, David, and Lant Pritchett. 1998. *Assessing Aid—What Works, What Doesn't, and Why* (English). World Bank policy research report. Washington, DC: The World Bank.

Doucouliagos, Hristos, and Martin Paldam. 2008. "Aid Effectiveness on Growth: A Meta Study." *European Journal of Political Economy* 24, no. 1: 1–24.

———. 2009. "The Aid Effectiveness Literature: The Sad Results of 40 Years of Research." *Journal of Economic Surveys* 23, no. 3: 433–61.

Doyle, Michael W. 1986. "Liberalism and World Politics." *The American Political Science Review* 80, no. 4: 1151–69.

Doyle, Michael W., and Nicholas Sambanis. 2006. *Making War and Building Peace: United Nations Peace Operations*. Princeton, NJ: Princeton University Press.

Drake, William J., and Kalypso Nicolaïdis. 1992. "Ideas, Interests, and Institutionalization: 'Trade in Services' and the Uruguay Round." *International Organization* 46, no. 1: 37–100.

Drazen, Allan. 2000. "The Political Business Cycle After 25 Years." In *NBER Macroeconomics Annual*, vol. 15, edited by Ben S. Bernanke and Kenneth Rogoff, 75–138. Cambridge, MA: MIT Press.

———. 2005. "Lying Low During Election: Political Pressure and Monetary Accommodation." Working paper. University of Maryland.

Dreher, Axel, and Andreas Fuchs. 2015. "Rogue Aid? An Empirical Analysis of China's Aid Allocation." *Canadian Journal of Economics* 48, no. 3: 988–1023.

Dreher, Axel, Andreas Fuchs, Roland Hodler, Bradley C. Parks, Paul A. Raschky, and Michael J. Tierney. 2019. "African Leaders and the Geography of China's Foreign Assistance." *Journal of Development Economics* 140: 44–71.

Drezner, Daniel W. 1999. *The Sanctions Paradox: Economic Statecraft and International Relations*. New York: Cambridge University Press.

———. 2006. *U.S. Trade Strategy: Free Versus Fair*. New York: Council on Foreign Relations.

———. 2009. "Bad Debts: Assessing China's Financial Influence in Great Power Politics." *International Security* 34, no. 2: 7–45.

———. 2011. *Theories of International Politics and Zombies*. Princeton, NJ: Princeton University Press.

———. 2014a. "The System Worked: Global Economic Governance during the Great Recession." *World Politics* 66, no. 1: 123–64.

———. 2014b. *The System Worked: How the World Stopped Another Great Depression*. New York: Oxford University Press.

Drury, A. Cooper, and Dursun Peksen. 2014. "Women and Economic Statecraft: The Negative Impact International Economic Sanctions Visit on Women."ʿ *European Journal of International Relations* 20, no. 2: 463–90.

Dunning, Thad. 2004. "Conditioning the Effects of Aid: Cold War Politics, Donor Credibility, and Democracy in Africa." *International Organization* 58, no. 2: 409–23.

Dupuy, Kendra, James Ron, and Aseem Prakash. 2014. "Stop Meddling in My Country! Governments' Restrictions on Foreign Aid to Non-Governmental Organizations." Available at SSRN: https://ssrn.com/abstract=2529620.

Easterly, William, Ross Levine, and David Roodman. 2004. "Aid, Policies, and Growth: Comment." *American Economic Review* 94, no. 3: 774–80.

Easterly, William, and Claudia R. Williamson. 2011. "Rhetoric versus Reality: The Best and Worst of Aid Agency Practices." *World Development* 39, no. 11: 1930–49.

Editors. 2003. "American Realism and the Real World." *Review of International Studies* 29: 401–2.

Ehrlich, Paul R., and Anne Ehrlich. 1968. *The Population Bomb*. New York: Ballantine Books.

Ehrlich, Paul R., and John P. Holdren. 1972. "Impact of Population Growth." In *Population, Resources, and the Environment*, edited by Ronald G. Ridker, 365–377. Washington, DC: Commission on Population Growth and the American Future.

Eichengreen, Barry. 2013. "Currency War or International Policy Coordination?" *Journal of Policy Modeling* 35, no. 3: 425–33.

Eichengreen, Barry, and Jeffry A. Frieden. 2000. *The Political Economy of European Monetary Unification*. Boulder, CO: Westview Press.

Elkus, Adam. 2015. "The Problem of Bridging the Gap." *Medium* (blog). September 5, 2015. https://medium.com/@Aelkus/the-problem-of-bridging-the-gap-5498d5f25581.

Elsig, Manfred, and Mark A. Pollack. 2012. "Agents, Trustees, and International Courts: The Politics of Judicial Appointment at the World Trade Organization." *European Journal of International Relations* 20, no. 2: 391–415.

Enders, Walter, Todd Sandler, and Khusrav Gaibulloev. 2011. "Domestic versus Transnational Terrorism: Data, Decomposition, and Dynamics." *Journal of Peace Research* 48, no. 3: 319–37.

Eriksson, Johan, and Ludvig Norman. 2011. "Political Utilisation of Scholarly Ideas: The 'Clash of Civilisations' vs. 'Soft Power' in US Foreign Policy." *Review of International Studies* 37, no. 1: 417–36.

Eriksson, Johan, and Bengt Sundelius. 2005. "Molding Minds that Form Policy: How to Make Research Useful." *International Studies Perspectives* 6, no. 1: 51–71.

Estevadeordal, Antoni, Caroline Freund, and Emanuel Ornelas. 2008. "Does Regionalism Affect Trade Liberalization Towards Non-Members?" *Quarterly Journal of Economics* 123: 1531–75.

Evangelista, Matthew. 1995. "The Paradox of State Strength: Transnational Relations, Domestic Structures, and Russia and the Soviet Union." *International Organization* 49, no. 1: 1–38.

Farber, Henry S., and Joanne Gowa. 1995. "Polities and Peace." *International Security* 20, no. 2: 123–46.

Fariss, Christopher J. 2014. "Respect for Human Rights has Improved Over Time: Modeling the Changing Standard of Accountability." *American Political Science Review* 108, no. 2: 1–22.

Farley, Robert. 2007. "What the New U.S.-Russia Fight is Really About." *The American Prospect*. June 7. http://prospect.org/article/what-new-us-russia-fight-really-about-0.

Farrell, Henry, and Jack Knight. 2019. "How Political Science Can Be Most Useful." *Chronicle of Higher Education*. March 10. www.chronicle.com/article/How-Political-Science-Can-Be/245852.

Fearon, James D. 1995. "Rationalist Explanations for War." *International Organization* 49, no. 3: 379–414.

Feaver, Peter D. 1993. "Proliferation Optimism and Theories of Nuclear Operations." *Security Studies* 2, no. 3–4: 159–91.

———. 1995. "Optimists, Pessimists, and Theories of Nuclear Proliferation: Debate." *Security Studies* 4, no. 4: 754–72.

———. 1999. "The Theory-Policy Debate in Political Science and Nuclear Proliferation." *National Security Studies Quarterly* 5, no. 3: 69–82.

Findley, Michael G., Allen Hicken, Daniel L. Nielson, and Joel S. Selway. 2014. "Electing to Develop: A Field Experiment on Legislator's Endorsements of Aid." Unpublished design.

Findley, Michael G., Daniel L. Nielson, and J. C. Sharman. 2013. "Using Field Experiments in International Relations: A Randomized Study of Anonymous Incorporation." *International Organization* 67, no. 4: 657–93.

Findley, Michael G., James Piazza, and Joseph K. Young. 2012. "Games Rivals Play: Terrorism in International Rivalries." *Journal of Politics* 74, no. 1: 235–48.

Findley, Michael G., and Tze Kwang Teo. 2006. "Rethinking Third-Party Intervention into Civil Wars: An Actor-Centric Approach." *Journal of Politics* 68, no. 4: 828–37.

Findley, Michael G., and Joseph K. Young. 2012. "Terrorism and Civil War: A Spatial and Temporal Approach to a Conceptual Problem." *Perspectives on Politics* 10, no. 2: 285–305.

Finkel, James P. 2014. "Atrocity Prevention at the Crossroads: Assessing the President's Atrocity Prevention Board after Two Years." *Center for the Prevention of Genocide, Series of Occasional Papers*, no. 2. US Holocaust Memorial Museum.

Finkel, Steven E., Aníbal Pérez-Liñán, and Mitchell A. Seligson. 2007. "The Effects of U.S. Foreign Assistance on Democracy Building, 1990–2003." *World Politics* 59, no. 3: 404–39.

Finlayson, Jock A., and Mark W. Zacher. 1981. "The GATT and the Regulation of Trade Barriers: Regime Dynamics and Functions." *International Organization* 35, no. 4: 561–602.

Fisher, Max. 2016. "The Credibility Trap." *Vox*. April 29, 2016. www.vox.com/2016/4/29/11431808/credibility-foreign-policy-war.

Fligstein, Neil, Jonah Stuart Brundage, and Michael Schultz. 2014. "Why the Federal Reserve Failed to See the Financial Crisis of 2008: The Role of 'Macroeconomics' as a Sensemaking and Cultural Frame." *Institute for Research on Labor and Employment Working Paper No. 111–14*. Berkeley: University of California.

Flory, Peter C. W., Keith Payne, Pavel Podvig, Alexei Arbatov, Karl A. Lieber, and Daryl G. Press. 2006. "Nuclear Exchange: Does Washington Really Have (or Want) Nuclear Primacy?" *Foreign Affairs*, September/October 2006. www.foreignaffairs.com/articles/united-states/2006-09-01/nuclear-exchange-does-washington-really-have-or-want-nuclear.

Foot, Rosemary, and Andrew Walter. 2011. *China, the United States, and Global Order*. New York: Cambridge University Press.

Ford Foundation. 2015. "Louis Bickford." The Ford Foundation. www.fordfoundation.org/people/louis-bickford/.

Fortna, Virginia Page. 2015. "Do Terrorists Win? Rebels' Use of Terrorism and Civil War Outcomes." *International Organizations* 69, no. 3: 519–56.

Founex Report on Development and Environment. 1971. www.unedforum.org/file
   admin/files/Earth%20Summit%202012new/Publications%20and%20Reports
   /founex_report_on_development_and_environment_1972.pdf.
Fox, Jonathan, and Shmuel Sandler, eds. 2004. *Bringing Religion into International
   Relations.* New York: Palgrave Macmillan.
Fransen, Luc. 2011. "Why Do Private Governance Organizations Not Converge? A
   Political–Institutional Analysis of Transnational Labor Standards Regulation."
   *Governance* 24, no. 2: 359–87.
Freedman, Lawrence. 1983. *The Evolution of Nuclear Strategy.* New York: St. Martins.
Freund, Caroline, and Emanuel Ornelas. 2009. "Regional Trade Agreements." *Cen-
   tre for Economic Performance Discussion Paper No. 961.*
Frieden, Jeffry A. 1991. *Debt, Development, and Democracy: Modern Political Econ-
   omy in Latin America.* Princeton, NJ: Princeton University Press.
———. 2006. *Global Capitalism: Its Fall and Rise in the Twentieth Century.* New
   York: W. W. Norton.
Frieden, Jeffry A., and J. Lawrence Broz. 2001. "The Political Economy of Interna-
   tional Monetary Relations." *Annual Review of Political Science* 4: 317–43.
Frieden, Jeffry A., and David Lake. 2005. "International Relations as a Social Science: Rigor and Relevance." *Annals of the American Academy of Political and
   Social Science* 600: 136–56.
Friedman, Thomas L. 2015. "Time for a Pause." *New York Times.* January 6. www
   .nytimes.com/2015/01/07/opinion/thomas-friedman-time-for-a-pause.html
   ?rref=collection%2Fcolumn%2Fthomas-l-friedman&_r=0.
Friedman, Uri. 2012. "Democratic Platform Swaps 'American Exceptionalism' for
   'Indispensable Nation.'" *Foreign Policy,* September 4. https://foreignpolicy
   .com/2012/09/04/democratic-platform-swaps-american-exceptionalism-for
   -indispensable-nation/.
Friman, H. Richard. 1990. *Patchwork Protectionism: Textile Trade Policy in the
   United States, Japan, and West Germany.* Ithaca, NY: Cornell University Press.
Gaddis, John L. 1992. "International Relations Theory and the End of the Cold War."
   *International Security* 17, no. 3: 5–58.
Gadinis, Stavros. 2015. "Three Pathways to Global Standards: Private, Regulator,
   and Ministry Networks." *The American Journal of International Law* 109,
   no. 1: 1–57.
Galaz, Victor, Per Olsson, Thomas Hahn, Carl Folke, and Uno Svedin. 2008. "The
   Problem of Fit among Biophysical Systems, Environmental and Resource Re-
   gimes, and Broader Governance Systems: Insights and Emerging Challenges."
   In *Institutions and Environmental Change: Principal Findings, Applications,
   and Research Frontiers,* edited by Heiki Schroeder, Leslie A. King, and Oran R.
   Young, 147–86. Cambridge, MA: MIT Press.
Galiani, Sebastian, Stephen Knack, Lixin Colin Xu, and Ben Zou. 2014. "The Effect
   of Aid on Growth: Evidence from a Quasi-experiment." *World Bank Policy Re-
   search Paper No. 6865.*
Gallagher, Kevin P., José Antonio Campo, Ming Zhang, and Yu Yongding. 2014.
   "Capital Account Liberalization in China." *A Global Economic Governance Ini-
   tiative Policy Brief,* no. 002. Pardee School of Global Studies.
Gallucci, Robert L. 2012. "How Scholars Can Improve International Relations."
   *Chronicle of Higher Education,* November 26. http://chronicle.com/article
   /How-Scholars-Can-Improve/135898/.

Galula, David. 1964. *Counterinsurgency Warfare: Theory and Practice.* Westport, CT: Praeger.

Garand, James C., and Michael W. Giles. 2003. "Journals in the Discipline: A Report on a New Study of American Political Scientists." *P.S.: Political Science and Politics* 36, no. 2: 293–308.

Gartzke, Erik. 1998. "Kant We All Just Get Along? Opportunity, Willingness, and the Origins of the Democratic Peace." *American Journal of Political Science* 42, no. 1: 1–27.

———. 2007. "The Capitalist Peace." *American Journal of Political Science* 51, no. 1: 166–91.

———. 2011. "Zombie Relevance." *Foreign Policy.* February 27. www.foreignpolicy .com/posts/2011/02/27/gartzke_on_policy_political_science_and_zombies.

Gartzke, Erik, and Matthew Kroenig. 2016. "Nukes with Numbers: Empirical Research on the Consequences of Nuclear Weapons for International Conflict." *Annual Review of Political Science* 19: 397–412.

Gavin, Francis J. 2012. *Nuclear Statecraft: History and Strategy in America's Atomic Age.* Ithaca, NY: Cornell University Press.

———. 2014. "What We Talk About When We Talk About Nuclear Weapons." *The Monkey Cage* (blog). July 8, 2014. www.washingtonpost.com/news/monkey -cage/wp/2014/07/08/what-new-academic-research-can-teach-us-about-nuclear -weapons/.

———. 2015. "Strategies of Inhibition: U.S. Grand Strategy, the Nuclear Revolution, and Nonproliferation." *International Security* 40, no. 1: 9–46.

Gawande, Kishore, Bernard M. Hoekman, and Yue Cui. 2014. "Global Supply Chains and Trade Policy Responses to the 2008 Crisis." *World Bank Economic Review* 29, no. 1: 102–28.

Geithner, Tim. 2009. "Press Briefing at the Conclusion of the Pittsburg G20 Summit." *G20 Information Centre. G20 Research Group.* September 24. www.g20 .utoronto.ca/2009/2009geithner0924.html.

Gelpi, Christopher, Jason Reifler, and Peter Feaver. 2009. *Paying the Human Costs of War: American Public Opinion and Casualties in Military Conflicts.* Princeton, NJ: Princeton University Press.

Gent, Stephen E. 2007. "Strange Bedfellows: The Strategic Dynamics of Major Power Military Interventions." *Journal of Politics* 69, no. 4: 1089–102.

George, Alexander L. 1993. *Bridging the Gap: Theory and Practice in Foreign Policy.* Washington, DC: United States Institute of Peace.

———. 1997. "Knowledge for Statecraft: The Challenge for Political Science and History." *International Security* 22, no. 1: 44–52.

Germain, Randall D. 2001. "Global Financial Governance and the Problem of Inclusion." *Global Governance* 7, no. 4: 411–26.

Ghamari-Tabrizi, Sharon. 2005. *The Worlds of Herman Khan: The Intuitive Science of Thermonuclear War.* Cambridge, MA: Harvard University Press.

Gibney, Mark, Linda Cornett, Reed Wood, Peter Haschke, Daniel Arnon, and Attilio Pisanò. 2018. "The Political Terror Scale 1976–2017." July 1. From the Political Terror Scale website: www.politicalterrorscale.org.

Gilligan, Michael J. 1997. *Empowering Exporters: Reciprocity, Delegation, and Collective Action in American Trade Policy.* Ann Arbor: University of Michigan Press.

Gilpin, Robert. 1962. *American Scientists & Nuclear Weapons Policy.* Princeton, NJ: Princeton University Press.

_____. 1975. *US Power and the Multinational Corporation.* New York: Basic Books.

Glaser, Charles L. 2003. "Structural Realism in a More Complex World." *Review of International Studies* 29, no. 3: 403–14.

Gleditsch, Kristian S., and Michael D. Ward. 2013. "Forecasting Is Difficult, Especially about the Future: Using Contentious Issues to Forecast Interstate Disputes." *Journal of Peace Research* 50, no. 1: 17–31.

Goel, Vindu, and Andrew E. Kramer. 2015. "Web Freedom Is Seen as a Growing Global Issue." *The New York Times.* January 1. www.nytimes.com/2015/01/02/business/international/web-freedom-is-seen-to-be-growing-as-a-global-issue-in-2015.html.

Golden, Miriam A. 2003. "Electoral Connections: The Effects of the Personal Vote on Political Patronage, Bureaucracy and Legislation in Postwar Italy." *British Journal of Political Science* 33, no. 2: 189–212.

Goldgeier, James. 2012. "The Academic and Policy Worlds." In *Security Studies: An Introduction,* edited by Paul D. Williams, 555–67. London: Routledge.

Goldman, Emily O. 2006. "Closing the Gap: Network the Policy and Academic Communities." *Asia Policy* 1, no. 1: 16–24.

Goldstein, Judith, and Robert Keohane, eds. 1993. *Ideas and Foreign Policy: Beliefs, Institutions, and Political Change.* Ithaca, NY: Cornell University Press.

Goldstein, Judith, Douglas Rivers, and Michael Tomz. 2007. "Institutions in International Relations: Understanding the Effects of the GATT and the WTO on World Trade." *International Organization* 61, no. 1: 37–67.

Gomez-Mera, Laura, and Andrea Molinari. 2014. "Overlapping Institutions, Learning, and Dispute Initiation in Regional Trade Agreements: Evidence from South America." *International Studies Quarterly* 58, no. 2: 269–81.

Goodman, Ryan, Derek Jinks, and Andrew K. Woods, eds. 2012. *Understanding Social Action, Promoting Human Rights.* New York: Oxford University Press.

Google. 2016a. "Top Publications-Law." https://scholar.google.com/citations?view_op=top_venues&hl=en&vq=soc_law.

_____. 2016b. "Top Publications-Political Science." https://scholar.google.com/citations?view_op=top_venues&hl=en&vq=soc_politicalscience.

Gorvin, Ian. 2009. "Producing the Evidence that Human Rights Advocacy Works: First Steps Towards Systematized Evaluation at Human Rights Watch." *Journal of Human Rights Practice* 1, no. 3: 477–87.

Gowa, Joanne. 1994. *Allies, Adversaries, and International Trade.* Princeton, NJ: Princeton University Press.

Gowa, Joanne, and Edward D. Mansfield, 1993. "Power Politics and International Trade." *American Political Science Review* 87, no. 2: 408–20.

Gray, Julia. 2013. *The Company States Keep: International Economic Organizations and Investor Perceptions.* Cambridge: Cambridge University Press.

Green, Brendan, and Austin Long. 2017. "The MAD Who Wasn't There: Soviet Reactions to the Late Cold War Nuclear Balance." *Security Studies* 26, no. 4: 606–41.

Green, Jessica F. 2008. "Delegation and Accountability in the Clean Development Mechanism: The New Authority of Non-State Actors." *Journal of International Law and International Relations* 4, no. 2: 21–55.

_____. 2014. *Rethinking Private Authority: Agents and Entrepreneurs in Global Environmental Governance.* Princeton, NJ: Princeton University Press.

Green, Jessica F., and Thomas Hale. 2017. "Reversing the Marginalization of Global Environmental Politics in International Relations: An Opportunity for the Discipline." *PS: Political Science & Politics* 50, no. 2: 473–79.

Griffith-Jones, Stephany, Eric Helleiner, and Ngaire Woods, eds. 2010. "The Financial Stability Board: An Effective Fourth Pillar of Global Economic Governance?" *CIGI Special Report.* Waterloo, UK: Centre for International Governance Innovation.

Gupta, Joyeeta. 2008. "Global Change: Analyzing Scale and Scaling in Environmental Governance." In *Institutions and Environmental Change: Principal Findings, Applications, and Research Frontiers,* edited by Heike Schroeder, Leslie A. King, and Oran R. Young, 225–58. Cambridge, MA: MIT Press.

Gurr, Ted R. 1970. *Why Men Rebel.* Princeton, NJ: Princeton University Press.

H-Diplo. 2014. "What We Talk About When We Talk About Nuclear Weapons." ISSF Forum no. 2. June 15. https://issforum.org/forums/2-what-we-talk-about -when-we-talk-about-nuclear-weapons.

Haack, Allison. 2014. *The Papers of Lynton K. Caldwell.* Indiana University Archives. https://blogs.libraries.indiana.edu/iubarchives/2011/09/13/lynton-k-caldwell -papers/.

Haas, Peter M. 1989. "Do Regimes Matter? Epistemic Communities and Mediterranean Pollution Control." *International Organization* 43, no. 3: 377–403.

———. 1990. *Saving the Mediterranean: The Politics of International Environmental Cooperation.* New York: Columbia University Press.

———. 1992. "Introduction: Epistemic Communities and International Policy Coordination." *International Organization* 46, no. 1: 1–35.

Haas, Peter M., and Emanuel Adler. 1992. "Conclusions: Epistemic Communities, World Order, and the Creation of Reflective Research Program." *International Organization* 46, no. 1: 367–90.

Haas, Peter M., Robert Keohane, and Marc Levy. 1993. *Institutions for the Earth: Sources of Effective International Environmental Protection.* Cambridge, MA: MIT Press.

Haass, Richard N. 2002. "Think Tanks and US Foreign Policy: A Policy-maker's Perspective." *US Foreign Policy Agenda* 7, no. 3: 5–8.

Hadden, Jennifer. 2015. *Networks in Contention: The Divisive Politics of Climate Change.* New York: Cambridge University Press.

Hafner-Burton, Emilie M. 2012. "International Regimes for Human Rights." *Annual Review of Political Science* 15, 265–86.

———. 2014. "A Social Science of Human Rights." *Journal of Peace Research* 51, no. 2: 273–86.

Hafner-Burton, Emilie M., Laurence R. Helfer, and Christopher J. Fariss. 2011. "Emergency and Escape: Explaining Derogations from Human Rights Treaties." *International Organization* 65, no. 4: 673–707.

Hafner-Burton, Emilie M., and James Ron. 2009. "Seeing Double: Human Right Impact through Qualitative and Quantitative Eyes." *World Politics* 61, no. 2: 360–401.

Hafner-Burton, Emilie M., and Kiyoteru Tsutsui. 2005. "Human Rights in a Globalizing World: The Paradox of Empty Promises." *American Journal of Sociology* 110, no. 5: 1373–411.

Haftel, Yoram Z. 2007. "Designing for Peace: Regional Integration Arrangements, Institutional Variation, and Militarized Interstate Disputes." *International Organization* 61, no. 1: 217–37.

Hakim, Danny. 2014. "Once Celebrated in Russia, the Programmer Pavel Durov Chooses Exile." *The New York Times.* December 2. www.nytimes.com/2014 /12/03/technology/once-celebrated-in-russia-programmer-pavel-durov-chooses -exile.html.

Halberstam, David. 1993. *The Best and the Brightest*. New York: Ballantine Books.

Hale, Thomas, David Held, and Kevin Young. 2013. *Gridlock: Why Multilateralism Is Failing When We Need It Most*. Cambridge: Polity.

Hale, Thomas, and Charles Roger. 2014. "Orchestration and Transnational Climate Governance." *The Review of International Organizations* 9, no. 1: 59–82.

Hall, Peter A. 1989. *The Political Power of Economic Ideas: Keynesianism across Nations*. Princeton, NJ: Princeton University Press.

Hampson, Fen Osler, and Paul Heinbecker. 2011. "The 'New' Multilateralism of the Twenty-First Century." *Global Governance* 17, no. 3: 299–310.

Hansen, Henrik, and Finn Tarp. 2000. "Aid Effectiveness Disputed." *Journal of International Development* 12, no. 3: 375–98.

Hardin, Garrett. 1968. "The Tragedy of the Commons." *Science* 162, no. 3859: 1243–48.

Harff, Barbara. 2003. "No Lessons Learned from the Holocaust? Assessing Risks of Genocide and Political Mass Murder Since 1955." *American Political Science Review* 97, no. 1: 57–73.

Hasnain, Zahid, and Yasuhiko Matsuda. 2011. "The Politics of Power: The Political Economy of Rent-Seeking in Electric Utilities in the Philippines." *World Bank Policy Research Working Papers*, no. WPS 5704. World Bank.

Heger, Lindsay. 2014. "A Gap Exists! (But It Is Smaller and More Specific Than You Might Think)." Discussion paper. One Earth Future Foundation.

Helleiner, Eric. 1994. *States and the Reemergence of Global Finance*. Ithaca, NY: Cornell University Press.

Henderson, Errol A., and Richard Tucker. 2001. "Clear and Present Strangers: The Clash of Civilizations and Interstate Conflict." *International Studies Quarterly* 45, no. 2: 317–38.

Hendrix, Cullen S., and Sarah M. Glaser. 2007. "Trends and Triggers: Climate, Climate Change and Civil Conflict in Sub-Saharan Africa." *Political Geography* 26, no. 6: 695–715.

Hendrix, Cullen S., and Jon Vreede. 2019. "US Dominance in International Relations and Security Scholarship in Leading Journals." *Journal of Global Security Studies* 4, no. 3: 310–20.

Herken, Gregg. 1985. *Counsels of War*. New York: Alfred A. Knopf.

Hernandez, Diego. 2017. "Are 'New' Donors Challenging World Bank Conditionality?" *World Development* 96: 529–49.

Heyns, Christof, and Frans Viljoen, eds. 2002. *The Impact of the United Nations Human Rights Treaties on the Domestic Level*. Boston: Martinus Nijhoff.

Higgins, Andrew, and Andrew E. Kramer. 2015. "Ukraine Leader Was Defeated Even before He Was Ousted." *The New York Times*. January 3. www.nytimes.com/2015/01/04/world/europe/ukraine-leader-was-defeated-even-before-he-was-ousted.html?ref=europe.

Hill, Christopher, and Pamela Beshoff. 1994. *Two Worlds of International Relations: Academics, Practitioners and Trade in Ideas*. London: Routledge.

Hill, Daniel W. Jr. 2010. "Estimating the Effects of Human Rights Treaties on State Behavior." *The Journal of Politics* 72, no. 4: 1161–74.

Hilsman, Roger. 1967. *To Move a Nation: The Politics of Foreign Policy in the Administration of John F. Kennedy*. Garden City, NJ: Doubleday and Co.

Hirschman, Albert O. 1945. *National Power and the Structure of Foreign Trade*. Berkeley: University of California.

———. 1970. *Exit, Voice and Loyalty: Responses to Decline in Firms, Organizations, and States.* Cambridge, MA: Harvard University Press.

Hoagland, John, Elizabeth Martin, and Amy Oakes. 2017. "Mapping the International Security Subfield." Paper presented to the Annual Meeting of the International Studies Association. Baltimore.

Hoffman, Bruce. 2006. *Inside Terrorism (Columbia Studies in Terrorism and Irregular Warfare).* New York: Columbia University Press.

Hoffman, Matthew J. 2011. *Climate Governance at the Crossroads: Experimenting with a Global Response after Kyoto.* Cambridge: Oxford University Press.

Homer-Dixon, Thomas F. 1991. "On the Threshold: Environmental Changes as Causes of Acute Conflict." *International Security* 16, no. 2: 76.

Honig, Dan. 2018. *Navigation by Judgment: Why and When Top Down Management of Foreign Aid Doesn't Work.* Oxford: Oxford University Press.

Hook, Steven W. 2008. "Ideas and Change in U.S. Foreign Aid: Inventing the Millennium Challenge Corporation." *Foreign Policy Analysis* 4, no. 2: 147–67.

Hopf, Ted. 1995. *Peripheral Visions: Deterrence Theory and American Foreign Policy in the Third World, 1965–1990.* Ann Arbor: University of Michigan Press.

Hopgood, Stephen. 2013. The *Endtimes of Human Rights.* Ithaca, NY: Cornell University Press.

———. 2014. "The End of Human Rights." *The Washington Post.* January 3. www .washingtonpost.com/opinions/the-end-of-human-rights/2014/01/03/7f8fa83c -6742-11e3-ae56-22de072140a2_story.html.

Horowitz, Michael C. 2013. "Policy Relevance, the Academy, and Nuclear Weapons." Working paper. *SSRN.* October 7, 2013. https://papers.ssrn.com/sol3 /papers.cfm?abstract_id=2574269.

———. 2015. "What Is Policy Relevance?" *War on the Rocks* (blog). June 17, 2015. https://warontherocks.com/2015/06/what-is-policy-relevance/.

Horowitz, Michael C., William Burke-White, Laurie Jensen, Katelyn Leader, and Mira Patel. 2015. "The Role of Academic International Affairs Institutes in the Public Policy Landscape." Working paper. Perry World House. University of Pennsylvania.

Horsburgh, Nicola, Astrid Nordin, and Shaun Breslin, eds. 2014. *Chinese Politics and International Relations: Innovation and Invention.* New York: Routledge Studies in Globalisation.

Howard-Hassmann, Rhoda E. 2012. "Human Security: Undermining Human Rights?" *Human Rights Quarterly* 34, no. 1: 88–112.

Hufbauer, Gary Clyde, Jeffre J. Schott, and Kimberly Ann Elliott. 1990. *Economic Sanctions Reconsidered: History and Current Policy.* Washington, DC: Institute for International Economics.

Human Rights Data Analysis Group. n.d. HRDAG website. https://hrdag.org.

Human Rights Measurement Initiative. n.d. HRMI website. https://humanrights measurement.org/.

Huntington, Samuel P. 1993. "The Clash of Civilizations?" *Foreign Affairs* 72, no. 3: 22–49.

Hurrell, Andrew. 2011. "The Theory and Practice of Global Governance: The Worst of All Possible Worlds?" *International Studies Review* 13, no. 1: 144–54.

Hyde, Susan. 2015. "Experiments in International Relations: Lab, Survey, and Field." *Annual Review of Political Science* 18: 403–24.

IBRD. 2015. "Mind, Society, and Behavior." *World Development Report 2015.* Washington, DC: IBRD/The World Bank.

IGM Forum. 2012. "Gold Standard." *IGM Forum.* January 12. www.igmchicago.org /surveys/gold-standard.

_____. 2014. "Chairman Bernanke." *IGM Forum.* January 28. www.igmchicago.org /surveys/chairman-bernanke.

Ikenberry, G. John. 1992. "A World Economy Restored: Expert Consensus and the Anglo-American Postwar Settlement." *International Organization* 46, no. 1: 289–321.

_____. 2003. "Is American Multilateralism in Decline?" *Perspectives on Politics* 1, no. 3: 533–50.

International Center for Transitional Justice. 2014. *Failing to Deal with the Past: What Cost to Lebanon?* International Center for Transitional Justice. www.ictj .org/sites/default/files/ICTJ-Lebanon-Impunity-Report-2014.pdf.

Jablonski, Ryan S. 2014. "How Aid Targets Votes: The Effect of Electoral Strategies on the Distribution of Foreign Aid." *World Politics* 66, no. 2: 293–330.

Jacobson, Harold K., and Edith Brown Weiss. 1995. "Strengthening Compliance with International Environmental Accords: Preliminary Observations from a Collaborative Project." *Global Governance* 1, no. 2: 119–48.

Jalali, Rita. 2013. "Financing Empowerment? How Foreign Aid to Southern NGOs and Social Movements Undermines Grass-Roots Mobilization." *Sociology Compass* 7, no. 1: 55–73.

Jaschik, Scott. 2013. "What to Do About Congress." *Inside Higher ED.* September 3. www.insidehighered.com/news/2013/09/03/political-scientists-consider-strategies -deal-ban-nsf-support.

Javeline, Debra. 2014. "The Most Important Topic Political Scientists Are Not Studying: Adapting to Climate Change." *Perspectives on Politics* 12, no. 2: 420–34.

Jensen, J. Bradford, Dennis P. Quinn, and Stephen Weymouth. 2015. "The Influence of Firm Global Supply Chains and Foreign Currency Undervaluations on US Trade Disputes." *International Organization* 69, no. 4: 913–47.

Jentleson, Bruce W. 2002. "The Need for Praxis: Bringing Policy Relevance Back In." *International Security* 26, no. 4: 169–83.

Jentleson, Bruce W., and Ely Ratner. 2011. "Bridging the Beltway–Ivory Tower Gap." *International Studies Review* 13, no. 1: 6–11.

Jervis, Robert. 1989. *The Meaning of the Nuclear Revolution: Statecraft and the Prospect of Armageddon.* Ithaca, NY: Cornell University Press.

_____. 2004. "Security Studies: Ideas, Policy, and Politics." In *The Evolution of Political Knowledge,* edited by Edward D. Mansfield and Richard Sisson, 100–26. Columbus: The Ohio State University Press.

_____. 2006. "Commentary." Review of *Blind Oracles: Intellectuals and War from Kennan and Kissinger,* by Bruce Kuklick. H-Diplo | ISSF Roundtable. Available from: https://issforum.org/roundtables/PDF/Jervis-KuklickRoundtable.pdf.

Johnson, Simon, and James Kwak. 2010. *13 Bankers: The Wall Street Takeover and the Next Financial Meltdown.* New York: Vintage Books.

Jones, Lee. 2009. "International Relations Scholarship and the Tyranny of Policy Relevance." *Journal of Critical Globalisation Studies* 1, no. 1: 125–31.

Jordan, Lisa, and Peter van Tuijl. 2000. "Political Responsibility in Transnational NGO Advocacy." *World Development* 28, no. 12: 2051–65.

Jordan, Richard, Daniel Maliniak, Amy Oakes, Susan Peterson, and Michael J. Tierney. 2009. *TRIP 2008 Faculty Survey.* Teaching, Research, and International Policy Project, Institute for the Theory and Practice of International Relations, Williamsburg, VA. https://trip.wm.edu/data/our-surveys/faculty-surveys.

Kahl, Colin H. 2014. "How Worried Should U.S. Policymakers be about Nuclear Blackmail." *The Monkey Cage* (blog). July 9, 2014. www.washingtonpost.com /news/monkey-cage/wp/2014/07/09/how-worried-should-u-s-policymakers-be -about-nuclear-blackmail/.

Kaplan, Fred. 1983. *The Wizards of Armageddon.* Palo Alto, CA: Stanford University Press.

Karl, David J. 2011. "Proliferation Optimism and Pessimism Revisited." *Journal of Strategic Studies* 34, no. 4: 619–41.

Katzenstein, Peter J. (ed.). 1978. *Between Power and Plenty: Foreign Economic Policies of Advanced Industrialized Countries.* Ithaca, NY: Cornell University Press.

Katzenstein, Peter J., Robert Keohane, and Stephen D. Krasner, eds. 1999. *Exploration and Contestation in the Study of World Politics.* Cambridge, MA: MIT Press.

Kaufmann, Daniel, Aart Kraay, and Massimo Mastruzzi. 2009. "Governance Matters VIII: Aggregate and Individual Governance Indicators, 1996–2008." The World Bank Policy Research Working Paper 4978.

Kaufmann, William W. 1956. "The Requirements of Deterrence." In *Military Police and National Security,* edited by William W. Kaufman, 12–38. Princeton, NJ: Princeton University Press.

Keck, Margaret E., and Kathryn Sikkink. 1998. *Activists Beyond Borders: Advocacy Networks in International Politics.* Ithaca, NY: Cornell University Press.

Kee, Hiau Looi, Cristina Neagu, and Alessandro Nicita. 2013. "Is Protectionism on the Rise? Assessing National Trade Policies during the Crisis of 2008." *Review of Economics and Statistics* 95, no. 1: 342–46.

Kelly, Claire, and Roberta S. Karmel. 2009. "The Hardening of Soft Law in Securities Regulation." Brooklyn Law School Legal Studies Paper No. 241. http://ssrn .com/abstract=1371188.

Kennan, George F. "To Prevent a World Wasteland." *Foreign Affairs,* April 1970. www.foreignaffairs.com/articles/1970-04-01/prevent-world-wasteland.

Keohane, Robert O. 1982. "The Demand for International Regimes." *International Organization* 36, no. 2: 325–55.

———. 1984. *After Hegemony: Power and Discord in International Politics.* Princeton, NJ: Princeton University Press.

———. 1986. *Neorealism and Its Critics.* New York: Columbia University Press.

———. 2014. "The Global Politics of Climate Change: Challenge for Political Science." *The James Madison Lecture.* Annual Meeting of the American Political Science Association. www.apsanet.org/archives/James_Madison.

Kiai, Maina. 2015. "2014: The Year in Assembly and Association Rights." *The United Nations Special Rapporteur.* http://freeassembly.net/rapporteurreports /2014-year-in-review/.

Kim, Rakhyun E. 2013. "The Emergent Network Structure of the Multilateral Environmental Agreement System." *Global Environmental Change* 23, no. 5: 980–91.

Kindleberger, Charles. 1973. *The World in Depression: 1929–1939.* Berkeley: University of California Press.

King, Gary, Robert O. Keohane, and Sidney Verba. 1994. *Designing Social Inquiry: Scientific Inference in Qualitative Research.* Princeton, NJ: Princeton University Press.

Kingdon, John W. 2003. *Agendas, Alternatives, and Public Policies.* 2nd ed. New York: Longman.

Kirshner, Jonathan. 1995. *Currency and Coercion: The Political Economy of International Monetary Power.* Princeton, NJ: Princeton University Press.

———. 2012. "The Tragedy of Offensive Realism: Classical Realism and the Rise of China." *European Journal of International Relations* 18, no. 1: 52–74.

Kissinger, Henry. 1959. "The Policymaker and the Intellectual." *The Reporter,* March 5, 30–35.

Klein, Daniel B., Ryan Daza, and Hannah Mead. 2013. "Ideological Profiles of the Economics Laureates." *Econ Journal Watch* 10, no. 3: 255–682.

Klein, Michael W., and Jay C. Shambaugh. 2006. "Fixed Exchange Rates and Trade." *Journal of International Economics* 70, no. 2: 359–83.

Knack, Stephen. 2004. "Does Foreign Aid Promote Democracy?" *International Studies Quarterly* 48, no. 1: 251–66.

Knack, Stephen, F., Halsey Rogers, and Nicholas Eubank. 2011. "Aid Quality and Donor Ranking." *World Development* 29, no. 11: 1907–17.

Kraft, Joseph. 1960. "RAND: Arsenal for Ideas." *Harper's Magazine* 221, no. 1322 (July): 69–71.

———. 1962. "The War Thinkers." *Esquire* 58, no. 9 (September 1): 102–5.

Krain, Matthew. 1997. "State-Sponsored Mass Murder the Onset and Severity of Genocides and Politicides." *Journal of Conflict Resolution* 41, no. 3: 331–60.

———. 2005. "International Intervention and the Severity of Genocides and Politicides." *International Studies Quarterly* 49, no. 3: 363–88.

———. 2012, "J'accuse! Does Naming and Shaming Perpetrators Reduce the Severity of Genocides or Politicides?" *International Studies Quarterly* 56, no. 3: 574–89.

Krasner, Stephen D. 1976. "State Power and the Structure of International Trade." *World Politics* 28, no. 3: 317–47.

———. 1982. "Structural Causes and Regime Consequences: Regimes as Intervening Variables." *International Organization* 36, no. 2: 185–205.

———. 1983. *International Regimes.* Ithaca, NY: Cornell University Press.

Krasner, Stephen D., Joseph S. Nye, Janice Gross Stein, and Robert O. Keohane. 2009. "Autobiographical Reflections on Bridging the Policy-Academy Divide." *Cambridge Review of International Affairs* 22, no. 1: 111–28.

Kreps, Sarah E. 2011. *Coalitions of Convenience: United States Military Interventions After the Cold War.* Oxford: Oxford University Press.

Kristof, Nicholas. 2014. "Professors, We Need You!" *The New York Times.* February 15. www.nytimes.com/2014/02/16/opinion/sunday/kristof-professors -we-need-you.html.

Kroenig, Matthew. 2009. "Exporting the Bomb: Why States Provide Sensitive Nuclear Assistance." *American Political Science Review* 103, no. 1: 113–33.

———. 2013a. "Debating the Benefits Nuclear Superiority for Crisis Bargaining, Part I." *Duck of Minverva* (blog). March 25, 2013. https://duckofminerva.com/2013/03 /debating-the-benefits-nuclear-superiority-for-crisis-bargaining-part-i.html.

———. 2013b. "Nuclear Superiority and the Balance of Resolve: Explaining Nuclear Outcomes." *International Organization* 67, no. 1: 141–71.

———. 2015. "The History of Proliferation Optimism: Does It Have a Future?" *Journal of Strategic Studies* 38, no. 1–2: 98–125.

Kruzel, Joseph. 1994. "More a Chasm Than a Gap, But Do Scholars Want to Bridge It?"' *Mershon International Studies Review* 38, no. 1: 179–81.

Kucik, Jeffrey. 2012. "The Domestic Politics of Institutional Design: Producer Preferences over Trade Agreement Rules." *Economics & Politics* 24, no. 2: 95–118.

Kuklick, Bruce. 2006. *Blind Oracles: Intellectuals and War from Kennan to Kissinger.* Princeton, NJ: Princeton University Press.

Kurth, James. 1998. "Inside the Cave: The Banality of IR Studies." *The National Interest* 53 (September):29–40.

Lake, David A. 1992. "Power Pacifists: Democratic States and War." *American Political Science Review* 86, no. 1: 24–37.

Landman, Todd. 2004. "Measuring Human Rights: Principle, Practice and Policy." *Human Rights Quarterly* 26, no. 4: 906–31.

——. 2005. "The Political Science of Human Rights." *British Journal of Political Science* 35, no. 3: 549–72.

Lanoszka, Alexander. 2018. *Atomic Assurance: The Alliance Politics of Nuclear Proliferation.* Ithaca, NY: Cornell University Press.

Larson, Deborah W. 1995. "Deterrence Theory and the Cold War." *Radical History Review* 63, no. 3: 86–109.

Latham, Michael. 1998. "Ideology, Social Science, and Destiny: Modernization and the Kennedy-Era Alliance for Progress." *Diplomatic History* 22, no. 2: 199–229.

Latin America Centre. 2016. "Professor Leigh A. Payne." University of Oxford. www.lac.ox.ac.uk/professor-leigh-payne.

Lavoy, Peter R. 1995. "The Strategic Consequences of Nuclear Proliferation: A Review Essay." *Security Studies* 4, no. 4: 695–753.

Leblang, David, and Shanker Satyanath. 2008. "Politically Generated Uncertainty and Currency Crises: Theory, Tests, and Forecasts." *Journal of International Money and Finance* 27, no. 3: 480–97.

Lebow, Richard Ned. 1994. "The Long Peace, the End of the Cold War, and the Failure of Realism." *International Organization* 48, no. 2: 249–77.

Legro, Jeffrey. 2000. "The Transformation of Policy Ideas." *American Journal of Political Science* 44, no. 3: 419–32.

Leites, Nathan, and Charles Wolf. 1970. *Rebellion and Authority: An Analytic Essay on Insurgent Conflicts.* Santa Monica, CA: The Rand Corporation.

Lepgold, Joseph. 1998. "Is Anyone Listening? International Relations Theory and the Problem of Policy Relevance." *Political Science Quarterly* 113, no. 1: 43–62.

Lerner, Michael A. M., and Ethan Hill. 2007. "The New Nostradamus." *Good.* October 4. www.good.is/articles/the-new-nostradamus.

Levy, Jack S. 1989. "The Causes of War: A Review of Theories and Evidence." In *Behavior, Society, and Nuclear War,* vol. 1, edited by Philip E. Tetlock, Jo L. Husbands, Robert Jervis, Paul C. Stern, and Charles Tilly, 209–303. Oxford: Oxford University Press.

Lieber, Karl A., and Daryl G. Press. 2006a. "The End of MAD? The Nuclear Dimension of U.S. Primacy." *International Security* 30, no. 4: 7–44.

——. 2006b. "The Rise of U.S. Nuclear Primacy." *Foreign Affairs* 95, no. 2: 42–54.

——. 2017. "The New Era of Counterforce: Technological Change and the Future of Nuclear Deterrence." *International Security* 41, no. 4: 9–49.

Lieberthal, Kenneth. 2006. "Initiatives to Bridge the Gap." *Asia Policy* 1, no. 1: 7–15.

Lipson, Charles. 1982. "The Transformation of Trade: The Sources and Effects of Regime Change." *International Organization* 36, no. 2: 417–55.

Liu, Li-gang, and Laurent Pauwels. 2012. "Do External Political Pressures Affect the Renminbi Exchange Rate?" *Journal of International Money and Finance* 31, no. 6: 1800–18.

Lowenthal, Abraham F., and Mariano E. Bertucci. 2014. *Scholars, Policymakers, and International Affairs: Finding Common Cause*. Baltimore, MD: Johns Hopkins University Press.

Lupton, Danielle L. 2014. "Leaders, Perceptions and Reputations for Resolve." Ph.D. diss., Duke University.

Lyons, Gene M., and Louis Morton. 1965. *Schools for Strategy: Education and Research in National Security Affairs*. New York: Frederick A. Praeger.

Mack, Andrew. 2002. "Civil War: Academic Research and the Policy Community." *Journal of Peace Research* 39, no. 5: 515–25.

Mahnken, Thomas G. 2010. "Bridging the Gap Between the Worlds of Ideas and Action." *Orbis* 54, no. 1: 4–13.

Maliniak, Daniel, Amy Oakes, Susan Peterson, and Michael J. Tierney. 2011. "International Relations in the US Academy." *International Studies Quarterly* 55, no. 2: 437–64.

Maliniak, Daniel, Susan Peterson, Ryan Powers, and Michael J. Tierney. 2013. *Codebook and User's Guide for TRIP 2.0 Journal Article Database*. Teaching, Research, and International Policy Project, Global Research Institute, Williamsburg, VA.

Maliniak, Daniel, Susan Peterson, and Michael J. Tierney. 2012. *TRIP 2011 Faculty Survey*. Teaching, Research, and International Policy Project, Institute for the Theory and Practice of International Relations, Williamsburg, VA. https://trip.wm.edu/data/our-surveys/faculty-surveys.

———. 2019. "Policy-Relevant Publications and Tenure Decisions in International Relations." *PS: Political Science & Politics* 52, no. 2: 318–24.

Maliniak, Daniel, Ryan Powers, and Barbara F. Walter. 2013. "The Gender Citation Gap in International Relations." *International Organization* 67, no. 4: 889–922.

———. 2014. *TRIP 2014 Faculty Survey*. Teaching, Research, and International Policy Project, Global Research Institute, Williamsburg, VA. https://trip.wm.edu/data/our-surveys/faculty-survey.

———. 2018. "Is International Relations a Global Discipline? Hegemony, Insularity, and Diversity in the Field." *Security Studies* 27, no. 3: 448–84.

Malthus, Thomas. 2013/1798. *An Essay on the Principle of Population*. Berkeley, CA: Malthus Press.

Manger, Mark S., Mark A. Pickup, and Tom A. B. Snijders. 2012. "A Hierarchy of Preferences: A Longitudinal Network Analysis Approach to PTA Formation." *Journal of Conflict Resolution* 56, no. 5: 853–78.

Mansfield, Edward D. 1998. "The Proliferation of Preferential Trading Arrangements." *Journal of Conflict Resolution* 42, no. 5: 523–43.

Mansfield, Edward D., and Helen V. Milner. 2012. *Votes, Vetoes, and the Political Economy of International Trade Agreements*. Princeton, NJ: Princeton University Press.

Mansfield, Edward D., Helen V. Milner, and B. Peter Rosendorff. 2002. "Why Democracies Cooperate More: Electoral Control and Preferential Trade Agreements." *International Organization* 56, no. 3: 477–513.

Mansfield, Edward D., and Jon C. W. Pevehouse. 2000. "Trade Blocs, Trade Flows, and International Conflict." *International Organization* 54, no. 4: 775–808.

———. 2008. "Quantitative Approaches." In *The Oxford Handbook of International Relations*, edited by Christian Reus-Smith and Duncan Snidal, 481–98. New York: Oxford University Press.

———. 2013. "The Expansion of Preferential Trading Arrangements." *International Studies Quarterly* 57, no. 3: 592–604.

Mansfield, Edward D., and Eric Reinhardt. 2008. "International Institutions and the Volatility of International Trade." *International Organization* 62, no. 4: 621–52.

Maoz, Zeev, and Bruce Russett. 1993. "Normative and Structural Causes of Democratic Peace, 1946–1986." *American Political Science Review* 87, no. 3: 624–38.

Martin, Lisa L. 1992. *Coercive Cooperation: Explaining Multilateral Economic Sanctions.* Princeton, NJ: Princeton University Press.

———. 1999. "The Contributions of Rational Choice: A Defense of Pluralism." *International Security* 24, no. 2: 74–83.

Mastanduno, Michael. 1992. *Economic Containment: COCOM and the Politics of East-West Trade.* Ithaca, NY: Cornell University Press.

Mathews, Jessica T. "Power Shift." *Foreign Affairs*, January/February 1997. www.foreignaffairs.com/articles/52644/jessica-t-mathews/power-shift.

McDonald, Patrick J. 2009. *The Invisible Hand of Peace: Capitalism, the War Machine, and International Relations Theory.* New York: Cambridge University Press.

———. 2015. "Great Powers, Hierarchy, and Endogenous Regimes: Rethinking the Domestic Causes of Peace." *International Organization* 69, no. 3: 557–88.

McKeown, Timothy J. 1984. "Firms and Tariff Regime Change: Explaining the Demand for Protection." *World Politics* 36, no. 2: 215–33.

McNamara, Kathleen R. 1999. *The Currency of Ideas: Monetary Politics in the European Union.* Ithaca, NY: Cornell University Press.

Meadows, Dennis, Jørgen Randers, Donella Meadows, and William W. Behrens III. 1974. *The Limits to Growth.* 2nd ed. New York: Universe Books.

Mearsheimer, John J., and Stephen M. Walt. 2013. "Leaving Theory Behind: Why Simplistic Hypothesis Testing Is Bad for International Relations." *European Journal of International Relations* 19, no. 3: 427–57.

Meckling, Jonas. 2011. *Carbon Coalitions: Business, Climate Politics, and the Rise of Emissions Trading.* Cambridge, MA: The MIT Press.

Mehta, Rupal N. 2019. *Delaying Doomsday: The Politics of Nuclear Reversal.* New York: Oxford University Press.

Melitz, Marc J. 2003. "The Impact of Trade on Intra-industry Reallocations and Aggregate Industry Productivity." *Econometrica* 71, no. 6: 1695–725.

"Membership Roster." 2014. *Council on Foreign Relations.* www.cfr.org/about/membership/roster.html.

Mendelson, Sarah E. 1998. *Changing Course: Ideas, Politics, and the Soviet Withdrawal from Afghanistan.* Princeton, NJ: Princeton University Press.

———. 2009. "Dusk or Dawn for the Human Rights Movement?" *The Washington Quarterly* 32, no. 2: 103–20.

———. 2015. *Why Governments Target Civil Society and What Can Be Done in Response: A New Agenda.* Washington, DC: Center for Strategic and International Studies. April 2015. https://csis-prod.s3.amazonaws.com/s3fs-public/legacy_files/files/publication/150422_Mendelson_GovTargetCivilSociety_Web.pdf.

Mendelson, Sarah E., and Theodore Gerber. 2007. "Activist Culture and Transnational Diffusion: An Experiment in Social Marketing among Human Rights Groups in Russia." *Post-Soviet Affairs* 23, no. 1: 50–75.

Mendelson, Sarah E., and John R. Harvey. 2014. "Responding to Putin's Plan Post-Crimea." *CSIS Commentary* July 24. http://csis.org/publication/responding-putins-plan-post-crimea.

Mercer, Jonathan. 1996. *Reputation and International Politics.* Ithaca, NY: Cornell University Press.

Merton, Robert C. 1997. "Applications of Option Pricing Theory: Twenty-Five Years Later." *Nobel Prize Lecture.* www.nobelprize.org/nobel_prizes/economic-sciences/laureates/1997/merton-lecture.html.

Metternich, Nils W., Cassy Dorff, Max Gallop, Simon Weschle, and Michael D. Ward. 2013. "Antigovernment Networks in Civil Conflicts: How Network Structures Affect Conflictual Behavior." *American Journal of Political Science* 57, no. 4: 892–911.

Miles, Edward, Steinar Andresen, Elaine M. Carlin, Jon Birger Skjaerseth, A. Underdal, and Jørgen Wettestad. 2001. *Environmental Regime Effectiveness: Confronting Theory with Evidence.* Cambridge, MA: MIT Press.

Miller, D. W. 2001. "Storming the Palace in Political Science." *Chronicle of Higher Education.* September 21. www.chronicle.com/article/Storming-the-Palace-in /36137/.

Miller, Nicholas L. 2018. *Stopping the Bomb: The Sources and Effectiveness of US Nonproliferation Policy.* Ithaca, NY: Cornell University Press.

Milner, Helen V. 1988. *Resisting Protectionism: Global Industries and the Politics of International Trade.* Princeton, NY: Princeton University Press.

Milner, Helen V., and David B. Yoffie. 1989. "Between Free Trade and Protectionism: Strategic Trade Policy and a Theory of Corporate Trade Demands." *International Organization* 42, no. 2: 239–72.

Mitchell, Ronald B. 1994. "Regime Design Matters: Intentional Oil Pollution and Treaty Compliance." *International Organization* 48, no. 3: 452–58.

———. 2002–16. "Data from Ronald B. Mitchell." *International Environmental Agreements Database Projects.* http://iea.uoregon.edu/project-related-publications.

———. 2003. "International Environmental Agreements: A Survey of Their Features, Formation, and Effects." *Annual Review of Environment and Resources* 28, no. 1: 429–61.

———. 2006. *Global Environmental Assessments: Information and Influence.* Cambridge, MA: MIT Press.

———. 2010. *International Politics and the Environment.* London: Sage Publishing.

Monroe, Bunt L., and Philip A. Schrodt. 2008. "Introduction to the Special Issue: The Statistical Analysis of Political Text." *Political Analysis* 16, no. 4: 351–55.

Monroe, Kristen. 2005. *Perestroika! The Raucous Rebellion in Political Science.* New Haven, CT: Yale University Press.

Monteiro, Nuno P. 2014. *Theory of Unipolar Politics.* New York: Cambridge University Press.

Moore, Barrington. 1966. *Social Origins of Dictatorship and Democracy.* Boston, MA: Beacon Press.

Moore, Will H. 2000. "The Repression of Dissent: A Substitution Model of Government Coercion." *Journal of Conflict Resolution* 44, no. 1: 107–27.

———. 2006. "A Problem with Peace Science: The Dark Side of COW." *Paper presented to the 48th Annual Convention of the International Studies Association,* Chicago, IL.

Moravcsik, Andrew. 1998. *The Choice for Europe.* Ithaca, NY: Cornell University Press.

Moreland, Will. 2017. "The Geopolitics of Democracy Promotion." *Order from Chaos* (blog), *Brookings Institution.* June 31. www.brookings.edu/blog/order -from-chaos/2017/07/31/the-geopolitics-of-democracy-promotion/.

Morgan, Rhiannon. 2012. "Human Rights Research and the Social Sciences." In *Interpreting Human Rights: Social Science Perspectives,* edited by Rhiannon Morgan and Bryan Turner, 1–22. New York: Routledge.

Most, Benjamin A., and Harvey Starr. 1984. "International Relations Theory, Foreign Policy Substitutability, and 'Nice' Laws." *World Politics* 36, no. 3: 383–406.

Moyn, Samuel. 2010. *The Last Utopia: Human Rights in History*. Cambridge: Harvard University Press.

Mundell, Robert A. 1961. "A Theory of Optimum Currency Areas." *American Economic Review* 51, no. 4: 657–65.

Murdie, Amanda. 2014. *Help or Harm: The Human Security Effects of International NGOs*. Stanford, CA: Stanford University Press.

Nacht, Michael. 1980. "The War in Vietnam: The Influence of Concepts on Policy." *ACIS Working Paper* 26, no. 16, Center for International and Strategic Affairs, UCLA, Los Angeles.

Naím, Moisés. 2013. *The End of Power: From Boardrooms to Battlefields and Churches to States, Why Being in Charge Isn't What It Used to Be*. New York: Basic Books.

Najam, Adil. 2005. "Developing Countries and Global Environmental Governance: From Contestation to Participation to Engagement." *International Environmental Agreements: Politics, Law and Economics* 5, no. 3: 303–21.

Narang, Vipin. 2014. *Nuclear Strategy in the Modern Era: Regional Powers and International Conflict*. Princeton, NJ: Princeton University Press.

National Science Foundation. 2013. "Notice: Implementation of the 2013 Federal Continuing Appropriations Act provisions affecting the NSF Political Science Program." Directorate for Social, Behavioral & Economic Sciences, *National Science Foundation*. June 7. www.nsf.gov/pubs/2013/nsf13101/nsf13101.jsp.

Nau, Henry R. 2008. "Conservative Internationalism." *Policy Review*, no. 150: 3–44.

Nelson, Stephen C. 2014. "Playing Favorites: How Shared Beliefs Shape the IMF's Lending Decisions." *International Organization* 68, no. 2: 297–328.

Nelson, Stephen C., and Peter J. Katzenstein. 2014. "Uncertainty, Risk, and the Financial Crisis of 2008." *International Organization* 68, no. 2: 361–92.

Neumayer, Eric. 2005. "Do International Human Rights Treaties Improve Respect for Human Rights?" *Journal of Conflict Resolution* 49, no. 6: 925–53.

Neustadt, Richard, and Ernest May. 1986. *Thinking in Time: The Uses of History for Decision-Makers*. New York: The Free Press.

*New Zealand Herald*. 2014. "Qatar 'Most Peaceful Nation' in Mena Region." April 4, 2014.

Nexon, Daniel. 2011. "State of the Field." *Duck of Minerva* (blog). August 5. http://duckofminerva.com/2011/08/state-of-field.html.

Nichols, Tom. 2013. *No Use: Nuclear Weapons and U.S. National Security*. Philadelphia: University of Pennsylvania Press.

———. 2014. "Response to What We Do, and Why It Matters." *H-Diplo | ISSF*. https://networks.hnet.org/node/28443/discussions/32070/%E2%80%9Cwhat-we-do-and-why-it-matters-response-fks%E2%80%9D-response-h-diploissf.

Nussle, Jim, and Peter Orszag, eds. 2015. *Moneyball for Government*. Washington, DC: Results for America.

Nye, Joseph S. 2008a. "Bridging the Gap between Theory and Policy." *Political Psychology* 29, no. 4: 593–603.

———. 2008b. "International Relations: the Relevance of Theory to Practice." In *The Oxford Handbook of International Relations*, edited by Christian Reus-Smit and Duncan Snidal, 648–60. New York: Oxford University Press.

———. 2009. "Scholars on the Sidelines." *The Washington Post*. April 13. www.belfercenter.org/publication/scholars-sidelines.

O'Brien, Denis Patrick. 2007. *The Development of Monetary Economics: A Modern Perspective on Monetary Controversies*. Cheltenham: Edward Elga.

O'Brien, Sean P. 2010. "Crisis Early Warning and Decision Support: Contemporary Approaches and Thoughts on Future Research." *International Studies Review* 12, no. 1: 87–104.

O'Neill, Kate. 2009. *The Environment and International Relations.* New York: Cambridge University Press.

Oatley, Thomas, Kindred Winecoff, Andrew Pennock, and Sarah Bauerle Danzman. 2013. "The Political Economy of Global Finance: A Network Model." *Perspectives on Politics* 11, no. 1: 133–53.

Office of the White House. 1994. *A National Security Strategy of Engagement and Enlargement.* http://nssarchive.us/NSSR/1994.pdf.

———. 2002. *The National Security Strategy of the United States of America.* http://nssarchive.us/NSSR/2002.pdf.

Oren, Ido. 2004. "The Enduring Relationship Between the American (National Security) State and the State of the Discipline." *PS: Political Science and Politics* 37, no. 1: 51–55.

———. 2006. "Can Political Science Emulate the Natural Sciences? The Problem of Self-Disconfirming Analysis." *Polity* 38, no. 1: 72–100.

———. 2015. "How Can We Make Political Science Less Techno-Centric? Widen Rather than Narrow Its Distance from the Government." *Perspectives on Politics* 13, no. 2: 394–95.

Ostrom, Elinor. 1990. *Governing the Commons: The Evolution of Institutions for Collective Action.* Cambridge: Cambridge University Press.

Owen, Erica, and Dennis P. Quinn. 2013. "Does Economic Globalization Influence the US Policy Mood?: A Study of US Public Sentiment, 1956–2011." *British Journal of Political Science* 46, no. 1: 1–31.

Owen, John M. 1994. "How Liberalism Produces Democratic Peace." *International Security* 19, no. 2: 87–125.

Oye, Kenneth A., and James H. Maxwell. 1994. "Self-Interest and Environmental Management." *Journal of Theoretical Politics* 6, no. 4: 593–624.

Pahre, Robert. 2008. *Politics and Trade Cooperation in the Nineteenth Century: The "'Agreeable Customs'" of 1815–1914.* New York: Cambridge University Press.

Pape, Robert A. 1997. "Why Economic Sanctions Do Not Work." *International Security* 22, no. 2: 90–136.

Parks, Bradley C., and Alena Stern. 2013. "In-and-Outers and Moonlighters: An Evaluation of the Impact of Policy-Making Exposure on IR Scholarship." *International Studies Perspectives* 15, no. 1: 73–93.

Parson, Edward A. 2003. *Protecting the Ozone Layer: Science and Strategy.* New York: Oxford University Press.

Paterson, Matthew. 2014. "Theoretical Perspectives on International Environmental Politics." In *Palgrave Advances in International Environmental Politics*, edited by Michele M. Betsill, Kathryn Hochstetler, and Dimitris Stevis, 45–77. New York: Palgrave Macmillan.

Peksen, Dursun. 2009. "Better or Worse? The Effect of Economic Sanctions on Human Rights." *Journal of Peace Research* 46, no. 1: 59–77.

———. 2011. "Economic Sanctions and Human Security: The Public Health Effect of Economic Sanctions." *Foreign Policy Analysis* 7, no. 3: 237–51.

Pepinsky, Thomas B. 2008. "Capital Mobility and Coalitional Politics: Authoritarian Regimes and Economic Adjustment in Southeast Asia." *World Politics* 60, no. 3: 438–74.

_____. 2009. *Economic Crises and the Breakdown of Authoritarian Regimes: Indonesia and Malaysia in Comparative Perspective.* New York: Cambridge University Press.

_____. 2014. "The Politics of Capital Flight in the Global Economic Crisis." *Economics and Politics* 26, no. 3: 431–36.

Peterson, Susan. 1995. "How Democracies Differ: Public Opinion, State Structure, and the Lessons of the Fashoda Crisis." *Security Studies* 5, no. 1: 3–37.

Peterson, Susan, and Christopher Wenk. 2001. "Domestic Institutional Change and Foreign Policy: A Comparative Study of U.S. Intervention in Guatemala and Nicaragua." *Security Studies* 11, no. 1: 53–76.

Peterson, Timothy M., and Leah Graham. 2011. "Shared Human Rights Norms and Military Conflict." *Journal of Conflict Resolution* 55, no. 2: 248–73.

Peterson, Timothy M., and Cameron Thies. 2012. "Beyond Ricardo: The Link between Intra-industry Trade and Peace." *British Journal of Political Science* 42, no. 4: 747–67.

Petranov, Borislav, and Monette Zard. 2014. "Keeping Defenders Safe: A Call to Donor Action." *International Human Rights Funders Group.* https://human rightsdefenders.blog/2014/11/08/important-report-keeping-defenders-safe-a -call-to-donor-action/.

Pieczara, Kamila, and Yong-Soo Eun. 2013. "What Is 'Vintage' in IR? A Writer's Note." *PS: Political Science and Politics* 46, no. 3: 611–14.

Piewitt, Martina, Meike Rodekamp, and Jens Steffek. 2010. "Civil Society in World Politics: How Accountable Are Transnational CSOs?" *Journal of Civil Society* 6, no. 3: 237–58.

Piketty, Thomas. 2014. *Capital in the Twenty-First Century.* Translated by Arthur Goldhammer. Cambridge, MA: The Belknap Press of Harvard University Press.

Pirages, Dennis. 1977. "Scarcity and International Politics: An Introduction." *International Studies Quarterly* 21, no. 4: 563–67.

Platteau, Jean-Philippe, and Frederic Gaspart. 2003. "The Risk of Resource Misappropriation in Community-Driven Development." *World Development* 31, no. 10: 1687–1703.

_____. 2005. "Disciplining Local Leaders in Community-Based Development." Working paper.

Poe, Steven C., and C. Neal Tate. 1994. "Repression of Human Rights to Personal Integrity in the 1980s: A Global Analysis." *The American Political Science Review* 88, no. 4: 853–72.

Pollins, Brian M. 1989. "Does Trade Still Follow the Flag?" *American Political Science Review* 83, no. 2: 465–80.

Powell, Robert. 2006. "War as a Commitment Problem." *International Organization* 60, no. 1: 169–203.

Press, Daryl G. 2007. *Calculating Credibility: How Leaders Assess Military Threats.* Ithaca, NY: Cornell University Press.

Proctor, Robert N. 1991. *Value-Free Science? Purity and Power in Modern Knowledge.* Cambridge, MA: Harvard University Press.

Putnam, Robert D. 2003. "APSA Presidential Address: The Public Role of Political Science." *Perspectives on Politics* 1, no. 2: 249–55.

Radaelli, Claudio M. 1999. "The Public Policy of the European Union: Whither Politics of Expertise?" *Journal of European Public Policy* 6, no. 5: 757–74.

Radelet, Steven. 2006. "A Primer on Foreign Aid." *Center for Global Development Working Paper no. 92,* Center for Global Development, Washington, DC.

Rajan, Raghuram. 2010. *Fault Lines: How Hidden Fractures Still Threaten the World Economy*. Princeton, NJ: Princeton University Press.

Rajan, Raghuram, and Arvind Subramanian. 2008. "Aid and Growth: What Does the Cross-Country Evidence Really Show?" *Review of Economics and Statistics* 90, no. 4: 643–65.

Raman, Narayanan, Lucy Qian Liu, and Sonali Das. 2016. "International Policy Coordination: Why, When, and How." In *Managing Complexity: Economic Policy Cooperation After the Crisis*, edited by Tamim Bayoumi, Stephen Pickford, and Paola Subacchi, 353–84. Washington, DC: Brookings Institution Press.

Ramírez, Carlos D. 2013. "The Political Economy of 'Currency Manipulation' Bashing." *China Economic Review*. 27, no. C: 227–237.

Raskin, Marcus G. 1963. "The Megadeath Intellectuals." *The New York Review of Books*. November 14. www.nybooks.com/articles/1963/11/14/the-megadeath-intellectuals/.

Rathbun, Brian C. 2011. "The 'Magnificent Fraud': Trust, International Cooperation, and the Hidden Domestic Politics of American Multilateralism after World War II." *International Studies Quarterly* 55, no. 1: 1–21.

Raustiala, Kal, and David G. Victor. 2004. "The Regime Complex for Plant Genetic Resources." *International Organization* 58, no. 2: 277–309.

Ravallion, Martin. 2014. "On the Role of Aid in the Great Escape." *Review of Income and Wealth* 60, no. 4: 967–84.

Reiter, Dan, and Allan C. Stam. 2002. *Democracies at War*. Princeton, NJ: Princeton University Press.

Research Excellence Framework (UK). 2012. *Assessment Framework and Guidance on Submissions*. Research Excellence Framework. www.fapesp.br/avaliacao/manuais/ref_guidelines.pdf.

Ribar, Matthew. 2016 "Keeping Up with the Times: How the Discipline of International Relations Responds to Benchmark Events." *International Studies Perspectives* 18, no. 3: 304–22.

Richards, David, email correspondence to author, August 15, 2014.

Richards, David L., and K. Chad Clay. 2012. "An Umbrella with Holes: Respect for Non-Derogable Human Rights during Declared States of Emergency, 1996–2004." *Human Rights Review* 13, no. 4: 443–71.

Richardson, J. David. 1990. "The Political Economy of Strategic Trade Policy." *International Organization* 44, no. 1: 107–35.

Ricks, Thomas E. 2014. "Given All That Is Going On, Why Is 'International Security' So Boring?" *Foreign Policy*. September 15. http://foreignpolicy.com/2014/09/15/given-all-that-is-going-on-why-is-international-security-so-damn-boring/.

Risse, Thomas, Stephen C. Ropp, and Kathryn Sikkink. 1999. *The Power of Human Rights: International Norms and Domestic Change*. New York: Cambridge University Press.

Risse-Kappen, Thomas. 1991. "Public Opinion, Domestic Structure, and Foreign Policy in Liberal Democracies." *World Politics* 43, no. 4: 479–512.

———. 1995. "Democratic Peace—Warlike Democracies? A Social Constructivist Interpretation of the Liberal Argument." *European Journal of International Relations* 1, no. 4: 491–517.

Rodrik, Dani. 1995. "Political Economy of Trade Policy." In *Handbook of International Economics*, vol. III, edited by Gene M. Grossman and Kenneth Rogoff, 1457–94. Amsterdam: North-Holland.

Ron, James. n.d. "James Ron." *James Ron and Team.* http://jamesron.com/.

Ron, James, and David Crow. 2015. "Who Trusts Local Human Rights Organizations? Evidence from Three World Regions." *Human Rights Quarterly* 37, no. 1: 188–239.

———. 2014a. "Human Rights Familiarity and Socio-Economic Status: A Four Country Study." *SUR – International Journal on Human Rights* 11, no. 20. https://papers.ssrn.com/sol3/papers.cfm?abstract_id=2553365.

———. 2014b. "The Struggle for Truly Grassroots Human Rights Movement." *Open Democracy.net.* November 18. www.opendemocracy.net/openglobalrights/james -ron-david-crow-shannon-golden/struggle-for-truly-grassroots-human-rights -move.

Rosato, Sebastian. 2003. "The Flawed Logic of Democratic Peace Theory." *American Political Science Review* 97, no. 4: 585–602.

Rose, Gideon. 1998. "Neoclassical Realism and Theories of Foreign Policy." *World Politics* 51, no. 1: 144–72.

Rosendorff, B. Peter. 2005. "Stability and Rigidity: Politics and Design of the WTO's Dispute Settlement Procedure." *American Political Science Review* 99, no. 3: 389–400.

Roth, Kenneth. 2004. "Defending Economic, Social and Cultural Rights: Practical Issues Faced by an International Human Rights Organization." *Human Rights Quarterly* 26, no. 1: 63–73.

———. 2014. "The End of Human Rights?" *The New York Review of Books.* October 23. www.nybooks.com/articles/archives/2014/oct/23/end-human-rights/.

Rothkopf, David (@djrothkopf). 2014. "Kristof gets why we at FP are dialing back academic contributions—too many are opaque, abstract, incremental, dull." Twitter post, February 16. https://twitter.com/djrothkopf/status/435028506984980480.

Ruggie, John G. 1982. "International Regimes, Transactions, and Change: Embedded Liberalism in the Postwar Economic Order." *International Organization* 36, no. 2: 379–415.

———. 2004. "Reconstituting the Global Public Domain—Issues, Actors, and Practices." *European Journal of International Relations* 10, no. 4: 499–531.

Russett, Bruce M. 1985. "The Mysterious Case of Vanishing Hegemony." *International Organization* 39, no. 2: 207–31.

———. 1993. *Grasping the Democratic Peace: Principles for a Post-Cold War World.* Princeton, NJ: Princeton University Press.

———. 2005. "Bushwhacking the Democratic Peace." *International Studies Perspectives* 6, no. 4: 395–408.

———. 2010. "Capitalism or Democracy? Not So Fast." *International Interactions* 36, no. 2: 198–205.

Russett, Bruce M., John R. Oneal, and Michaelene Cox. 2000. "Clash of Civilizations, or Realism and Liberalism Déjà Vu? Some Evidence." *Journal of Peace Research* 37, no. 5: 583–608.

Rutzen, Douglas. 2015. "Civil Society Under Assault." *Journal of Democracy* 26, no. 4: 28–39.

Sagan, Scott D. 1995. "Responses and Reflections." *Security Studies* 4, no. 4: 805–10.

———. 2014. "Two Renaissances in Nuclear Security Studies." *H-Diplo | ISSF Forum.* http://issforum.org/ISSF/PDF/ISSF-Forum-2.pdf.

Sagan, Scott D., and Kenneth N. Waltz. 2013. *The Spread of Nuclear Weapons: An Enduring Debate,* 3rd ed. New York: W.W. Norton.

Saideman, Stephen M. 1997. "Explaining the International Relations of Secession-ist Conflicts: Vulnerability versus Ethnic Ties." *International Organization* 51, no. 4: 721–53.

Sambanis, Nicholas. 2008. "Short- and Long-Term Effects of United Nations Peace Operations." *World Bank Economic Review* 22, no. 1: 9–32.

Sánchez-Cuenca, Ignacio, and Luis De la Calle. 2009. "Domestic Terrorism: The Hidden Side of Political Violence." *Annual Review of Political Science* 12: 31–49.

Satterthwaite, Margaret L., and Justin Simeone. 2014. "An Emerging Fact-Finding Discipline? A Conceptual Roadmap for Social Science Methods in Human Rights Advocacy." In *The Future of Human Rights Fact-Finding*, edited by Philip Altson and Sarah Knuckey, 14–33. Cambridge: Oxford University Press.

Schattschneider, Elmer Eric. 1935. *Politics, Pressures, and the Tariff*. New York: Prentice Hall.

Schelling, Thomas C. 1966. *Arms and Influence*. New Haven, CT: Yale University Press.

———. 1978. "Bernard Brodie (1910–1978)." *International Security* 3, no. 3: 2–3.

———. 2004. "Academics, Decision Makers, and Security Policy during the Cold War: A Comment on Jervis." In *The Evolution of Political Knowledge*, edited by Edward D. Mansfield and J. Richard Sisson, 137–39. Columbus: The Ohio State University Press.

Schlesinger, James R. 1963. "Quantitative Analysis and National Security." *World Politics* 15, no. 2: 295–315.

Schmitz, Hans Peter. 2010. "Transnational Human Rights Networks: Significance and Challenges." In *International Studies Encyclopedia, Volume XI*, edited by Robert A. Denmark, 7189–208. New York: Wiley-Blackwell.

———. 2011. "Transnational NGOs and Human Rights in a post-9/11 World." In *Human Rights in the 21st Century: Continuity and Change since 9/11*, edited by Michael Goodhart and Anja Mihr, 203–21. New York: Palgrave Macmillan.

Schweller, Randall L. 1998. *Deadly Imbalances: Tripolarity and Hitler's Strategy of World Conquest*. New York: Columbia University Press.

Schweller, Randall L., and Xiaoyu Pu. 2011. "After Unipolarity: China's Visions of International Order in an Era of U.S. Decline." *International Security* 36, no. 1: 41–72.

Sechser, T. S., and M. Fuhrmann. 2017. *Nuclear Weapons and Coercive Diplomacy*. New York: Cambridge University Press.

Seng, Jordan. 1997. "Less Is More: Command and Control Advantages of Minor Nuclear States." *Security Studies* 6, no. 4: 50–92.

Sex Worker Forum of Vienna, Austria. 2013. *Austria: Discriminations against Sex Workers in the Rights to Work and to Health*. Presented to the United Nations Committee on Economic, Social and Cultural Rights. tbinternet.ohchr .org/Treaties/CESCR/Shared%20Documents/AUT/INT_CESCR_NGO _AUT_14625_E.docx.

Shah, Raj, and Michael Gerson. 2014. "Foreign Assistance and the Revolution of Rigor." In *Moneyball for Government*, 2nd ed., edited by Jim Nussle and Peter Orszag, 74–105. Washington, DC: Results for America.

Shapiro, Ian. 2007. *The Flight from Reality in the Human Sciences*. Princeton, NJ: Princeton University Press.

Shapley, Deborah. 1993. *Promise and Power: The Life and Times of Robert McNamara*. Boston, MA: Little Brown.

Sharman, J. C., and Catherine E. Weaver. 2013. "Between the Covers: International Relations in Books." *PS: Political Science and Politics* 46, no. 1: 124–28.

Shellman, Stephen M. 2008. "Coding Disaggregated Intrastate Conflict: Machine Processing the Behavior of Sub-state Actors Over Time and Space." *Political Analysis* 16, no. 4: 464–77.

Shetty, Salil. 2014. "'Human Rights Organizations Should Have a Closer Pulse to the Ground,' or How We Missed the Bus." *SUR – International Journal on Human Rights* 11, no. 20: 531–36.

Sides, John. 2007. "Why This Blog?" *The Monkey Cage* (blog). November 20. http://themonkeycage.org/2007/11/why_this_blog/.

Sikkink, Kathryn. 2011. "The Case for Human Rights Prosecutions." *The International Herald Tribune*, September 16, 2011.

Simmons, Beth A. 1994. *Who Adjusts? Domestic Sources of Foreign Economic Policy during the Interwar Years, 1923–1939*. Princeton, NJ: Princeton University Press.

———. 2009. *Mobilizing for Human Rights: International Law in Domestic Politics.* New York: Cambridge University Press.

Singer, David A. 2007. *Regulating Capital: Setting Standards for the International Financial System*. Ithaca, NY: Cornell University Press.

Siverson, Randolph M. 2000. "A Glass Half-Full? No, but Perhaps a Glass Filling: The Contributions of International Politics Research to Policy." *PS: Political Science and Politics* 33, no. 1: 59–64.

Sjoberg, Laura. 2015. "Locating Relevance in Security Studies." *Perspectives on Politics* 13, no. 2: 396–98.

Skocpol, Theda. 1979. *States and Social Revolutions: A Comparative Analysis of France, Russia and China*. Cambridge: Cambridge University Press.

Slaughter, Anne-Marie. 1992. "Toward an Age of Liberal Nations." *Harvard Journal of International Law* 33, no. 2: 393–493.

Slezkine, Peter. 2014. "From Helsinki to Human Rights Watch: How an American Cold War Monitoring Group Became an International Human Rights Institution." *Humanity: An International Journal of Human Rights, Humanitarianism, and Development* 5, no. 3: 345–70.

Smeltz, Dina, Ivo Daalder, and Craig Kafura. 2014. "Foreign Policy in the Age of Retrenchment." *The Chicago Council on Global Affairs*. www.thechicagocouncil.org/sites/default/files/2014_CCS_Report_1.pdf.

Smith, Bruce L. R. 1966. *The RAND Corporation: Case Study of a Nonprofit Advisory Corporation*. Cambridge, MA: Harvard University Press.

Snyder, Jack. 2017. "Empowering Rights with Mass Movements, Religion, and Reform Parties." In *Human Rights Futures*, edited by Stephen Hopgood, Leslie Vinjamuri, and Jack Snyder, 88–113. Cambridge: Cambridge University Press.

Sobek, David, Rodwan Abouharb, and Christopher G. Ingram. 2006. "The Human Rights Peace: How the Respect for Human Rights at Home Leads to Peace Abroad." *Journal of Politics* 68, no. 3: 519–29.

Solomon, Richard H., and Nigel Quincy. 2010. *American Negotiating Behavior*. Washington, DC: US Institute of Peace.

Sprout, Harold, and Margaret Sprout. 1971. *Towards a Politics of the Planet Earth*. New York: Van Nostrand Reinhold Co.

Steinberg, David. 2015. *Demanding Devaluation: Exchange Rate Politics in the Developing World*. Ithaca, NY: Cornell University Press.

Steinberg, David, Karrie J. Koesel, and Nicolas W. Thompson. 2015. "Political Regimes and Currency Crises." *Economics and Politics*, 27: 337–61.

Steiner, Barry H. 1991 *Bernard Brodie and the Foundations of American Nuclear Strategy*. Lawrence: The University Press of Kansas.

Stern, Robert M. 1987. *US Trade Policies in a Changing World Economy*. Cambridge, MA: MIT Press.

Stevis, Dimitris. 2014. "The Trajectory of International Environmental Politics." In *Palgrave Advances in International Environmental Politics*, edited by Michele M. Betsill, Kathryn Hochstetler, and Dimitris Stevis, 13–44. New York: Palgrave Macmillan.

Strange, Austin M., Axel Dreher, Andreas Fuchs, Bradley C. Parks, and Michael J. Tierney. 2017. "Tracking Underreported Financial Flows: China's Development Finance and the Aid-Conflict Nexus Revisited." *Journal of Conflict Resolution* 61, no. 5: 935–63.

Strange, Susan. 1982. "Cave! Hic Dragones: A Critique of Regime Analysis." *International Organization* 36, no. 2: 479–96.

———. 1988. *States and Markets: An Introduction to International Political Economy*. London: Pinter Publishers.

Strom, Stephanie. 2011. "World Bank Is Opening Its Treasure Chest of Data." *The New York Times*. July 2. www.nytimes.com/2011/07/03/business/global /03world.html?pagewanted=all.

Tallberg, Jonas, Thomas Sommerer, Theresa Squatrito, and Christer Jönsson. 2013. *The Opening Up of International Organizations: Transnational Access in Global Governance*. Cambridge: Cambridge University Press.

Talmadge, Caitlin. 2017. "Would China Go Nuclear?: Assessing the Risk of Chinese Nuclear Escalation in a Conventional War with the United States." *International Security* 40, no. 4: 50–92.

Teaching, Research and International Policy (TRIP) Project. 2017. *TRIP Journal Article Database Release (Version 3.1)*. Available from: https://trip.wm.edu/.

Terviö, Marko. 2011. "Divisions within Academia: Evidence from Faculty Hiring and Placement." *Review of Economics and Statistics* 93, no. 3: 1053–62.

Thomas, Jakana. 2014. "Rewarding Bad Behavior: How Governments Respond to Terrorism in Civil War." *American Journal of Political Science* 58, no. 4: 804–18.

Tierney, Michael J., Daniel L. Nielson, Darren G. Hawkins, J. Timmons Roberts, Michael G. Findley, Ryan M. Powers, Bradley Parks, Sven E. Wilson, and Robert L. Hicks. 2011. "More Dollars than Sense: Refining our Knowledge of Development Finance Using AidData." *World Development* 39, no. 11: 1891–906.

Tilly, Charles. 1978. *From Mobilization to Revolution*. Boston, MA: Addison-Wesley.

Tomz, Michael R. 2007. "Domestic Audience Costs in International Relations: An Experimental Approach." *International Organization* 6, no. 4: 821–40.

Tomz, Michael R., and Jessica Weeks. 2013. "Public Opinion and the Democratic Peace." *American Political Science Review* 107, no. 4: 849–65.

Trachtenberg, Marc. 1991. *History and Strategy*. Princeton, NJ: Princeton University Press.

Tullock, Gordon. 1972. "Economic Imperialism." In *Theory of Public Choice: Political Applications of Economics*, edited by James M. Buchanan, 17–29. Ann Arbor: University of Michigan Press.

Turton, Helen Louise. 2015. "'Please Mind the Gap': Policy Relevance and British IR." *Perspectives on Politics* 13, no. 2: 399–401.

———. 2016. *International Relations and American Dominance*. London: Routledge.

Tushabomwe, Denis. 2014. "NGO Accountability in Uganda: Analyzing the Reasons, Challenges, and Remedial Postulates." *The International Journal of Humanities and Social Studies* 2, no. 7: 390–98.

Tyson, Laura D. 1993. *Who's Bashing Whom? Trade Conflict in High Technology Industries.* Washington, DC: Peterson Institute.

United Nations Department of Economic and Social Affairs. 2003. *Human Rights and Humanitarian Law.* Available from: www.un.org/esa/socdev/enable/comp 210.htm.

United Nations Economic and Social Council. 2000. *Economic and Social Council Official Records, 200 Supplement No. 2.* E/2000/22 E/C.12/1999/11.

United Nations General Assembly. 1972. *Institutional and Financial Arrangements for International Environmental Cooperation.* A/RES/27/2997.

———. 1974. *Declaration on the Establishment of a New International Economic Order.* A/RES/S-6/3201.

———. 1983. *International Co-Operation in the Field of the Environment.* A/RES/38/165.

———. 2010. *Implementation of the Outcome of the United Nations Conference on Human Settlements (Habitat II) and Strengthening of the United Nations Human Settlements Programme (UN-Habitat).* A/RES/65/165.

———. 2014. *Report of the Independent Expert on Human Rights and International Solidarity, Virginia Dandan. Preliminary Text of a Draft Declaration on the Right of Peoples and Individuals to International Solidarity.* A/HRC/26/34/Add.1.

United Nations Human Rights Council. 2014a. *Preliminary Research-Based Report on Human Rights and Unilateral Coercive Measures.* A/HRC/AC/13/CRP.2.

———. 2014b. *Preliminary Study on Enhancement of International Cooperation.* A/HRC/AC/12/CRP.2.

———. 2009. *Informal Background Paper.* www2.ohchr.org/english/bodies/HRTD /docs/Informal_background_paper_Dublin_meeting.pdf.

———. 2014. *Preliminary Study on Enhancement of International Cooperation.* A/HRC/AC/12/CRP.2.

United States Department of Defense. 2008. *Broad Agency Announcement: Department of Defense (DoD) Minerva Research Initiative.* Washington, DC. www.arl .army.mil/www/pages/362/08-R-0007.pdf.

———. 2014. *Climate Change Adaptation Report.* Washington, DC. www.scribd .com/doc/242845848/Read-DoD-report-2014-Climate-Change-Adaptation -Roadmap.

Uppsala Conflict Data Program. 2018. UCDP Conflict Encyclopedia: www.ucdp .uu.se. Uppsala University. Accessed September 20, 2019.

USAID. 2013. *USAID Strategy on Democracy, Human Rights, and Governance.* USAID. www.usaid.gov/sites/default/files/documents/1866/USAID%20DRG _%20final%20final%206-24%203%20%281%29.pdf.

"USAID Learning Lab." n.d. *United States Agency for International Development.* https://usaidlearninglab.org/.

Van Evera, Stephen. 1997. *Guide to Methods for Students of Political Science.* Ithaca, NY: Cornell University Press.

———. 2015. "U.S. Social Science and International Relations." *War on the Rocks* (blog). February 9, 2015. https://warontherocks.com/2015/02/u-s-social-science -and-international-relations/.

Vasak, Karel. 1979. "For the Third Generation of Human Rights: The Rights of Solidarity." Inaugural Lecture to the Tenth Study Session of the International Institute of Human Rights, Strasbourg, 2–27.

Verdier, Pierre-Hugues. 2013. "The Political Economy of International Financial Regulation."' *Indiana Law Journal* 88, no. 4: 1405–74.

Verdun, Amy. 1999. "The Role of the Delors Committee in the Creation of EMU: An Epistemic Community?" *Journal of European Public Policy* 6, no. 2: 308–28.

Vermeiren, Mattias. 2013. "Monetary Power and EMU: Macroeconomic Adjustment and Autonomy in the Eurozone." *Review of International Studies* 39, no. 3: 729–61.

Victor, David G. 2011 *Global Warming Gridlock: Creating More Effective Strategies for Protecting the Planet.* New York: Cambridge University Press.

Victor, David G., and Leslie A. Coben. 2005. "A Herd Mentality in the Design of International Environmental Agreements?" *Global Environmental Politics* 5, no. 1: 24–57.

Viner, Jacob. 1950. *The Customs Union.* New York: Carnegie Endowment for International Peace.

Voeten, Erik. 2015. "Rigor Is Not the Enemy of Relevance." *Perspectives on Politics* 13, no. 2: 402–3.

Vogel, David. 2008. "Private Global Business Regulation." *Annual Review of Political Science* 11: 261–82.

Von Stein, Jana. 2005. "Do Treaties Constrain or Screen? Selection Bias and Treaty Compliance." *American Political Science Review* 99, no. 4: 611–22.

Wagner, R. Harrison. 2007. *War and the State: The Theory of International Politics.* Ann Arbor: Michigan University Press.

Walt, Stephen M. 1999. "Rigor or Rigor Mortis? Rational Choice and Security Studies." *International Security* 23, no. 4: 5–48.

―――. 2005. "The Relationship between Theory and Policy in International Relations." *Annual Review of Political Science* 8, no. 1: 23–48.

―――. 2009. "The Cult of Irrelevance." *Foreign Policy.* April 15. http://foreignpolicy .com/2009/04/15/the-cult-of-irrelevance/.

―――. 2015a. "The Credibility Addiction." *Foreign Policy.* January 6. http:// foreignpolicy.com/2015/01/06/the-credibility-addiction-us-iraq-afghanistan -unwinnable-war/.

―――. 2015b. "Comment on Michael Desch, 'Technique Trumps Relevance.'" *Perspectives on Politics* 13, no. 2: 406–7.

Walter, Stefanie. 2013. *Financial Crises and the Politics of Macroeconomic Adjustment.* New York: Cambridge University Press.

Waltz, Kenneth. 1979/2010. *Theory of International Politics.* Long Grove, IL: Waveland Press.

―――. 1959. *Man, the State, and War: A Theoretical Analysis.* New York: Columbia University Press.

―――. 2000. "Structural Realism after the Cold War." *International Security* 25, no. 1: 5–41.

Waltz, Susan E. 2001. "Universalizing Human Rights: The Role of Small States in the Construction of the Universal Declaration of Human Rights." *Human Rights Quarterly* 23, no. 1: 44–72.

Weaver, Catherine. 2014. "Mind–and Measure–the Gap." *International Studies Quarterly Online.* August 30. www.isanet.org/Publications/ISQ/Posts/ID/1421 /Mind–and-Measure–the-Gap.

Weaver, Catherine, and Christian Peratsakis. 2014. "Engineering Policy Norm Implementation: The World Bank's Transparency Transformation." In *Implementation and World Politics: How International Norms Change Practice*, edited by Alexander Betts and Phil Orchard, Oxford: Oxford University Press.

Weaver, Catherine E., and J. C. Sharman. 2013. "RIPE, the American School, and Diversity in Global IPE." *Review of International Political Economy* 20, no. 5: 1082–100.

Wellman, Carl. 2000. "Solidarity, the Individual and Human Rights." *Human Rights Quarterly* 22, no. 3: 639–57.

Wells, Tom. 2001. *Wild Man: The Life and Times of Daniel Ellsberg*. New York: St. Martins.

White House Office of the Press Secretary. 2014. "Presidential Memorandum—Civil Society." September 23. https://obamawhitehouse.archives.gov/the-press-office/2014/09/23/presidential-memorandum-civil-society.

Whitlark, Rachel E. 2017. "Nuclear Beliefs: A Leader-focused Theory of Counter-proliferation." *Security Studies* 26, no. 4: 545–674.

Wilson, EJ III. 2007. "Is There Really a Scholar-Practitioner Gap? An Institutional Analysis." *PS: Political Science & Politics* 40, no. 1: 147–51.

Winecoff, William K. (@whinecough), "6 years since the onset of the global financial crisis, and International Organization has published zero articles related to it. #IPEfail," Twitter, April 24, 2013, 8:05 p.m., https://twitter.com/whinecough/status/327211705878851584.

Wohlforth, William C. 1999. "The Stability of a Unipolar World." *International Security* 24, no. 1: 5–41.

Wohlstetter, Albert. 1959. "The Delicate Balance of Terror." *Foreign Affairs* 37, no. 2: 211–34.

Wood, Reed M. 2008. "'A Hand Upon the Throat of the Nation': Economic Sanctions and State Repression, 1976–2001. *International Studies Quarterly* 52, no. 3: 489–513.

Wood, Reed M., and Mark Gibney. 2010. "The Political Terror Scale (PTS): A Re-Introduction and a Comparison to CIRI." *Human Rights Quarterly* 32, no. 2: 367–400.

World Bank. 2001. *World Development Report 2000/2001: Attacking Poverty.* World Bank. New York: Oxford University Press.

———. 2011. *World Development Report 2011: Conflict, Security, and Development – overview (English).* World Development Report. Washington, DC: World Bank Group.

World Commission on Environment and Development: Brundtland Commission. 1987. *Our Common Future.* World Commission on Environment and Development. www.un-documents.net/our-common-future.pdf.

World Trade Organization. 2011. *World Trade Report 2011: The WTO and Preferential Trade Agreements: From Co-existence to Coherence.* World Trade Organization.

Yarhi-Milo, Keren. 2014. *Knowing the Adversary: Leaders, Intelligence Organizations, and Assessments of Intentions in International Relations.* Princeton, NJ: Princeton University Press.

Yarhi-Milo, Keren, and Alex Weisiger. 2015. "Revisiting Reputation: How Do Past Actions Matter in International Politics?" *International Organization* 69, no. 2: 473–95.

Yeshanew, Sisay Alemahu. 2012. "CSO Law in Ethiopia: Considering Its Constraints and Consequences." *Journal of Civil Society* 8, no. 4: 349–84.

Young, Joseph K. 2013. "Repression, Dissent, and the Onset of Civil War." *Political Research Quarterly* 66, no. 3: 516–32.

_____. 2014. "What Is Terrorism?" *Paper presented at the Annual Meeting of the American Political Science Association.* Washington, DC.

_____. 2019. "Measuring Terrorism." *Terrorism and Political Violence* 31, no. 2: 323–45.

Young, Joseph K., and Michael G. Findley. 2011. "Promise and Pitfalls of Terrorism Research." *International Studies Review* 13, no. 3: 411–31.

Young, Oran R. 1989. "The Politics of International Regime Formation: Managing Natural Resources and the Environment." *International Organization* 43, no. 3: 349–75.

_____. 2002. *The Institutional Dimensions of Environmental Change: Fit, Interplay, and Scale.* Cambridge, MA: MIT Press.

Zagare, Frank C. 1999. "All Mortis, No Rigor." *International Security* 24, no. 2: 107–14.

Zeng, Ka. 2013. "Legal Capacity and Developing Country Performance in the Panel Stage of the WTO Dispute Settlement System." *Journal of World Trade* 47, no. 1: 187–213.

Zoellick, Robert. 2012. "The Currency of Power." *Foreign Policy*, no. 196: 67–73.

Zürn, Michael. 1998. "The Rise of International Environmental Politics: A Review of Current Research." *World Politics* 50, no. 4: 617–49.

# CONTRIBUTORS

**Paul C. Avey** is an assistant professor of political science at Virginia Tech. His research interests include US foreign policy and nuclear politics. He was a 2018–19 Council on Foreign Relations International Affairs Fellow based in the Office of the Under Secretary of Defense for Policy.

**Dimitri G. Demekas** is a visiting senior fellow at the Institute of Global Affairs, London School of Economics and Political Science and a special adviser with the Bank of England. He had a thirty-year career at the International Monetary Fund, ending in 2017 as assistant director of the Monetary and Capital Markets department working on global financial stability policies. He holds a PhD in economics from Columbia University.

**Michael C. Desch** is the Packey J. Dee Professor of Political Science and the Brian and Jeannelle Brady Family Director of the Notre Dame International Security Center. His research interests include international relations, American foreign policy, and international security.

**Scott Edwards** is a senior adviser for Amnesty International's Crisis Response and a lecturer at George Washington University's Elliott School of International Affairs. He holds a PhD in political science from the University of Illinois, Urbana-Champaign, with a focus on violent political conflict.

**Peter D. Feaver** is a professor of political science and public policy at Duke University and director of the Triangle Institute for Security Studies and the Program in American Grand Strategy. He has previously served as special advisor for strategic policy and institutional reform on the National Security Council (NSC) staff, director for defense policy and arms control on the NSC staff, and a reservist in the US Naval Reserve Intelligence Program.

**Michael G. Findley** is a professor in the Department of Government at the LBJ School of Public Affairs at the University of Texas at Austin. He conducts research on civil wars, terrorism, international development, and illicit finance.

**Jessica F. Green** is an associate professor in the Department of Political Science and the School of the Environment at the University of Toronto. Her research focuses on climate change, private regulation, and interactions between public and private authority.

**Thomas Hale** is an associate professor at Oxford University's Blavatnik School of Government. He studies the management of transnational problems and how political institutions evolve in response to globalization and interdependence, with a particular emphasis on environmental and economic issues.

**John R. Harvey** served as principal deputy assistant secretary of defense for nuclear, chemical, and biological defense programs. He is a physicist who worked for thirty-five years on nuclear weapons and national security issues at Lawrence Livermore National Laboratory, at Stanford University's Center for International Security and Arms Control, and in senior government positions in the departments of Defense and Energy.

**Sarah Kreps** is a professor of government and adjunct professor of law at Cornell University. Her research interests include international relations, international conflict and cooperation, alliance politics, and nuclear proliferation. She previously served in the United States Air Force.

**Marc A. Levy** serves as deputy director of the Center for International Earth Science Information Network (CIESIN) at the Earth Institute at Columbia University. He has worked with the US government and the United Nations on climate-related security problems and was a lead author on the Intergovernmental Panel for Climate Change Fifth Assessment.

**Daniel Maliniak** is an assistant professor of government at William & Mary. He works on the political economy of the environment, public opinion, the politics of energy policy, and the international politics of the Russian and post-Soviet region.

**Edward D. Mansfield** is the Hum Rosen Professor of Political Science and director of the Christopher H. Browne Center for International Politics at the University of Pennsylvania. His research focuses on international security and international political economy.

**Sarah E. Mendelson** is a distinguished service professor of public policy and head of Carnegie Mellon's Heinz College in Washington, DC. Previously she served as the US representative to the Economic and Social Council at the United Nations, as a deputy assistant administrator at the US Agency for International Development, and as senior adviser and director of the Human Rights Initiative at the Center for Strategic and International Studies. She holds a PhD in political science from Columbia University.

**Amanda Murdie** is the Thomas P. and M. Jean Lauth Public Affairs Professor and professor of international affairs in the School of Public and International Affairs at the University of Georgia. Her research focuses on human rights, human security, and nongovernmental organizations.

**Thomas B. Pepinsky** is a professor of government at Cornell University. He works on comparative and international political economy, identity and politics, and emerging markets with a special focus on Southeast Asia.

**Susan Peterson** is the Wendy and Emery Reves Professor of Government and International Relations and the codirector of the Global Research Institute at William & Mary. She studies the domestic sources of foreign and security policy, the nexus between global health and national security, and the role of scholars and scholarly research in the policy process.

**Jon C. W. Pevehouse** is the Vilas Distinguished Achievement Professor of Political Science, University of Wisconsin–Madison. He studies the politics of international organizations, international agreements, trade, democratization, and political economy.

**Ryan Powers** is an assistant professor of international affairs at the University of Georgia's School of Public and International Affairs. He studies international relations, political economy, international organization, and the domestic politics of trade policy.

**Steven Radelet** is the Donald F. McHenry Chair in Global Human Development and is the director of the Global Human Development Program at Georgetown University, former chief economist of the United States Agency for International Development, and senior advisor for development to the secretary of state.

**Christina J. Schneider** is a professor of political science and Jean Monnet Chair at the University of California, San Diego. Her research focuses on international cooperation and bargaining in international organizations, with a focus on distributional bargaining in the European Union and multilateral aid.

**David A. Steinberg** is an associate professor of international political economy at Johns Hopkins University's School of Advanced International Studies. His research focuses on the politics of international money and finance.

**Michael J. Tierney** is the George and Mary Hylton Professor of Government and codirector of the Global Research Institute at William & Mary. He works on international organizations, foreign aid, Chinese development finance, and the role of international relations scholars in the policy process.

**Jessica Weeks** is an associate professor of political science and Trice Family Faculty Scholar at the University of Wisconsin–Madison. Her research focuses on the domestic sources of foreign policy in both democracies and dictatorships, the link between public opinion and foreign policy, and related topics.

**Joseph K. Young** is a professor in the School of Public Affairs and School of International Service at American University. His research seeks to understand the cross-national causes and consequences of political violence.

**Robert B. Zoellick** is a senior counselor at the Brunswick and a senior fellow at the Belfer Center for Science and International Affairs at Harvard University's Kennedy School of Government. Previously he served as US trade representative, deputy and under secretary of state, counselor to the secretary of the Treasury, deputy chief of staff at the White House, and president of the World Bank Group.

# INDEX